D0435702

UNDERSTANDING
ETF
OPTIONS

UNDERSTANDING
ETF
OPTIONS

Profitable Strategies for Diversified, Low-Risk Investing

Kenneth R. Trester

New York   Chicago   San Francisco   Lisbon   London
Madrid   Mexico City   New Delhi   San Juan
Seoul   Singapore   Sydney   Toronto

1 2 3 4 5 6 7 8 9 0   QFR/QFR   1 6 5 4 3 2 1

ISBN: 978-0-07-176030-0
MHID: 0-07-176030-X

e-ISBN: 978-0-07-176043-0
e-MHID: 0-07-176043-1

This publication is designed to provide accurate and authoritative information in regard to the subject matter covered. It is sold with the understanding that neither the author nor the publisher is engaged in rendering legal, accounting, or other professional service. If legal advice or other expert assistance is required, the services of a competent professional person should be sought.
  —*From a Declaration of Principles Jointly Adopted by a Committee of the American Bar Association and a Committee of Publishers and Associations*

McGraw-Hill books are available at special quantity discounts to use as premiums and sales promotions, or for use in corporate training programs. To contact a representative, please e-mail us at bulksales@mcgraw-hill.com.

This book is printed on acid-free paper.

Contents

CONTENTS

Introduction

All investors need to know how to survive in the colossal cosmos, on the predatory planet, and inside the bewildering wilderness of finance.

INVESTING IN A DANGEROUS ENVIRONMENT

Investing today has become a dangerous venture. Real estate, considered a sure investment, has almost collapsed in price. Stocks are now at the same price they were at 12 years ago, and the U.S. dollar is now worth less than $0.60 in 1990 measures. In 2008, several blue-chip stocks went out of business, and credit markets were on the brink of disaster.

As you can see, the market has become a far more volatile place. One day in 2010, we saw a flash crash. The Dow Jones

Industrial Average dropped 1,000 points, plunging 500 points in 15 minutes and then bouncing back in 15 minutes. Some blue chips, like Procter & Gamble, dropped from 60 down to 30. Other stocks dropped to pennies on the dollar. Exchange-traded funds (ETFs) took on even more damage during that same 15 minutes. Then all of them bounced back.

Lots contributed to the volatility: high-frequency trading, computer-run markets, and ETFs that increased at two and three times what the market was doing at the upside and downside. The investment markets have become a minefield where an investment can blow up at any time.

These wild markets have scared many investors away. Many are hiding money in the U.S. dollar or Treasury bills and bonds, but inflation is beating them. The dollar has suffered from inflation averaging about 5 percent per year. This inflation may expand dramatically in the future.

WHAT TO DO?

The only way to protect yourself from a dangerous environment is to diversify so that if an investment blows up, you will be able to return to fight another day.

There has been an explosion of exchange-traded funds (ETFs), and they offer an investor an efficient means to diversify. Not only do they offer a way to diversify, but they allow you to diversify in an extraordinary variety of investments, for now you can use them to invest in commodities, currencies, bonds, and many other types of investments that were not available before now.

Besides diversification with ETFs, there is another survival tool in the arsenal that enables you to use the great volatility in the market to your advantage. This, of course, is options. The versatility of options is quite remarkable. You can buy them and sell them. You can use them to buy bargain-priced stocks or ETFs, and you can use them to sell stocks and ETFs at bonus prices. You can insure your portfolio with options, and you can enhance your portfolio with a steady income. Options are indeed useful!

Then put them together. ETFs and options together can be formidable weapons in your arsenal and will help you in your survival and success in this very difficult financial world. Each one, option or ETF, has its own rules and purposes. Each one functions in a different way, yet both serve in achieving financial security.

THE JOURNEY

Yes, the financial world now appears to be a colossal cosmos with ever-expanding financial vehicles. This can seem overwhelming, but if we can get to the moon and travel regularly to a space station, we can master this figurative cosmos. In fact, ETFs give nonprofessional investors much easier access to financial value, and options give them the means to handle, acquire, and safeguard that financial value.

The financial world has expanded incredibly but so has our ability to handle it.

First, you have to know the appropriate attitude you should have to be financially successful. Though our access to the financial world has improved, giving us great mobility and reach, it still is a dangerous environment. You have to be aware of the rogue waves and the series of don'ts one should beware. Then we will go on a wondrous tour of the expanding universe of ETFs.

We'll visit an immense variety of ETFs, so that you will have an idea of how expansive and inclusive ETFs are. Next we'll more specifically point out the ETFs that could pull you into a black hole or at least give you a sigh of resignation. Not all ETFs are of good value.

From the ETF cosmos you will be introduced to some hard truths in the markets, truths that have made the financial markets the dangerous environment they are. Then we'll get down to earth and meet the elephants and whales and the computers. You will need methods to operate among these elephants and whales and computers, and those methods are presented.

At last, you are introduced to options, get a quick introductory course, and are sent on your way to serious basic training in option buying and option writing. You'll learn the secrets of the professional traders. You'll learn how to create your own hedge fund and, thus, live a more secure financial life.

We hope that you'll emerge from the wilderness an effective investor. As with great commanders of the past, know-how and confidence are essential for you to reach your goals. With know-how and confidence, you can get command of your future and, in your own world of finance, become a great commander.

Part I

RECOGNITION OF OBSTACLES = THE RIGHT ATTITUDE

1

Rogue Waves

The phenomenon of rogue waves shows you why the environment is dangerous and how precautions must be in place. Rogue waves are ocean waves that are about 100 feet high. Such waves based on linear models should occur only once every 10,000 years, but based on recent historical observations, these waves may occur more often. Some have even hit cruise ships. One ship disappears every week in the ocean. Once thought to be caused by human error or mechanical failure, many of these disappearances are now blamed on rogue waves. Rogue waves can appear anywhere in the oceans without warning.

We see the same phenomenon in the investment markets. Rogue waves hit stocks all the time. These waves are unexpected news events. Such events cause stocks to leap up or drop down in price.

The book *The Black Swan* by Nassim Nicholas Taleb (Random House, 2007) helps explain the impact of improbable events. Black swans were thought not to exist until they were discovered in Australia. Today the term refers to highly improbable events, and the book indicated that these events occur much more often than you would expect and that they can have a dramatic effect.

Furthermore, chaos theory indicates that small changes can have big impacts. This is also true of the markets. In other words, certain events, even small ones, can have a dramatic impact on the daily markets today. When we see these improbable events, most people call them black swans, but because of the havoc they can wreak, I call them *rogue waves*.

An Example: Subprime Mortgages

An example of a rogue wave is the severe recession of 2008–2009. One of the major causes was the subprime mortgage bubble. Part of that problem was that the rating agencies were giving all these subprime mortgages a triple A rating. One of the reasons that these agencies were giving these AAA ratings to subprime mortgage packages, which were purchased all over the world, was that their models for determining the ratings had a worst-case scenario of a decline in real estate prices by only 15 percent. Unfortunately, what we saw was a decline in real estate prices by 40 percent, something totally improbable, but again one of these rogue waves.

Defensive Moves

In such an investment environment, it is critical that you make investments that have a lot of upside gain and minimal downside loss. Here, options are the answer. The option market is one of the places where you have greater safety to participate in the market. Also in options, diversification is necessary, and ETFs will help you diversify.

An important lesson learned here is that you need to make an honest appraisal of the worst thing that could happen to an investment that you are considering making. It is always more important to know the worst-case scenario rather than the best-case scenario. This is a key element in determining whether you will be a successful investor or not. This factor also tells you to be well diversified and to seek some protection in the options you buy so that rogue waves do not cause your major investments to tip over and sink out of sight forever.

2

Avoid Wall Street Pitfalls

I n the movie *Wall Street*, the main character, Gordon Gecko (played by Michael Douglas), made a pronouncement that you should always remember. "Money managers cannot beat the S&P 500 index because they are sheep, and sheep get slaughtered."

Don't Follow the Money Managers

Not following the money managers makes a lot of sense. If we go back to the 1960s, mutual funds and money managers have had a difficult time beating the action of the S&P 500 index. In fact, numerous studies over the years have demonstrated that 80 percent of the managed funds have been unable to beat the market. (The difficulty of beating the market is probably why so many money managers leave the profession.) Actually, money managers are not sheep, but they still have a very difficult time beating the market.

The big question is: why are the best professionals on Wall Street not able to beat the market? One reason is that we are faced with a very efficient market. With computers becoming almost as intelligent as people and with an ever-increasing large number of skilled professionals analyzing stocks, most information about a stock is already in the market, and the price of a stock reflects all the information that is currently available to the public.

Don't Underestimate the Wisdom of a Crowd

There is another reason the market is so efficient—a smart crowd. For commanders, underestimating the enemy can be fatal. General Robert E. Lee underestimated the morale and skill of the Union forces at Gettysburg, and his army was defeated. General Ulysses S. Grant underestimated the strength of the Confederate forces at Cold Harbor, and thousands of his men were slaughtered. Don't underestimate your fellow investors or your competitors. You ignore them at your own risk. The crowd is smart.

There is an old saying that goes something like this: he (or she) who keeps his (or her) head while those around him (or her) are losing theirs, probably doesn't fully understand the situation. This is usually the case. If a stock is falling, the crowd knows something. Check it out. It's sort of like if you see a crowd of people running in the opposite direction you're headed—take note. There probably is a good reason for their flight, maybe wild elephants stampeding.

In most investment markets the crowd is very smart, smarter than the most intelligent people within the crowd. It is the crowd that determines the stock price, and when stock prices drop dramatically for no reason, beware! Indymac, WorldCom, and Enron all signaled that they were headed off a cliff by their price action, even though these corporations denied having any critical problems. The FDIC didn't even have Indymac on its watch list of troubled banks. Nevertheless, you knew the bank was in trouble when its stock price dropped below $2 a share. Knowing the fundamentals was useless to the investor, but the technical action of the stock price revealed the truth. The stock price action will always tell you if a company is in trouble.

In horse racing, the crowd is so smart that it picks the winner of a race 33 percent of the time and has done so for over 100 years. In the TV show *Who Wants to Be a Millionaire*, when members of the audience were asked a question, they were right over 90 percent of the time. *Wisdom of the Crowd* (Doubleday, 2004), a book written by James Surowiecki, will give you even more evidence of crowd intelligence. One important point he made in this book was that a group's decisions are better than the decisions made individually by the smartest people in the group; groups can make quite intelligent decisions.

Because the crowd is so smart and the crowd determines the stock price, it is difficult to win in the investment game. All the available information is reflected in that stock price. Therefore, the only time you get an opportunity for a bargain (and you should always be looking for bargains) is when the market overshoots on the upside or downside. Determining when it will do that is difficult, particularly when you're trying to predict the bottom of a market. You are supposed to buy stock when there is blood in the street, but in 2008 there was blood in the street for a long time, yet stock prices kept falling.

Don't Underestimate Lady Luck

In addition to the efficient market and the smart crowd, another factor to consider is Lady Luck. Many of the successful money managers of mutual funds are successful, not based so much on skill as on luck. There are hot funds and cold funds, but the hot fund today may not be a hot fund tomorrow.

The investment world is particularly affected by Lady Luck because of a term used in the science community—*statistically significant*. Statistically significant tells us if a specific drug treatment has any meaningful effect on a patient. If the event is statistically significant, it will, in general, improve the health or reduce the symptoms of a medical condition. If not, it tells you that the treatment is probably based on luck, which is random or has no significance. However, to be statistically significant, you need a large number of events, and in the investment world, there are not a large number of events available to make a statistically significant judgment.

An investor picks four stocks in a row that bring him profits. He thinks he is an incredible investor and deserves a place, if there was such a place, in the Investors Hall of Fame. But four or even more successful stock picks in a row are not statistically significant and could be caused by the mischievous Lady Luck. Investors run hot and cold just like our water faucets. In other words, Lady Luck has a powerful influence in the cosmos, and the cosmos includes us, the investors. Don't allow Lady Luck to toy with you. She can be a ruthless trickster, deluding you, making you believe you are brilliant or dumb, and enticing you to calculate wrongly your odds of real investment success.

Lady Luck, the trickster, can make finding a winning investment system very hard to do. She can give you a winning streak when your system is actually a losing system, but you might not find that out until you're in trouble. And vice versa. You might have a losing streak when your system in the long run is a good one, but you might never find that out because you probably will have thrown the book that suggested it in the trash.

Testimonials and gurus are of no help in a cosmos influenced by the power of Lady Luck. Because we live in an uncertain world, the average investor has a tendency to give too much credence to testimonials and put too much faith in gurus. Lady Luck affects all, including gurus, and one can't tell if their claims of success are based on luck or the real thing. Investment markets are a big gambling game, and Lady Luck is the house.

Beware the Soothsayer, Even If It's You

Trying to predict the future is not a way to beat the market. Many investors subconsciously (or consciously) believe they can do this. But you cannot know the future until you are there, and no one, so far, has invented a time machine. We can dream like H. G. Wells, but we live in the present.

The soothsayer warning Caesar of his dastardly demise is either a myth or luck. (Maybe the soothsayer eavesdropped on the conspirators.) Whatever. Don't trust soothsayers, particularly if they are money managers. No matter what tools they use, they cannot claim infallible knowledge of the future. As you have already been told, money managers don't have a good track record.

Despite knowing that we can't predict the future, everyone tries to beat the market by doing exactly that. Unfortunately, 90 percent of all investors are terrible failures at trying to predict short-term moves in stocks, indexes, and futures. Remember, year after year, 80 percent of stock mutual funds underperform the indexes and stock market averages. It is wiser to invest in an index fund, where no management is involved, than in a mutual fund of stocks where you have to pay management fees. If the professionals can't beat the averages, how can the unprofessional investor do so? Future stock price actions are unpredictable.

This, of course, doesn't stop the professionals from trying to find systems that will predict future stock and commodities prices. Brokerage firms spend millions of dollars trying to find the system and have failed. Scientists, too, have tried to develop a system for predicting stock prices, also spending millions of dollars, and they have not succeeded. However, check out *The Predictors* (Henry Holt, 1999) by Thomas Bass, which shows how a system to predict index prices was developed by scientists after extensive research and testing.

And then there are the trend followers. Chaos theory does them in. Chaos theory says that small unrelated events can have a major impact on future events or trends. The unrelated small events are impossible to detect. Thus you can't foresee their impact or plan for it. Having chaos theory attack and change the course of a trend can be mind-boggling, or at least disappointing, to the trend follower.

Self-Reliance

Many investors are in search of a neat, wide path through the wilderness of investing and are looking for a reliable guide to lead them. They have high expectations for their guide, the Hawkeye of finance, a guru. They believe that this guide will lead them to the hidden gold or at least point them in the right direction.

Here we're talking about investment analysts and their systems. However, as you know by now, there is a difficult truth. There are no systems that will work all the time, and although there are good analysts, they, too, will have their losing streaks.

What it comes down to is that being successful in the market depends on you. The only way to find a path to success in the markets is to forge ahead, relying on yourself to make a path and earn your success. Of course, you can use the wisdom of the experts, but make your own decisions and be willing to take the responsibility for those decisions.

Part II

THE ETFs = THE ASSETS

Exchange-Traded Funds (ETFs)

The hottest phenomenon on Wall Street is the explosion of exchange-traded funds (ETFs), and they have made a revolutionary change in the investment environment. For whatever grouping can be imagined, a fund has been created. Like the canning of a huge variety of foods that are easily bought over the counter, ETFs package an incredible variety of products that are easily bought on the stock market exchanges. ETFs have also increased our financial mobility. The barriers are down for investors. We can zoom around in the new expanding universe of ETFs at speeds that were not possible before. The whole universe of investing is affected. As the 1960s gave us the mutual fund boom and the 1990s gave us the hedge fund boom, the beginning of the twenty-first century has given us the ETF boom.

The Expanding Universe of ETFs

Not only do ETFs allow you to buy funds on every type of investment under the sun, but you can now buy a fund the way you would buy stock or metals, such as gold, silver, platinum, or copper. Also, you no longer have to understand how to trade futures to participate in that market. Even if you want to buy stocks in emerging markets, with ETFs you have numerous choices. In some cases, there are several ETFs that you can choose from in just one country. A short search on the Web will reveal an unbelievable number of ETFs in the many emerging market countries. But let's start with the most basic investments—cash and currencies.

Minding the Money: Cash and Currency ETFs

Without traveling to countries that have desirable currency and stuffing your suitcase with it, how do you invest in cash or other currencies? Consider using ETFs. It's easy, and the choices are numerous.

To invest in the U.S. dollar, you can buy the UUP, the PowerShares DB US Dollar Index Bullish Fund. To buy other currencies, you again have ETFs to invest in. If you are interested in the euro, you can buy the FXE, the CurrencyShares Euro Trust. If you are interested in the Canadian dollar, you can buy the FXC, the CurrencyShares Canadian Dollar Trust. And if you are interested in the Japanese yen, you can buy the FXY, the CurrencyShares Japanese Yen Trust. Another fund you may be interested in is the FXA, the CurrencyShares Australian Dollar Trust, and the list goes on.

The beauty here is not only that all these funds can be purchased the way stocks are, but also that the funds closely follow the value of the currencies. In addition, with ETFs, there is no need to get involved in the futures market. Furthermore, ETFs allow you to invest a lot money in any currency.

Commodity ETFs

The new ETFs also allow you to get involved in purchasing commodities such as grains, crude oil, gasoline, and natural gas. Again, you do not have to get involved in the futures markets, and you can invest a small amount if you desire.

One example of grains is the DBA, the PowerShares DB Agriculture Fund. This fund tracks the performance of the Deutsche Bank Liquid Commodity Index. The DBA index is composed of futures contracts on commodities such as corn, wheat, soybeans, and sugar. As indicated above, you can buy DBA just like a stock, and if you wish, you can buy just a few shares.

One problem with commodity ETFs is that the funds invest in futures contracts. These contracts may not track the commodity prices closely. The same would be true with the crude oil ETFs such as the USO (U.S. Oil Fund), or the UNG (the U.S. Natural Gas Fund). Over the longer term, these funds may not trade or track oil or gas prices. Instead, these funds say that they will track the prices during that trading day. One way to stabilize the return on the fund is to select one with longer-term futures contracts. An example would be USL, the U. S. 12-Month Oil Fund.

With respect to the limitations of these funds, you will find that commodity ETFs are an easy way to get into the market. Commodity ETFs are certainly better than storing the grain in your garage. It is said that one trader bought and stored sugar in order to corner the sugar market; but this might be an urban myth. Regardless, many would think that it's better that the ETF involve itself in futures contracts than the individual investor doing it.

Index ETFs

If commodity trading is not to your taste, try trading indexes. The best way to play the stock market may be to play with the many indexes. If you want to buy the Dow Jones Industrial Average (DJIA), you can buy the SPDR, which is the SPDR Dow Jones Industrial Average ETF Trust. If you want to buy the S&P 500 index, you can buy the SPY, SPDR S&P 500 Trust, Series 1 (one of the first ETFs). For a more widespread index, the Russell 2000 Index can be traded by buying the IWM, iShares Russell 2000 Index Fund (ETF). All these ETFs trade as stocks and are usually priced at under $100 a share, with some trading for less than $10 a share.

Trading the indexes, particularly if you're successful, can be very entertaining; watching cable business channels, while the indexes go up and down, can create hours of suspense. Indexes are probably still the best way to play the stock market. But trading indexes can be quite expensive. Investing in the indexes for the longer term is fine, but trading the indexes from day to day is a crap shoot.

Stock Indexes for Emerging Markets

If you wish to travel far and wide to the stocks of countries all over the world, there are a large number of ETFs from the emerging markets. For example, Brazil offers a lot of ETFs. The

BRF, Brazil Small-Cap ETF, replicates the price and yield performance of the Market Vectors Brazil Small-Cap Index. This example of one of its ETFs is a brief glimpse of what is out there. The Emerging Market Funds offered at iShares will open up a universe of possibilities for investing in emerging market ETFs.

Staying Close to Home

The U.S. Treasury market also offers a range of ETFs. For example, if you wanted to buy inflation-protected Treasury bonds, you could buy the Treasury Inflation-Protected Securities (TIP) ETF, which is (by the way) a very liquid ETF.

Following are three additional U.S. Treasury ETFs. Note that there are many more:

1. TLT—the iShares Barclays 20+-Year Treasury Bond Fund
2. IEF—the iShares Barclays 7–10-Year Treasury Bond Fund
3. SHY—the iShares Barclays 1–3-Year Treasury Bond Fund

Bonding with Bond ETFs?

The availability of different bond funds is very large and still expanding. For corporate bonds, currently the three most popular are:

1. LQD—the iShares iBoxx $ Investment Grade Corporate Bond Fund
2. HYG—the iShares iBoxx $ High-Yield Corporate Bond Fund
3. JNK—the SPDR Barclays Capital High-Yield Bond Fund.

Mortgage-Backed Securities

Here are two mortgage-backed security ETFs:

1. VMBS—the Vanguard Mortgage-Backed Securities ETF
2. MBG—the SPDR Barclays Capital Mortgage-Backed ETF

U.S. Municipal Bond ETFs

Following is a list of U.S. municipal bond ETFs currently available, along with many other ETFs:

U.S. Broad Market

Note: A *broad market* is a market with a large number of issues.

Dow Jones U.S. Index Fund (IYY)

MSCI USA Index Fund (EUSA)

NYSE Composite Index Fund (NYC)

Russell 3000 Growth Index Fund (IWZ)

Russell 3000 Index Fund (IWV)

Russell 3000 Value Index Fund (IWW)

S&P 1500 Index Fund (ISI)

Large Cap

Note: *Large cap* refers to the capitalization of the stocks. Large caps are companies with a large value or price tag, and small caps have a small price tag.

Morningstar Large Core Index Fund (JKD)

Morningstar Large Growth Index Fund (JKE)

Morningstar Large Value Index Fund (JKF)

NYSE 100 Index Fund (NY)

Russell 1000 Growth Index Fund (IWF)

Russell 1000 Index Fund (IWB)

Russell 1000 Value Index Fund (IWD)

Russell Top 200 Growth Index Fund (IWY)

Russell Top 200 Index Fund (IWL)

Russell Top 200 Value Index Fund (IWX)

S&P 500 Growth Index Fund (IVW)

S&P 500 Index Fund (IVV)

S&P 100 Index Fund (OEF)

S&P 500 Value Index Fund (IVE)

Mid Cap

Note: *Mid cap* refers to the capitalization of the stocks. Mid caps are companies with a medium value or price tag.

Morningstar Mid Core Index Fund (JKG)

Morningstar Mid Growth Index Fund (JKH)

Morningstar Mid Value Index Fund (JKI)

Russell Midcap Growth Index Fund (IWP)

Russell Midcap Index Fund (IWR)

Russell Midcap Value Index Fund (IWS)

S&P MidCap 400 Growth Index Fund (IJK)

S&P MidCap 400 Index Fund (IJH)

S&P MidCap 400 Value Index Fund (IJJ)

Small Cap

Morningstar Small Core Index Fund (JKJ)

Morningstar Small Growth Index Fund (JKK)

Morningstar Small Value Index Fund (JKL)

Russell Microcap(R) Index Fund (IWC)

Russell 2000 Growth Index Fund (IWO)

Russell 2000 Index Fund (IWM)

Russell 2000 Value Index Fund (IWN)

S&P SmallCap 600 Growth Index Fund (IJT)

S&P SmallCap 600 Index Fund (IJR)

S&P SmallCap 600 Value Index Fund (IJS)

Sectors/Industries

Sectors refer to the industry the stocks are in such as health care or retail.

Consumer Staples/Discretionary

This is an industry of stocks that handles services and products that are not necessities. It includes high-end products, cars, hotels, and restaurants.

Dow Jones U.S. Consumer Goods Sector Index Fund (IYK)

Dow Jones U.S. Consumer Services Sector Index Fund (IYC)

Dow Jones U.S. Home Construction Index Fund (ITB)

MSCI ACWI ex US Consumer Discretionary Sector Index Fund (AXDI)

MSCI ACWI ex US Consumer Staples Sector Index Fund (AXSL)

S&P Global Consumer Discretionary Sector Index Fund (RXI)

S&P Global Consumer Staples Sector Index Fund (KXI)

Energy

This includes oil, natural gas, and refiner stocks.

Dow Jones U.S. Energy Sector Index Fund (IYE)

Dow Jones U.S. Oil Equipment & Services Index Fund (IEZ)

Dow Jones U.S. Oil & Gas Exploration & Production Index Fund (IEO)

MSCI ACWI ex US Energy Sector Index Fund (AXEN)

S&P Global Clean Energy Index Fund (ICLN)

S&P Global Energy Sector Index Fund (IXC)

Financial

This includes banks and brokerage stocks.

Dow Jones U.S. Broker-Dealers Index Fund (IAI)

Dow Jones U.S. Financial Sector Index Fund (IYF)

Dow Jones U.S. Financial Services Index Fund (IYG)

Dow Jones U.S. Insurance Index Fund (IAK)

Dow Jones U.S. Regional Banks Index Fund (IAT)

MSCI ACWI ex US Financials Sector Index Fund (AXFN)

MSCI Emerging Markets Financials Sector Index Fund (EMFN)

MSCI Europe Financials Sector Index Fund (EUFN)

MSCI Far East Financials Sector Index Fund (FEFN)

S&P Global Financials Sector Index Fund (IXG)

Health Care

Dow Jones U.S. Healthcare Providers Index Fund (IHF)

Dow Jones U.S. Healthcare Sector Index Fund (IYH)

Dow Jones U.S. Medical Devices Index Fund (IHI)

Dow Jones U.S. Pharmaceuticals Index Fund (IHE)

MSCI ACWI ex US Health Care Sector Index Fund (AXHE)

Nasdaq Biotechnology Index Fund (IBB)

S&P Global Healthcare Sector Index Fund (IXJ)

Industrials

This includes the railroad, defense, aerospace, and transportation industries.

Dow Jones Transportation Average Index Fund (IYT)

Dow Jones U.S. Aerospace & Defense Index Fund (ITA)

Dow Jones U.S. Industrial Sector Index Fund (IYJ)

MSCI ACWI ex US Industrials Sector Index Fund (AXID)

S&P Global Industrials Sector Index Fund (EXI)

Materials

This includes natural resources stocks, including rare metals.

Dow Jones U.S. Basic Materials Sector Index Fund (IYM)

MSCI ACWI ex US Materials Sector Index Fund (AXMT)

MSCI Emerging Markets Materials Sector Index Fund (EMMT)

S&P Global Materials Sector Index Fund (MXI)

S&P North American Natural Resources Sector Index Fund (IGE)

Technology

This includes the computer and software stocks.

Dow Jones U.S. Technology Sector Index Fund (IYW)

MSCI ACWI ex US Information Technology Sector Index Fund (AXIT)

PHLX SOX Semiconductor Sector Index Fund (SOXX)

S&P Global Technology Sector Index Fund (IXN)

S&P North American Technology-Multimedia Networking Index Fund (IGN)

S&P North American Technology Sector Index Fund (IGM)

S&P North American Technology-Software Index Fund (IGV)

Telecommunications

This includes stocks involved in the transmission of information, including wireless communications.

Dow Jones U.S. Telecommunications Sector Index Fund (IYZ)

MSCI ACWI ex US Telecommunication Services Sector Index Fund (AXTE)

S&P Global Telecommunications Sector Index Fund (IXP)

Utilities

Dow Jones U.S. Utilities Sector Index Fund (IDU)

MSCI ACWI ex US Utilities Sector Index Fund (AXUT)

S&P Global Utilities Sector Index Fund (JXI)

Real Estate

This includes stocks in the residential and commercial housing and raw real estate.

International Real Estate

FTSE EPRA/NAREIT Developed Asia Index Fund (IFAS)

FTSE EPRA/NAREIT Developed Europe Index Fund (IFEU)

FTSE EPRA/NAREIT Developed Real Estate ex-U.S. Index Fund (IFGL)

FTSE EPRA/NAREIT North America Index Fund (IFNA)

S&P Developed ex-U.S. Property Index Fund (WPS)

U.S. Real Estate

Cohen & Steers Realty Majors Index Fund (ICF)

Dow Jones U.S. Real Estate Index Fund (IYR)

FTSE NAREIT Industrial/Office Capped Index Fund (FIO)

FTSE NAREIT Mortgage Plus Capped Index Fund (REM)

FTSE NAREIT Real Estate 50 Index Fund (FTY)

FTSE NAREIT Residential Plus Capped Index Fund (REZ)

FTSE NAREIT Retail Capped Index Fund (RTL)

International/Global

Broad Market

FTSE Developed Small Cap ex-North America Index Fund (IFSM)

MSCI ACWI ex US Index Fund (ACWX)

MSCI ACWI Index Fund (ACWI)

MSCI EAFE Growth Index Fund (EFG)

MSCI EAFE Index Fund (EFA)

MSCI EAFE Small Cap Index Fund (SCZ)

MSCI EAFE Value Index Fund (EFV)
MSCI Emerging Markets Index Fund (EEM)
MSCI Kokusai Index Fund (TOK)
S&P Global 100 Index Fund (IOO)

Market Cap

FTSE Developed Small Cap ex-North America Index Fund
  (IFSM)
MSCI EAFE Small Cap Index Fund (SCZ)
MSCI Japan Small Cap Index Fund (SCJ)

Global Sectors

S&P Global Clean Energy Index Fund (ICLN)
S&P Global Consumer Discretionary Sector Index Fund
  (RXI)
S&P Global Consumer Staples Sector Index Fund (KXI)
S&P Global Energy Sector Index Fund (IXC)
S&P Global Financials Sector Index Fund (IXG)
S&P Global Healthcare Sector Index Fund (IXJ)
S&P Global Industrials Sector Index Fund (EXI)
S&P Global Infrastructure Index Fund (IGF)
S&P Global Materials Sector Index Fund (MXI)
S&P Global Nuclear Energy Index Fund (NUCL)
S&P Global Technology Sector Index Fund (IXN)
S&P Global Telecommunications Sector Index Fund (IXP)
S&P Global Timber & Forestry Index Fund (WOOD)
S&P Global Utilities Sector Index Fund (JXI)

International Sectors

MSCI ACWI ex US Consumer Discretionary Sector Index Fund (AXDI)

MSCI ACWI ex US Consumer Staples Sector Index Fund (AXSL)

MSCI ACWI ex US Energy Sector Index Fund (AXEN)

MSCI ACWI ex US Financials Sector Index Fund (AXFN)

MSCI ACWI ex US Health Care Sector Index Fund (AXHE)

MSCI ACWI ex US Industrials Sector Index Fund (AXID)

MSCI ACWI ex US Information Technology Sector Index Fund (AXIT)

MSCI ACWI ex US Materials Sector Index Fund (AXMT)

MSCI ACWI ex US Telecommunication Services Sector Index Fund (AXTE)

MSCI ACWI ex US Utilities Sector Index Fund (AXUT)

MSCI Emerging Markets Financials Sector Index Fund (EMFN)

MSCI Emerging Markets Materials Sector Index Fund (EMMT)

MSCI Europe Financials Sector Index Fund (EUFN)

MSCI Far East Financials Sector Index Fund (FEFN)

S&P Emerging Markets Infrastructure Index Fund (EMIF)

Emerging Markets

This includes stocks in the emerging markets such as China, Russia, Brazil, and India.

FTSE/Xinhua China 25 Index Fund (FXI)

MSCI All Peru Capped Index Fund (EPU)

MSCI Brazil Index Fund (EWZ)

MSCI BRIC Index Fund (BKF)

MSCI Chile Investable Market Index Fund (ECH)

MSCI Emerging Markets Eastern Europe Index Fund (ESR)

MSCI Emerging Markets Financials Sector Index Fund (EMFN)

MSCI Emerging Markets Index Fund (EEM)

MSCI Emerging Markets Materials Sector Index Fund (EMMT)

MSCI Indonesia Investable Market Index Fund (EIDO)

MSCI Israel Capped Investable Market Index Fund (EIS)

MSCI Malaysia Index Fund (EWM)

MSCI Mexico Investable Market Index Fund (EWW)

MSCI Poland Investable Market Index Fund (EPOL)

MSCI South Africa Index Fund (EZA)

MSCI South Korea Index Fund (EWY)

MSCI Taiwan Index Fund (EWT)

MSCI Thailand Investable Market Index Fund (THD)

MSCI Turkey Investable Market Index Fund (TUR)

S&P Emerging Markets Infrastructure Index Fund (EMIF)

S&P India Nifty 50 Index Fund (INDY)

S&P Latin America 40 Index Fund (ILF)

Africa/Middle East

MSCI Israel Capped Investable Market Index Fund (EIS)

MSCI South Africa Index Fund (EZA)

MSCI Turkey Investable Market Index Fund (TUR)

Americas

FTSE EPRA/NAREIT North America Index Fund (IFNA)

MSCI All Peru Capped Index Fund (EPU)

MSCI Brazil Index Fund (EWZ)

MSCI Canada Index Fund (EWC)

MSCI Chile Investable Market Index Fund (ECH)

MSCI Mexico Investable Market Index Fund (EWW)

S&P Latin America 40 Index Fund (ILF)

Asia

FTSE China (HK Listed) Index Fund (FCHI)

FTSE EPRA/NAREIT Developed Asia Index Fund (IFAS)

FTSE/Xinhua China 25 Index Fund (FXI)

MSCI All Country Asia ex Japan Index Fund (AAXJ)

MSCI Australia Index Fund (EWA)

MSCI Far East Financials Sector Index Fund (FEFN)

MSCI Hong Kong Index Fund (EWH)

MSCI Indonesia Investable Market Index Fund (EIDO)

MSCI Japan Index Fund (EWJ)

MSCI Japan Small Cap Index Fund (SCJ)

MSCI Malaysia Index Fund (EWM)

MSCI Pacific ex-Japan Index Fund (EPP)

MSCI Singapore Index Fund (EWS)

MSCI South Korea Index Fund (EWY)

MSCI Taiwan Index Fund (EWT)

MSCI Thailand Investable Market Index Fund (THD)

S&P Asia 50 Index Fund (AIA)

S&P/TOPIX 150 Index Fund (ITF)

Europe

FTSE EPRA/NAREIT Developed Europe Index Fund (IFEU)

MSCI Austria Investable Market Index Fund (EWO)

MSCI Belgium Investable Market Index Fund (EWK)

MSCI EMU Index Fund (EZU)

MSCI Europe Financials Sector Index Fund (EUFN)

MSCI France Index Fund (EWQ)

MSCI Germany Index Fund (EWG)

MSCI Ireland Capped Investable Market Index Fund (EIRL)

MSCI Italy Index Fund (EWI)

MSCI Netherlands Investable Market Index Fund (EWN)

MSCI Poland Investable Market Index Fund (EPOL)

MSCI Spain Index Fund (EWP)

MSCI Sweden Index Fund (EWD)

MSCI Switzerland Index Fund (EWL)

MSCI United Kingdom Index Fund (EWU)

S&P Europe 350 Index Fund (IEV)

Fixed Income

This includes bonds and notes.

Broad Market

Barclays Aggregate Bond Fund (AGG)

Treasury

These include U.S. Treasury bonds, notes, and bills.

Barclays 1–3 Year Treasury Bond Fund (SHY)

Barclays 3–7 Year Treasury Bond Fund (IEI)

Barclays 7–10 Year Treasury Bond Fund (IEF)

Barclays 10–20 Year Treasury Bond Fund (TLH)

Barclays 20+ Year Treasury Bond Fund (TLT)

Barclays Agency Bond Fund (AGZ)

Barclays Short Treasury Bond Fund (SHV)

Barclays TIPS Bond Fund (TIP)

S&P/Citigroup 1–3 Year International Treasury Bond Fund (ISHG)

S&P/Citigroup International Treasury Bond Fund (IGOV)

Government/Credit

These are government obligations.

Barclays Agency Bond Fund (AGZ)

Barclays Government/Credit Bond Fund (GBF)

Barclays Intermediate Government/Credit Bond Fund (GVI)

iShares 10+ Year Government/Credit Bond Fund (GLJ)

Credit

Barclays 1–3 Year Credit Bond Fund (CSJ)

Barclays Credit Bond Fund (CFT)

Barclays Intermediate Credit Bond Fund (CIU)

iBoxx $ High Yield Corporate Bond Fund (HYG)
iBoxx $ Investment Grade Corporate Bond Fund (LQD)
iShares 10+ Year Credit Bond Fund (CLY)

Municipal Bond

These are tax-free city and state bond funds.

iShares 2012 S&P AMT-Free Municipal Series (MUAA)
iShares 2013 S&P AMT-Free Municipal Series (MUAB)
iShares 2014 S&P AMT-Free Municipal Series (MUAC)
iShares 2015 S&P AMT-Free Municipal Series (MUAD)
iShares 2016 S&P AMT-Free Municipal Series (MUAE)
iShares 2017 S&P AMT-Free Municipal Series (MUAF)
S&P California AMT-Free Municipal Bond Fund (CMF)
S&P National AMT-Free Municipal Bond Fund (MUB)
S&P New York AMT-Free Municipal Bond Fund (NYF)
S&P Short-Term National AMT-Free Municipal Bond Fund
    (SUB)

Mortgages

Barclays MBS Bond Fund (MBB)

International/Global

JPMorgan USD Emerging Markets Bond Fund (EMB)
S&P/Citigroup 1–3 Year International Treasury Bond Fund
    (ISHG)
S&P/Citigroup International Treasury Bond Fund (IGOV)

Commodities

COMEX Gold Trust (IAU)
S&P GSCI(R) Commodity-Indexed Trust (GSG)
Silver Trust (SLV)

Asset Allocation

These are funds that can be involved in asset allocations providing diversification for your portfolio.

S&P Aggressive Allocation Fund (AOA)
S&P Conservative Allocation Fund (AOK)
S&P Growth Allocation Fund (AOR)
S&P Moderate Allocation Fund (AOM)
S&P Target Date 2015 Index Fund (TZE)
S&P Target Date 2020 Index Fund (TZG)
S&P Target Date 2025 Index Fund (TZI)
S&P Target Date 2030 Index Fund (TZL)
S&P Target Date 2035 Index Fund (TZO)
S&P Target Date 2040 Index Fund (TZV)
S&P Target Date Retirement Income Index Fund (TGR)

Dividend

These funds try to get you a good return from dividend payouts.

Dow Jones International Select Dividend Index Fund (IDV)
Dow Jones Select Dividend Index Fund (DVY)
S&P U.S. Preferred Stock Index Fund (PFF)

Environmental—Social

FTSE KLD 400 Social Index Fund (DSI)
FTSE KLD Select Social Index Fund (KLD)

Bonds

Barclays Aggregate Bond Fund (AGG)

Treasury

Barclays 1–3 Year Treasury Bond Fund (SHY)
Barclays 3–7 Year Treasury Bond Fund (IEI)
Barclays 7–10 Year Treasury Bond Fund (IEF)
Barclays 10–20 Year Treasury Bond Fund (TLH)
Barclays 20+ Year Treasury Bond Fund (TLT)
Barclays Agency Bond Fund (AGZ)
Barclays Short Treasury Bond Fund (SHV)
Barclays TIPS Bond Fund (TIP)

Government

Barclays Agency Bond Fund (AGZ)
Barclays Government/Credit Bond Fund (GBF)
Barclays Intermediate Government/Credit Bond Fund (GVI)

Credit

Barclays 1–3 Year Credit Bond Fund (CSJ)
Barclays Credit Bond Fund (CFT)

Barclays Intermediate Credit Bond Fund (CIU)
Barclays MBS Bond Fund (MBB)
iShares 10+ Year Credit Bond Fund (CLY)
iShares 10+ Year Government/Credit Bond Fund (GLJ)

Other ETFs

Every day new ETFs are added. Many are unique and do not fit into any specific category. Here is just a sampling:

Cohen & Steers Realty Majors Index Fund (ICF)
Dow Jones International Select Dividend Index Fund (IDV)
Dow Jones Select Dividend Index Fund (DVY)
Dow Jones U.S. Aerospace & Defense Index Fund (ITA)
Dow Jones U.S. Basic Materials Sector Index Fund (IYM)
Dow Jones U.S. Broker-Dealers Index Fund (IAI)
Dow Jones U.S. Consumer Goods Sector Index Fund (IYK)
Dow Jones U.S. Consumer Services Sector Index Fund (IYC)
Dow Jones U.S. Energy Sector Index Fund (IYE)
Dow Jones U.S. Financial Sector Index Fund (IYF)
Dow Jones U.S. Financial Services Index Fund (IYG)
Dow Jones U.S. Healthcare Providers Index Fund (IHF)
Dow Jones U.S. Healthcare Sector Index Fund (IYH)
Dow Jones U.S. Home Construction Index Fund (ITB)
Dow Jones U.S. Index Fund (IYY)
Dow Jones U.S. Industrial Sector Index Fund (IYJ)
Dow Jones U.S. Insurance Index Fund (IAK)
Dow Jones U.S. Medical Devices Index Fund (IHI)
Dow Jones U.S. Oil & Gas Exploration & Production Index Fund (IEO)

Dow Jones U.S. Oil Equipment & Services Index Fund (IEZ)

Dow Jones U.S. Pharmaceuticals Index Fund (IHE)

Dow Jones U.S. Real Estate Index Fund (IYR)

Dow Jones U.S. Regional Banks Index Fund (IAT)

Dow Jones U.S. Technology Sector Index Fund (IYW)

Dow Jones U.S. Telecommunications Sector Index Fund (IYZ)

Dow Jones U.S. Transportation Average Index Fund (IYT)

Dow Jones U.S. Utilities Sector Index Fund (IDU)

FTSE China (HK Listed) Index Fund (FCHI)

FTSE Developed Small Cap ex-North America Index Fund (IFSM)

FTSE EPRA/NAREIT Developed Asia Index Fund (IFAS)

FTSE EPRA/NAREIT Developed Europe Index Fund (IFEU)

FTSE EPRA/NAREIT Developed Real Estate ex-U.S. Index Fund (IFGL)

FTSE EPRA/NAREIT North America Index Fund (IFNA)

FTSE KLD 400 Social Index Fund (DSI)

FTSE KLD Select Social Index Fund (KLD)

FTSE NAREIT Industrial/Office Capped Index Fund (FIO)

FTSE NAREIT Mortgage Plus Capped Index Fund (REM)

FTSE NAREIT Real Estate 50 Index Fund (FTY)

FTSE NAREIT Residential Plus Capped Index Fund (REZ)

FTSE NAREIT Retail Capped Index Fund (RTL)

FTSE/Xinhua China 25 Index Fund (FXI)

iBoxx $ High Yield Corporate Bond Fund (HYG)

iBoxx $ Investment Grade Corporate Bond Fund (LQD)

iShares 2012 S&P AMT-Free Municipal Series (MUAA)

iShares 2013 S&P AMT-Free Municipal Series (MUAB)

iShares 2014 S&P AMT-Free Municipal Series (MUAC)

iShares 2015 S&P AMT-Free Municipal Series (MUAD)

iShares 2016 S&P AMT-Free Municipal Series (MUAE)

iShares 2017 S&P AMT-Free Municipal Series (MUAF)

JPMorgan USD Emerging Markets Bond Fund (EMB)

Morningstar Large Core Index Fund (JKD)

Morningstar Large Growth Index Fund (JKE)

Morningstar Large Value Index Fund (JKF)

Morningstar Mid Core Index Fund (JKG)

Morningstar Mid Growth Index Fund (JKH)

Morningstar Mid Value Index Fund (JKI)

Morningstar Small Core Index Fund (JKJ)

Morningstar Small Growth Index Fund (JKK)

Morningstar Small Value Index Fund (JKL)

MSCI ACWI ex US Index Fund (ACWX)

MSCI ACWI ex US Consumer Discretionary Sector Index Fund (AXDI)

MSCI ACWI ex US Consumer Staples Sector Index Fund (AXSL)

MSCI ACWI ex US Energy Sector Index Fund (AXEN)

MSCI ACWI ex US Financials Sector Index Fund (AXFN)

MSCI ACWI ex US Health Care Sector Index Fund (AXHE)

MSCI ACWI ex US Industrials Sector Index Fund (AXID)

MSCI ACWI ex US Information Technology Sector Index Fund (AXIT)

MSCI ACWI ex US Materials Sector Index Fund (AXMT)

MSCI ACWI ex US Telecommunication Services Sector Index Fund (AXTE)

MSCI ACWI ex US Utilities Sector Index Fund (AXUT)

MSCI ACWI Index Fund (ACWI)

MSCI All Country Asia ex Japan Index Fund (AAXJ)

MSCI All Peru Capped Index Fund (EPU)

MSCI Australia Index Fund (EWA)

MSCI Austria Investable Market Index Fund (EWO)

MSCI Belgium Investable Market Index Fund (EWK)

MSCI Brazil Index Fund (EWZ)

MSCI BRIC Index Fund (BKF)

MSCI Canada Index Fund (EWC)

MSCI Chile Investable Market Index Fund (ECH)

MSCI EAFE Growth Index Fund (EFG)

MSCI EAFE Index Fund (EFA)

MSCI EAFE Small Cap Index Fund (SCZ)

MSCI EAFE Value Index Fund (EFV)

MSCI Emerging Markets Eastern Europe Index Fund (ESR)

MSCI Emerging Markets Financials Sector Index Fund (EMFN)

MSCI Emerging Markets Index Fund (EEM)

MSCI Emerging Markets Materials Sector Index Fund (EMMT)

MSCI EMU Index Fund (EZU)

MSCI Europe Financials Sector Index Fund (EUFN)

MSCI Far East Financials Sector Index Fund (FEFN)

MSCI France Index Fund (EWQ)

MSCI Germany Index Fund (EWG)

MSCI Hong Kong Index Fund (EWH)

MSCI Indonesia Investable Market Index Fund (EIDO)

MSCI Ireland Capped Investable Market Index Fund (EIRL)

MSCI Israel Capped Investable Market Index Fund (EIS)

MSCI Italy Index Fund (EWI)

MSCI Japan Index Fund (EWJ)

MSCI Japan Small Cap Index Fund (SCJ)

MSCI Kokusai Index Fund (TOK)

MSCI Malaysia Index Fund (EWM)

MSCI Mexico Investable Market Index Fund (EWW)

MSCI Netherlands Investable Market Index Fund (EWN)

MSCI Pacific ex-Japan Index Fund (EPP)

MSCI Poland Investable Market Index Fund (EPOL)

MSCI Singapore Index Fund (EWS)

MSCI South Africa Index Fund (EZA)

MSCI South Korea Index Fund (EWY)

MSCI Spain Index Fund (EWP)

MSCI Sweden Index Fund (EWD)

MSCI Switzerland Index Fund (EWL)

MSCI Taiwan Index Fund (EWT)

MSCI Thailand Investable Market Index Fund (THD)

MSCI Turkey Investable Market Index Fund (TUR)

MSCI United Kingdom Index Fund (EWU)

MSCI USA Index Fund (EUSA)

MSCI United Kingdom Index Fund (EWU)

Nasdaq Biotechnology Index Fund (IBB)

NYSE Composite Index Fund (NYC)

NYSE 100 Index Fund (NY)

Russell Microcap(R) Index Fund (IWC)

Russell Midcap Growth Index Fund (IWP)

Russell Midcap Index Fund (IWR)

Russell Midcap Value Index Fund (IWS)

Russell 1000 Growth Index Fund (IWF)

Russell 1000 Index Fund (IWB)

Russell 1000 Value Index Fund (IWD)

Russell 2000 Growth Index Fund (IWO)

Russell 2000 Index Fund (IWM)

Russell 2000 Value Index Fund (IWN)

Russell 3000 Growth Index Fund (IWZ)

Russell 3000 Index Fund (IWV)

Russell 3000 Value Index Fund (IWW)

Russell Top 200 Growth Index Fund (IWY)

Russell Top 200 Index Fund (IWL)

Russell Top 200 Value Index Fund (IWX)

S&P Aggressive Allocation Fund (AOA)

S&P Asia 50 Index Fund (AIA)

S&P California AMT-Free Municipal Bond Fund (CMF)

S&P/Citigroup International Treasury Bond Fund (IGOV)

S&P/Citigroup 1–3 Year International Treasury Bond Fund (ISHG)

S&P Conservative Allocation Fund (AOK)

S&P Developed ex-U.S. Property Index Fund (WPS)

S&P Emerging Markets Infrastructure Index Fund (EMIF)

S&P Europe 350 Index Fund (IEV)

S&P 1500 Index Fund (ISI)

S&P 500 Growth Index Fund (IVW)

S&P 500 Index Fund (IVV)

S&P 500 Value Index Fund (IVE)

S&P Global Clean Energy Index Fund (ICLN)

S&P Global Consumer Discretionary Sector Index Fund (RXI)

S&P Global Consumer Staples Sector Index Fund (KXI)

S&P Global Energy Sector Index Fund (IXC)

S&P Global Financials Sector Index Fund (IXG)

S&P Global Healthcare Sector Index Fund (IXJ)

S&P Global Industrials Sector Index Fund (EXI)

S&P Global Infrastructure Index Fund (IGF)

S&P Global Materials Sector Index Fund (MXI)

S&P Global Nuclear Energy Index Fund (NUCL)

S&P Global 100 Index Fund (IOO)

S&P Global Technology Sector Index Fund (IXN)

S&P Global Telecommunications Sector Index Fund (IXP)

S&P Global Timber & Forestry Index Fund (WOOD)

S&P Global Utilities Sector Index Fund (JXI)

S&P Growth Allocation Fund (AOR)

S&P GSCI(R) Commodity-Indexed Trust (GSG)

S&P India Nifty 50 Index Fund (INDY)

S&P Latin America 40 Index Fund (ILF)

S&P MidCap 400 Growth Index Fund (IJK)

S&P MidCap 400 Index Fund (IJH)

S&P MidCap 400 Value Index Fund (IJJ)

S&P Moderate Allocation Fund (AOM)

S&P National AMT-Free Municipal Bond Fund (MUB)

S&P New York AMT-Free Municipal Bond Fund (NYF)

S&P North American Natural Resources Sector Index Fund (IGE)

S&P North American Technology-Multimedia Networking Index Fund (IGN)

S&P North American Technology Sector Index Fund (IGM)

S&P North American Technology-Semiconductors Index Fund (IGW)

S&P North American Technology-Software Index Fund (IGV)

S&P 100 Index Fund (OEF)

S&P Short Term National AMT-Free Municipal Bond Fund (SUB)

S&P SmallCap 600 Growth Index Fund (IJT)

S&P SmallCap 600 Index Fund (IJR)

S&P SmallCap 600 Value Index Fund (IJS)

S&P Target Date 2015 Index Fund (TZE)

S&P Target Date 2020 Index Fund (TZG)

S&P Target Date 2025 Index Fund (TZI)

S&P Target Date 2030 Index Fund (TZL)

S&P Target Date 2035 Index Fund (TZO)

S&P Target Date 2040 Index Fund (TZV)

S&P Target Date Retirement Income Index Fund (TGR)

S&P/TOPIX 150 Index Fund (ITF)

S&P U.S. Preferred Stock Index Fund (PFF)

Mining the Metals

Why invest in metals? You can now buy ETFs on the precious metals exchange, but why would you not just buy a gold or silver mining stock? The problem with these stocks is the external and internal factors (unrelated to the price of gold or silver) that influence the price of the stock. Politics, taxes, and management are some of the factors. One gold firm went out of business when Montana prevented it from working its largest mine. The government of Australia put a heavy tax on mining companies in its country. No one can make predictions or estimate odds when politics is involved. Rational thinking does not generally apply to politics.

There are a couple of other routes you could take. If you only want to bet on the price of gold, silver, or platinum, you could buy the futures contract. Or you could pick an easier alternative and buy an ETF, as many have done. The most liquid ETF for the price of gold is the GLD, the SPDR Gold Shares. Here, the GLD invests in gold futures contracts to replicate the price of gold. To invest in silver, you can buy the SLV ETF.

To invest in platinum, you can buy ETFS Physical Platinum Shares. The problem with platinum ETFs is that there is a very limited supply of platinum in the world. As a result, the ETF will draw more money into the platinum futures, causing the prices to rise for industrial users. Another popular metal is palladium. You can buy the ETFS Physical Palladium Shares. Finally, you can directly buy copper by purchasing JJC, iPath Dow Jones–UBS Copper Subindex Total Return ETN shares.

These ETFS invest in the futures contracts. As easily as you can buy stock, you can buy shares in gold, silver, platinum, palladium, or copper. Sometimes the cookie jar is not the only place to store valuable metals. You might not want to replace that strategic cookie jar plan, but trading in metal ETFs could enhance it.

ETFs

Buying ETFs is easy, but how do you bet on the opposite direction? If the broker can borrow the stock and you are responsible for the dividends, you could sell short the ETF. But that is not necessary. There are "inverse ETFs." These are ETFs that go up in price when the underlying index, commodity, currency, or futures goes down in price. So when you buy the DOG, which is the short of the Dow 30 Industrials ETF, you are betting that the Dow 30 will go down in price. This means that the DOG rises when the Dow 30 falls, and the DOG falls in price when the Dow 30 rises in price.

Other inverse ETFs include PSG, Short QQQ or Nasdaq 100, Short S&P 500 or SH, Short Small Cap 600 or SBB, and Short Russell 2000. In the commodities arena, you have the DNO, the United States Short Oil ETF, the DGZ, and the PowerShares DB Gold Short ETN. And, as usual, the list goes on.

Ultra ETFs

As you have seen, ETFs can come in different forms, and one type is more explosive than your regular ETF. This kind of ETF is designed to give you more leverage. In other words, these ETFs give you two and three times the move of the underlying index, commodity, bonds, or groups of stocks. They are called *ultra ETF's* and create leverage by using futures and derivative contracts.

Here is an example of how ultra ETFs work. Let's say you think that interest rates will rise, and as a result, Treasuries will fall in price. You could then buy the TBT, The Pro Shares Ultra Short 20+ Year Treasury ETF. This ETF should rise twice as fast as Treasury bonds will fall in price. In a sense, you are short Treasury bonds but get twice the firing power of such a short position.

Here is another example. If you think that financial stocks will fall in price, you could buy The Direxion Daily Bear 3 × Shares ETF. On a daily basis, this ETF should move up three times as fast as the amount that financial stocks fall in price. Of course, if financial stocks rise in price, the reverse is true.

Currently, one of the most popular inverse ultra funds is the SDS, ProShares UltraShort S&P 500 ETF. When you buy this ETF, you are betting that the S&P 500 index will fall in price, but at twice the rate of the S&P 500 index. Again, because futures and derivative contracts are used to do this, this ETF may not perfectly track the index in reverse.

Of course, you can also buy ultra ETFs that move on the upside. In other words, the ETF moves up when the underlying index, bonds, or commodity moves up. For example, you could buy the UBT, Ultra 20+ Year Treasury ETF, which should rise twice as fast as the 20+ Year Treasury bond rises in price. The UST, Ultra 7–10 Year Treasury ETF works the same way. The Ultra Gold Fund is UGL, and likewise, on a daily basis will or should move up twice as fast as the price of gold.

There is a drawback. The promise of the funds' manager is that the ETFs will make the proper move on any specific day. However, over longer periods of time, such moves are not usually likely. Although these ETFs are quite popular, over time they do not make the promised moves. Ultra ETFs can deliver some enormous gains. However, like quasars, ultra ETFs' power can be dangerous. It can burn you as well as enrich you. Beware!

ETFs on Stock Sectors

As you have seen, exchange-traded funds create an expanding universe of choices. You can bet on an incredible variety of groupings, and this includes stock groupings. ETFs can be purchased on stock sectors, such as the retail sector or the real estate sector; and that's just a glimpse of the variety that's available.

For example, you could buy the health-care sector by buying ETF ticker XLV, the Telecom sector with ETF ticker ITV, or the Utilities ETF ticker XLU. The list continues:

- The financials—ETF ticker XLF
- The basic materials—ETF ticker XLB
- The consumer staples—ETF ticker XLP
- The energy—ETF ticker XLE
- The technology—ETF ticker XLK
- The industrial—ETF ticker XLI
- The consumer discretionary—ETF ticker XLY

So you have a lot of choices regarding the different stock groups. Also, you have an extra bonus; because stock sector ETFs are not actively traded internally, management fees are quite low.

Exchange-Traded Notes (ETNs)

What are ETNs? They are not ETFs; they are exchange-traded *notes*. They are debt instruments. Debt instruments do not own anything except the promise to track an instrument. With an ETN, you only have a promise from the firm or provider that created the ETN—a promise that it will pay the investor. But here is the disadvantage: if the provider goes bankrupt, you lose everything. So there is an extra danger in buying these notes. Obviously, then, ETNs are not the same as ETFs. With ETFs you actually own something, like the futures contracts or the stocks in a sector or the actual bonds in an index.

Two interesting ETNs are the VXX and the VXZ. The VXX is the iPath S&P 500 VIX Short-Term Future ETN and the VXZ is the iPath S&P 500 VIX Mid-Term Futures ETN. The VIX is the volatility index of the stocks in the S&P 500. It tells you the overall volatility of the stock prices in the S&P 500 index. The volatility measure is derived from the implied volatility of the stock's put and call options. When the VIX is high, there is a lot of fear in the market. When it is low, there is a lot of complacency in the market. In the recent recession, the VIX almost reached 90 percent, although it was as low as 10 percent for a few years before.

How to Select ETFs

ETFs give you the opportunity to dramatically diversify your portfolio, but how should you approach the selection process?

Management fees are always an important consideration. Mutual funds have always had high management fees that greatly cut into your returns, especially actively managed funds. ETFs have low fees, but you still need to shop around. One of the best rates right now is at Vanguard, but this will change, so check the fees at each ETF you are considering. You need to do your homework here.

Do not select ETFs or funds of any kind that are actively traded internally. Money managers cannot beat the market, so don't bet on them! Most money managers that actively manage their holdings cannot better the S&P 500 index. The explosion of ETFs will give you the opportunity to truly diversify and to do as well as the money managers.

Mutual Funds versus ETFs

There are many advantages of ETFs over mutual funds. Mutual funds are usually actively managed, and such funds do not do well. As mentioned earlier, with ETFs, the management fees are usually far less. You also have much more control of the tax consequences with ETFs, an important consideration. Finally, ETFs usually have options listed on them. That gives you better ways to increase your income and reduce your risks.

ETFs offer new advantages for the investor. With ETFs, there is less complexity, greater flexibility, easier diversification, and generally more power to the investor.

You have to put the odds in your favor. You, as a small investor, have an immense variety of investments that are easy to get at because they are now packaged and available to be easily bought on the stock exchanges. You have the ability to run your portfolio like your own hedge fund. And to do this, along with options, the main element in your portfolio should be ETFs. Plan well with ETFs and you will be able to say as we do in war, space, and now in finance, mission accomplished!

4

Master Limited
Partnerships

Another choice for exchange-traded funds is the master limited partnership (MLP). MLPs are similar to real estate investment trusts (REITs) in that they do not pay income taxes and are traded on exchanges, like the New York Stock Exchange. However, they are different because they are a partnership. This means that a general partner operates the partnership and the investors are limited partners.

MLPs receive special tax treatment. Unlike listed stocks that have double taxation, MLPs do not pay income taxes. (Almost all U.S. corporations pay a corporate tax on profits, plus a tax on dividends and distributions paid out by the corporation.) They pay out all their profits, and the investor pays a tax on the distribution or dividend. In order to get this special benefit, the master limited partnership must get 90 percent of its income on activities in real estate, commodities, or natural resources.

When choosing an MLP, try to select larger ones that have a long history of consistent distribution.

Here is a sampling of exchange-traded master limited partnerships:

Natural Gas MLPs

Atlas Pipeline Partners (APL) Based in Pennsylvania and formed in 1999; owns and operates approximately 8,600 miles of active intrastate gas gathering and processing assets in Oklahoma, west Texas, southern Kansas, and Tennessee.

Boardwalk Pipeline Partners (BWP) Based in Houston, Texas, with initial public offering occurring in 2005; owns and operates approximately 14,000 miles of natural gas pipelines and underground storage fields in 11 states, including Texas and Louisiana.

Copano Energy (CPNO) Operates natural gas pipelines and a processing plant in the Texas Gulf region. Copano is a limited liability company (LLC).

Crosstex Energy (XTEX) Operates natural gas pipelines and processing plants in Texas, Louisiana, and Mississippi.

DCP Midstream (DPM) Transports natural gas and natural gas liquids (propane) in the Gulf Coast area. Also handles a wholesale propane distribution business.

Duncan Energy Partners (DEP) Operates natural gas pipelines in Texas and Louisiana.

Eagle Rock Energy Partners (EROC) Operates natural gas pipeline in Texas and Louisiana.

El Paso Pipeline Partners (EPB) Has an interstate pipeline system including interest in the Colorado Interstate Gas Company and the Southern Natural Gas Company, both of which operate pipelines in the region.

Hiland Partners (HLND) Has natural gas processing services in the Rocky Mountain regions of the United States.

MarkWest Energy Partners (MWE) Operates natural gas pipelines in the Northeast and South Central areas of the United States.

Oneok Partners (OKS) Has natural gas pipelines, mostly in the Midwest.

Quicksilver Gas Services (KGS) Has natural gas facilities in Texas.

Regency Energy Partners (RGNC) Has natural gas pipelines in several southern states.

Spectra Energy Partners (SEP) Has natural gas pipelines in Tennessee and Florida.

Targa Resources Partners (NGLS) Operates natural gas pipelines in Louisiana and Texas.

TC PipeLines (TCLP) Transports natural gas from Oregon to northern Nevada, plus has an interest in other pipeline companies.

Western Gas Partners (WES) Handles the business of processing natural gas for Anadarko and other producers.

Williams Partners (WPZ) Has natural gas processing assets in New Mexico, Colorado, and Alabama.

Williams Pipeline Partners (WMZ) Owns an interest in a natural gas pipeline system from New Mexico to the northwestern United States.

Oil Pipeline MLPs

Buckeye Partners (BPL) Has petroleum products pipelines and operates pipelines owned by major oil and chemical companies.

Holly Energy Partners (HEP) Has crude oil/refined product pipelines in the West.

Magellan Midstream Partners (MMP) Operates oil pipelines.

Martin Midstream Partners (MMLP) Operates a variety of services for producers and suppliers of petroleum products in the Gulf Coast region.

Plains All American Pipeline (PAA) Has crude oil and refined products pipelines.

SemGroup Energy Partners (SGLP) Has crude oil pipelines in Oklahoma, Kansas, and Texas.

Sunoco Logistics Partners (SXL) Has crude oil and refined products pipelines in the Midwest and eastern states.

Pipeline MLPs

Enbridge Energy Partners (EEP) Has liquid petroleum pipelines and operates natural gas facilities.

Energy Transfer Partners (ETP) Has natural gas pipelines and sells propane in many states.

Enterprise Product Partners (EPD) Has many different pipelines including natural gas and crude oil.

Genesis Energy (GEL) Operates and has crude oil and natural gas pipelines.

Kinder Morgan Energy Partners (KMP) Operates and owns a wide variety of pipelines including natural gas, gasoline, and other petroleum products.

NuStar Energy (NS) NuStar has crude oil and refined product pipelines in North America and Europe.

TransMontaigne Partners (TLP) Operates pipeline services for refined petroleum products and crude oil on the Gulf Coast.

Propane MLPs

AmeriGas Partners (APU) Sells propane to over a million customers in most states.

Ferrellgas Partners (FGP) Sells propane to a million customers in all states.

Inergy (NRGY) Sells propane to 700,000 customers in the eastern states.

Star Gas Partners (SGU) Sells heating oil to customers in 40 states.

Suburban Propane Partners (SPH) Sells propane to a million customers in many states.

Oil and Natural Gas MLPs

Alliance Resource Partners (ARLP) Runs coal mines in Illinois, Indiana, Kentucky, and Maryland.

BreitBurn Energy Partners (BBEP) Has oil and natural gas reserves in California, Wyoming, Florida, Indiana, Kentucky, and Texas.

Constellation Energy Partners (CEP) This is an LLC that produces oil and natural gas.

Dorchester Minerals (DMLP) Has producing and nonproducing oil and natural gas lands in many states.

Encore Energy Partners (ENP) Has producing and non-producing oil and natural gas properties in Wyoming, Montana, and Texas.

EV Energy Partners (EVEP): Operates a natural gas and oil exploration and production partnership.

Legacy Reserves (LGCY) Has oil and gas deposits in Texas and New Mexico.

LINN Energy (LINE) Has natural gas reserves in Texas, Oklahoma, and California.

Natural Resources Partners (NRP) Has coal properties in the United States. Also leases its properties to mine operators.

Penn Virginia Resource Partners (PVR) Owns coal properties and generates revenues from the sale of timber growing on its properties. Also operates natural gas facilities.

Pioneer Southwest Energy Partners (PSE) Has oil and natural gas reserves in Texas and New Mexico.

Vanguard Natural Resources (VNR) Has producing and nonproducing natural gas and oil reserves.

Tanker MLPs

Capital Product Partners (CPLP) Operates tankers capable of carrying crude and refined oil products.

K-Sea Transportation Partners (KSP) Runs tank barges and tugboats for transporting refined petroleum products.

Teekay LNG Partners (TGP) Runs liquefied natural gas carriers and crude oil tankers.

Teekay Offshore Partners (TOO) Runs shuttle tankers that transport oil from offshore fields to onshore processing plants.

Mortgage MLPs

America First Tax Exempt Investors (ATAX) Buys federally tax-exempt mortgage revenue bonds.

Municipal Mortgage & Equity (MMAB) Conveys financing to developers of multifamily housing.

New England Realty Associates (NEN) Has residential apartment buildings, condominium units, and commercial properties.

Other MLPs

AllianceBernstein Holding L.P. (AB) Manages mutual funds and provides investment management services to private clients, individual investors, and institutional investors.

Blackstone Group (BX) A private equity company with interest in many firms. It also manages mutual funds.

Calumet Specialty Products Partners (CLMT) Produces all types of fuels and oils.

Cedar Fair (FUN) Manages and owns amusement parks, outdoor water parks, and hotels.

Cheniere Energy Partners (CQP) Owns a liquid natural gas (LNG) receiving terminal in Louisiana.

Exterran Partners (EXLP) Generates compression services to transport natural gas.

Global Partners (GLP) Distributes petroleum products wholesale.

ML Macadamia Orchards (NNUT) Manages and has macadamia orchards in Hawaii.

Pope Resources (POPE) Manages and has timberland property in the Northwest.

Terra Nitrogen (TNH) Produces nitrogen fertilizer products.

Real Estate Investment Trusts (REITs)

Real estate investment trusts(REITs) are similar to master limited partnerships because they can avoid or reduce corporate income taxes. They are also traded on an exchange, like the New York Stock Exchange. To get the tax advantage, REITs must invest in real estate and are required to distribute 90 percent of their income. The key things to evaluate are net asset value, adjusted funds from operations, and cash available for distribution. Try to find REITs that are larger and have a good stream of distribution for a longer period of time.

Here is a sampling of real estate investment trusts and the properties they own or manage:

> **Acadia Realty Trust (AKR)** Based in White Plains, New York and founded in 1998; owns and operates community shopping centers totaling more than 10 million square feet of retail space across the United States.

Shopping Center and Other Retail REITs

> **Agree Realty (ADC)** Based in Farmington, Michigan; initial public offering was made in 1994; owns and operates community shopping centers and tenant properties totaling more than 3.5 million square feet in 17 states, mostly in the Midwest.
>
> **CBL & Associates Properties (CBL)** Regional malls and community shopping centers.
>
> **Cedar Shopping Centers (CDR)** Community and neighborhood shopping centers.
>
> **Developers Diversified Realty (DDR)** Shopping centers, minimalls, and lifestyle centers.
>
> **Equity One (EQY)** Community shopping centers.
>
> **Federal Realty Investment Trust (FRT)** Shopping centers and street retail properties.
>
> **General Growth Properties (GGP)** Handles regional shopping centers in 45 states, plus Brazil and Turkey.

Glimcher Realty Trust (GRT) Regional and super-regional malls and community centers.

Inland Real Estate (IRC) Neighborhood, community, and single-tenant retail centers.

Kimco Realty (KIM) Neighborhood and community shopping centers in most states, plus Puerto Rico, Canada, Mexico, and Chile.

Kite Realty Group (KRG) Neighborhood and community shopping centers.

Macerich (MAC) Regional shopping centers.

National Retail Properties (NNN) Properties in most states where tenant is under long-term lease.

Pennsylvania Real Estate Investment (PEI) Retail strip centers and shopping malls.

Ramco-Gershenson Properties Trust (RPT) Regional malls plus community shopping centers.

Realty Income (O) Retail properties leased to regional and national chains.

Regency Centers (REG) Neighborhood retail centers.

Saul Centers (BFS) Office properties and neighborhood shopping centers.

Simon Property Group (SPG) Regional malls, outlet centers, lifestyle centers, and community shopping centers all over the world.

Tanger Factory Outlet (SKT) Factory outlet centers.

Taubman Centers (TCO) Urban, suburban regional, and super-regional shopping centers.

Urstadt Biddle Properties (UBP) Community shopping centers.

Weingarten Realty Investors (WRI) Community shopping centers and industrial properties.

Healthcare REITs

Care Investment Trust (CRE) Nursing, assisted living, and Alzheimer facilities.

HCP (HCP) Hospitals and senior housing.

Healthcare Realty Trust (HR) Numerous medical care facilities.

Health Care REIT (HCN) Assisted living and nursing facilities.

LTC Properties (LTC) Buys long-term care and other health-care investments.

Medical Properties Trust (MPW) A wide variety of medical care facilities.

Nationwide Health Properties (NHP) A wide variety of medical care facilities.

Omega Healthcare Investors (OHI) Finances and invests in nursing homes.

Senior Housing Properties Trust (SNH) Nursing homes, senior apartments, etc.

Universal Health Realty Income Trust (UHT) Owns acute care hospitals, behavioral health-care facilities, rehabilitation hospitals, subacute care facilities, surgery centers, childcare centers, and medical office buildings in 15 states.

Ventas (VTR) Medical care facilities.

Hotel REITs

DiamondRock Hospitality (DRH) Premium hotels.

FelCor Lodging Trust (FCH) All-suite hotels.

Hersha Hospitality Trust (HT) Full-service hotels.

Hospitality Properties Trust (HPT) Midscale suite hotels.

Host Hotels & Resorts (HST) Large REIT that owns upscale hotels.

LaSalle Hotel Properties (LHO) Upscale, full-service hotels.

MHI Hospitality Corporation (MDH): Full-service hotels

Strategic Hotels & Resorts (BEE) Luxury hotels and resorts.

Sunstone Hotel Investors (SHO) Upscale hotels.

Supertel Hospitality (SPPR) Hotels.

Industrial Facilities REITs

Alexandria Real Estate Equities (ARE) Leases out R&D labs.

AMB Property (AMB) Industrial facilities.

BioMed Realty Trust (BMR) Leases out R&D labs.

DCT Industrial Trust (DCT) Light industrial properties.

Digital Realty Trust (DLR) Data centers used by information technology.

DuPont Fabros Technology (DFT) Data centers used by information technology.

EastGroup Properties (EGP) Industrial properties.

First Industrial Realty Trust (FR) Industrial properties.

Mission West Properties (MSW) R&D properties.

Monmouth Real Estate Investment (MNRTA) Industrial properties and REIT securities.

ProLogis (PLD) Distribution facilities.

Office Property REITs

Boston Properties (BXP) Office properties.

Brandywine Realty Trust (BDN) Office properties.

Brookfield Properties (BPO) Office properties.

CommonWealth REIT (CWH) Office and industrial properties.

Corporate Office Properties Trust (OFC) Office properties.

Government Properties Income Trust (GOV) Government-owned properties.

Mack-Cali Realty (CLI) Office properties.

Maguire Properties (MPG) Office properties.

Pacific Office Properties (PCE) Office properties.

Parkway Properties (PKY) Office properties.

SL Green Realty (SLG) Office properties.

Office and Industrial Properties REITs

Duke Realty (DRE) Office and industrial properties.

First Potomac Realty Trust (FPO) Office and industrial properties.

Kilroy Realty (KRC) Office and industrial properties.

Liberty Property Trust (LRY) Office and industrial properties.

PS Business Parks (PSB) Office and industrial properties.

Mortgage-Backed Securities REITs

American Capital Agency (AGNC) Mortgage-backed securities.

Annaly Capital Management (NLY) Mortgage-backed securities.

Anworth Mortgage Asset (ANH) Mortgage-backed securities.

Apollo Commercial Real Estate Finance (ARI) Mortgage-backed securities.

Arbor Realty Trust (ABR) Specialty financing.

Ashford Hospitality Trust (AHT): Hospitality properties through equity investments.

BRT Realty Trust (BRT) Secured financial loans.

CapLease (LSE) Finances commercial real estate.

Capstead Mortgage (CMO) Mortgage-backed securities.

Chimera Investment (CIM) Mortgage-backed securities.

CIFC (DFR) Mortgage-backed securities.

Colony Financial (CLNY) Commercial mortgages.

CreXus Investment Corp. (CXS) Commercial mortgages.

Cypress Sharpridge Investments (CYS) Mortgage-backed securities.

Dynex Capital (DX) Mortgage-backed securities.

Franklin Street Properties (FSP) Real estate, investment banking, and office properties.

Invesco Mortgage Capital (IVR) Mortgage-backed securities.

iStar Financial (SFI) Mortgage-backed securities.

MFA Mortgage Investments (MFA) Mortgage-backed securities.

National Health Investors (NHI) Mortgages for healthcare properties.

Newcastle Investment (NCT) Mortgages for a variety of properties.

NorthStar Realty Finance (NRF) Mortgage-backed securities.

PennyMac Mortgage Investment Trust (PMT) Mortgages.

PMC Commercial Trust (PCC) Loans to small businesses.

RAIT Investment Trust (RAS) Invests in commercial mortgages.

Redwood Trust (RWT) Residential and commercial real estate loans.

Resource Capital (RSO) Commercial real estate–related loans.

Starwood Property Trust (STWD) Commercial mortgage loans and related assets.

Two Harbors Investment (TWO) Mortgage-backed securities.

W. P. Carey (WPC) Long-term financing.

Vestin Realty Mortgage I (VRTA) Commercial real estate loans.

Vestin Realty Mortgage II (VRTB) Commercial real estate loans.

Apartment REITs

American Campus Communities (ACC) Student housing communities.

Apartment Investment & Management (AIV) Apartment communities.

Associated Estates Realty (AEC) Apartment communities.

AvalonBay Communities (AVB) Upscale apartment communities.

BRE Properties (BRE) Apartment communities.

Camden Property Trust (CPT) Apartment communities.

Education Realty Trust (EDR) Student housing communities.

Equity LifeStyle Properties (ELS) Recreational vehicle and resort communities.

Equity Residential (EQR) Apartment communities.

Essex Property Trust (ESS) Apartment communities.

Home Properties (HME) Apartment communities.

Mid-America Apartment Communities (MAA) Apartment communities.

Post Properties (PPS) Apartment communities.

Sun Communities (SUI) Apartment communities.

UDR (UDR) Apartment communities.

UMH Properties (UMH) Apartment communities and REIT securities.

Self-Storage and Other REITs

Entertainment Properties Trust (EPR) Movie theaters and entertainment.

Extra Space Storage (EXR) Self-storage properties.

Getty Realty (GTY) Store/gas station properties and oil distribution.

Pittsburgh & West Virginia Railroad (PW) Business and property of a railroad.

Plum Creek Timber (PCL) Lumber producing timberlands

Public Storage (PSA) Storages and self-storage properties.

Rayonier (RYN) Lumber-producing timberlands.

Sovran Self Storage (SSS) Self-storage properties.

U-Store-It Trust (YSI) Self-storage properties.

The Danger of ETFs

Every tool that enables you to achieve success in an endeavor is not perfect. We can't afford to think only idealistically in the real world. Although there are a vast number of ETFs of every shape and color, some of the ETFs do not do a good job of following the underlying assets they represent. Remember that ETFs can be traded on an exchange and so can be traded above or below their true value. Many of the bad ETFs use futures contracts to duplicate the actions of their underlying assets. The problem occurs when they must roll into the new contracts as the old one expires, and the price of the new contract may be different.

For example, if the old contract was selling at 40, you might have to pay 50 for the new contract. This puts a drag on the price of the ETF. One glaring example of this is the ETF for natural gas—the UNG. This ETF was once priced as high as 60, but dropped down to a price below 6—a much larger decline than the price of natural gas. When the large ETFs roll over and have to pay a higher price, the whole market can be affected.

Avoid ETFs that are actively managed. Managers who move in and out of positions do not do well; even the skilled ones can't beat the market.

The Real Danger: Futures and Derivatives

A real danger can occur with inverse ETFs and double and triple ETFs. These ETFs use leverage to get their desired effect, which means that they use futures and derivatives to duplicate two or three times the action of their underlying assets.

These derivatives are complex and difficult to understand. Adding to the confusion, the market, of course, is determining the ETF's price. These ETFs start to look like the subprime mortgage packages that were sold to the world investment community and were rated AAA by Moody's and Standard & Poor's, even though they were worthless. These volatile, confusing ETFs are not long-term investments and should be handled with care, or at the least held for only a short period of time.

ETFs should be evaluated based on the positions they hold. The ETF SPY is good because this ETF owns the stocks in the S&P 500 index. This is an example of the type of ETF that you should own. You want to remove yourself from the morass of futures and derivatives. You want to get as close as you can to that gold hidden in a cookie jar, simple and concrete.

Have a discriminating eye when reviewing possible ETFs for investment. There are a lot of stars out there in the cosmos. Pick the brightest and safest one. Never forget to be wary of ETFs that use futures or derivatives. You don't want to step into an ETF black hole.

As you were advised before, do your homework.

Part III

RECOGNITION OF THE ELEPHANTS, WHALES, AND COMPUTERS = DEFENSIVE MEASURES

7

Elephants and Whales

The investment markets have changed over the years. The biggest change has been the increase in the size and number of funds. The institutions truly control the market. We just discussed the explosion of ETFs. In the 1960s, it was an explosion of mutual funds. Then we had an explosion of pension funds and annuities. In the 1990s we saw an explosion of hedge funds, which continues today. How many funds are there? Who knows? At the very least, there are 15,000 funds, but probably more. These are the elephants in the room. In this chapter, we analyze the effect they have on you.

First, let me introduce the whales. These are the billionaire investors, many of whom manage hedge funds, and some are activist shareholders. The whales include individuals such as Warren Buffett, George Soros, and Carl Icahn. Take note of what the whales are doing. For example, when I saw that George Soros was taking a position in the gold-mining stock, Novogold (NG), I purchased shares at about $7 a share. The stock then rose to above $15 a share.

With so many huge funds trading in the market, you are trading in a dangerous environment. The first sign of this danger occurred in 1987 with the severe crash of 1987, a crash that was deeper than that of 1929. Another like it has not occurred since. Then we saw a severe decline in 2000 and, of course, a deep decline in 2008–2009.

But we can't stop there. In 2010, we saw a flash crash where, in one day, the Dow Jones Industrial Average declined by over 1,000 points and rebounded by 500 points. In 15 minutes, the Dow declined 500 points and retracted 500 points. This left the anchors on at least one cable financial station open-mouthed (except for an investment advisor, being interviewed at the time, who, while the Dow was falling, kept urging the viewers to buy). We were all stunned; no doubt, many hearts were pounding.

Why did this happen? One of the big reasons was the influence of elephants and whales. In a stable market, these huge chunks of money merge well, but when panic strikes look out! All the elephants head for the exit at the same time with volume the market cannot handle. This is when we see markets crash.

What is really frightening is that you don't need lots of elephants heading for the exits. One can do a lot of damage all by itself. This elephant, the Waddell & Reed Asset Strategy Fund, a $27-billion hedge fund, sold 75,000 S&P 500 futures contracts on May 6, 2010–the flash crash day. It seemed to have triggered a 700-point decline in the Dow in 7 minutes. The market recovered most of the loss in 15 minutes, but this shows you how just one elephant can wreak havoc on Wall Street.

The Role of the Computer

The elephants and whales are abetted by technology. Over the years, computers have developed a far greater influence on the market than ever before. They provide algorithms and formulas that can influence many of the decisions investors make. In past decades, the specialists on the floor of the New York Stock Exchange (NYSE) were there to provide stability to the market. They would buy stocks when the market was falling and sell stocks when the market was rising. However, today there are far more exchanges, all run by computers. The human element is not there to provide stability for the market. This is why we saw the flash crash. This evokes the image of elephants stampeding with no humans on their back to direct their flight.

The Stock Influence

The elephants also have a strong influence on individual stocks. A surprise negative news event about a stock can cause the elephants to rush toward the exits, causing stock prices to fall dramatically. For example, Wellcare Health Plans dropped overnight from 120 to 30 on surprise negative news about a Federal investigation; the institutional money managers ran to the exits all at the same time.

With this great influx of institutional money managed funds (elephants), we have much greater volatility. The Volatility Index (VIX) measures the amount of volatility in the market. There were several years where the VIX was close to 10 percent. During the 2008–2009 market decline, the VIX reached a high of 90 percent. Never had it been that high.

The flash crash is further evidence of the large number of elephants in the market, elephants that panic easily and stampede briskly to the closest way out. With so many more elephants in the game, volatility has greatly increased. You must be aware and take advantage of the new volatility, but you must also protect yourself against it.

The stock market is a wilder ride, a dangerous safari among some very nervous mammals. Because of computer programs, they don't have complete control of their hysteria. How do you protect yourself? The first safeguard is to *diversify*.

8

Diversify, Diversify, Diversify

Your first and most important safeguard against the risk of high volatility and risky positions is to diversify. And with the explosion of ETFs, it is now far easier to diversify. With effective diversification, you should be able to easily withstand any surprise move in the wrong direction of a specific asset or investment, so you'll be able to return to invest another day. The problem is that most investors have a tendency to plunge into a few positions because they are sure that those investments will rise in price. Unfortunately, such great confidence is a sure sign that these investments will fall in price.

The 50 Percent Rule

No matter how you feel about any investment, always assume there is only a 50 percent chance that the investment will increase in price. Definitely avoid plunging into the market. The one major error, even made by some of the best traders, is that at some point they plunged all their money into one investment and lost everything. This was a lesson they never forgot. So don't plunge. Think of a tourist wading into the Nile, forgetting that big crocodiles are out there. Plunging in with your whole financial life at stake is not a good idea.

Contrary Investing

A very successful investor, who over many years turned $1,000 into over $20 million in the stock market, gave me one secret to success: buy only when there is blood in the streets; buy only when in the pit of your stomach you believe the financial world is coming to an end or that the worst is yet to come. This secret is called *contrary investing*; when everyone believes something is about to happen, always bet the other way. You have to be as crafty as a panther.

Many of these situations are called *crowded trades*. So when you are in a crowded trade, plan to get out. When everybody loves a stock, he or she has already bought that stock, so there are now few buyers available to buy the stock. Therefore, any negative news event could cause the stock price to fall apart. In other words, try to buy when the investment is out of favor, especially when it is a superficial news event that caused the stock to fall in price and out of favor in the first place.

The key to successful contrary investing is to buy only at the depths of despair, *but* (and this is a big but) only buy stocks or ETFs where there is still true value. Don't try to catch the falling knife! Don't buy stocks that could easily go into bankruptcy or disappear into the night, for example, stocks that are small and unstable that make a big move down for no reason at all. Try to stay with blue-chip stocks where a decline in price is easy to understand. Here, due diligence is important. Always try to stand alone in the crowd, but don't be an eccentric hunter who is also reckless. Pick your game carefully. Make it worth your tracking expertise. In racing parlance, don't bet on a dead horse.

Part IV

THE OPTIONS = THE TOOLS

10

Options Made Easy

The most important survival tools that you will use to manage your portfolio in this wilderness of finance are options. Most investors will not touch options because they do not understand them, nor do they want to attempt to understand them. Second, they may have heard horror stories about options; yet options can be safer than stocks or other investments.

However, like any tool, options must be used wisely. A chain saw is an effective tool, but if you don't use it wisely, you can hurt yourself or wreak havoc on your immediate surroundings. You don't want to haphazardly attack any tree in sight. Likewise, with options, don't overdo it.

Actually, trading options is easy because an option trades like a stock. Happily for the investor, options trade more like low-priced stocks. An option controls 100 shares of stock or an ETF. If an option sells for 2, that is $200 (2 × 100), as you control 100 shares of the underlying stock or ETF. *Control* is the key word here. You don't actually own the stock or ETF unless certain criteria are met.

You might ask if options trade just like stocks and, if not, what the differences are. First, an option controls a specific stock or ETF, but the option has no intrinsic value unless the stock price is across the strike price of the option. With call and put options, the strike price is the stock price where the option takes on real value. For calls, if the stock price is above the strike price, it is worth $100 for each point above that price. For put options, the option increases in value $100 for each point it is below that price. Second, there are two types of options: puts and calls. Call options are bets that the stock will rise in price; puts are bets that the stock price will fall in price. Call options got their name because they give the owner of the option the right to call (buy) 100 shares of the stock at the strike price. Owners of put options have the right to put (sell) the stock to someone else at the strike price, and, so these options are called puts.

There are two types of option traders: option buyers and option writers (sellers). If you make a bet, someone has to take that bet. Obviously, the buyer makes the bet and the writer (seller) takes the bet. You have to decide what side of the bet you want to be on. This book should help you decide when it is appropriate and beneficial for you to be the buyer or the writer (seller).

Finally, and most importantly, options, unlike stocks or ETFs, die after a certain time. An option is a tool that you use or lose. However, if you lose, you don't lose much. And if you use, you profit or save yourself from losing a lot of accumulated profit. This is explained more thoroughly in subsequent chapters.

To be an option trader, you must know the necessary terms. The following vocabulary list should help you on your way in double-quick time. (When I say stock, think ETF too.)

Assigned: The writer (option seller) is being assigned the obligation to deliver or buy the stock.

Assignment: The process of exercise.

Exercise: For a call option, this means you are calling from the writer of the option the 100 shares as specified in the option at the specified strike price.

Expiration date: The date your right to the option ends or expires.

In-the-money: For calls, when the strike price is lower than the current market price. The reverse applies to puts.

Intrinsic value: If you exercise your call option contract, you will purchase 100 shares of the common stock at a lower price than the current market price of the common stock. The opposite is true if you would sell 100 shares of stock at a higher price than the current market price. This is real value. But the option does not have this value unless it crosses the strike price in a given time span. That is why we say options by themselves have no intrinsic value and yet use this term to explain the pricing of options.

Liquid: If an option is liquid, it can be bought and sold at any time in an option exchange (auction market like the New York Stock Exchange).

Listed option: A stock option that can be bought and sold at any time in an auction market, such as the New York Stock Exchange. A listed option is liquid, standardized, and continually created at the changing price levels of the common stock.

Option price: The price you paid for the right to buy or sell 100 shares at an exercise (strike) price until an expiration date.

Out-of-the-money: For calls, when the strike price is higher than the current market price. The reverse applies to puts.

Price: The cost of a listed option on the options exchange according to two values: intrinsic value and time value.

Price volatility: The amount the stock price moves up and down.

Right: Ability/opportunity to buy or sell 100 shares of a specific stock or ETF.

Strike price: The price at which you can buy or sell the stock.

Time value: An option exists only for a period of time, and you pay for that time. As time passes, the value of an option decreases.

To sum up, an option is the vehicle that gives you the right to buy or sell specific stocks or ETFs if the price of that stock or ETF goes above or below a particular price. Put simply, you're betting that a stock or ETF will go up or go down in a given time. You can see how options, as a result, are perfect tools for foraging in a volatile market.

Options on Real Estate

You can buy options on almost any asset, even on a home. For example, let's say that you want to buy a house for $500,000, but you don't have the money. If the seller is willing, he could sell you the option on the house for $10,000. This option would be good for two years. The option would give you the right to buy the house for $500,000 up to two years in the future. The price of the house is called the "strike price." If the house stays at $500,000 over the next two years, you lose the $10,000. But if the house falls in price to $480,000, you made a good move because you can now buy the house for $20,000 less. And if the house rises in price to $540,000, you made a good move because you still can buy the home for $500,000. You lose if the house price is the same in two years. You lose if the price is less than $510,000 or more than $490,000. The movement of the price of the house is called "volatility." Options are best in volatile markets.

The problem with an option on a house is that it is not listed on an exchange, and so you cannot buy or sell the option freely during that two-year period.

Options Are Like $2 Bets at a Horse Race

Another way to look at options is as $2 bets at a horse race. Betting that a horse will win is like an option. If the horse wins, it gets across the finish line first. The finish line is like the strike price. If the stock gets across the strike price, you are the winner. If you have a call option, you want the stock (or ETF) price to move above the strike price before the option expires. If you have a put option, you want the stock (or ETF) price to move below the strike price. For both, the game is over when the race finishes, which for options is when the expiration date arrives. So options are like making a $2 bet, and like at a race track when you make a $2 bet, the most you can lose is the $2 and nothing more.

Another Look

If you are still having trouble understanding options, the next section may help. The first step in becoming an effective options' player is to gain a complete understanding of the focal point of the game, the listed option. A listed option is a stock or ETF option (remember, think futures, too), and an option is simply a contract—one that gives you the right to buy or sell 100 shares of stock at a specific price for a specific period of time. While stock options have been with us for a long time, the brilliant idea of creating listed options opened up a whole new investment medium.

As a result, listed options are stock or ETF options that are liquid, standardized, and continually created at the changing price levels of the common stock. When we say a listed option is liquid, we mean that it can be bought and sold at any time in an auction market similar to the New York Stock Exchange.

Formerly in the old over-the-counter (OTC) market, if you could find a seller, a stock option could be purchased, but in order to have taken your profits from that option, you would have had to exercise the option, actually buying the 100 shares of the stock that you had the right to purchase. Now with the options exchanges, this costly process of actually buying the stock or selling the stock is not necessary. All you have to do is go back to the exchange and sell your option.

The Listed Call and Put

There are two types of listed options: the listed call option that gives you the right to buy stock and the listed put option that gives you the right to sell stock. When you purchase a call, you are betting that the underlying stock price will move up. When you purchase a put, you are betting that the underlying stock price will move down.

Using stock options, a listed option has four major segments:

1. The *right* to buy or sell 100 shares of a specific stock.

2. The *expiration date*—the date that your right ends or expires.

3. The *strike price*—the price at which you can buy or sell.

4. The *option price*—the price you paid for the right to buy or sell 100 shares at an exercise (strike) price until the expiration date.

Let's look at each part of IBM Jul 60 (at) 3:

Part 1— IBM: This represents the stock name. This option is the right to buy 100 shares of IBM Corporation common stock.

Part 2—Jul: This represents the time when your right expires. This is the expiration date which falls on the Saturday immediately following the third Friday of the expiration month. In this case, it is the month of July.

Part 3—60: This represents the exercise price at which the IBM stock can be purchased. This price is also referred to as the strike price.

Part 4—(at) 3: This refers to the last transaction price at which this option was bought or sold with one qualifying point. The 3 represents $3, the price it cost to buy one share of stock. All listed options carry the right to buy or sell 100 shares of stock. Therefore, always multiply the price by 100 to get the true price of the option. In this case, the true price is $300 ($3 × 100 = $300).

The Price of an Option

The price is the most important element of a listed option. The price of an option is set on the options exchange according to two different values: intrinsic value and time value.

Intrinsic Value

The intrinsic value is the real value of the option. This means that if you exercise your call option contract (which you normally never do in the options market), you will purchase 100 shares of the common stock at a lower price than the current market price of the common stock. Thus the call option has some real value.

If you were to exercise a put option contract with intrinsic value, you would sell 100 shares of common stock at a higher price than the current market value of the common stock. The put option would then have real value.

Time Value

Remember that an option is a right you have for a period of time. You must pay for that right, and the amount of money you must pay is referred to as time value. This is what the market thinks the intrinsic value of an option will be in the future.

As time passes, the value of an option will decrease. In fact, the time value of an option continually declines as time passes and the option reaches the end of its life. The time value is the most important factor that we work with. In many cases, the options you buy will be options with time value only—and no intrinsic value.

Intrinsic Value + Time Value = Option Price

Here, two concepts need to be explained: in-the-money and out-of-the-money. A call option is *in-the-money* when the *strike price* (the price at which you can buy the stock) is lower than the current market price. *Out-of-the-money* is, of course, the opposite; the strike price is higher than the current market price.

The option will probably be cheaper to buy when it is out-of-the-money, but by buying the option, you are hoping that time will cure this and bring you in-the-money before your time (the option) is up. An experienced player, whether she is a buyer or a writer (the seller of the option, the role of the casino owner), will spend most of her time with out-of-the-money options—options that have only time value.

To summarize, the option price is determined by adding intrinsic value to time value. Intrinsic value is the real value of the option. Time value is the value that you place on the possibility that the option will attain some intrinsic value by having the stock price move through the strike price and into-the-money.

Volatility

An obvious truth to achieving success in betting a stock that will move up or down is that you have to bet on stocks that are known to move up or down. Therefore, another element that controls the price of a listed option is the price volatility of the underlying common stock—the amount that the stock price moves up and down.

A common stock price that has high volatility normally moves in very wide ranges over a period of time. A volatile stock may move from 40 to 60 percent off its base price annually. Such wide price movements give it a much greater probability of moving through the strike price of a listed option, and as a result, that option will take on premium (time value).

On the other hand, a stock with low volatility normally trades within a narrow range—not moving very far in any one direction. This will have a negative effect on the option price because the probability of the stock price moving through the strike price is diminished. However, understanding stock volatility in the options market can be tricky. In some cases, a common stock that has been historically quite volatile may reach periods in which it is somewhat dormant, and conversely, stocks that are normally quite low in price volatility will suddenly move dramatically in one direction or another. These shifts in price behavior will alter the influence of this factor on the listed option.

Liquidity

Though the price of the underlying stock, the time left in the life of an option, and the volatility of the underlying stock can be factors that constitute 90 percent of the price of the stock option, another factor that has a powerful indirect influence on option price behavior is the amount of liquidity that exists in a specific listed option. Liquidity refers to trading volume or the ability to move in and out of an option position easily.

Liquidity requires that plenty of buyers and sellers be available to ensure such transactions. Options that do not have liquidity may trap you into a position or prevent you from taking a large enough position to make the transaction worthwhile. Liquidity in the options market can be measured by the number of specific listed options that are traded every day and the "open interest." Open interest refers to the number of contracts that have not been closed out and are currently open.

For example, how many IBM Jul 60 calls are traded on an average day? Calculating this average would give you an idea of this option's liquidity. Note that liquidity changes throughout the life of a specific option. The IBM Jul 60 call may have no liquidity at all when the stock is at 90 because the option is so far in-the-money that no one is interested in that option.

On the other hand, it may not have any liquidity at all if the stock is at 30 because now the option is so far out-of-the-money that it hardly has any value at all.

Also, if there are eight months left in that IBM Jul 60 call, its price may be so high that it will lack the necessary liquidity to be an effective trading vehicle. In fact, options that have lives of seven, eight, or nine months normally do not have the liquidity that options of two or three months maintain.

11

Playing the Odds

The beautiful characteristic of options is that—like wild animals such as lions, wolves, and crocodiles—they are most successful for buyers in a wild, dangerous, and volatile environment. To function in such an environment, the investor must have the heart and head of an adventurer, one who is wise and courageous. Like leading a Special Forces unit into enemy territory or flying a NASA mission, the investor has to have the coping skills to successfully handle the dangerous terrain of the unexpected, the confusing wilderness of the complex, and the challenges of a huge ever-expanding universe of finance.

For investors to improve their coping skills in this dangerous environment, they must understand odds or the probability of profit. For many years, one of the most successful hedge funds used quantitative analysis to identify mispriced investments. In other words, it used science and mathematics to gain an advantage in the market. Identifying mispriced stocks or ETFs is important to a good investor. However, doing so is a difficult task, especially for an individual investor. The market is so intelligent, especially with sophisticated computer models, that the average investor has little chance of competing with the pros. But options are a different story. With the vast number of options, there are many more mispriced opportunities available. To take advantage of these opportunities, you must understand the odds.

Understand the Odds

Most investors don't realize how important luck is in determining their successes because many investors don't understand the laws of probability. When you toss a coin, you have a 50 percent chance of getting a head or tail. If you flip a coin a thousand times, you should get 500 heads and 500 tails. However, on the journey to that point, the number of heads and tails will vary dramatically. In fact, the pattern looks like the price chart of a stock rather than a simple random process. Lady Luck has a big influence on what happens in the future.

In the casinos of Nevada, there is an old Chinese game called Keno. One of the bets is to select 15 numbers out of 20 numbers picked from 1 to 80. If you get the 15 numbers, you win $100,000 for a $1 bet. What are the odds of hitting the 15 numbers? Your odds are 4.5 billion to 1. No one has ever won this bet, nor is it likely that anyone will in the future.

When you buy options on stocks, what are your odds of winning? Most investors think they are much better than 50 percent. But the real odds for options are always under 50 percent and usually much lower than that. When investing in stocks themselves, a money manager can have a hot streak, but, in the long run, is only right 50 percent of the time.

Computer Simulation

To gain an advantage in option investing, you need to use some form of statistical analysis. Computer simulation is one way to gain that advantage. Almost a half century ago, math professor Dr. Jim Thorpe discovered how to beat the game of blackjack in the casinos. He did it by using computer simulations and then published his results in the world famous book, *Beat the Dealer*. Blackjack, today, is the only game where you can beat the casinos in casinos that still use fair blackjack rules. You gain a statistical advantage when the cards in the decks have more high cards (10s and pictures) than usual, and by counting the cards, you can determine when there is a high count of high cards in the deck. Then you have a slight advantage. Dr. Jim Thorpe went on to create one of the first hedge funds that dealt with mispriced options; the fund was very successful.

What Is Variance?

Even when you have a slight advantage, there still is a lot of variance. And variance confuses everyone. Variance relates to the example of flipping a coin. Although there is a 50 percent chance of getting heads, you could get heads or tails many times in a row. So you can have long winning streaks and losing streaks when your chances of profiting are only 50–50. Such variance can cause many investors to think they are brilliant or total failures, when actually Lady Luck is calling all the shots.

Computer simulation gives you a much more accurate measure of your chances to make a profit. Just like when you play Blackjack, you will have a better view of your chances of profiting with each of your plays.

If Exxon (XOM) is at 46, what are the chances that XOM will hit 50 within the next three months? Running simulations will tell you that there is a 31 percent chance of hitting the price some time during the next three months. This is done by simulating the three-month price action of XOM—hundreds or thousands of times.

Computer Simulation Programs

There are several simulation programs available. The Institute for Options Research Inc. (Gooptions.com) developed four such programs: Option Master, the Push-Button Option Trader, the Push-Button Option Writer, and the Push-Button Spread Trader. There is now even a Stock and ETF Simulator app for the iPhone, iPod Touch, and the iPad. Such simulations will tell you what your true odds of profiting are. With such information, you will be a much more intelligent investor. But, because of variance, you will still have winning streaks and losing streaks.

The importance of simulation cannot be overstated. Later you are given more specific details about how to use this tool. In this mad and dangerous world of finance among the elephants and whales, the computer is essential. You have seen how computers have enabled the whales and elephants to drastically influence the markets. Using the computers for simulation, at least, gives you a fighting chance and can keep you from being trampled or drowned by these bulky mammals.

12

Secrets to Successful Option Buying

In any endeavor, always know what you're up against. This is vital in war and investing. A Sun Tzu (an ancient Chinese general) imperative, "Know your enemy" applies to buying options. The two major obstacles to success when buying options are *time* and *movement*. They will try to beat you.

The Disadvantages of Option Buying

When you buy an option, you are betting on the movement of the underlying asset such as a stock or an ETF. If the underlying stock does not move in your direction, you lose! Then there is the other obstacle, and that is time. Options expire after a set amount of time, so when you buy options, you are betting on the clock. Options are a depreciating asset; they fade away as time passes.

I get a lot of letters from prisoners and for good reason. They are interested in options because when they buy options time seems to fly. The reason time seems to fly is that when you buy options, you need a lot of movement in a short period of time. Like an ice cube, an option melts away over time.

Quick Action

Quick action is essential in option investing. If you don't respond adroitly, you are likely to suffer bad consequences. The problems may not be as dire as they are for a soldier, but they are certainly annoying in the least. Quick action has to be one of your skills. As professional soldiers are trained to react quickly and skillfully to events, so must you, the investor, train yourself to react quickly and skillfully to market conditions and the time limitations of options.

Option buying is a tough game, and success is dependent on quick actions because you are always fighting the factor of time. Options usually have a short life, so you must take profits during the life of an option and not wait until expiration. That is why it is important to use a simulator. The simulator will tell you when to take profits or cut losses during the life of the option.

For example: If Freeport McMoRan Copper & Gold (FCX) is at 70, select a price where you want to take profits and a price where you would cut losses. With a call option, let's say that you would take profits at 75 and stop losses at 67. Now run a simulation. If the probability of hitting 75 during the life of the option is 31 percent, that is pretty good. If you don't like that probability, set another profit goal until you are satisfied.

Just remember that you must be active when you buy options or else your results will be disappointing. Don't stick those options in a closet and forget them.

Get a Big Bang for Your Buck

When you buy options, you are making a bet. Don't make that bet too big. Luckily, option prices can be as low as 5 cents for one share or $5 for any option. That $5 will control 100 shares of stock or an ETF. Low-priced options give you the chance for a big bang for your buck or investment.

In 1987, I recommended in *The Trester Complete Option Report*, a Dec 55 put option on ITT when it was 62 in the month of August. The option was priced at 1/8 or $12.50, the price of two cups of coffee. I wrote an article about this option because of its low price and said that it would make an excellent insurance policy. In October we saw the crash of 1987, and ITT dropped to 47 overnight. Because of the fear in the market, that option was selling for 16, or $1,600, when its intrinsic value was only 8. So if you purchased that option, you had a gain of over 10,000 percent. This means you could lose the next hundred option positions in a row and still come out ahead. That is a big bang for your buck. The lesson to learn here is to buy cheap, underpriced options that have the chance for big percentage gains.

Avoid expensive options. The wrong move of the underlying stock will cause these options to vanish. An investor once told me that he bought 100 call options on Microsoft with a strike of 110 when the stock was 100 because he was confident the stock would move above 110. He paid 10 ($1,000) for each option and invested $100,000 in these options. Microsoft did move above 110, but after the expiration date of the options. The investor lost everything. Buying expensive options is a dangerous game you don't want to play.

Slow Movement—Not a Big Winner

When you buy options, you are betting on price movement of the underlying asset. The more price movement there is, the better your chance is to make a big gain. Therefore, you don't want to buy options on slow-moving stocks or ETFs. In fact, you should avoid buying options on ETFs, as most ETFs neutralize volatility. Indexes (or ETFs that represent indexes, such as the S&P 500 index) are perfect examples. Indexes are a large number of stocks, and a sudden move by one of the stocks in the index will have little effect on the movement of the index. This is not good. You need movement. Don't bet on a stock or ETF that has a small chance of making a big move.

The Secret Advantage

The key to successful option trading is to identify mispriced options. A lot of research has gone into identifying such options. The one that has won a Nobel Prize is the Black-Scholes model. This model assumes that stock and ETF prices move according to a log-normal curve. However, there is one problem with this model. Stocks and ETFs don't move according to such a curve. This model assumes that stock prices move in a continuous pattern with no gap up or gap down in prices, but stocks can move dramatically in price.

One example in recent years is Wellcare Health Plans; it dropped overnight from 120 down to 30. No model anticipates these kinds of moves. The model only projects moves of up to 3 standard deviations in the stock price, not 10 standard deviations. The crash of 1987 is another example of gigantic moves, a gap down, of the whole market.

These gigantic unexpected moves of the underlying stocks I call *surprise volatility*. You could call some of these rogue wave events. Surprise earning reports or news events will cause such volatility with big gap ups and big gap downs in price. This is where big gains can be made buying options. The fair value of options does not reflect these moves. Thus they give the option buyer a secret advantage.

Some of these options are mispriced, but the fair value, according to the model, says they are not. Therefore, the wise option player should always be looking for stocks that have the chance for a surprise move. These are stocks in industries that are unstable, where a discovery could cause a surprise move. Technology or biotech stocks would meet these requirements.

For example, Dendreon (DNDN) had a pending prostate cancer drug and was priced at 3.5 per share. I started buying call options on the stock. The drug was approved by the FDA (Food and Drug Administration), and the stock made a big move that reached a high of 57.

Other stocks, besides those in unstable industries such as technology and biotech, have chances of surprise volatility. These are stocks that have small capitalization. In other words, stocks whose total value is small (the smaller the better) are open to a takeover. You have to know approximately where to look for stocks that are most susceptible to a big move.

The secret advantage of buying options is that there is more opportunity for options than other investments to be mispriced.

The fair value of options is upset by surprise moves, and when the weakness in the fair value is discovered, the investor, like a general who catches the enemy off-guard, attacks. But the investor, like the general, must be vigilant and probe for the weaknesses and put himself in a position to take advantage of any disparity between fair value and sudden volatility.

Looking for underlying stocks that will be most vulnerable to a surprise event is the strategy. General Sun Tzu always found the most vulnerable part of the enemy force. He was great at using reconnaissance and secret intelligence to determine where to attack. That is how he won against overwhelming enemy strength. That is how you can win in the financial environment.

Survival Checklist for the Option Buyer

1. Be an activist.
2. Act quickly.
3. Take profits during the life of the option.
4. Use simulations.
5. Buy cheap, underpriced options.
6. Avoid expensive options.
7. Set profit goals and stop-loss prices.
8. Buy options a month *before* earnings reports are issued; later, everyone else gets in and pushes up the option price.

9. Buy puts.

10. Avoid large, blue-chip stocks and ETFs.

11. Buy when the Volatility Index is rising.

12. Bet on explosive, unstable, small stocks.

13. Always think about the chances of a surprise move, a surprise news event, or a surprise report.

14. Go for the home run. When you buy, you will lose more than you will win. You will have losing streaks, so once in a while, when you do win, you will win big.

15. Be patient!

13

If You Are a Bear, Be a Grizzly

One of the most important functions of options is to provide protection for your portfolio.

In a conversation with the famed investment author, Joseph Granville, I discussed my love for put options (bets that stocks or ETFs will fall in price.) Joe cited the fact that when stocks rise in price, it is like walking up the stairs of the Empire State Building. And when they fall in price, it is like jumping off the top of the Empire State Building. When the market falls, you can see dramatic declines like the flash crash and the crashes of 1929 and 1987.

Panic causes stocks and ETFs to fall much faster than they rise. This is ideal for the put option buyer. When you buy options, you need action or volatility. Major market declines give you that action. So when you turn bearish, look at buying puts. Puts are a good insurance policy for your portfolio. However, puts are options, and as you have learned, when you buy options, you must be very aggressive; act like a grizzly bear and not a teddy bear.

Puts should not be held until expiration. Follow the rules we set earlier.

Do not buy puts and put them in the closet and forget about them. Watch them like a hawk. The major error of the option buyer is holding options too long. Remember that an option is a depreciating asset. Have a trigger finger, take profits quickly, and exit when prices move against you. Be aggressive; be very aggressive.

When to Buy Puts

During a major decline in the market, puts can become very expensive. Check the Volatility Index; when it gets above 25 percent, puts are getting too expensive.

You should always have some puts in your portfolio, but try to buy puts that are cheap. Increase the number of puts you own during a market decline. Remember, a put acts like a stock when the stock price is below the strike price. So if you own 10 puts, this is like being short 1,000 shares of stock. And if the stock is below the strike price, you earn $1,000 for each point the stock falls in price. Try buying puts when one of your stocks or ETFs has risen too far, too fast.

For example, on November 9, 2010, SLV, the Silver ETF, had made almost a parabolic move up in price. Such moves do not sustain themselves. Holding a position in the SLV, I bought an SLV put position. The SLV was over 28, so I bought a January 23 put that was only 0.37 ($37). By the end of that day, the option had doubled in price. Being like a grizzly bear, I took profits. So try to buy puts in the midst of a rising market and not when the market is falling.

Deductible Insurance

Try to buy a deductible insurance policy. Try to buy further out-of-the-money puts; they won't give you full coverage, but you will pay a lot less for those options just as we did with the out-of-the-money put options we bought on the SLV.

You do not have to buy puts on the stocks or ETFs that you own. In fact, there could be negative tax consequences to such actions. Try to buy puts on the weak members of your industry group. Try to buy puts on unstable individual stocks that have more potential for surprise volatility. This volatility is what you want. If you buy undervalued puts, your put portfolio could show a profit even in a bull market.

Alternative Bear Plays

If puts are too expensive, what do you do? The answer is turn to ETFs. There are ETFs that will rise when the market falls. Some move point-for-point in reverse of the market, such as the DOG that moves inversely to the Dow Jones Industrial Average; it does this by using futures.

Others are designed to move against the market in a double manner, such as the SDS that moves twice the inverse to the S&P 500 index. So if he S&P 500 index declines, the SDS should move up twice as much. Here it does this by using futures and options.

Get even more bang for your buck with ETFs that move up three times the action of market indexes. For example, the Direxion Daily Financial Bear 3× Shares (FAZ) move up three times the downside action of financial stocks.

Debit Spreads

You can be even more aggressive and buy put debit spreads. These spreads reduce the cost of buying put options, but they provide less bang for your buck. When you buy a debit spread, you are buying a put, but you are reducing the cost of that put by selling a further out-of-the-money put, usually in the same month. The disadvantage is that you limit your profit.

For example, you might buy a January 100 put at 3, but to reduce your cost, you sell me the January 95 put at 1. Now your cost is reduced to two points (3 − 1 = 2). But you limit your profit if the SPY (S&P 500 index) drops below 95, and all your profits usually cannot be generated until expiration. Again be aggressive here, for if the SPY moves down long before expiration, a bird in the hand is better than two in the bush. Take your profits quickly, even if the profits may be smaller. Be a grizzly bear!

Another alternative play is to sell stocks and ETFs short, but here you do not have a risk-reward advantage. In addition, sometimes you cannot short sell stocks because you must borrow stocks to short them, and they may not be available.

Finally, you can write calls against the stocks and ETFs you own. This will generate income and provide a little cushion for downside damage; however, this does not provide much downside insurance.

14

The Secret Path of the Professional

Professional option traders, like the West Point elite of the military, know the quickest route with the fewest obstacles to success. Yet, to the nonprofessional, that route appears to be just the opposite of safe; that route appears to be mined and ready to blow up when it is tread upon by the poor option-trader-bloke willing to take the chance. Not so.

At the beginning of the American Civil War, the northern politicians and the public looked down on the professional West Point officers. The politicians and public sneered at the strategy of maneuver, and as a result, the war lasted longer with more casualties than was necessary. The South didn't have this problem and so was successful at the beginning of the war. Only when the North began to value the professionals' expertise did victory come. Victory can come to you, too, if you know what the professionals know.

So what is this secret route? Simple. Be an option writer. Most professional option traders are option writers. They want more control; they want to be Mr. Big, or, in Las Vegas parlance, they want to be the casino instead of the gambler. They want to deal the cards. It is option writing that is the hidden path to profits that professional option traders follow.

Option Writing

Since 1973, when the option exchanges began, many investors were given the opportunity to be option writers. The extraordinary part of this development is that option writing is the only investment in which you can be the house and take the bets instead of just making the bets. This access to power is to be noted because, like any officer on the battlefield, a trader gropes for any tactic that can give him or her more control and, in the end, success.

So what is option writing? *Option writing* is a game in which you take the option buyer's bet, and guarantee that you will pay off the bet if the bet is a winner. Imagine yourself on a couch with friends watching Monday Night Football. One friend wants to bet you $10 that the Green Bay Packers will win, but not only win—win by scoring a certain number of points over the opponent. You, thinking the Packers are looking a bit sluggish and haven't been performing sprightly on the field lately, believe that there's no way they will acquire the number of points your friend believes they will get. What is in your favor? The game is going to end, so your friend has a limited time for his team to sprint across the field or sail the football between the goal posts. Second, lately his team has not been performing with a great deal of alacrity; chances are that will continue. The team has to perform well to allow your friend to win the bet. You can sit back and wait.

Although there are some differences, the role of option writer is as simple as the above scenario.

When you take the bet of the option buyer, you're called the option writer. As noted above, the two disadvantages of option buying are time and movement; however, time and movement are *advantages* for the option writer. Time: the game will end —the option will expire. Movement: the team has to hustle to win—the stock or ETF on which the option is based has to go up or down past a strike price before the option buyer can profit. If this doesn't happen, in the case of the football bet, you pocket the $10—in the case of options, the option writer wins.

Now note: If you buy an option that is out-of-the-money— has a strike price that is far away from the present stock price— the stock price has to move a long way to put you in-the-money, and it must do that within the time left on the option. Translation: you're probably going to be the loser. This indicates the huge advantage for the option writer. A majority of the time, the option will not pay off for its buyer, but this means that it will pay off for its writer.

There are five scenarios the stock price can follow:

1. The stock price can stay the same.
2. The stock price can move up a little.
3. The stock price can move up a lot.
4. The stock price can move down a little.
5. The stock price can move down a lot.

When option writers write out-of-the-money options, only one of the five scenarios will hurt them, so in a sense, the odds are stacked in their favor. Therefore, we need to look deeply at option writing and see the advantages and disadvantages of this game.

15

Thinking Like the Professionals

Option buying is easy to understand. You are making a bet on what a stock price or ETF price will do. But who takes that bet and pays off if that bet is a winner? We all know the answer by now—the option writer. The option writer must pay if the option you have bought has any value at expiration: in other words, if the stock price is across the strike price.

This means that if you're an option writer, you have an obligation to pay if you're buying customer wins the bet. If this happened on the streets, a failure to fulfill this obligation might mean broken bones. Of course, here the option writer is safe from physical violence. But even more advantageous, the option writer has recourse.

The Contingency Plan

An option writer has an escape hatch from impending financial obligations. A thoughtful commander always has contingency plans. Sometimes they're as simple as, "Let's get the hell out of here!"

The uniqueness of writing options gives the trader an if-all-else-fails maneuver. Options, like stocks or ETFs, are traded on an exchange like the Chicago Board Option Exchange (CBOE). The price of the specific option changes throughout the trading day. This means that the option writer can exit the option position at any time during trading hours and remove the obligation.

To extend the Monday Night Football bet metaphor from the previous chapter, if the Green Bay Packers start looking too frisky and it appears as though your friend with the $10 bet will win, you can give Charley, another friend watching the Monday night game, your friend's $10 and, with it, this other friend will have the obligation to pay off. Thus you would prevent yourself from losing $10. It is unlikely you'll get Charley to take your friend's bet—but not so with options.

Again, an option writer can exit the option position at any time during the trading hours and remove the obligation. In Las Vegas parlance, he can close the casino doors at any time. He is the boss: Mr. Big.

Collateral

In order to write options, you must have collateral in your brokerage account to ensure that you will meet your obligations. You need to set up a margin account which requires at least $2,000. (A margin brokerage account is one in which the broker lends you cash to purchase securities. The loan in the account is collateralized by cash and securities.) But, today such accounts are larger, sometimes as high as $100,000. (I know, some of you would rather chance a broken bone than set up such an account, but we have to be civilized here.)

In a margin account, cash and securities are used to ensure that the option writer will pay off if assigned.

One Word

The mechanics of writing options are quite easy. When you buy options, you say that you want to buy to open. When you write options, you just change one word. You say you want to *sell* to open. And to exit an option position, you buy to close.

Writing options is just like shorting stock. When you short a stock, you sell to open and to cover; you buy to close. Just remember that buying and selling options is just like buying and selling stock. The only difference is that the prices will likely be lower or similar to penny stocks.

For example, let's say that you want to write an Apple Apr 220 put at a price of 2. Let's also say that the bid price is 1.9 and that the ask price in the market right now is 2.2. You could put an order in to sell to open the Apple Apr 220 put at 2. You probably will get it executed at 2. If not, you will change your limit to 1.9 or change it to a market order. Once the order is executed at 2, $200 less commissions will go into your account. Now you are obligated to buy the stock at 220 at expiration in April or if the stock is below 220 before expiration and you are assigned, which does not happen very often. However, what if the stock price right now is 250? You will have to pay off only if the stock falls below 220 at expiration. If it doesn't, you keep the $200.

If you are an option writer, this is a great game. You win with this put if the stock price stays unchanged, moves up a little or a lot, or moves down a little. You lose only if the stock price moves down a lot, and that has a limited time to happen. Besides, if it appears as though it will move down a lot, you can bail.

In other words, you can lose if the Apple stock price drops below 220, but you can get out of this game at any time and close the casino door by buying back the option and thereby removing your obligation.

Risk Is the Major Disadvantage

"The best laid plans ..." as the poem goes, can be upset by the dangerous environment a trader is operating in. Whales, elephants, and rogue waves come to mind. As well prepared as a commander might be, as diligent as a wilderness guide is, or as thorough and professional as an astronaut will surely be, unexpected events can happen. Thus the major disadvantage for the option writer is risk. The call option writer has unlimited risk, and the put option writer has extensive risk. The big risk is a large gap up or large gap down in the price of the stock or ETF.

Examples of the Dire Gap

As we mentioned before, Wellcare Health Plans dropped overnight from 120 to 30. If you were writing a 100 put, you would incur a paper loss of 70 or $7,000 instantly. In the flash crash, the stocks and ETFs dropped to pennies on the dollar. Even if you had a market stop-loss in place on an option writing position, you likely would have incurred a major loss.

If you are a call writer, you are always in danger of a buyout offer in which a stock price will gap up in price, sometimes even doubling the price of the underlying stock. Of course big blue-chip companies will not get buyout offers, nor will ETFs. So, in those cases you will have the opportunity to close the casino door. Yet, that still leaves a lot of stocks vulnerable to buyout offers.

Naked Writers versus Covered Writers

There are two types of option writers: the covered option writer and the uncovered (naked) writer. The difference between a naked writer and covered writer is like the difference between a soldier protected behind a sturdy bush and a soldier who is standing out in the open. The naked writer is more vulnerable than the protected or covered one. That is where the similarity ends.

Covered option writers sell an option on 100 shares of stock that they have bought (own). This is a "comfy" arrangement. They benefit from selling the option, having the time value of the option on their side. At the same time, the writers profit from the upward move of the stock, offsetting any possible losses from the option that was just written; however, that does limit profits.

For example, if you owned 100 shares of FCX (Freeport McMoRan) at $70 a share, you could write the January 70 call at 4. Now if FCX is at 70 or above at option expiration, you would get the $400, but limit your profit above 74.

Uncovered (naked) writers, however, write (sell) the option on 100 shares of stock that they do not own. This is very speculative. If the robot from *Lost in Space* were on hand, he would be flashing lights and waving his robotic arms shouting, "Danger! Danger!" There is unlimited risk to the naked call writer (betting the stock won't go up) and extensive risk to the naked put writer (betting the stock won't go down).

This is why you need collateral or a margin account. Naked writers must be able to guarantee to both the options buyer and to the options exchange that they will make good on the options that they write.

The Options Exchange

Where does all this option action happen, be it buying, writing, naked or covered? Logically, the venues for trading listed options are called the *options exchanges*. Like a stock exchange, an option exchange is an auction market where buyers and sellers gather to trade securities that are listed options. The Chicago Board Options Exchange (CBOE) was the first of these exchanges and was established in April 1973. (I remember a day I was on the floor when the professional traders. were crumbling paper and trying to make baskets using waste paper containers. It was an extraordinarily slow day.) Because of its success, others have been established. Options are also available on stock market indexes, such as the Dow Jones Industrial Average, S&P 500 index, and the S&P 100 index.

The stocks that are listed on the options exchanges must meet a set of criteria. Each individual stock must have at least three different options listed on the exchange, though it can have many more than three. Each common stock has listed options that expire in the next two months, every three months, and up to nine months in the future.

In 1990, long-term options called LEAPS (long-term equity anticipation securities) were introduced. Such long-term options can run more than two years before they expire.

These are options that have a lot more time before they expire so you have more time to wait for a stock or ETF to make a move. However, still watch your position like a hawk, and don't pay a lot for such options.

Some stocks have more options and more strike prices than others. When options for a stock are first listed on an exchange, options with one or two strike prices will become available. According to the rules, each will have four to eight listed options for a specific stock. However, if there is a significant change in the market price of the underlying common stock, new options with new strike prices will become available.

Generally, options with new strike prices are established at 5-point intervals, unless the stock is below 50. Then strike prices are usually available at 2.5-point intervals. Now some slow-moving stocks have strikes at 1-point intervals. As a result, many stocks have hundreds of different options available.

16

The Secret to Buying Low and Selling High

Because of the risk of "naked" option writing, you probably are crossing it off your list of things to do. The image of mines blowing up if you tread that path or of the *Lost in Space* robot warning you hysterically to keep away might be putting you off a little about indulging in naked option writing. Sometimes what may be a risk in one form can be used to your advantage in another form. This is true of naked option writing.

An old and famous adage on Wall Street says, "Buy low and sell high." However, what some investors don't realize is that you can get paid for waiting to buy low and sell high. The secret, of course, involves option writing. Few understand this technique, and that is the place you want to be—on the opposite side of the investment crowd.

The secret way of trying to buy stocks and ETFs at lower prices is to write naked puts. The further out-of-the-money or the further the strike price is from the current market price, the better. Remember, you will be trying to buy stocks or ETFs at real bargain prices.

When you write or sell a put, you are obligated to buy the stock if it is below the strike price at expiration. In most circumstances that wouldn't be a good thing. But in this case, that is exactly what you want—to buy the stock at that much lower price. On the other hand, if the stock price does not fall very far, you get a consolation prize. You get the premium or price at which you wrote the option.

On the other side of the coin, if you own a stock or an ETF and have a target price at which you wish to sell, you could write or sell a call. This is "covered" option writing because you own the underlying stock or ETF. As the writer of the call, you are obligated to sell the stock if it is above the strike price of the call at expiration. But if the stock doesn't get to that strike price at expiration, you again receive a consolation prize—the premium (or price of the option) from writing the call option.

When you write naked puts or covered options, you can keep earning income as you try to buy or sell stocks or ETFs. This is a much more lucrative way to buy or sell than just putting in limited orders and waiting for the stocks to hit those limits. This way you are getting paid to wait for lower or higher prices. This also builds patience into your investment practices.

One warning: at times you may need to take action immediately. Then, writing puts and calls will not work. To buy an ETF to protect your downside *right now*, don't write a put.

Just buy the ETF. Or if you want to sell a stock right now, sell it and don't write a call.

For example, during the big decline in the market in 2008 and 2009, I was trying to buy Freeport McMoRan (FCX) at a much lower price. So I was writing puts with a strike price of 25 when FCX was at about 35. FCX kept dropping in price down below 20, so at expiration of the put options I received the stock at a price of 25. I was a winner because I wanted the stock at 25. Also, I received a premium on top of that. Then during the recovery in the market, the FCX stock price returned to much higher levels, and I set a target price for the stock on part of my position at $70 a share. There I wrote call options with a strike price of 70. FCX was above 70 at expiration. As a result, I lost the stock at that price. In addition to the big profit I made from selling the stock, I received the premium from writing the call option. In fact, I had written several calls before losing the stock. This is the way you apply the old adage, "buy low and sell high!"

The Secret

Now you know the secret to taking what is otherwise a risky investment—naked option writing—and turning it into a winning strategy. Covered option writing, while not as risky, is also a part of the winning strategy and more profitable than when used in the conventional way. The professionals handle the tools of finance to their best advantage. They know how to tiptoe around the mines underfoot.

And even if you don't want to plunge down the option writing path, when you desire a stock or ETF or want to rid yourself of a stock or ETF, you have this secret route available.

To sum up, this is the secret to buying and selling stocks and ETFs—write naked puts and covered calls. This strategy forces you to buy stocks and ETFs at lower prices and sell stocks and ETFs at higher prices. This is the investor's ideal.

17

The Win-Win Strategy

In Chapter 16, I share the secret to successful investing, a method by which you can earn money as you try to buy stocks or ETFs at lower and sometimes much lower prices and sell the stocks or ETFs that you own at higher or much higher prices.

This is truly a win-win situation. You win if you buy the stock or ETF at a much lower price, but you also win if you don't get the prized stock or ETF at a lower price because you get the consolation prize of the option premium. In addition, you can write another put over and over again until you finally get the stock or ETF, while all along earning income as you write each put.

On the other side of the coin, when you write covered calls to sell stock, if you sell the stock by it being exercised or assigned, you should be happy because you have taken profits on your stock. But if the stock is not assigned, you should still be happy because you have earned income from the calls you have written, and, again, you can keep writing more calls and earn more income.

This approach to writing options is *safe*. (Not a lot of investment strategies are safe.) This investment strategy is safe because you realize income, get the stock or ETF at a lower price, or take profits on the stock or ETF you own. Though the strategy is safe, you still can wander off the secure path onto a dangerous one if you do not use common sense. Investors get in trouble when they write too many puts, that is, more puts than they can afford to buy stock, or sell calls naked where they don't have stock to sell. In these cases, sirens should be going off, warning you that your financial life is on the line and that financial doom is close.

The Big Challenge

Timing is everything. Commanders are well aware of this and so must you be as an investor when writing options. The big challenge is to pick the right time to try to buy stocks or ETFs, and, more than that, the right time to pick the right stocks and ETFs to purchase. Try to increase your attempts to buy stocks and ETFs when there is blood in the streets and stocks are in a deep bear market. That is when I was trying to buy Freeport McMoRan stock (FCX).

Always take a contrary view. Commanders try to do the unexpected, and in a way, so should you as the investor. Be aware of what the crowd is telling you; the information garnered is probably accurate, but don't do the expected. You want to be standing away from the crowd.

General Sun Tzu always struck large enemy forces in places where an attack wasn't expected, and, as a result, won the war against an enemy who had overwhelming numbers. General

Robert E. Lee tried always to surprise the enemy, constantly defying common military rules and, as a result, won victory after victory, until he did the expected at Gettysburg and lost. (General Grant was so exasperated with his generals' fear of Robert E. Lee that he said something like, "Do you think Lee can jump over our army and come up behind us?" Those probably are not his exact words, but something on that order.) You want to be that type of investor, a contrarian.

If you are a conservative investor, try to buy only big, blue-chip stocks or ETFs. They have less downsize risk. Also, only write puts that are far out-of-the-money but that still give you enough premium to make the practice worthwhile. One money manager who follows this secret practice handles money for technology billionaires. She writes puts on the big, blue-chip stocks and tries to get her clients into these stocks at lower prices that can earn an income for them. Investors like Warren Buffett also write puts to collect blue-chip stocks at lower prices and earn an income along the way. Now you can do the same.

The Hidden Risk

The only hidden risk to this strategy is buying stocks or ETFs that have greater risks than you think they have. An example of this would be Wellcare Health Plans (mentioned earlier), which dropped almost 100 points overnight. So a careful analysis of your selected stocks and ETFs is a helpful step in your writing program.

Also remember to have wide diversification in case you make a mistake in the stocks or ETFs you select. Then you'll avoid getting seriously hurt. Diversification has been mentioned before, and certainly will be mentioned again, because it is essential for your financial success and security.

Math and Science

Here is another slightly relevant tidbit about the Civil War. General Lee, besides being a skillful military man, was a skillful topographical engineer. This enabled him to pick just the right ground for his army to fight on. West Point was known for its advanced courses in math and science and to graduate as a military engineer was to be at the top of the graduating class, as was General Lee.

Now we come to the important part of the secret program—applying math and science to the selection process. Math and science were as necessary to the nineteenth-century military as it is to twenty-first–century investor. General Lee picked the best ground to fight on, and the investor must pick the best stocks and ETFs for options. In order to pick the right stocks and ETFs for options, you need to know the 80-percent rule.

The 80 Percent Rule

In order to buy stocks and ETFs at low prices, you should write put options that will expire 80 percent of the time worthless without needing to buy the stock. Then you will get the stock at low enough prices and, of course, earn a lot of income as you wait to try to buy the stock.

Also don't forget to apply the contrarian theory here. Write put options when stocks or ETFs are at true undervalued status. Of course, the question is how do you know if your written puts will expire as worthless 80 percent of the time? The answer is computer simulation.

The Magic of Computer Simulation

Computer simulation will tell you over a certain time frame what the probability is of a stock or ETF price hitting a specific target price during that time period. The one input you will need is the volatility of the underlying stock. Believe it or not, volatility is usually stable. The VIX (Volatility Index) gives you the "implied" volatility of a combination of all the stocks in the S&P 500 index. "Implied" means that the volatility is derived from the option prices or premiums of the underlying puts and calls.

There are many computer programs that will calculate implied volatility and historical volatility. Historical volatility is the underlying volatility of the underlying stock over a certain time frame in the past. You can also go to CBOE.com, the Web site of the Chicago Board Options Exchange. Click on "tools" and then click on "volatility."

A simulation is also an easy task. Programs like Option Master, the Push-Button Option Trader, and the Push-Button Option Writer all have simulators. If you have an iPhone, and an iPod touch, or an iPad, there is a simulator in the App Store called *The Stock and ETF Simulator* for only $14.95. Make sure you are using a simulator and not a probability calculator because the calculator will tell you what will happen only at the expiration of the option.

Using a Simulator

Using a simulator is easy. You enter the stock price, the volatility, your target price (the stock price you set as your profit goal or stop-loss point), and the date the option expires or your target date. Once you have done this, just click simulate.

The results of your simulation will be printed out, giving you what percent chance you have that the target will be hit.

For example, if Apple Computer is at 250 and you want to write the Apr 215 put when it is Oct 1, what is the chance that 215 will be hit during that time period? The simulator will give you that information. With a volatility of 35 percent, your chances of Apple hitting 215 are about 32 percent.

Try to find an option where the probability of hitting the target is less than 20 percent. Then your options will expire worthless about 80 percent of the time. Here you have created a simulation in which you will collect premiums from the option you have written 80 percent of the time, and the worst that can happen is that you get the stock or ETF at a much lower price less than 20 percent of the time. This is a win-win situation.

Let's say that you want to write an FCX Apr 50 put when the stock is $70 a share with a volatility of 40 percent and it is still Oct 1. Your chance of hitting the target of 50 is 16 percent. This means that there is an 84 percent chance that the option will expire without the strike price being hit. Even though your probability of winning is high, you still need to get a high enough option price for the option you write to make the effort worthwhile. Keep in mind that we're talking about option writing here; computer simulation is also an extremely valuable tool for the option buyer.

Regardless of option writing or buying, you must always be very active in managing your options. Option writing or buying is not for the passive investor. You have to be involved in the adventure, and part of that involvement is made easier with computer simulations.

18

The Art of Valuing Options

By using computer simulation, we can measure the odds of any option expiring worthless. But to really apply math and science to option trading, we must measure the true value of an option.

As an option buyer, you know that you want to find cheap undervalued options. As an option writer, you should always be in search of overvalued options. Even if you are writing options to buy stocks or ETFs, it is critical that you write only overvalued options.

When considering buying stocks, you should be looking for undervalued stocks. The best time to do this is when there is blood in the street and you can sniff panic in the air. However, you can't rely on your nose. Obviously plunging markets are a sure sign of panic that is hard to miss. However, there is a more subtle gauge of fear in the market. Option prices themselves are an excellent gauge of how much fear there is in the market. High option prices reflect a lot of fear, and when fear is high, stocks and ETFs decline and become undervalued.

The first place to look to determine if options are over-valued is the Volatility Index (VIX). The Volatility Index has ranged from 10 percent all the way up to 90 percent in 2008–2009. When the VIX is above 30 percent, options are over-valued. When the VIX is below 15 percent, the options are undervalued. Try to write options when the VIX is near or above 30. By following this guideline, you will find the perfect environment to buy stocks, ETFs, and options. This, in the fine tradition of *contrarianism*, is when everyone is running away from them.

Fair Value Tables

However, for options, there is an extra twist. Individual stocks and ETFs have different volatilities, and some options are over-valued all the time. This is where fair value tables come in. At the back of this book, you will find a set of fair value tables to guide you.

There are several models that try to determine the fair value of an option. I used the Nobel Prize–winning Black-Scholes model to develop our tables. The tables give you the fair value of options on a stock with an average volatility of 32 percent. Try to write options that are higher priced than those in the fair value tables. (You will learn how to use the tables in the final chapter.)

Other Ways to Measure Fair Value

The best way to measure the value of an option is with a computer program such as Option Master (gooptions.com). In addition, online stock and option brokerage houses have tools for measuring the fair value of options.

Here are several methods to determine if an option is overvalued:

1. Check the Volatility Index (VIX).
2. Use the fair value tables.
3. Use a computer program such as Option Master.
4. Use an online service from a brokerage house.

And here are some points to remember about options:

1. The most important consideration in writing options is not the option price, but the price of the underlying stock or ETF.
2. Before you write an option, make sure you have the funds and the desire to buy the stock or ETF. Then you will always be in a win–win situation.
3. Because you are choosing to operate when the market is panicky (a dangerous environment), be careful to avoid stocks that could go bankrupt or decline dramatically in value. To avoid this, try to stick with the blue-chip stocks and ETFs that are indexes of stocks, bonds, or currency.

In the end, your risk tolerance will determine which stocks and ETFs you select. How adventurous are you going to be? Are you going to go down the "River of Doubt" or are you going to prefer a healthy hike on a park trail? Whether aggressive or conservative, your adventure in finance can be profitable if you approach it with the right attitude—vigilance and patience; the right tools—options, simulators, and this book; and, the right preparation—research and know-how.

Part V

THE PORTFOLIO = HOLDING AND HEDGING

19

Long-Term
Investments Are
Dead, or Are They?

The big theme on Wall Street today is that long-term investments are dead. The advice given is that you should jump in and out of stocks as the markets change. However, there is one big factor being ignored—*taxes*. Of course, if you are working in a tax-exempt account, taxes are not an issue.

The common belief among analysts is that taxes should not be considered in any investment decision. Yet you can't avoid the fact that you incur a tax when you take profits on any investment. A casino's take isn't as large as what the IRS takes. Such a fact is hard to ignore. (Taxes, in general, are hard to ignore.) So even though it is everyone's desire to banish thoughts of impending taxes, taxes are a consideration. To the grave, they need to be a consideration. You know the old saying—something about death and taxes and a sure thing.

Of course, investments are not taxed until they are sold. Therefore, the longer you hold an investment, the better off you will be. This means that long-term investments are the only way to fly. Naturally, they should be good long-term investments. You won't fly very far on losing investments, particularly with the price of gasoline; in your bad investment plane you would eventually take a dive, or at least be grounded.

However, a leaky plane, to continue the metaphor, can surprise you. This is where the familiar statement, "Abandon the leaky plane" comes from. No, sorry, the metaphor is getting away from me. The real quote and popular truism is, "Cut your losses, and let your profits run."

Near the end of the tax year, take losses in your losing positions to offset profits you have taken during the year. Try to avoid paying any investment taxes each year. But, above all else, hold onto your winning positions for the long term. And if the market declines, you can hedge your winning positions with ETFs. Long-term investing is the only way to avoid the big tax bite. Always have a long-term perspective.

However, sometimes a commander must abandon his strategy if the situation gets precarious. You should be able to do the same. You shouldn't fall in love with a particular tactic or stock. Like commanders, you must be flexible. So if you have a profitable position that has some dire consequences, sell it and forget the tax situation.

Regardless of the adaptability advice, here is the car sticker you should have, "Long-term investing is not dead! Do not suffer the tax consequences!"

20

Develop Your Own Hedge Fund

Hedge funds seem to dominate the investment environment today. Designed to neutralize risk and help you prosper, regardless of what the market is doing, hedge funds use options, futures, and the shorting of stock.

You can develop your own hedge fund by investing in a wide variety of ETFs and option strategies. With the right balance you should prosper in all environments. That means that if the market moves up or down or stays where it is, you would prosper. (Such a portfolio is developed in Chapter 21.)

In the early twentieth century, France built sturdy extensive fortifications (known as the Maginot Line) to prevent Germany from invading. The French were very confident in these fortifications. They lost their confidence when the Germans went around them. That is about how the hedge fund professionals and customers feel when they lose a lot of money.

How did the markets get around the hedge fund fortifications? The hedge funds' fallibility was that they had taken one side or the other of the market and did not stay neutral, or they entered markets that did not have enough liquidity. How bad was this? In 1997, one fund, Long Term Capital, almost caused the whole market to crash, and that fund was run by Nobel Prize winners!

You should always be concerned about the market getting around your defensive fortifications. Again, always ask, "What is the worst that can happen to each of my investments?" Then build defenses such as put options and inverse ETFs to protect your downside.

A hedge fund should be designed to stay neutral—not bullish or bearish—and still prosper. The whole strategy of this book is to do that: to reduce risk, earn a good income, and grow. We do that by writing puts on the stocks and ETFs you want to own and slowly collecting stocks and ETFs over time as we continue to earn a lot of income by writing these puts. This formula should be familiar to you by now.

To reduce your risks, you must diversify. This advice is critical and should also, by now, be familiar to you. Try to take a lot of diverse positions. The key words here are "a lot" and "diverse." You don't want to make the mistake the hedge funds made. France probably shouldn't have relied on its fortifications. Working on advanced technology might have helped. The wise people in the South during the Civil War not only bought Confederate bonds, but they also hid some Yankee greenbacks and gold away some place. However, a lot of Southern people didn't have this much forethought. You don't want to be stuck (figuratively) with a lot of worthless Confederate bonds or watch the enemy sidestep your fortifications. Have forethought. No matter what the market does, if you follow this advice, you will prosper.

The next bit of advice should also be familiar to you now. Diversify by trying to buy stocks and ETFs at much lower prices than expected. Use the option tactics presented to make sure that when you do get the stock or ETF, it will be at a bargain price. Be patient and build your portfolio slowly. Just keep writing those puts!

How to Select a Broker

If you are just starting to trade, selecting a broker is an important step. Select a broker who can help you with the mechanics of the game, but don't let the broker lead you astray. When selecting a broker, there are two important considerations—commissions and margin. Use online brokers who have very low commissions—never more than $3 an option—and that have low margin requirements. If the broker requires all the cash to buy the underlying stock or ETF in the account, go to another broker. Eventually your stocks and ETFs will be used as margin.

Evasive Action

As you manage your own portfolio, there will be times when you will not be able to write puts. Instead, you will need to go in and just buy the stock or ETF. For example, you might have to do this when you need immediate downside protection. Then you may need to buy something like the ProShares Ultra Short S&P 500 (ETF), which gives you double the downside action of the S&P 500 index to offset the risks to the rest of your portfolio.

Why Build Your Own Hedge Fund?

Hedge your own bets. Don't rely on professional hedge funds. You want control; you want to ensure that you are neutral; and you always include some downside bets with your upside positions. ETFs and options can help you build up a fortification that can't be sidestepped. Besides stocks, own ETFs in bonds, currency, gold, silver, and T-bills. This is how ETFs help you diversify. Use options to insure your investments and to pop in and out of the markets, giving you more control, and ultimately putting undervalued and bargain priced assets into your portfolio.

21

The Perfect ETF Portfolio

L et's design a portfolio that has the look of a well-balanced hedge fund: diversified and truly hedged—one that should prosper in any environment.

Cash

The first position to consider is your cash position. Americans tend to hold too much of their cash in U.S. dollars. You need to diversify your cash position. This means putting some of your cash into other countries' currencies. For example, put some of your cash into currencies like the Australian dollar or the Canadian dollar by adding the FXA (Rydex Currency Shares Australian) and the FXC (Rydex Currency Shares Canadian D) ETFs to your portfolio.

Bonds

In an attempt to get your best cash return, put some money into bonds. Select short-term bond funds or ETFs. Then you will not be at the mercy of the whims of interest-rate fluctuations. One such ETF is CSJ (iShares Barclays 1–3 Credit Bond Fund). When interest rates are very low, avoid Treasury bonds unless they are inflation-protected like the TIP (iShares Barclays TIPS Bond Fund).

To protect your portfolio from interest-rate increases, buy the TBT (ProShares UltraShort 20+ Year Treasury) when interest rates are very low. This ETF moves double to the inverse of Treasury bond prices. So as interest rates rise, TBT should rise twice as fast as the Treasury bond prices fall. For longer-term Treasury bonds, you can buy the TLT (iShares Barclays 20+ Year Treasury Bond Fund), but use the TBT to hedge that position when rates are low. When it comes to inverse ETFs like the TBT, be like a grizzly bear: take profits quickly and monitor the positions closely.

Other higher-yielding Bond ETFs to consider are: LQD (iShares IBOXX $ Investment Grade Corporate Bond Fund) and HYG (iShares IBOXX $ High Yield Corporate Bond Fund). However, lighten up on these positions when interest rates are very low. (These bond funds will drop like a rock when interest rates rise.) Other bond ETFs to consider are emerging market bond ETFs such as the iShares JPMorgan USD Emerging Markets Bond Fund (EMB).

Stocks

You have a lot of options when it comes to putting stock positions into your portfolio.

U.S. Index ETFs

Investing in SPY, the S&P 500 Index Fund ETF; QQQ, the Nasdaq Index ETF; or DIA, the Dow Jones Industrial Index ETF are good choices. But here you need to dollar average. (Dollar averaging involves putting money into the market slowly.)

For example, buying stocks once every month helps to build your portfolio, slowly, so that you're not stuck in a situation in which you put all your money into the market at the top. It is much wiser to add to your portfolio slowly, so that you can take advantage of healthy corrections and major declines in the market. Markets tend to rise on the last day of the month and the first four trading days of the next month; try to take advantage of this historical trend.

Emerging Market ETFs

In addition to U.S. indexes, you can add ETFs from the emerging markets with an ETF like EEM (iShares MSCI Emerging Markets Index Fund). There are a lot of choices when considering stocks of specific countries. For example, to buy stocks in countries such as Brazil, you can buy the EWZ (iShares MSCI Brazil Index Fund) or the BRF (Market Sectors Brazil Small-Cap) ETFs, which are Brazilian small-cap stocks. To be more aggressive, you could try the Russian stock market by buying the RSX (Market Vectors Russia). (Just remember to dollar-average when you enter these positions and try to buy on weakness.)

Sector ETFs

When selecting stock ETFs, make sure to include some sector ETFs in your portfolio.

For example, the XLE (Energy Select Sector SPDR Fund) can add energy stocks to your portfolio. To put health stocks on your team, you could buy the XLV (Select Sector Health Care Select Sector SPDR Fund). To add semiconductor stocks, you can buy the SMH (Merrill Lynch Semiconductor HOLDRS Trust). Try to buy sector ETFs that are in the weakest industries. Always try to find bargain-priced ETFs.

Another sector to consider adding to your portfolio is metals. You can buy a mining stock ETF like GDX (Market Vectors Gold Miners ETF). But if you really want to buy the gold, silver, or copper directly, you can buy the GLD (SPDR Gold Shares), SLV (iShares Silver Trust), and JJC (iPath Dow Jones-AIG Copper Total Return Sub-Index ETN).

These ETFs tend to rise with the spot price of gold, silver, and copper. The problem is that these ETFs use futures contracts to duplicate the action of the metals. However, to get the real, physical metals, you need to look at the PSLV (Sprott Physical Silver Trust ET) and SGOL (ETFs Physical Swiss Gold Shares). When you purchase these particular ETFs, you are actually buying physical gold and physical silver; so you will not have the disadvantage of handling futures contracts.

In order to include agricultural products like corn, soybeans, wheat, or other commodities such as coffee and sugar, consider the DBA (PowerShares DB Agriculture Fund). Again, try to buy these ETFs on pullbacks or weaknesses, always making sure to dollar-cost average. To get a *specific* commodity such as corn, you could buy CORN by way of the Teucrium Corn Fund (ETF).

To include crude oil and natural gas in your portfolio, buy energy stocks such as XLE (mentioned earlier.) But where can you buy crude oil directly? Purchase the USO (United States Oil Fund) or the USL (United States 12 Month Oil Fund, LP).

These ETFs use futures contracts. The USO has a lot more liquidity, but the USL has 12 month contracts, which gives it more stability.

To buy natural gas, you could buy the UNG (United States Natural Gas Fund, LP) or the UNL (United States 12 Month Natural Gas, LP). Again, the UNL has more stability than the UNG.

Master Limited Partnerships (MLPs)

You should include some master limited partnerships in your portfolio, as they allow for some specific tax advantages. They avoid the problem of double taxation where the corporation is taxed, and then you are taxed again on the distribution you receive. You can also take advantage of the rising demand for oil and gas with some of these master limited partnerships. Such MLPs include KMP (Kinder Morgan Energy Partners) and ETP (Energy Transfer Partners).

Real Estate Investment Trusts (REITS)

Real estate investment trusts also avoid double taxation, and these kinds of trusts center on facilities or housing in both commercial and residential real estate and also land and timber. Commercial real estate includes healthcare facilities and industrial facilities.

Some of the safer trusts can be found in the healthcare real estate market. For example, OHI (Omega Healthcare) is one choice in this market. Another industry that has REITs is the timber market, with an excellent choice being PCL (Plum Creek Timber). This is a good way to put hard assets into your portfolio.

Acquiring ETFs

Now you have a widely diversified portfolio, but to put ETFs into that portfolio, you should write naked puts. What do you do if you don't have the funds to write puts? Buy just a few shares of each ETF, but make sure to acquire them slowly, using dollar-cost averaging.

The Hedge

Any good portfolio should be "hedged" or have some downside insurance. I already explained how to protect against rising interest rates. Here you would buy TBT (ProShares UltraShort 20+ Year Treasury ETF), but you also must have enough cash in your account to be able to buy other inverse ETFs such as the SDS (ProShares UltraShort S&P 500) that will move up twice as fast in price when the S&P 500 index falls in price.

Finally, have some insurance in place at all times, be it ETFs or put options. But when it is put options, buy on volatile, unstable, small stocks. These will give you the biggest bang for your buck.

22

Are You a Gunslinger?

There are some traders who don't want to play it safe. Adventure is their middle name. They probably enjoy the adrenaline rush or yearn for a challenge and enjoy the resulting suspense. I call them the gunslingers. So if there is a gunslinger reading this book, he or she may be asking, "What if I am more aggressive?"

Safeguards, Even for the Gunslingers

Here is my advice. You still need to be defensive. I am more aggressive when I trade, but nevertheless I always have the funds to buy the underlying assets if I must. Also, I always have "mental stops" to exit put writing positions. This way the only time that I have to buy a stock or ETF is if it gaps down in price—an unlikely occurrence.

By mental stops, I mean stops you put into your head and then write down to make them more concrete. Mental stops, specifically, are the stock prices you reach that tell you to exit the positions and close the doors of the casino. You have to discipline yourself to make sure that once you establish your mental stops, you stick to them.

Why mental stops? Mental stops should be in place in case another flash crash occurs because regular stop-losses could cause disaster to your portfolio in that situation.

Because I'm aggressive, I try to write short-term options, usually less than two months before expiration and, according to the simulator, that have less than a 15 percent chance of the underlying stock or ETF hitting the strike price. Here you must diversify and also be prepared to have a gap down once in a while, where you will then incur a fat loss.

Whatever type of investor you fashion yourself to be, gunslinger or gun-phobic, how aggressive you are depends on your risk tolerance. Be realistic about how much risk you can take and still sleep at night.

Warning, Warning

If you decide you are a gunslinger, one big warning is necessary. Many option traders have been, figuratively of course, carried off the option floor in body bags because they overdosed on option writing. Your opponent in a shootout is the very dangerous, unpredictable, fickle, predatory, bewildering, extensive, and growing world market. Don't underestimate it!

Part VI

THE BEST MOVE = THE WIN-WIN STRATEGY

23

Put Writing with Insurance

If you are writing puts to acquire stocks or ETFs, or if you are writing puts for pure speculation, there is a way to reduce the risk of the position. The answer is the "credit spread." The credit spread can prevent a huge loss when a stock or ETF shows a big gap down in price. The function of a credit spread is to limit your maximum risk.

Credit Spreads

When you write put options, you are obligated to buy the underlying stock or ETF if the stock price is below the strike price of the put at expiration. But just as we discussed in the grizzly bear chapter, you can buy a further out-of-the-money put to protect your position.

163

The key is to buy cheap puts to offset that risk. To do this, you need to write short-term puts. The protective puts should be really cheap. Sometimes finding such opportunities is difficult.

Let's review a play I recommended in my market letter.

I suggested writing the RIG (Transocean) 65 put at 0.5 when the stock was at about a 67.5 with one week before expiration. However, to protect the position from a possible gap down in price, I purchased a 62.5 put at 0.1. This action reduced my credit by $10. I may still receive a credit of 0.4 instead of 0.5. This is a credit spread that limited my maximum to 2.5 points less the credit I got off 0.4, giving me a maximum risk of 2.1; and that, only if the stock would gap down below 62.5 in the next week.

Here is how you would enter this order:

1. Buy to open the RIG Nov 62.5 put.
2. Sell to open the RIG Nov 65 put.
3. Minimum credit of 0.4.

Here you earn $40 for each position if RIG does not drop below 65 by the end of the week which it did not do.

I use credit spreads when I am writing puts on stocks or ETFs that have some downside risk. But the key to success is to find a very cheap put to buy and offset the downside risk. When you are playing with risky stocks where you are writing puts just to earn income, credit spreads are a very useful tool.

24

In Search of the
Sure Thing

One of the goals of my put writing portfolio is to select puts that have a low probability of ever acquiring the stock or ETF. It is a win-win strategy because if I am assigned to the stock or ETF, I am a winner because I have purchased the stock at a lower, more attractive price.

However, my goal is to keep writing puts to generate a lot of income for the portfolio. Slowly I will build a portfolio, and that is what I want. Like dollar-cost averaging, where you invest the same number of dollars in stocks each month, I will slowly acquire stocks during market declines or major pullbacks. But along the way I will generate a lot of income. Similarly, when you buy an ETF, you'll purchase shares every month for a long period of time. Writing put options should have the same effect and force you to buy at lower prices.

How to Pick the Winning Puts

Puts that will expire worthless are winning puts. The most important tool to use is a stock and ETF simulator. As mentioned previously, I will also set a stop-loss price, but make it a "mental" stop-loss price so that a flash crash will not give me a horrible price to get out of the position. If a stock or ETF gaps down below my stop-loss price, I will wait and be assigned the stock or ETF—but only then will I buy the stock. I only select puts that will expire worthless 85 percent of the time or better, without hitting the stop-loss price (and the simulator will tell me that.)

With this strategy, in a sense, I have almost found the sure thing. About 85 percent of the time the puts that I write (sell) will expire, and I will pocket the proceeds. Far less than 15 percent of the time, I will acquire the stock or the ETF at a lower price. Once in a while, I will take a small loss when the stock hits a stop-loss price, and I decide to exit the position.

Following are some ETF positions I took over a short time span during the fall of 2010:

1. On November 26, 2010—Sell to open the FXI (iShares FTSE/Xinhua China 25 Index Fund). Dec 40 Put at 0.3. FXI price is 43.5. Here I wrote an FXI put. This is a China stock index fund. The chance of the option expiring worthless was over 95 percent according to our computer simulations; almost a sure thing.

.

2. On November 26, 2010—Sell to open the FXA (currency shares Australian Dollar Trust). Dec 93 put at 0.45. FXA price is 96.6. Here we wrote an FXA put on the Australian Dollar The chance of the option expiring worthless was over 94 percent according to our computer simulations; almost a sure thing.

3. On November 11, 2010—Sell to open the IJR (iShares S&P SmallCap 600 Index Fund). Feb 52 put at 0.8. IJR price is 62.2. Here I wrote an IJR put on the small-cap stock fund. The chance of the option expiring worthless was almost 99 percent according to our computer simulations; almost a sure thing.

All these plays were on conservative funds. So the only downside was that I would get funds at attractive prices—a win-win strategy.

25

Pep Talk for Option Writers

A put strategy can be quite conservative. For example, as we discussed earlier, if you wanted to convert U.S. dollars, you could write (sell) an FXA (Australian dollar) put. I did this, writing the Nov 83 put at 0.7 in the middle of September. At this time, FXA was selling for 91. Using the Apple App computer simulation, The Stock & ETF Simulator, the chances that FXA would hit 83 before Nov expiration were about 4 percent (using a volatility of 14 percent.) This was almost a sure bet that the option would expire worthless, and the worst that could happen was that I would have the ETF at a bargain price of 83, moving my U.S. dollars into Australian dollars at a great price.

This is one of the surest and best plays you could ever make. That is why the professional option investors I know love option writing. Sometimes the odds against gamblers and investment traders appear to be similar and insurmountable; however, the house has been beaten. Ed Thorp found a way to beat the casinos playing blackjack. Jeffrey Ma, author of the excellent book, *The House Advantage*, was on the MIT blackjack team that won millions of dollars in Las Vegas and was the inspiration for the book, *Bringing Down the House* and the movie *21*. He said that when he first started playing blackjack, he was a trader on the Chicago Board Options Exchange. He added that option trading was a gamble, but blackjack was not.

Despite Jeffrey Ma's skeptical attitude toward option trading, I have tried to build a system that could beat Wall Street. Option writing is that system, because with computer simulation you can identify winning trades.

Jeffrey Ma could at one time beat the casino with blackjack, but he would have had to suffer through some long losing streaks. And, of course, on any hand he would only have a so-so chance of winning. However, with options markets, you can create option strategies that will win 96 percent of the time, as I just demonstrated. The downside of this isn't even a downside. The downside, if you lose the bet, is that you receive the ETF at a bargain price. This is the strategy that can beat the house. In other words, this is how you can beat Wall Street!

Part VII

THE MISSION = SUCCESS

26

In Search of the Holy Grail of Investing

Now is the time to develop your game plan and find the Holy Grail of investing. The first step on this path of discovery is recognizing the importance of defense.

Just as military commanders try to plan for all possible contingencies, so must investors. However, most commanders realize that not all contingencies can be planned for. There are just too many variables. The unexpected can and will happen. You need to recognize and understand what the risks are. If you have wealth, you must protect it; your aim should be to protect what you have.

Thus the question that everyone should ask about any investment is: What is my maximum downside risk? Understanding this risk is your ultimate goal.

Fickle, Frail World

First, however, you have to be aware of the dangerous, fickle world we live in.

History will repeat itself; over the past 100 years, the world has suffered two world wars and many other major conflicts. During such times, much wealth was lost. Yet the United States has been somewhat immune from such losses. However, we can't get comfortable with that thought. Not only may we not stay immune, but there are myriad catastrophes that could affect us. Various rogue waves could change the picture: a major terrorist attack, a nuclear attack, a plague, a financial collapse, an electronic system collapse—and the list continues!

All could endanger your wealth. No one knows when or where the next rogue wave will hit, but you must be prepared for such an event.

Consider the growth of the world's population. At 6.5 billion people, we are pressing the limits of our world's resources. Rogue waves have hit many times in the past, ripping out huge amounts of wealth; we are in a prime place for new rogue waves.

Consider the fallibility of governments. In the last century, over 100 million people died at the hands of communists and socialists. Communist-socialist governments centralize economic power, which gives them absolute control of all individuals. This makes the governments vulnerable to a zealous or corrupt, all-powerful leader or oligarchy. In such societies, the market doesn't control human behavior; the government does. In the name of "for the people," these governments have "killed

174

the people." If they don't kill you, they just take most or all of your wealth. Then individualism becomes a crime.

When will a wave hit home? Even now the United States is becoming a socialist country. Based on the amount of money the government is spending as compared to that spent in the private sector, the United States is more socialistic now than England, France, or Germany. There are always those who try to redistribute the country's wealth. Bernie Madoff said that the U.S. government is running the greatest Ponzi scheme of all time. (And this from the most notorious con man in history who ran his own multibillion dollar scheme.)

Understanding Risk

Rogue waves threaten, and inflation creeps or leaps onward.

Bonds

In such an environment, debt is a bad investment. You do not want to be a lender; therefore, long-term bonds are not a good investment. Equities have fared better even during desperate times; however, U.S. debt was a good investment only during the 1930's depression and some other short periods in our financial history.

Real Estate

Real estate has its advantages because you are holding real assets. However, during World War II in Europe, few were able to collect rent. In addition, much real estate was confiscated. Even in the United States, Japanese Americans were forced to sell their personal real estate and business property and were sent to camps. Governments may get desperate during war times and perform outrageous acts.

Hard Assets

Hard assets like gold, silver, copper, and oil are like currency; they rarely decline in real value. However, though gold, silver, and copper have better purchasing power than paper currencies, they also have had long, bear markets.

Again, what to do? The dollar, no; long-term bonds, no. Real estate and hard assets have their good points, but they aren't the best answers either. A possible answer is equities. Equities or stocks seem to fare best in the long run. However, *stocks are not forever*.

Stocks

Stocks are a good investment, but specific stocks in general are not a good very-long-term hold. Out of the top 100 stocks in the S&P index more than 100 years ago, almost all did not survive. Only two stocks survived. One is General Electric.

Why? As stocks grow in value and size, they become less efficient, less innovative, less competitive, and less adaptable. They are too big to adjust to a radically changing environment, so they eventually disappear. In fact, one of the best financial decisions is to buy a stock that is breaking into several smaller companies. These smaller companies, then, do not have size as a disadvantage.

Here are two points about buying stocks:

1. Depending on professionals, the media or analysts will lead you astray.

2. It is far better to buy indexes such as the S&P 500 index or the Dow Jones Industrial Average. (The indexes drop the weak players, so you are not betting on a dead horse.)

Option Writing and Diversification

With such flaws in a variety of investments, defense should always be on your mind, but how does this get us to the Holy Grail of investing?

The answer could be wide diversification. And as you have discovered, ETFs are the answer to getting such diversification. Investing in the markets is a tough game. Most players have a difficult time of winning 50 percent of the time. Lady Luck seems to dictate how well you will do. Getting a return of 10 percent per year is almost impossible. So is diversification alone the Holy Grail?

The financial regulators do not believe you can win 90 percent of the time, but you can when you *write puts* (using a simulator to make sure you have a 90 percent chance of winning). You *can* win 90 percent of the time, and the remaining 10 percent will get you the underlying stock or ETF at an attractive price.

This is the Holy Grail of investing. This is the secret weapon. Add diversification, and you have the perfect game plan.

27

The Mission

ETFs and options offer you, the investor, a chance to more carefully and creatively control your portfolio. They allow you to plan.

During the French and Indian Wars, Robert Rogers (who formed Rogers' Rangers, the first American special forces' unit) had a rule: before going on a mission, don't forget anything! This rule still applies. Astronauts taking off on a NASA mission have to plan. It's hard to send home for something once the rocket takes off. So, too, when investors are navigating in the treacherous universe of finance, an unstable environment, they cannot afford to forget anything. Planning is essential. The existence of ETFs and options make the planning easier and more effective.

Sun Tzu, the very wise and successful Chinese general, once wrote, "Every battle is won before it is fought." ETFs and options help you win your battles before you fight them.

Appendix

The Fair Value Option Tables

The fair value option tables are one of the most indispensible aids to the option player. They will tell you when to buy, when to sell, and project what a specific price will be in the future. Fair value option tables are your crystal ball. They are critical to your success (if you don't have an option pricing computer program). They will identify bargain price options as well as options that are ripe for naked or covered writing. The fair value option tables will give you the true option price based on the underlying common stock or ETF price and the number of weeks left in the life of the option.

Options with strike prices as high as $150 are provided in the tables. Very few common stocks are priced above $150, and those that do reach those heights are normally split in order to make their shares more attractive to the market. So if you are evaluating a listed option with a strike price at 150 or lower, you should be able to easily determine the true value of that option today or at any time in the option's life.

The fair option prices presented in these tables are to be used as *guidelines*—not as an absolute measure of value. The prices given are based on an underlying common stock or ETF with average volatility.

Volatility is a key you will have to input in evaluating these fair prices. Common stocks with a higher-than-average volatility usually have a higher price than the prices listed in the fair value option tables. Underlying common stocks with low volatility should have a lower price than the listed option prices in the tables. Therefore, volatility should be carefully considered when you view the fair values given to each option. Use the volatility formula presented or look at the underlying common stock's Beta factor (provided by most chart services).

When the volatility is much greater than 32 percent or the Beta factor is much greater than 1.00, the corresponding option price should be adjusted accordingly. The same adjustment should be made for underlying common stocks or ETFs that have a volatility that is significantly below 30 percent or that maintains a Beta factor well below 1.00.

Remember, the fair value prices are to be used as guidelines— a beacon to guide you in this fast-moving and confusing game. You will find these tables invaluable, both in strategy design and in making tactical maneuvers. These tables will clearly tell you when option prices are out of line. So keep these tables at your side when you play the options game.

Interpolation

Under certain conditions, you will encounter an option exercise (strike) price not listed in the fair value option tables, such as 55 or 22.5, and so on. In order to measure the fair price of options with abnormal exercise prices, interpolation is required. This means that you make an estimate based on the values in the tables.

For example, you are evaluating an EXXON Oct 55 put with six weeks until expiration, with the stock price at 55. This option is not presented in the tables. Therefore, identify the two option prices with the closest exercise prices and the same number of weeks to expiration. Add these two prices together and, in this case, divide by two. This will give you the fair value of the Oct 55 option with six weeks remaining until expiration.

1. The fair value of the Oct 50 put is 1.7 when the underlying stock is 50.
2. Add the fair value of the Oct 60 +2.1 put when the underlying stock is 60.

$$\text{Fair value} = 3.8 \div 2 = 1.9$$

3. The sum of (1) and (2) divided by 2 equals the fair value of the Oct 55 put option, which is 1.9 ($190).

You can also use interpolation to measure the fair value of an option for a specific number of days rather than a specific number of weeks before expiration. However, I feel that the fair value prices given for each week will provide quite adequate guidelines, and such interpolation is probably unnecessary.

How to Use the Fair Option Tables

Finding the fair value of an option using the fair value option tables is an easy task.

For example, to find the real value of a Sears July 40 call with 10 weeks remaining, with Sears priced at $40 a share, turn to the call tables and the page with the exercise (strike) price of 40. Look down the table to the point where the common stock price is 40. Move across to the column which states that 10 weeks are remaining, and you will find the fair value of the Sears July 40 call, which is 2.3 ($230).

Practice with a few more options, and you will get the hang of using these tables quite rapidly. But remember, I highly recommend that you use an options pricing computer program, such as Option Master when you really get serious about trading options.

THE NORMAL VALUE LISTED CALL OPTION TABLES

LISTED CALL OPTION PRICE WHEN EXERCISE PRICE IS 10

NUMBER OF WEEKS BEFORE THE OPTION EXPIRES

Common Stock Price	1	2	3	4	5	6	7	8	9	10	11	12	13	14	15	16	17	18	19	20	21	22	23	24	25	26	27	28	29	30	31	32	33	34	35	36	37	38	39
14	4.0	4.0	4.0	4.0	4.0	4.0	4.0	4.1	4.1	4.1	4.1	4.1	4.1	4.1	4.1	4.1	4.1	4.1	4.1	4.1	4.1	4.1	4.2	4.2	4.2	4.2	4.2	4.2	4.2	4.2	4.2	4.2	4.2	4.2	4.2	4.2	4.2	4.2	4.3
13.5	3.5	3.5	3.5	3.5	3.5	3.6	3.6	3.6	3.6	3.6	3.6	3.6	3.6	3.6	3.6	3.6	3.7	3.7	3.7	3.7	3.7	3.7	3.7	3.7	3.7	3.7	3.7	3.8	3.8	3.8	3.8	3.8	3.8	3.8	3.8	3.8	3.8	3.8	3.9
13	3.0	3.0	3.0	3.0	3.1	3.1	3.1	3.1	3.1	3.1	3.1	3.1	3.2	3.2	3.2	3.2	3.2	3.2	3.2	3.2	3.2	3.3	3.3	3.3	3.3	3.3	3.3	3.3	3.3	3.4	3.4	3.4	3.4	3.4	3.4	3.4	3.4	3.4	3.5
12.5	2.5	2.5	2.5	2.6	2.6	2.6	2.6	2.6	2.6	2.6	2.7	2.7	2.7	2.7	2.7	2.7	2.7	2.8	2.8	2.8	2.8	2.8	2.8	2.8	2.9	2.9	2.9	2.9	2.9	2.9	2.9	3.0	3.0	3.0	3.0	3.0	3.0	3.0	3.1
12	2.0	2.0	2.1	2.1	2.1	2.1	2.1	2.1	2.2	2.2	2.2	2.2	2.2	2.2	2.3	2.3	2.3	2.3	2.3	2.3	2.4	2.4	2.4	2.4	2.4	2.4	2.5	2.5	2.5	2.5	2.5	2.5	2.6	2.6	2.6	2.6	2.6	2.6	2.7
11.5	1.5	1.5	1.6	1.6	1.6	1.6	1.6	1.7	1.7	1.7	1.7	1.7	1.8	1.8	1.8	1.8	1.8	1.8	1.9	1.9	1.9	1.9	1.9	2.0	2.0	2.0	2.0	2.0	2.1	2.1	2.1	2.1	2.1	2.2	2.2	2.2	2.2	2.2	2.3
11	1.0	1.1	1.1	1.2	1.2	1.2	1.2	1.2	1.3	1.3	1.3	1.3	1.3	1.4	1.4	1.4	1.4	1.5	1.5	1.5	1.5	1.5	1.6	1.6	1.6	1.6	1.6	1.6	1.7	1.7	1.7	1.7	1.7	1.8	1.8	1.8	1.8	1.9	1.9
10.5	0.6	0.7	0.7	0.7	0.8	0.8	0.8	0.8	0.9	0.9	0.9	0.9	0.9	1.0	1.0	1.0	1.0	1.0	1.1	1.1	1.1	1.1	1.2	1.2	1.2	1.2	1.2	1.2	1.3	1.3	1.3	1.3	1.3	1.4	1.4	1.4	1.4	1.4	1.5
10	0.2	0.3	0.3	0.4	0.4	0.4	0.5	0.5	0.6	0.6	0.6	0.6	0.6	0.7	0.7	0.7	0.7	0.8	0.8	0.8	0.8	0.8	0.9	0.9	0.9	0.9	0.9	0.9	1.0	1.0	1.0	1.0	1.0	1.0	1.1	1.1	1.1	1.1	1.1
9.5	0.0	0.1	0.1	0.2	0.2	0.2	0.3	0.3	0.4	0.4	0.4	0.4	0.4	0.5	0.5	0.5	0.5	0.6	0.6	0.6	0.6	0.6	0.7	0.7	0.7	0.7	0.7	0.7	0.8	0.8	0.8	0.8	0.8	0.8	0.9	0.9	0.9	0.9	0.9
9	0.0	0.0	0.0	0.0	0.0	0.0	0.1	0.1	0.2	0.2	0.2	0.2	0.2	0.3	0.3	0.3	0.3	0.4	0.4	0.4	0.4	0.4	0.5	0.5	0.5	0.5	0.5	0.5	0.6	0.6	0.6	0.6	0.6	0.6	0.7	0.7	0.7	0.7	0.7
8.5	0.0	0.0	0.0	0.0	0.0	0.0	0.0	0.0	0.0	0.0	0.0	0.0	0.0	0.1	0.1	0.1	0.1	0.2	0.2	0.2	0.2	0.2	0.3	0.3	0.3	0.3	0.3	0.3	0.4	0.4	0.4	0.4	0.4	0.4	0.5	0.5	0.5	0.5	0.5
8	0.0	0.0	0.0	0.0	0.0	0.0	0.0	0.0	0.0	0.0	0.0	0.0	0.0	0.0	0.0	0.0	0.0	0.0	0.0	0.0	0.0	0.1	0.1	0.1	0.1	0.1	0.1	0.1	0.2	0.2	0.2	0.2	0.2	0.2	0.2	0.3	0.3	0.3	0.3
7.5	0.0	0.0	0.0	0.0	0.0	0.0	0.0	0.0	0.0	0.0	0.0	0.0	0.0	0.0	0.0	0.0	0.0	0.0	0.0	0.0	0.0	0.0	0.0	0.0	0.0	0.0	0.0	0.0	0.0	0.0	0.0	0.0	0.0	0.0	0.1	0.1	0.1	0.1	0.1
7	0.0	0.0	0.0	0.0	0.0	0.0	0.0	0.0	0.0	0.0	0.0	0.0	0.0	0.0	0.0	0.0	0.0	0.0	0.0	0.0	0.0	0.0	0.0	0.0	0.0	0.0	0.0	0.0	0.0	0.0	0.0	0.0	0.0	0.0	0.0	0.0	0.0	0.0	0.0
6.5	0.0	0.0	0.0	0.0	0.0	0.0	0.0	0.0	0.0	0.0	0.0	0.0	0.0	0.0	0.0	0.0	0.0	0.0	0.0	0.0	0.0	0.0	0.0	0.0	0.0	0.0	0.0	0.0	0.0	0.0	0.0	0.0	0.0	0.0	0.0	0.0	0.0	0.0	0.0
6	0.0	0.0	0.0	0.0	0.0	0.0	0.0	0.0	0.0	0.0	0.0	0.0	0.0	0.0	0.0	0.0	0.0	0.0	0.0	0.0	0.0	0.0	0.0	0.0	0.0	0.0	0.0	0.0	0.0	0.0	0.0	0.0	0.0	0.0	0.0	0.0	0.0	0.0	0.0

LISTED CALL OPTION PRICE WHEN EXERCISE PRICE IS 15

NUMBER OF WEEKS BEFORE THE OPTION EXPIRES

Common Stock Price	1	2	3	4	5	6	7	8	9	10	11	12	13	14	15	16	17	18	19	20	21	22	23	24	25	26	27	28	29	30	31	32	33	34	35	36	37	38	39
21	6.0	6.0	6.0	6.0	6.0	6.1	6.1	6.1	6.1	6.1	6.1	6.1	6.1	6.1	6.1	6.2	6.2	6.2	6.2	6.2	6.2	6.2	6.2	6.2	6.2	6.3	6.3	6.3	6.3	6.3	6.3	6.3	6.3	6.3	6.3	6.4	6.4	6.4	6.4
20	5.0	5.0	5.0	5.1	5.1	5.1	5.1	5.1	5.1	5.1	5.2	5.2	5.2	5.2	5.2	5.2	5.3	5.3	5.3	5.3	5.3	5.3	5.3	5.4	5.4	5.4	5.4	5.4	5.4	5.4	5.5	5.5	5.5	5.5	5.5	5.5	5.6	5.6	5.6
19	4.0	4.0	4.1	4.1	4.1	4.1	4.1	4.2	4.2	4.2	4.2	4.2	4.3	4.3	4.3	4.3	4.3	4.4	4.4	4.4	4.4	4.4	4.5	4.5	4.5	4.5	4.5	4.6	4.6	4.6	4.6	4.6	4.7	4.7	4.7	4.7	4.7	4.8	4.8
18	3.0	3.1	3.1	3.1	3.1	3.2	3.2	3.2	3.2	3.3	3.3	3.3	3.3	3.3	3.4	3.4	3.4	3.5	3.5	3.5	3.5	3.6	3.6	3.6	3.6	3.7	3.7	3.7	3.7	3.8	3.8	3.8	3.8	3.9	3.9	3.9	3.9	4.0	4.0
17	2.0	2.1	2.1	2.1	2.2	2.2	2.2	2.2	2.3	2.3	2.3	2.4	2.4	2.4	2.5	2.5	2.5	2.5	2.6	2.6	2.6	2.7	2.7	2.7	2.8	2.8	2.8	2.8	2.9	2.9	2.9	3.0	3.0	3.0	3.1	3.1	3.1	3.2	3.2
16	1.1	1.2	1.2	1.3	1.3	1.4	1.4	1.5	1.5	1.5	1.6	1.6	1.6	1.7	1.7	1.8	1.8	1.8	1.9	1.9	1.9	1.9	2.0	2.0	2.0	2.0	2.0	2.1	2.1	2.1	2.1	2.2	2.2	2.3	2.3	2.4	2.4	2.5	2.5
15	0.3	0.4	0.5	0.6	0.6	0.7	0.7	0.8	0.8	0.8	0.9	0.9	1.0	1.0	1.0	1.1	1.1	1.1	1.2	1.2	1.2	1.3	1.3	1.3	1.3	1.4	1.4	1.4	1.4	1.5	1.5	1.5	1.5	1.6	1.6	1.6	1.6	1.6	1.7
14.5	0.1	0.2	0.3	0.4	0.4	0.5	0.5	0.6	0.6	0.7	0.7	0.7	0.8	0.8	0.8	0.9	0.9	0.9	1.0	1.0	1.0	1.1	1.1	1.1	1.1	1.2	1.2	1.2	1.2	1.3	1.3	1.3	1.3	1.4	1.4	1.4	1.4	1.4	1.5
14	0.0	0.0	0.1	0.2	0.3	0.3	0.3	0.4	0.4	0.4	0.5	0.5	0.5	0.6	0.6	0.6	0.7	0.7	0.7	0.8	0.8	0.8	0.9	0.9	0.9	1.0	1.0	1.0	1.0	1.0	1.1	1.1	1.1	1.1	1.2	1.2	1.2	1.2	1.3
13.5	0.0	0.0	0.0	0.0	0.0	0.0	0.0	0.0	0.0	0.1	0.1	0.1	0.2	0.2	0.2	0.3	0.3	0.3	0.4	0.4	0.4	0.5	0.5	0.5	0.6	0.6	0.6	0.7	0.7	0.7	0.8	0.8	0.8	0.9	0.9	0.9	1.0	1.0	1.1
13	0.0	0.0	0.0	0.0	0.0	0.0	0.0	0.0	0.0	0.0	0.0	0.0	0.0	0.0	0.0	0.1	0.1	0.1	0.2	0.2	0.2	0.3	0.3	0.3	0.4	0.4	0.4	0.5	0.5	0.5	0.6	0.6	0.6	0.7	0.7	0.7	0.8	0.8	0.9
12.5	0.0	0.0	0.0	0.0	0.0	0.0	0.0	0.0	0.0	0.0	0.0	0.0	0.0	0.0	0.0	0.0	0.0	0.0	0.0	0.0	0.0	0.1	0.1	0.1	0.2	0.2	0.2	0.3	0.3	0.3	0.4	0.4	0.4	0.5	0.5	0.5	0.6	0.6	0.7
12	0.0	0.0	0.0	0.0	0.0	0.0	0.0	0.0	0.0	0.0	0.0	0.0	0.0	0.0	0.0	0.0	0.0	0.0	0.0	0.0	0.0	0.0	0.0	0.0	0.0	0.0	0.1	0.1	0.1	0.2	0.2	0.2	0.3	0.3	0.3	0.4	0.4	0.4	0.5
11.5	0.0	0.0	0.0	0.0	0.0	0.0	0.0	0.0	0.0	0.0	0.0	0.0	0.0	0.0	0.0	0.0	0.0	0.0	0.0	0.0	0.0	0.0	0.0	0.0	0.0	0.0	0.0	0.0	0.0	0.0	0.1	0.1	0.1	0.2	0.2	0.2	0.3	0.3	0.3
11	0.0	0.0	0.0	0.0	0.0	0.0	0.0	0.0	0.0	0.0	0.0	0.0	0.0	0.0	0.0	0.0	0.0	0.0	0.0	0.0	0.0	0.0	0.0	0.0	0.0	0.0	0.0	0.0	0.0	0.0	0.0	0.0	0.0	0.0	0.0	0.1	0.1	0.1	0.1
10.5	0.0	0.0	0.0	0.0	0.0	0.0	0.0	0.0	0.0	0.0	0.0	0.0	0.0	0.0	0.0	0.0	0.0	0.0	0.0	0.0	0.0	0.0	0.0	0.0	0.0	0.0	0.0	0.0	0.0	0.0	0.0	0.0	0.0	0.0	0.0	0.0	0.0	0.0	0.0
10	0.0	0.0	0.0	0.0	0.0	0.0	0.0	0.0	0.0	0.0	0.0	0.0	0.0	0.0	0.0	0.0	0.0	0.0	0.0	0.0	0.0	0.0	0.0	0.0	0.0	0.0	0.0	0.0	0.0	0.0	0.0	0.0	0.0	0.0	0.0	0.0	0.0	0.0	0.0
9.5	0.0	0.0	0.0	0.0	0.0	0.0	0.0	0.0	0.0	0.0	0.0	0.0	0.0	0.0	0.0	0.0	0.0	0.0	0.0	0.0	0.0	0.0	0.0	0.0	0.0	0.0	0.0	0.0	0.0	0.0	0.0	0.0	0.0	0.0	0.0	0.0	0.0	0.0	0.0
9	0.0	0.0	0.0	0.0	0.0	0.0	0.0	0.0	0.0	0.0	0.0	0.0	0.0	0.0	0.0	0.0	0.0	0.0	0.0	0.0	0.0	0.0	0.0	0.0	0.0	0.0	0.0	0.0	0.0	0.0	0.0	0.0	0.0	0.0	0.0	0.0	0.0	0.0	0.0

LISTED CALL OPTION PRICE WHEN EXERCISE PRICE IS 20

NUMBER OF WEEKS BEFORE THE OPTION EXPIRES

Common Stock Price	1	2	3	4	5	6	7	8	9	10	11	12	13	14	15	16	17	18	19	20	21	22	23	24	25	26	27	28	29	30	31	32	33	34	35	36	37	38	39
28	8.0	8.0	8.0	8.1	8.1	8.1	8.1	8.1	8.1	8.1	8.1	8.2	8.2	8.2	8.2	8.2	8.2	8.2	8.2	8.3	8.3	8.3	8.3	8.3	8.3	8.3	8.4	8.4	8.4	8.4	8.4	8.4	8.4	8.4	8.5	8.5	8.5	8.5	8.5
27	7.0	7.0	7.1	7.1	7.1	7.1	7.1	7.1	7.2	7.2	7.2	7.2	7.2	7.3	7.3	7.3	7.3	7.3	7.3	7.4	7.4	7.4	7.4	7.4	7.5	7.5	7.5	7.5	7.5	7.5	7.6	7.6	7.6	7.6	7.6	7.7	7.7	7.7	7.7
26	6.0	6.0	6.1	6.1	6.1	6.1	6.2	6.2	6.2	6.2	6.3	6.3	6.3	6.3	6.4	6.4	6.4	6.4	6.4	6.5	6.5	6.5	6.5	6.6	6.6	6.6	6.6	6.7	6.7	6.7	6.7	6.8	6.8	6.8	6.8	6.9	6.9	6.9	6.9
25	5.0	5.1	5.1	5.1	5.1	5.1	5.2	5.2	5.3	5.3	5.3	5.3	5.4	5.4	5.4	5.5	5.5	5.5	5.5	5.6	5.6	5.6	5.7	5.7	5.7	5.7	5.8	5.8	5.8	5.9	5.9	5.9	5.9	6.0	6.0	6.0	6.1	6.1	6.1
24	4.0	4.1	4.1	4.1	4.2	4.2	4.2	4.3	4.3	4.3	4.4	4.4	4.4	4.5	4.5	4.5	4.6	4.6	4.6	4.7	4.7	4.7	4.8	4.8	4.8	4.9	4.9	4.9	5.0	5.0	5.0	5.1	5.1	5.1	5.2	5.2	5.2	5.3	5.3
23	3.0	3.1	3.1	3.2	3.2	3.2	3.3	3.3	3.3	3.4	3.4	3.5	3.5	3.5	3.6	3.6	3.7	3.7	3.7	3.8	3.8	3.9	3.9	3.9	4.0	4.0	4.0	4.1	4.1	4.2	4.2	4.2	4.3	4.3	4.4	4.4	4.4	4.5	4.5
22	2.1	2.1	2.2	2.3	2.3	2.3	2.4	2.5	2.6	2.6	2.7	2.7	2.7	2.8	2.9	2.9	3.0	3.0	3.0	3.1	3.1	3.1	3.2	3.2	3.2	3.3	3.3	3.3	3.4	3.4	3.4	3.5	3.5	3.5	3.6	3.6	3.7	3.7	3.7
21	1.1	1.2	1.2	1.3	1.4	1.5	1.6	1.7	1.8	1.8	1.8	1.9	1.9	2.0	2.0	2.1	2.2	2.2	2.2	2.3	2.3	2.4	2.4	2.4	2.5	2.5	2.5	2.5	2.6	2.6	2.7	2.7	2.8	2.8	2.8	2.9	2.9	2.9	2.9
20	0.4	0.5	0.6	0.7	0.8	0.9	0.9	1.0	1.1	1.1	1.1	1.2	1.2	1.3	1.4	1.4	1.5	1.5	1.6	1.6	1.6	1.7	1.7	1.7	1.8	1.8	1.8	1.9	1.9	1.9	2.0	2.0	2.0	2.1	2.1	2.1	2.2	2.2	2.2
19	0.0	0.1	0.2	0.3	0.4	0.4	0.5	0.6	0.7	0.7	0.8	0.8	0.9	0.9	1.0	1.0	1.1	1.1	1.2	1.2	1.2	1.3	1.3	1.3	1.4	1.4	1.4	1.5	1.5	1.5	1.6	1.6	1.6	1.7	1.7	1.7	1.8	1.8	1.8
18	0.0	0.0	0.0	0.0	0.0	0.1	0.1	0.2	0.3	0.3	0.4	0.4	0.4	0.5	0.5	0.6	0.6	0.7	0.7	0.8	0.8	0.9	0.9	0.9	1.0	1.0	1.0	1.1	1.1	1.1	1.2	1.2	1.2	1.3	1.3	1.3	1.4	1.4	1.4
17	0.0	0.0	0.0	0.0	0.0	0.0	0.0	0.0	0.0	0.0	0.0	0.0	0.0	0.0	0.1	0.1	0.2	0.2	0.3	0.3	0.4	0.4	0.5	0.5	0.5	0.6	0.6	0.6	0.7	0.7	0.8	0.8	0.8	0.9	0.9	0.9	1.0	1.0	1.0
16	0.0	0.0	0.0	0.0	0.0	0.0	0.0	0.0	0.0	0.0	0.0	0.0	0.0	0.0	0.0	0.0	0.0	0.0	0.0	0.0	0.0	0.1	0.1	0.1	0.2	0.2	0.2	0.3	0.3	0.3	0.4	0.4	0.4	0.5	0.5	0.5	0.6	0.6	0.6
15	0.0	0.0	0.0	0.0	0.0	0.0	0.0	0.0	0.0	0.0	0.0	0.0	0.0	0.0	0.0	0.0	0.0	0.0	0.0	0.0	0.0	0.0	0.0	0.0	0.0	0.0	0.0	0.0	0.0	0.0	0.0	0.0	0.0	0.0	0.0	0.0	0.0	0.0	0.0
14.5	0.0	0.0	0.0	0.0	0.0	0.0	0.0	0.0	0.0	0.0	0.0	0.0	0.0	0.0	0.0	0.0	0.0	0.0	0.0	0.0	0.0	0.0	0.0	0.0	0.0	0.0	0.0	0.0	0.0	0.0	0.0	0.0	0.0	0.0	0.0	0.0	0.0	0.0	0.0
14	0.0	0.0	0.0	0.0	0.0	0.0	0.0	0.0	0.0	0.0	0.0	0.0	0.0	0.0	0.0	0.0	0.0	0.0	0.0	0.0	0.0	0.0	0.0	0.0	0.0	0.0	0.0	0.0	0.0	0.0	0.0	0.0	0.0	0.0	0.0	0.0	0.0	0.0	0.0
13.5	0.0	0.0	0.0	0.0	0.0	0.0	0.0	0.0	0.0	0.0	0.0	0.0	0.0	0.0	0.0	0.0	0.0	0.0	0.0	0.0	0.0	0.0	0.0	0.0	0.0	0.0	0.0	0.0	0.0	0.0	0.0	0.0	0.0	0.0	0.0	0.0	0.0	0.0	0.0
13	0.0	0.0	0.0	0.0	0.0	0.0	0.0	0.0	0.0	0.0	0.0	0.0	0.0	0.0	0.0	0.0	0.0	0.0	0.0	0.0	0.0	0.0	0.0	0.0	0.0	0.0	0.0	0.0	0.0	0.0	0.0	0.0	0.0	0.0	0.0	0.0	0.0	0.0	0.0
12.5	0.0	0.0	0.0	0.0	0.0	0.0	0.0	0.0	0.0	0.0	0.0	0.0	0.0	0.0	0.0	0.0	0.0	0.0	0.0	0.0	0.0	0.0	0.0	0.0	0.0	0.0	0.0	0.0	0.0	0.0	0.0	0.0	0.0	0.0	0.0	0.0	0.0	0.0	0.0
12	0.0	0.0	0.0	0.0	0.0	0.0	0.0	0.0	0.0	0.0	0.0	0.0	0.0	0.0	0.0	0.0	0.0	0.0	0.0	0.0	0.0	0.0	0.0	0.0	0.0	0.0	0.0	0.0	0.0	0.0	0.0	0.0	0.0	0.0	0.0	0.0	0.0	0.0	0.0

Common
Stock
Price

NUMBER OF WEEKS BEFORE THE OPTION EXPIRES

	1	2	3	4	5	6	7	8	9	10	11	12	13	14	15	16	17	18	19	20	21	22	23	24	25	26	27	28	29	30	31	32	33	34	35	36	37	38	39
35	10.0	10.0	10.0	10.1	10.1	10.1	10.1	10.1	10.1	10.2	10.2	10.2	10.2	10.2	10.2	10.3	10.3	10.3	10.3	10.3	10.3	10.4	10.4	10.4	10.4	10.4	10.4	10.5	10.5	10.5	10.5	10.5	10.5	10.6	10.6	10.6	10.6	10.6	10.6
34	9.0	9.0	9.1	9.1	9.1	9.1	9.2	9.2	9.2	9.2	9.2	9.3	9.3	9.3	9.3	9.3	9.4	9.4	9.4	9.4	9.5	9.5	9.5	9.5	9.5	9.6	9.6	9.6	9.6	9.6	9.7	9.7	9.7	9.7	9.8	9.8	9.8	9.8	9.8
33	8.0	8.1	8.1	8.1	8.1	8.2	8.2	8.2	8.2	8.3	8.3	8.3	8.3	8.4	8.4	8.4	8.5	8.5	8.5	8.5	8.6	8.6	8.6	8.6	8.7	8.7	8.7	8.7	8.8	8.8	8.8	8.9	8.9	8.9	8.9	9.0	9.0	9.0	9.0
32	7.0	7.1	7.1	7.1	7.2	7.2	7.2	7.3	7.3	7.3	7.3	7.4	7.4	7.4	7.5	7.5	7.5	7.6	7.6	7.6	7.7	7.7	7.7	7.8	7.8	7.8	7.9	7.9	7.9	8.0	8.0	8.0	8.0	8.1	8.1	8.1	8.2	8.2	8.2
31	6.0	6.1	6.1	6.1	6.2	6.2	6.3	6.3	6.3	6.4	6.4	6.4	6.5	6.5	6.6	6.6	6.6	6.7	6.7	6.7	6.8	6.8	6.8	6.9	6.9	7.0	7.0	7.0	7.1	7.1	7.1	7.2	7.2	7.3	7.3	7.3	7.4	7.4	7.4
30	5.0	5.1	5.1	5.2	5.2	5.3	5.3	5.3	5.4	5.4	5.5	5.5	5.5	5.6	5.6	5.7	5.7	5.8	5.8	5.8	5.9	5.9	6.0	6.0	6.0	6.1	6.1	6.2	6.2	6.3	6.3	6.3	6.4	6.4	6.5	6.5	6.6	6.6	6.6
29	4.0	4.1	4.1	4.2	4.2	4.3	4.3	4.4	4.4	4.5	4.5	4.6	4.6	4.7	4.7	4.8	4.8	4.8	4.9	4.9	5.0	5.0	5.1	5.1	5.2	5.2	5.3	5.3	5.4	5.4	5.5	5.5	5.6	5.6	5.6	5.7	5.7	5.8	5.8
28	3.1	3.1	3.2	3.2	3.3	3.3	3.4	3.4	3.5	3.5	3.6	3.6	3.7	3.7	3.8	3.8	3.9	3.9	4.0	4.0	4.1	4.1	4.2	4.3	4.3	4.4	4.4	4.5	4.5	4.6	4.6	4.7	4.7	4.8	4.8	4.9	4.9	5.0	5.0
27	2.2	2.3	2.4	2.4	2.5	2.6	2.7	2.7	2.7	2.8	2.9	2.9	3.0	3.0	3.1	3.1	3.2	3.2	3.2	3.3	3.3	3.4	3.4	3.5	3.5	3.6	3.6	3.7	3.7	3.8	3.8	3.9	3.9	4.0	4.1	4.1	4.1	4.2	4.2
26	1.3	1.4	1.6	1.7	1.8	1.9	1.9	1.9	1.9	2.0	2.1	2.1	2.2	2.3	2.4	2.5	2.5	2.5	2.6	2.6	2.7	2.7	2.7	2.8	2.8	2.9	2.9	3.0	3.0	3.0	3.1	3.1	3.2	3.2	3.2	3.3	3.3	3.3	3.4
25	0.4	0.6	0.8	0.9	1.0	1.1	1.2	1.3	1.3	1.4	1.5	1.5	1.6	1.7	1.7	1.8	1.8	1.9	1.9	2.0	2.0	2.1	2.1	2.2	2.2	2.3	2.3	2.4	2.4	2.4	2.5	2.5	2.6	2.6	2.6	2.7	2.7	2.7	2.8
24	0.0	0.2	0.4	0.5	0.6	0.7	0.8	0.9	0.9	1.0	1.1	1.1	1.2	1.3	1.3	1.4	1.4	1.5	1.5	1.6	1.6	1.7	1.7	1.8	1.8	1.9	1.9	2.0	2.0	2.0	2.1	2.1	2.2	2.2	2.2	2.3	2.3	2.3	2.4
23	0.0	0.0	0.0	0.1	0.2	0.3	0.4	0.5	0.5	0.6	0.7	0.7	0.8	0.9	0.9	1.0	1.0	1.1	1.1	1.2	1.2	1.3	1.3	1.4	1.4	1.5	1.5	1.6	1.6	1.6	1.7	1.7	1.8	1.8	1.8	1.9	1.9	1.9	2.0
22	0.0	0.0	0.0	0.0	0.0	0.0	0.0	0.1	0.1	0.2	0.3	0.3	0.4	0.5	0.5	0.6	0.6	0.7	0.7	0.8	0.8	0.9	0.9	1.0	1.0	1.1	1.1	1.2	1.2	1.2	1.3	1.3	1.4	1.4	1.4	1.5	1.5	1.5	1.6
21	0.0	0.0	0.0	0.0	0.0	0.0	0.0	0.0	0.0	0.0	0.0	0.0	0.0	0.1	0.1	0.2	0.2	0.3	0.3	0.4	0.4	0.5	0.5	0.6	0.6	0.7	0.7	0.8	0.8	0.8	0.9	0.9	1.0	1.0	1.0	1.1	1.1	1.1	1.2
20	0.0	0.0	0.0	0.0	0.0	0.0	0.0	0.0	0.0	0.0	0.0	0.0	0.0	0.0	0.0	0.0	0.0	0.0	0.0	0.0	0.0	0.1	0.1	0.2	0.2	0.3	0.3	0.4	0.4	0.4	0.5	0.5	0.6	0.6	0.6	0.7	0.7	0.7	0.8
19	0.0	0.0	0.0	0.0	0.0	0.0	0.0	0.0	0.0	0.0	0.0	0.0	0.0	0.0	0.0	0.0	0.0	0.0	0.0	0.0	0.0	0.0	0.0	0.0	0.0	0.0	0.0	0.0	0.0	0.0	0.1	0.1	0.2	0.2	0.2	0.3	0.3	0.3	0.4
18	0.0	0.0	0.0	0.0	0.0	0.0	0.0	0.0	0.0	0.0	0.0	0.0	0.0	0.0	0.0	0.0	0.0	0.0	0.0	0.0	0.0	0.0	0.0	0.0	0.0	0.0	0.0	0.0	0.0	0.0	0.0	0.0	0.0	0.0	0.0	0.0	0.0	0.0	0.0
17	0.0	0.0	0.0	0.0	0.0	0.0	0.0	0.0	0.0	0.0	0.0	0.0	0.0	0.0	0.0	0.0	0.0	0.0	0.0	0.0	0.0	0.0	0.0	0.0	0.0	0.0	0.0	0.0	0.0	0.0	0.0	0.0	0.0	0.0	0.0	0.0	0.0	0.0	0.0
16	0.0	0.0	0.0	0.0	0.0	0.0	0.0	0.0	0.0	0.0	0.0	0.0	0.0	0.0	0.0	0.0	0.0	0.0	0.0	0.0	0.0	0.0	0.0	0.0	0.0	0.0	0.0	0.0	0.0	0.0	0.0	0.0	0.0	0.0	0.0	0.0	0.0	0.0	0.0
15	0.0	0.0	0.0	0.0	0.0	0.0	0.0	0.0	0.0	0.0	0.0	0.0	0.0	0.0	0.0	0.0	0.0	0.0	0.0	0.0	0.0	0.0	0.0	0.0	0.0	0.0	0.0	0.0	0.0	0.0	0.0	0.0	0.0	0.0	0.0	0.0	0.0	0.0	0.0

LISTED CALL OPTION PRICE WHEN EXERCISE PRICE IS 30

NUMBER OF WEEKS BEFORE THE OPTION EXPIRES

Common Stock Price	1	2	3	4	5	6	7	8	9	10	11	12	13	14	15	16	17	18	19	20	21	22	23	24	25	26	27	28	29	30	31	32	33	34	35	36	37	38	39
42	12.0	12.0	12.0	12.1	12.1	12.1	12.1	12.2	12.2	12.2	12.2	12.2	12.3	12.3	12.3	12.3	12.4	12.4	12.4	12.4	12.4	12.4	12.5	12.5	12.5	12.5	12.5	12.5	12.6	12.6	12.6	12.6	12.6	12.7	12.7	12.7	12.7	12.7	12.8
41	11.0	11.0	11.0	11.1	11.1	11.1	11.1	11.2	11.2	11.2	11.2	11.3	11.3	11.3	11.4	11.4	11.4	11.4	11.5	11.5	11.5	11.5	11.6	11.6	11.6	11.6	11.7	11.7	11.7	11.7	11.8	11.8	11.8	11.8	11.9	11.9	11.9	11.9	12.0
40	10.0	10.1	10.1	10.1	10.1	10.2	10.2	10.2	10.3	10.3	10.3	10.4	10.4	10.4	10.4	10.5	10.5	10.5	10.6	10.6	10.6	10.7	10.7	10.7	10.7	10.8	10.8	10.8	10.9	10.9	10.9	11.0	11.0	11.0	11.1	11.1	11.1	11.1	11.2
39	9.0	9.1	9.1	9.1	9.1	9.2	9.2	9.3	9.3	9.3	9.3	9.4	9.4	9.5	9.5	9.5	9.6	9.6	9.6	9.7	9.7	9.7	9.8	9.8	9.9	9.9	9.9	9.9	10.0	10.0	10.1	10.1	10.1	10.2	10.2	10.3	10.3	10.3	10.4
38	8.0	8.1	8.1	8.2	8.2	8.2	8.3	8.3	8.4	8.4	8.4	8.5	8.5	8.6	8.6	8.6	8.7	8.7	8.7	8.8	8.8	8.9	8.9	9.0	9.0	9.0	9.1	9.1	9.2	9.2	9.2	9.3	9.3	9.4	9.4	9.4	9.5	9.5	9.6
37	7.0	7.1	7.1	7.2	7.2	7.3	7.3	7.3	7.4	7.4	7.5	7.5	7.6	7.6	7.7	7.7	7.8	7.8	7.9	7.9	8.0	8.0	8.0	8.1	8.1	8.2	8.2	8.3	8.3	8.4	8.4	8.5	8.5	8.5	8.6	8.6	8.7	8.7	8.8
36	6.1	6.1	6.2	6.2	6.3	6.3	6.4	6.4	6.5	6.5	6.5	6.6	6.6	6.7	6.7	6.8	6.8	6.9	6.9	7.0	7.0	7.1	7.1	7.2	7.2	7.3	7.3	7.4	7.4	7.5	7.5	7.6	7.6	7.7	7.7	7.8	7.8	7.9	8.0
35	5.1	5.1	5.2	5.2	5.3	5.3	5.4	5.4	5.5	5.5	5.6	5.6	5.7	5.7	5.8	5.8	5.9	5.9	6.0	6.0	6.1	6.2	6.2	6.3	6.3	6.4	6.4	6.5	6.6	6.6	6.7	6.7	6.8	6.9	6.9	7.0	7.0	7.1	7.2
34	4.1	4.1	4.2	4.2	4.3	4.3	4.4	4.5	4.5	4.6	4.6	4.7	4.7	4.8	4.8	4.9	5.0	5.0	5.1	5.2	5.2	5.3	5.3	5.4	5.5	5.5	5.6	5.6	5.7	5.8	5.8	5.9	6.0	6.1	6.1	6.2	6.2	6.3	6.4
33	3.2	3.2	3.2	3.3	3.4	3.4	3.5	3.6	3.6	3.7	3.8	3.8	3.9	4.0	4.0	4.1	4.2	4.2	4.3	4.4	4.4	4.5	4.6	4.6	4.7	4.8	4.8	4.9	4.9	5.0	5.0	5.1	5.2	5.3	5.3	5.4	5.4	5.5	5.6
32	2.2	2.3	2.4	2.5	2.6	2.7	2.8	2.9	2.9	3.0	3.1	3.1	3.2	3.3	3.4	3.4	3.5	3.6	3.6	3.7	3.8	3.8	3.9	3.9	4.0	4.0	4.1	4.1	4.2	4.3	4.3	4.3	4.4	4.4	4.5	4.5	4.6	4.7	4.8
31	1.3	1.5	1.6	1.8	1.9	2.0	2.1	2.2	2.2	2.3	2.4	2.5	2.6	2.7	2.7	2.8	2.9	2.9	3.0	3.0	3.1	3.1	3.2	3.2	3.3	3.3	3.4	3.4	3.5	3.5	3.6	3.6	3.6	3.7	3.8	3.9	3.9	4.0	4.0
30	0.5	0.8	0.9	1.1	1.2	1.3	1.4	1.5	1.6	1.7	1.8	1.8	1.9	2.0	2.1	2.2	2.2	2.3	2.4	2.4	2.5	2.5	2.6	2.6	2.7	2.7	2.8	2.8	2.9	2.9	3.0	3.0	3.0	3.1	3.2	3.2	3.2	3.3	3.3
29	0.1	0.4	0.5	0.7	0.9	1.0	1.0	1.1	1.2	1.3	1.4	1.4	1.5	1.6	1.7	1.7	1.8	1.9	1.9	2.0	2.0	2.1	2.2	2.2	2.3	2.3	2.4	2.4	2.5	2.5	2.6	2.6	2.7	2.7	2.8	2.8	2.8	2.9	2.9
28	0.0	0.0	0.1	0.3	0.5	0.5	0.6	0.7	0.8	0.9	0.9	1.0	1.1	1.1	1.2	1.3	1.3	1.4	1.4	1.5	1.6	1.6	1.7	1.7	1.8	1.8	1.9	1.9	2.0	2.0	2.1	2.1	2.2	2.2	2.3	2.3	2.4	2.5	2.5
27	0.0	0.0	0.0	0.1	0.3	0.4	0.5	0.6	0.6	0.7	0.8	0.8	0.9	1.0	1.0	1.1	1.2	1.2	1.3	1.3	1.4	1.4	1.5	1.5	1.6	1.6	1.7	1.7	1.8	1.8	1.9	1.9	1.9	2.0	2.0	2.0	2.0	2.1	2.1
26	0.0	0.0	0.0	0.0	0.1	0.2	0.3	0.4	0.5	0.5	0.6	0.7	0.7	0.8	0.9	0.9	1.0	1.0	1.1	1.1	1.2	1.2	1.3	1.3	1.4	1.4	1.4	1.5	1.5	1.5	1.6	1.6	1.6	1.6	1.6	1.7	1.7	1.7	1.7
25	0.0	0.0	0.0	0.0	0.0	0.1	0.1	0.2	0.3	0.3	0.4	0.5	0.5	0.6	0.6	0.7	0.7	0.8	0.9	0.9	1.0	1.0	1.0	1.1	1.1	1.1	1.2	1.2	1.2	1.2	1.3	1.3	1.3	1.3	1.3	1.3	1.3	1.3	1.3
24	0.0	0.0	0.0	0.0	0.0	0.0	0.0	0.1	0.1	0.2	0.2	0.3	0.3	0.4	0.4	0.5	0.5	0.6	0.6	0.6	0.7	0.7	0.7	0.8	0.8	0.8	0.8	0.8	0.8	0.8	0.9	0.9	0.9	0.9	0.9	0.9	0.9	0.9	0.9
23	0.0	0.0	0.0	0.0	0.0	0.0	0.0	0.0	0.0	0.0	0.1	0.1	0.1	0.2	0.2	0.2	0.3	0.3	0.3	0.4	0.4	0.4	0.4	0.5	0.5	0.5	0.5	0.5	0.5	0.5	0.5	0.5	0.5	0.5	0.5	0.5	0.5	0.5	0.5
22	0.0	0.0	0.0	0.0	0.0	0.0	0.0	0.0	0.0	0.0	0.0	0.0	0.0	0.0	0.0	0.0	0.0	0.0	0.0	0.0	0.0	0.0	0.0	0.0	0.0	0.0	0.0	0.0	0.1	0.1	0.1	0.1	0.1	0.1	0.1	0.1	0.1	0.1	0.1
21	0.0	0.0	0.0	0.0	0.0	0.0	0.0	0.0	0.0	0.0	0.0	0.0	0.0	0.0	0.0	0.0	0.0	0.0	0.0	0.0	0.0	0.0	0.0	0.0	0.0	0.0	0.0	0.0	0.0	0.0	0.0	0.0	0.0	0.0	0.0	0.0	0.0	0.0	0.0
20	0.0	0.0	0.0	0.0	0.0	0.0	0.0	0.0	0.0	0.0	0.0	0.0	0.0	0.0	0.0	0.0	0.0	0.0	0.0	0.0	0.0	0.0	0.0	0.0	0.0	0.0	0.0	0.0	0.0	0.0	0.0	0.0	0.0	0.0	0.0	0.0	0.0	0.0	0.0
19	0.0	0.0	0.0	0.0	0.0	0.0	0.0	0.0	0.0	0.0	0.0	0.0	0.0	0.0	0.0	0.0	0.0	0.0	0.0	0.0	0.0	0.0	0.0	0.0	0.0	0.0	0.0	0.0	0.0	0.0	0.0	0.0	0.0	0.0	0.0	0.0	0.0	0.0	0.0
18	0.0	0.0	0.0	0.0	0.0	0.0	0.0	0.0	0.0	0.0	0.0	0.0	0.0	0.0	0.0	0.0	0.0	0.0	0.0	0.0	0.0	0.0	0.0	0.0	0.0	0.0	0.0	0.0	0.0	0.0	0.0	0.0	0.0	0.0	0.0	0.0	0.0	0.0	0.0

LISTED CALL OPTION PRICE WHEN EXERCISE PRICE IS 35

Common Stock Price

NUMBER OF WEEKS BEFORE THE OPTION EXPIRES

Price	1	2	3	4	5	6	7	8	9	10	11	12	13	14	15	16	17	18	19	20	21	22	23	24	25	26	27	28	29	30	31	32	33	34	35	36	37	38	39
49	14.0	14.0	14.1	14.1	14.1	14.1	14.2	14.2	14.2	14.2	14.3	14.3	14.3	14.3	14.3	14.4	14.4	14.4	14.4	14.5	14.5	14.5	14.5	14.5	14.6	14.6	14.6	14.6	14.7	14.7	14.7	14.7	14.8	14.8	14.8	14.8	14.8	14.9	14.9
48	13.0	13.1	13.1	13.1	13.1	13.1	13.2	13.2	13.2	13.3	13.3	13.3	13.3	13.4	13.4	13.4	13.5	13.5	13.5	13.6	13.6	13.6	13.6	13.7	13.7	13.7	13.8	13.8	13.8	13.8	13.9	13.9	13.9	14.0	14.0	14.0	14.0	14.1	14.1
47	12.0	12.1	12.1	12.1	12.1	12.2	12.2	12.2	12.3	12.3	12.3	12.4	12.4	12.5	12.5	12.5	12.6	12.6	12.6	12.7	12.7	12.7	12.8	12.8	12.8	12.9	12.9	12.9	13.0	13.0	13.0	13.1	13.1	13.1	13.2	13.2	13.2	13.3	13.3
46	11.0	11.1	11.1	11.2	11.2	11.2	11.3	11.3	11.3	11.4	11.4	11.4	11.5	11.5	11.6	11.6	11.7	11.7	11.7	11.8	11.8	11.8	11.9	11.9	12.0	12.0	12.0	12.1	12.1	12.1	12.2	12.2	12.3	12.3	12.3	12.4	12.4	12.5	12.5
45	10.0	10.1	10.1	10.2	10.2	10.2	10.3	10.3	10.4	10.4	10.5	10.5	10.6	10.6	10.7	10.7	10.7	10.8	10.8	10.9	10.9	10.9	11.0	11.0	11.0	11.1	11.1	11.2	11.2	11.3	11.3	11.4	11.4	11.5	11.5	11.6	11.6	11.6	11.7
44	9.0	9.1	9.1	9.2	9.2	9.2	9.3	9.3	9.4	9.4	9.5	9.5	9.6	9.6	9.7	9.7	9.8	9.8	9.9	9.9	10.0	10.1	10.1	10.2	10.2	10.3	10.3	10.4	10.4	10.5	10.5	10.6	10.6	10.6	10.7	10.7	10.8	10.8	10.9
43	8.1	8.1	8.2	8.2	8.2	8.3	8.3	8.4	8.4	8.5	8.5	8.6	8.6	8.7	8.8	8.8	8.9	9.0	9.0	9.1	9.1	9.2	9.2	9.3	9.3	9.4	9.4	9.5	9.6	9.6	9.7	9.7	9.8	9.8	9.9	9.9	9.9	10.0	10.1
42	7.1	7.1	7.2	7.2	7.2	7.3	7.4	7.4	7.5	7.5	7.6	7.6	7.7	7.8	7.8	7.9	8.0	8.1	8.1	8.2	8.2	8.3	8.4	8.4	8.5	8.5	8.6	8.6	8.7	8.8	8.8	8.9	8.9	9.0	9.1	9.1	9.2	9.2	9.3
41	6.1	6.1	6.2	6.3	6.3	6.4	6.4	6.5	6.6	6.6	6.7	6.7	6.8	6.8	6.9	7.0	7.0	7.1	7.2	7.3	7.3	7.4	7.5	7.5	7.6	7.7	7.7	7.8	7.9	7.9	8.0	8.0	8.1	8.2	8.2	8.3	8.4	8.4	8.5
40	5.1	5.1	5.2	5.3	5.3	5.4	5.5	5.6	5.6	5.7	5.8	5.8	5.9	5.9	6.0	6.0	6.1	6.2	6.3	6.3	6.4	6.5	6.6	6.7	6.7	6.8	6.9	6.9	7.0	7.1	7.1	7.2	7.3	7.3	7.4	7.5	7.6	7.6	7.7
39	4.1	4.1	4.2	4.3	4.4	4.4	4.5	4.6	4.7	4.7	4.8	4.9	5.0	5.0	5.1	5.2	5.3	5.3	5.4	5.5	5.6	5.6	5.7	5.8	5.9	5.9	6.0	6.1	6.2	6.2	6.3	6.4	6.4	6.5	6.6	6.7	6.7	6.8	6.9
38	3.2	3.2	3.3	3.4	3.5	3.6	3.6	3.8	3.8	3.9	4.0	4.0	4.1	4.1	4.2	4.3	4.4	4.5	4.5	4.6	4.7	4.8	4.8	4.9	5.0	5.1	5.1	5.2	5.3	5.4	5.5	5.6	5.6	5.7	5.8	5.9	5.9	6.0	6.1
37	2.2	2.3	2.4	2.5	2.5	2.6	2.6	2.7	2.9	3.0	3.1	3.2	3.3	3.4	3.5	3.6	3.7	3.7	3.8	3.9	4.0	4.1	4.1	4.2	4.3	4.4	4.4	4.5	4.6	4.6	4.7	4.8	4.8	4.9	5.0	5.1	5.2	5.2	5.3
36	1.4	1.6	1.8	1.9	2.0	2.1	2.2	2.4	2.5	2.6	2.7	2.8	2.9	2.9	3.1	3.1	3.2	3.3	3.3	3.4	3.5	3.5	3.6	3.7	3.7	3.8	3.8	3.9	4.0	4.0	4.1	4.1	4.2	4.2	4.3	4.4	4.5	4.5	4.6
35	0.6	0.9	1.1	1.2	1.4	1.5	1.6	1.8	1.9	2.0	2.1	2.2	2.3	2.4	2.4	2.5	2.6	2.6	2.7	2.8	2.9	2.9	3.0	3.1	3.1	3.2	3.2	3.3	3.4	3.4	3.5	3.5	3.6	3.6	3.7	3.7	3.8	3.8	3.9
34	0.2	0.5	0.7	0.8	1.0	1.1	1.2	1.4	1.5	1.6	1.7	1.8	1.8	1.9	2.0	2.1	2.1	2.2	2.3	2.4	2.5	2.5	2.6	2.7	2.7	2.8	2.8	2.9	3.0	3.0	3.1	3.1	3.2	3.2	3.3	3.3	3.4	3.4	3.5
33	0.0	0.1	0.3	0.4	0.6	0.7	0.8	1.0	1.1	1.2	1.3	1.4	1.4	1.5	1.6	1.7	1.7	1.8	1.9	2.0	2.1	2.1	2.2	2.3	2.3	2.4	2.4	2.5	2.6	2.6	2.7	2.7	2.8	2.8	2.9	2.9	3.0	3.0	3.1
32	0.0	0.0	0.0	0.0	0.2	0.3	0.4	0.6	0.7	0.8	0.9	1.0	1.0	1.1	1.2	1.3	1.4	1.4	1.5	1.6	1.7	1.7	1.8	1.9	1.9	2.0	2.0	2.1	2.2	2.2	2.3	2.3	2.4	2.4	2.5	2.5	2.6	2.6	2.7
31	0.0	0.0	0.0	0.0	0.0	0.0	0.0	0.2	0.3	0.4	0.5	0.6	0.6	0.7	0.8	0.9	1.0	1.0	1.1	1.2	1.3	1.3	1.4	1.5	1.5	1.6	1.6	1.7	1.8	1.8	1.9	1.9	2.0	2.0	2.1	2.1	2.2	2.2	2.3
30	0.0	0.0	0.0	0.0	0.0	0.0	0.0	0.0	0.0	0.0	0.1	0.2	0.2	0.3	0.4	0.5	0.5	0.6	0.7	0.8	0.9	0.9	1.0	1.1	1.1	1.2	1.2	1.3	1.4	1.4	1.5	1.5	1.6	1.6	1.7	1.7	1.8	1.8	1.9
29	0.0	0.0	0.0	0.0	0.0	0.0	0.0	0.0	0.0	0.0	0.0	0.0	0.0	0.0	0.1	0.1	0.2	0.2	0.3	0.4	0.5	0.5	0.6	0.7	0.7	0.8	0.8	0.9	1.0	1.0	1.1	1.1	1.2	1.2	1.3	1.3	1.4	1.4	1.5
28	0.0	0.0	0.0	0.0	0.0	0.0	0.0	0.0	0.0	0.0	0.0	0.0	0.0	0.0	0.0	0.0	0.0	0.1	0.1	0.2	0.3	0.3	0.4	0.5	0.5	0.6	0.6	0.7	0.8	0.8	0.9	0.9	1.0	1.0	1.1	1.1	1.2	1.2	1.3
27	0.0	0.0	0.0	0.0	0.0	0.0	0.0	0.0	0.0	0.0	0.0	0.0	0.0	0.0	0.0	0.0	0.0	0.0	0.0	0.0	0.1	0.1	0.2	0.2	0.3	0.3	0.4	0.4	0.5	0.6	0.6	0.7	0.7	0.8	0.8	0.8	0.9	0.9	1.0
26	0.0	0.0	0.0	0.0	0.0	0.0	0.0	0.0	0.0	0.0	0.0	0.0	0.0	0.0	0.0	0.0	0.0	0.0	0.0	0.0	0.0	0.0	0.0	0.0	0.1	0.1	0.1	0.2	0.2	0.2	0.3	0.3	0.3	0.4	0.4	0.5	0.5	0.6	0.7
25	0.0	0.0	0.0	0.0	0.0	0.0	0.0	0.0	0.0	0.0	0.0	0.0	0.0	0.0	0.0	0.0	0.0	0.0	0.0	0.0	0.0	0.0	0.0	0.0	0.0	0.0	0.0	0.0	0.0	0.0	0.0	0.0	0.1	0.1	0.1	0.2	0.2	0.2	0.3
24	0.0	0.0	0.0	0.0	0.0	0.0	0.0	0.0	0.0	0.0	0.0	0.0	0.0	0.0	0.0	0.0	0.0	0.0	0.0	0.0	0.0	0.0	0.0	0.0	0.0	0.0	0.0	0.0	0.0	0.0	0.0	0.0	0.0	0.0	0.0	0.0	0.0	0.0	0.0
23	0.0	0.0	0.0	0.0	0.0	0.0	0.0	0.0	0.0	0.0	0.0	0.0	0.0	0.0	0.0	0.0	0.0	0.0	0.0	0.0	0.0	0.0	0.0	0.0	0.0	0.0	0.0	0.0	0.0	0.0	0.0	0.0	0.0	0.0	0.0	0.0	0.0	0.0	0.0
22	0.0	0.0	0.0	0.0	0.0	0.0	0.0	0.0	0.0	0.0	0.0	0.0	0.0	0.0	0.0	0.0	0.0	0.0	0.0	0.0	0.0	0.0	0.0	0.0	0.0	0.0	0.0	0.0	0.0	0.0	0.0	0.0	0.0	0.0	0.0	0.0	0.0	0.0	0.0
21	0.0	0.0	0.0	0.0	0.0	0.0	0.0	0.0	0.0	0.0	0.0	0.0	0.0	0.0	0.0	0.0	0.0	0.0	0.0	0.0	0.0	0.0	0.0	0.0	0.0	0.0	0.0	0.0	0.0	0.0	0.0	0.0	0.0	0.0	0.0	0.0	0.0	0.0	0.0

LISTED CALL OPTION PRICE WHEN EXERCISE PRICE IS 40

NUMBER OF WEEKS BEFORE THE OPTION EXPIRES

Common Stock Price	1	2	3	4	5	6	7	8	9	10	11	12	13	14	15	16	17	18	19	20	21	22	23	24	25	26	27	28	29	30	31	32	33	34	35	36	37	38	39
56	16.0	16.1	16.1	16.1	16.1	16.2	16.2	16.2	16.2	16.3	16.3	16.3	16.3	16.4	16.4	16.4	16.4	16.5	16.5	16.5	16.5	16.6	16.6	16.6	16.7	16.7	16.7	16.7	16.8	16.8	16.8	16.8	16.9	16.9	16.9	16.9	17.0	17.0	17.0
55	15.0	15.1	15.1	15.1	15.2	15.2	15.2	15.3	15.3	15.3	15.3	15.4	15.4	15.4	15.5	15.5	15.5	15.6	15.6	15.6	15.7	15.7	15.7	15.8	15.8	15.8	15.8	15.9	15.9	15.9	16.0	16.0	16.0	16.1	16.1	16.1	16.2	16.2	16.2
54	14.0	14.1	14.1	14.1	14.2	14.2	14.3	14.3	14.3	14.4	14.4	14.4	14.5	14.5	14.5	14.6	14.6	14.7	14.7	14.7	14.8	14.8	14.8	14.9	14.9	14.9	15.0	15.0	15.1	15.1	15.1	15.2	15.2	15.2	15.3	15.3	15.4	15.4	15.4
53	13.0	13.1	13.1	13.2	13.2	13.2	13.3	13.3	13.3	13.4	13.4	13.5	13.5	13.5	13.6	13.6	13.7	13.7	13.7	13.8	13.8	13.9	13.9	14.0	14.0	14.1	14.1	14.2	14.2	14.3	14.3	14.3	14.4	14.4	14.5	14.5	14.6	14.6	14.6
52	12.0	12.1	12.1	12.2	12.2	12.3	12.3	12.3	12.4	12.4	12.5	12.5	12.6	12.6	12.7	12.7	12.7	12.8	12.8	12.9	12.9	13.0	13.0	13.1	13.1	13.2	13.2	13.3	13.3	13.4	13.4	13.5	13.5	13.6	13.6	13.7	13.7	13.8	13.8
51	11.1	11.1	11.1	11.2	11.2	11.3	11.3	11.4	11.4	11.5	11.5	11.5	11.6	11.6	11.7	11.7	11.7	11.8	11.9	11.9	12.0	12.0	12.1	12.1	12.2	12.2	12.3	12.3	12.4	12.5	12.5	12.6	12.6	12.7	12.8	12.8	12.9	13.0	13.0
50	10.1	10.1	10.2	10.2	10.3	10.3	10.3	10.4	10.5	10.5	10.6	10.6	10.7	10.7	10.8	10.9	10.9	11.0	11.0	11.1	11.1	11.2	11.3	11.3	11.4	11.4	11.5	11.6	11.6	11.7	11.7	11.8	11.9	11.9	12.0	12.0	12.1	12.2	12.2
49	9.1	9.1	9.2	9.2	9.3	9.3	9.4	9.4	9.5	9.6	9.6	9.6	9.7	9.7	9.8	9.9	9.9	10.0	10.1	10.1	10.2	10.3	10.3	10.4	10.5	10.6	10.6	10.7	10.8	10.9	10.9	11.0	11.0	11.1	11.2	11.2	11.3	11.4	11.4
48	8.1	8.1	8.2	8.3	8.3	8.4	8.4	8.5	8.5	8.6	8.7	8.7	8.8	8.9	9.0	9.0	9.1	9.2	9.3	9.3	9.4	9.5	9.5	9.6	9.7	9.7	9.8	9.9	9.9	10.0	10.1	10.1	10.2	10.3	10.4	10.4	10.5	10.6	10.6
47	7.1	7.1	7.2	7.3	7.3	7.4	7.4	7.5	7.6	7.7	7.7	7.8	7.9	7.9	8.0	8.1	8.2	8.3	8.4	8.4	8.5	8.6	8.7	8.7	8.8	8.9	9.0	9.0	9.1	9.2	9.2	9.3	9.4	9.5	9.5	9.6	9.7	9.7	9.8
46	6.1	6.2	6.2	6.3	6.4	6.4	6.5	6.6	6.6	6.7	6.8	6.9	6.9	7.0	7.1	7.2	7.2	7.3	7.4	7.5	7.5	7.6	7.7	7.8	7.9	7.9	8.0	8.1	8.2	8.2	8.3	8.4	8.5	8.6	8.6	8.7	8.8	8.9	9.0
45	5.1	5.2	5.2	5.3	5.3	5.4	5.5	5.6	5.7	5.7	5.8	5.9	6.0	6.1	6.2	6.2	6.3	6.4	6.5	6.6	6.7	6.7	6.8	6.9	7.0	7.1	7.1	7.2	7.3	7.4	7.5	7.6	7.7	7.8	7.9	8.0	8.1	8.1	8.2
44	4.1	4.2	4.3	4.3	4.4	4.5	4.6	4.6	4.7	4.8	4.9	5.0	5.1	5.2	5.3	5.3	5.4	5.5	5.6	5.6	5.7	5.8	5.8	5.9	6.0	6.1	6.2	6.3	6.4	6.5	6.6	6.7	6.8	6.9	7.0	7.1	7.2	7.3	7.4
43	3.2	3.3	3.5	3.6	3.7	3.8	4.0	4.1	4.2	4.3	4.4	4.5	4.6	4.7	4.8	4.8	4.9	5.0	5.1	5.1	5.2	5.3	5.3	5.4	5.5	5.6	5.7	5.7	5.8	5.9	5.9	6.0	6.1	6.2	6.3	6.4	6.6	6.7	6.8
42	2.3	2.5	2.7	2.9	3.1	3.2	3.4	3.5	3.6	3.7	3.9	4.0	4.2	4.3	4.4	4.4	4.5	4.5	4.6	4.7	4.9	4.9	5.0	5.1	5.2	5.3	5.3	5.4	5.5	5.5	5.6	5.6	5.7	5.7	5.8	5.8	5.9	6.0	6.1
41	1.5	1.7	1.9	2.1	2.3	2.4	2.6	2.7	2.9	3.0	3.2	3.3	3.5	3.6	3.7	3.7	3.8	3.8	3.9	4.0	4.1	4.3	4.3	4.4	4.4	4.5	4.6	4.6	4.7	4.7	4.7	4.7	4.8	4.8	4.9	5.0	5.1	5.2	5.2
40	0.7	1.0	1.2	1.4	1.6	1.7	1.9	2.0	2.1	2.3	2.4	2.5	2.6	2.7	2.8	2.8	2.9	3.0	3.1	3.2	3.3	3.3	3.4	3.5	3.6	3.6	3.7	3.8	3.8	3.9	4.0	4.0	4.1	4.1	4.2	4.3	4.3	4.4	4.4
39	0.3	0.6	0.8	1.0	1.2	1.3	1.5	1.6	1.7	1.9	2.0	2.1	2.2	2.3	2.4	2.4	2.5	2.6	2.7	2.8	2.8	2.9	3.0	3.1	3.1	3.2	3.3	3.4	3.4	3.5	3.6	3.6	3.7	3.7	3.8	3.9	3.9	4.0	4.0
38	0.0	0.2	0.4	0.6	0.8	0.9	1.1	1.2	1.3	1.5	1.6	1.7	1.8	1.9	2.0	2.0	2.1	2.2	2.3	2.3	2.4	2.5	2.6	2.7	2.7	2.8	2.9	3.0	3.0	3.1	3.2	3.2	3.3	3.3	3.4	3.5	3.5	3.6	3.6
37	0.0	0.0	0.2	0.4	0.5	0.7	0.8	0.9	1.1	1.2	1.3	1.4	1.5	1.6	1.6	1.7	1.8	1.9	2.0	2.0	2.1	2.1	2.2	2.3	2.4	2.4	2.5	2.6	2.6	2.7	2.8	2.8	2.9	2.9	3.0	3.1	3.1	3.2	3.2
36	0.0	0.0	0.0	0.1	0.3	0.4	0.5	0.7	0.8	1.0	1.1	1.2	1.3	1.4	1.5	1.5	1.6	1.7	1.8	1.8	1.9	1.9	2.0	2.1	2.1	2.2	2.3	2.3	2.4	2.4	2.5	2.5	2.6	2.6	2.7	2.7	2.7	2.8	2.8
35	0.0	0.0	0.0	0.0	0.1	0.2	0.3	0.4	0.5	0.7	0.8	0.9	1.0	1.1	1.2	1.2	1.3	1.4	1.5	1.5	1.6	1.7	1.7	1.8	1.9	1.9	2.0	2.0	2.1	2.1	2.2	2.2	2.3	2.3	2.3	2.4	2.4	2.4	2.4
34	0.0	0.0	0.0	0.0	0.0	0.0	0.1	0.2	0.3	0.4	0.5	0.6	0.6	0.7	0.8	0.9	0.9	1.0	1.1	1.2	1.2	1.3	1.4	1.4	1.5	1.5	1.6	1.6	1.7	1.7	1.8	1.8	1.9	1.9	1.9	2.0	2.0	2.0	2.0
33	0.0	0.0	0.0	0.0	0.0	0.0	0.0	0.0	0.0	0.1	0.2	0.3	0.3	0.4	0.5	0.5	0.6	0.7	0.7	0.8	0.9	0.9	1.0	1.0	1.1	1.1	1.2	1.2	1.3	1.3	1.4	1.4	1.5	1.5	1.5	1.6	1.6	1.6	1.6
32	0.0	0.0	0.0	0.0	0.0	0.0	0.0	0.0	0.0	0.0	0.0	0.0	0.1	0.1	0.2	0.2	0.3	0.3	0.4	0.4	0.5	0.5	0.6	0.6	0.7	0.7	0.8	0.8	0.9	0.9	1.0	1.0	1.0	1.1	1.1	1.1	1.2	1.2	1.2
31	0.0	0.0	0.0	0.0	0.0	0.0	0.0	0.0	0.0	0.0	0.0	0.0	0.0	0.0	0.0	0.1	0.1	0.2	0.2	0.2	0.3	0.3	0.4	0.4	0.4	0.5	0.5	0.5	0.6	0.6	0.6	0.7	0.7	0.7	0.8	0.8	0.8	0.8	0.8
30	0.0	0.0	0.0	0.0	0.0	0.0	0.0	0.0	0.0	0.0	0.0	0.0	0.0	0.0	0.0	0.0	0.0	0.0	0.0	0.0	0.0	0.0	0.0	0.1	0.1	0.1	0.2	0.2	0.2	0.2	0.3	0.3	0.3	0.3	0.3	0.4	0.4	0.4	0.4
29	0.0	0.0	0.0	0.0	0.0	0.0	0.0	0.0	0.0	0.0	0.0	0.0	0.0	0.0	0.0	0.0	0.0	0.0	0.0	0.0	0.0	0.0	0.0	0.0	0.0	0.0	0.0	0.0	0.0	0.0	0.0	0.0	0.0	0.0	0.0	0.0	0.0	0.0	0.0

LISTED CALL OPTION PRICE WHEN EXERCISE PRICE IS 45

Common
Stock
Price

NUMBER OF WEEKS BEFORE THE OPTION EXPIRES

Price	1	2	3	4	5	6	7	8	9	10	11	12	13	14	15	16	17	18	19	20	21	22	23	24	25	26	27	28	29	30	31	32	33	34	35	36	37	38	39
63	18.0	18.1	18.1	18.1	18.1	18.2	18.2	18.2	18.3	18.3	18.3	18.4	18.4	18.4	18.4	18.5	18.5	18.5	18.6	18.6	18.6	18.6	18.7	18.7	18.7	18.8	18.8	18.8	18.9	18.9	18.9	18.9	19.0	19.0	19.0	19.1	19.1	19.1	19.1
62	17.0	17.1	17.1	17.1	17.2	17.2	17.2	17.3	17.3	17.3	17.4	17.4	17.4	17.5	17.5	17.5	17.6	17.6	17.7	17.7	17.7	17.8	17.8	17.8	17.9	17.9	17.9	18.0	18.0	18.0	18.1	18.1	18.1	18.2	18.2	18.2	18.3	18.3	18.3
61	16.0	16.1	16.1	16.2	16.2	16.2	16.3	16.3	16.4	16.4	16.4	16.5	16.5	16.6	16.6	16.6	16.7	16.7	16.8	16.8	16.8	16.9	16.9	16.9	17.0	17.0	17.1	17.1	17.2	17.2	17.2	17.3	17.3	17.3	17.4	17.4	17.5	17.5	17.5
60	15.0	15.1	15.1	15.2	15.2	15.2	15.3	15.3	15.4	15.4	15.4	15.5	15.5	15.6	15.6	15.6	15.7	15.7	15.8	15.8	15.9	15.9	16.0	16.0	16.1	16.1	16.2	16.3	16.3	16.3	16.4	16.4	16.5	16.5	16.6	16.6	16.7	16.7	16.7
59	14.0	14.1	14.1	14.2	14.2	14.3	14.3	14.4	14.4	14.5	14.5	14.6	14.6	14.7	14.7	14.7	14.8	14.8	14.9	14.9	15.0	15.0	15.1	15.2	15.2	15.3	15.3	15.4	15.4	15.5	15.5	15.5	15.6	15.7	15.7	15.8	15.8	15.9	15.9
58	13.1	13.1	13.2	13.2	13.3	13.4	13.4	13.4	13.5	13.6	13.6	13.7	13.7	13.8	13.8	13.9	13.9	14.0	14.0	14.1	14.2	14.2	14.3	14.3	14.4	14.4	14.5	14.5	14.6	14.7	14.7	14.8	14.8	14.9	14.9	15.0	15.1	15.1	15.1
57	12.1	12.1	12.2	12.2	12.3	12.3	12.4	12.4	12.5	12.5	12.6	12.6	12.7	12.7	12.8	12.9	12.9	13.0	13.1	13.2	13.3	13.3	13.4	13.4	13.5	13.6	13.6	13.7	13.7	13.8	13.9	13.9	14.0	14.1	14.1	14.2	14.2	14.3	14.3
56	11.1	11.1	11.2	11.3	11.3	11.4	11.4	11.5	11.5	11.6	11.6	11.7	11.7	11.8	11.8	11.9	12.0	12.0	12.1	12.2	12.3	12.3	12.4	12.5	12.6	12.6	12.7	12.8	12.8	12.9	12.9	13.0	13.1	13.2	13.2	13.3	13.4	13.4	13.5
55	10.1	10.1	10.2	10.3	10.3	10.4	10.4	10.5	10.6	10.6	10.7	10.7	10.8	10.8	10.9	11.0	11.1	11.1	11.2	11.3	11.4	11.5	11.5	11.6	11.7	11.7	11.8	11.9	12.0	12.0	12.1	12.2	12.3	12.3	12.4	12.5	12.5	12.6	12.7
54	9.1	9.2	9.2	9.3	9.3	9.4	9.5	9.5	9.6	9.7	9.7	9.8	9.9	9.9	10.0	10.1	10.2	10.2	10.3	10.4	10.5	10.5	10.6	10.7	10.8	10.8	10.9	11.0	11.1	11.1	11.2	11.3	11.4	11.5	11.6	11.6	11.7	11.8	11.9
53	8.1	8.2	8.2	8.3	8.3	8.4	8.4	8.5	8.6	8.7	8.7	8.8	8.9	9.0	9.0	9.1	9.2	9.2	9.3	9.4	9.5	9.6	9.7	9.8	9.9	10.0	10.1	10.1	10.2	10.3	10.4	10.5	10.6	10.7	10.8	10.9	11.0	11.1	11.1
52	7.1	7.2	7.3	7.3	7.4	7.5	7.6	7.6	7.7	7.8	7.9	7.9	8.0	8.1	8.2	8.3	8.4	8.5	8.5	8.6	8.7	8.8	8.9	9.0	9.1	9.1	9.2	9.3	9.4	9.5	9.6	9.7	9.8	9.8	10.0	10.1	10.2	10.3	10.3
51	6.1	6.2	6.3	6.4	6.4	6.5	6.5	6.6	6.7	6.8	6.9	6.9	7.0	7.1	7.2	7.3	7.4	7.5	7.5	7.6	7.7	7.8	8.0	8.1	8.2	8.3	8.4	8.5	8.5	8.6	8.7	8.8	8.9	9.0	9.1	9.2	9.3	9.4	9.5
50	5.1	5.2	5.3	5.4	5.5	5.5	5.6	5.7	5.8	5.8	6.0	6.0	6.1	6.2	6.2	6.4	6.5	6.6	6.7	6.8	6.9	7.0	7.1	7.1	7.3	7.4	7.5	7.6	7.7	7.8	7.9	8.0	8.1	8.2	8.3	8.4	8.5	8.6	8.7
49	4.2	4.3	4.3	4.5	4.6	4.7	4.8	4.9	5.0	5.1	5.2	5.3	5.4	5.4	5.5	5.6	5.7	5.8	5.9	6.0	6.1	6.2	6.3	6.4	6.4	6.5	6.7	6.8	7.0	7.0	7.1	7.2	7.3	7.4	7.5	7.6	7.8	7.9	8.0
48	3.3	3.4	3.4	3.6	3.7	3.8	3.9	4.1	4.2	4.3	4.4	4.5	4.5	4.6	4.7	4.8	4.9	5.0	5.1	5.2	5.3	5.4	5.5	5.6	5.7	5.8	5.9	6.0	6.1	6.2	6.3	6.4	6.5	6.6	6.7	6.8	7.0	7.1	7.2
47	2.4	2.6	2.6	2.8	3.1	3.3	3.4	3.6	3.7	3.8	3.9	4.0	4.1	4.2	4.3	4.4	4.4	4.5	4.6	4.7	4.7	4.8	4.9	5.0	5.0	5.1	5.2	5.3	5.4	5.4	5.5	5.6	5.7	5.8	5.9	6.0	6.2	6.3	6.4
46	1.6	1.8	2.0	2.2	2.4	2.6	2.7	2.9	3.0	3.1	3.3	3.4	3.5	3.6	3.7	3.8	3.9	4.0	4.1	4.2	4.2	4.3	4.4	4.5	4.6	4.7	4.8	4.9	5.0	5.1	5.2	5.2	5.3	5.4	5.4	5.5	5.6	5.6	5.6
45	0.8	1.1	1.4	1.6	1.8	2.0	2.1	2.3	2.4	2.5	2.7	2.9	3.0	3.1	3.2	3.2	3.4	3.5	3.5	3.6	3.6	3.7	3.8	3.9	3.9	4.0	4.1	4.2	4.2	4.3	4.3	4.4	4.5	4.6	4.7	4.7	4.8	4.9	5.0
44	0.4	0.7	1.0	1.2	1.4	1.6	1.7	1.9	2.0	2.1	2.3	2.4	2.5	2.6	2.7	2.8	2.9	3.0	3.1	3.2	3.3	3.4	3.4	3.5	3.6	3.7	3.8	3.8	3.9	4.0	4.1	4.1	4.2	4.3	4.3	4.4	4.5	4.5	4.6
43	0.0	0.3	0.6	0.8	1.0	1.2	1.3	1.5	1.6	1.7	1.9	2.0	2.1	2.2	2.3	2.4	2.5	2.6	2.6	2.7	2.8	2.9	3.0	3.1	3.2	3.3	3.3	3.4	3.5	3.6	3.7	3.7	3.8	3.9	3.9	4.0	4.1	4.1	4.2
42	0.0	0.0	0.2	0.4	0.6	0.8	0.9	1.1	1.2	1.3	1.5	1.6	1.7	1.8	1.9	2.0	2.1	2.2	2.3	2.4	2.5	2.6	2.6	2.7	2.8	2.9	2.9	3.0	3.1	3.2	3.3	3.3	3.4	3.5	3.5	3.6	3.7	3.7	3.8
41	0.0	0.0	0.0	0.0	0.2	0.4	0.5	0.7	0.8	1.1	1.1	1.2	1.3	1.4	1.5	1.6	1.7	1.8	1.9	2.0	2.0	2.1	2.2	2.3	2.4	2.5	2.6	2.6	2.7	2.8	2.9	2.9	3.0	3.1	3.1	3.2	3.3	3.3	3.4
40	0.0	0.0	0.0	0.0	0.0	0.0	0.2	0.3	0.4	0.5	0.7	0.8	0.9	1.1	1.2	1.2	1.3	1.4	1.5	1.6	1.7	1.8	1.8	1.9	2.0	2.1	2.2	2.2	2.3	2.4	2.4	2.5	2.6	2.6	2.7	2.8	2.9	2.9	3.0
39	0.0	0.0	0.0	0.0	0.0	0.0	0.0	0.0	0.1	0.1	0.3	0.4	0.5	0.6	0.7	0.8	0.9	0.9	1.0	1.1	1.2	1.3	1.4	1.4	1.5	1.6	1.7	1.8	1.8	1.9	2.0	2.1	2.1	2.2	2.3	2.4	2.4	2.5	2.6
38	0.0	0.0	0.0	0.0	0.0	0.0	0.0	0.0	0.0	0.0	0.1	0.2	0.3	0.4	0.5	0.6	0.7	0.8	0.8	0.9	1.0	1.0	1.1	1.2	1.3	1.3	1.4	1.4	1.5	1.6	1.7	1.7	1.8	1.8	1.9	2.0	2.1	2.1	2.2
37	0.0	0.0	0.0	0.0	0.0	0.0	0.0	0.0	0.0	0.0	0.0	0.0	0.0	0.2	0.3	0.4	0.5	0.6	0.7	0.7	0.8	0.9	1.0	1.0	1.1	1.2	1.3	1.3	1.4	1.4	1.5	1.6	1.6	1.7	1.7	1.8	1.8	1.8	1.8
36	0.0	0.0	0.0	0.0	0.0	0.0	0.0	0.0	0.0	0.0	0.0	0.0	0.0	0.0	0.0	0.2	0.3	0.4	0.5	0.6	0.6	0.7	0.8	0.9	0.9	1.0	1.1	1.2	1.2	1.3	1.4	1.4	1.5	1.6	1.6	1.7	1.7	1.3	1.4
35	0.0	0.0	0.0	0.0	0.0	0.0	0.0	0.0	0.0	0.0	0.0	0.0	0.0	0.0	0.0	0.0	0.1	0.2	0.3	0.4	0.4	0.5	0.6	0.7	0.7	0.8	0.9	1.0	1.0	1.1	1.1	1.2	1.3	1.3	1.4	1.1	1.2	1.3	1.0
34	0.0	0.0	0.0	0.0	0.0	0.0	0.0	0.0	0.0	0.0	0.0	0.0	0.0	0.0	0.0	0.0	0.0	0.0	0.1	0.2	0.2	0.3	0.3	0.4	0.4	0.5	0.5	0.6	0.6	0.7	0.7	0.8	0.9	0.9	0.5	0.7	0.7	0.8	0.6
33	0.0	0.0	0.0	0.0	0.0	0.0	0.0	0.0	0.0	0.0	0.0	0.0	0.0	0.0	0.0	0.0	0.0	0.0	0.0	0.0	0.0	0.0	0.1	0.1	0.2	0.2	0.3	0.3	0.4	0.4	0.5	0.1	0.1	0.2	0.3	0.4	0.5	0.3	0.2
32	0.0	0.0	0.0	0.0	0.0	0.0	0.0	0.0	0.0	0.0	0.0	0.0	0.0	0.0	0.0	0.0	0.0	0.0	0.0	0.0	0.0	0.0	0.0	0.0	0.0	0.0	0.0	0.0	0.0	0.0	0.0	0.0	0.0	0.0	0.0	0.0	0.0	0.0	0.0
31	0.0	0.0	0.0	0.0	0.0	0.0	0.0	0.0	0.0	0.0	0.0	0.0	0.0	0.0	0.0	0.0	0.0	0.0	0.0	0.0	0.0	0.0	0.0	0.0	0.0	0.0	0.0	0.0	0.0	0.0	0.0	0.0	0.0	0.0	0.0	0.0	0.1	0.1	0.0
30	0.0	0.0	0.0	0.0	0.0	0.0	0.0	0.0	0.0	0.0	0.0	0.0	0.0	0.0	0.0	0.0	0.0	0.0	0.0	0.0	0.0	0.0	0.0	0.0	0.0	0.0	0.0	0.0	0.0	0.0	0.0	0.0	0.0	0.0	0.0	0.0	0.5	0.5	0.0
29	0.0	0.0	0.0	0.0	0.0	0.0	0.0	0.0	0.0	0.0	0.0	0.0	0.0	0.0	0.0	0.0	0.0	0.0	0.0	0.0	0.0	0.0	0.0	0.0	0.0	0.0	0.0	0.0	0.0	0.0	0.0	0.0	0.0	0.0	0.0	0.0	0.1	0.1	0.0
28	0.0	0.0	0.0	0.0	0.0	0.0	0.0	0.0	0.0	0.0	0.0	0.0	0.0	0.0	0.0	0.0	0.0	0.0	0.0	0.0	0.0	0.0	0.0	0.0	0.0	0.0	0.0	0.0	0.0	0.0	0.0	0.0	0.0	0.0	0.0	0.0	0.0	0.0	0.0
27	0.0	0.0	0.0	0.0	0.0	0.0	0.0	0.0	0.0	0.0	0.0	0.0	0.0	0.0	0.0	0.0	0.0	0.0	0.0	0.0	0.0	0.0	0.0	0.0	0.0	0.0	0.0	0.0	0.0	0.0	0.0	0.0	0.0	0.0	0.0	0.0	0.2	0.2	0.0

LISTED CALL OPTION PRICE WHEN EXERCISE PRICE IS 50

NUMBER OF WEEKS BEFORE THE OPTION EXPIRES

Common Stock Price

Price	1	2	3	4	5	6	7	8	9	10	11	12	13	14	15	16	17	18	19	20	21	22	23	24	25	26	27	28	29	30	31	32	33	34	35	36	37	38	39
65	15.1	15.1	15.2	15.2	15.3	15.3	15.4	15.5	15.5	15.6	15.6	15.7	15.8	15.8	15.9	15.9	16.0	16.0	16.1	16.2	16.2	16.3	16.3	16.4	16.5	16.5	16.6	16.6	16.7	16.8	16.8	16.9	16.9	17.0	17.0	17.1	17.2	17.2	17.3
64	14.1	14.1	14.2	14.3	14.3	14.4	14.4	14.5	14.6	14.6	14.7	14.8	14.8	14.9	15.0	15.0	15.1	15.1	15.2	15.3	15.3	15.4	15.5	15.5	15.6	15.6	15.7	15.8	15.8	15.9	16.0	16.0	16.1	16.2	16.2	16.3	16.3	16.4	16.5
63	13.1	13.1	13.2	13.2	13.3	13.4	13.4	13.5	13.6	13.6	13.7	13.8	13.8	13.9	14.0	14.0	14.1	14.2	14.2	14.3	14.4	14.5	14.5	14.6	14.7	14.7	14.8	14.9	14.9	15.0	15.1	15.1	15.2	15.3	15.3	15.4	15.5	15.6	15.7
62	12.1	12.1	12.2	12.3	12.3	12.4	12.5	12.6	12.7	12.7	12.8	12.9	12.9	13.0	13.1	13.2	13.3	13.3	13.4	13.5	13.6	13.6	13.7	13.8	13.8	13.9	14.0	14.1	14.1	14.2	14.3	14.4	14.4	14.5	14.6	14.7	14.7	14.8	14.9
61	11.1	11.2	11.2	11.3	11.3	11.5	11.6	11.6	11.7	11.8	11.9	11.9	12.0	12.1	12.2	12.3	12.3	12.4	12.5	12.6	12.7	12.7	12.8	12.9	13.0	13.1	13.1	13.2	13.3	13.4	13.4	13.5	13.6	13.7	13.8	13.8	13.9	14.0	14.1
60	10.1	10.2	10.3	10.3	10.4	10.5	10.5	10.6	10.7	10.8	10.8	10.9	11.0	11.1	11.2	11.3	11.3	11.4	11.5	11.6	11.7	11.7	11.8	11.9	12.0	12.1	12.2	12.3	12.4	12.5	12.5	12.6	12.7	12.8	12.9	13.0	13.1	13.2	13.3
59	9.1	9.2	9.3	9.4	9.4	9.5	9.6	9.7	9.8	9.9	9.9	10.0	10.1	10.1	10.2	10.3	10.4	10.5	10.6	10.7	10.8	10.9	11.0	11.1	11.2	11.2	11.3	11.4	11.5	11.6	11.7	11.8	11.9	11.9	12.0	12.1	12.2	12.3	12.5
58	8.1	8.2	8.3	8.4	8.4	8.5	8.6	8.7	8.8	8.9	8.9	9.0	9.1	9.2	9.3	9.4	9.5	9.6	9.7	9.8	9.9	9.9	10.0	10.1	10.2	10.3	10.4	10.5	10.6	10.7	10.8	10.9	11.0	11.1	11.2	11.3	11.4	11.5	11.7
57	7.1	7.2	7.3	7.4	7.5	7.6	7.7	7.7	7.8	7.9	8.0	8.1	8.2	8.3	8.4	8.5	8.6	8.7	8.8	8.9	9.0	9.1	9.2	9.3	9.4	9.5	9.6	9.7	9.7	9.8	9.9	10.1	10.2	10.3	10.4	10.5	10.6	10.7	10.9
56	6.1	6.2	6.3	6.4	6.5	6.6	6.7	6.8	6.9	6.9	7.0	7.1	7.2	7.3	7.4	7.5	7.6	7.7	7.8	7.8	7.9	8.0	8.1	8.2	8.3	8.4	8.5	8.6	8.7	8.8	8.9	9.0	9.1	9.2	9.4	9.5	9.6	9.8	10.1
55	5.2	5.2	5.3	5.4	5.5	5.6	5.8	5.9	6.0	6.1	6.2	6.3	6.4	6.5	6.6	6.7	6.7	6.8	6.9	7.0	7.1	7.2	7.3	7.4	7.5	7.6	7.7	7.8	7.9	8.0	8.1	8.2	8.3	8.5	8.6	8.7	8.8	9.0	9.2
54	4.2	4.3	4.4	4.5	4.6	4.7	4.9	5.0	5.1	5.1	5.3	5.4	5.5	5.6	5.7	5.8	5.9	6.0	6.1	6.1	6.2	6.3	6.4	6.5	6.6	6.7	6.8	6.9	7.0	7.1	7.2	7.3	7.4	7.6	7.7	7.8	7.9	8.2	8.4
53	3.3	3.4	3.5	3.6	3.6	3.8	3.9	4.1	4.2	4.3	4.4	4.5	4.6	4.8	4.9	5.0	5.1	5.2	5.3	5.4	5.5	5.6	5.7	5.8	5.9	6.0	6.1	6.2	6.3	6.4	6.5	6.6	6.7	6.9	7.0	7.2	7.3	7.5	7.7
52	2.3	2.5	2.7	3.0	3.2	3.4	3.6	3.7	3.9	4.0	4.1	4.2	4.3	4.4	4.5	4.7	4.8	4.9	5.0	5.1	5.2	5.3	5.4	5.5	5.5	5.6	5.7	5.8	5.9	6.0	6.1	6.2	6.3	6.5	6.6	6.7	6.8	6.9	7.0
51	1.4	1.8	2.0	2.3	2.5	2.7	2.9	3.0	3.2	3.3	3.5	3.6	3.7	3.8	3.9	4.1	4.2	4.3	4.4	4.5	4.6	4.7	4.8	4.9	4.9	5.0	5.1	5.2	5.3	5.4	5.4	5.5	5.6	5.7	5.8	5.9	6.0	6.1	6.2
50	0.9	1.3	1.5	1.8	2.0	2.2	2.4	2.5	2.7	2.8	3.0	3.1	3.2	3.3	3.4	3.6	3.7	3.8	3.9	4.0	4.1	4.2	4.3	4.4	4.5	4.5	4.6	4.7	4.8	4.9	5.0	5.0	5.1	5.2	5.3	5.3	5.4	5.5	5.6
49	0.5	0.9	1.1	1.4	1.6	1.8	2.0	2.1	2.3	2.4	2.6	2.7	2.8	2.9	3.0	3.2	3.3	3.4	3.5	3.6	3.7	3.8	3.9	4.0	4.0	4.1	4.2	4.3	4.4	4.4	4.5	4.6	4.7	4.8	4.9	4.9	5.0	5.1	5.2
48	0.1	0.5	0.7	1.0	1.2	1.4	1.6	1.7	1.9	2.0	2.1	2.3	2.4	2.5	2.6	2.8	2.9	2.9	3.1	3.2	3.4	3.4	3.5	3.6	3.6	3.7	3.8	3.9	4.0	4.1	4.2	4.3	4.3	4.4	4.5	4.5	4.6	4.7	4.8
47	0.0	0.3	0.6	0.8	1.0	1.2	1.4	1.5	1.6	1.8	1.9	2.0	2.1	2.2	2.4	2.5	2.6	2.6	2.7	2.8	2.9	3.0	3.1	3.2	3.2	3.3	3.4	3.5	3.6	3.7	3.7	3.8	3.9	4.0	4.1	4.1	4.2	4.3	4.4
46	0.0	0.0	0.1	0.2	0.4	0.6	0.8	1.0	1.1	1.3	1.4	1.6	1.7	1.8	1.9	2.0	2.2	2.3	2.4	2.5	2.6	2.7	2.8	2.9	3.0	3.0	3.1	3.2	3.3	3.4	3.5	3.6	3.7	3.8	3.8	3.9	4.0	4.0	4.0
45	0.0	0.0	0.0	0.2	0.4	0.6	0.8	0.9	1.1	1.2	1.4	1.5	1.6	1.8	1.9	2.0	2.1	2.2	2.3	2.4	2.5	2.5	2.6	2.7	2.8	2.9	2.9	3.0	3.1	3.1	3.2	3.3	3.4	3.4	3.5	3.6	3.6	3.6	3.6
44	0.0	0.0	0.0	0.0	0.2	0.4	0.6	0.7	0.9	1.0	1.2	1.3	1.4	1.5	1.6	1.7	1.8	1.9	2.0	2.0	2.1	2.2	2.3	2.3	2.4	2.5	2.5	2.6	2.6	2.7	2.8	2.8	2.9	2.9	3.0	3.0	3.1	3.1	3.2
43	0.0	0.0	0.0	0.0	0.0	0.2	0.3	0.5	0.6	0.8	0.9	1.0	1.1	1.2	1.3	1.4	1.5	1.6	1.7	1.7	1.8	1.9	1.9	2.0	2.1	2.1	2.2	2.2	2.3	2.4	2.4	2.5	2.5	2.6	2.6	2.7	2.7	2.8	2.8
42	0.0	0.0	0.0	0.0	0.0	0.0	0.1	0.2	0.4	0.5	0.6	0.7	0.8	0.9	1.0	1.1	1.2	1.2	1.3	1.4	1.5	1.5	1.6	1.7	1.7	1.8	1.8	1.9	1.9	2.0	2.1	2.1	2.2	2.2	2.3	2.3	2.4	2.4	2.4
41	0.0	0.0	0.0	0.0	0.0	0.0	0.0	0.1	0.2	0.3	0.5	0.6	0.7	0.8	0.9	1.0	1.0	1.1	1.2	1.3	1.3	1.4	1.5	1.5	1.6	1.6	1.7	1.7	1.8	1.8	1.9	1.9	1.9	2.0	2.0	2.0	2.0	2.0	2.0
40	0.0	0.0	0.0	0.0	0.0	0.0	0.0	0.0	0.1	0.2	0.3	0.4	0.5	0.6	0.6	0.7	0.8	0.8	0.9	1.0	1.0	1.1	1.1	1.2	1.2	1.3	1.3	1.3	1.4	1.4	1.5	1.5	1.5	1.6	1.6	1.6	1.6	1.6	1.6
39	0.0	0.0	0.0	0.0	0.0	0.0	0.0	0.0	0.0	0.0	0.1	0.2	0.3	0.3	0.4	0.5	0.5	0.6	0.6	0.7	0.7	0.8	0.8	0.9	0.9	0.9	1.0	1.0	1.0	1.1	1.1	1.1	1.1	1.2	1.2	1.2	1.2	1.2	1.2
38	0.0	0.0	0.0	0.0	0.0	0.0	0.0	0.0	0.0	0.0	0.0	0.0	0.0	0.1	0.1	0.2	0.2	0.3	0.3	0.3	0.4	0.4	0.5	0.5	0.5	0.6	0.6	0.6	0.7	0.7	0.7	0.7	0.8	0.8	0.8	0.8	0.8	0.8	0.8
37	0.0	0.0	0.0	0.0	0.0	0.0	0.0	0.0	0.0	0.0	0.0	0.0	0.0	0.0	0.0	0.0	0.0	0.0	0.1	0.1	0.1	0.1	0.2	0.2	0.2	0.2	0.2	0.3	0.3	0.3	0.3	0.3	0.3	0.4	0.4	0.4	0.4	0.4	0.4
36	0.0	0.0	0.0	0.0	0.0	0.0	0.0	0.0	0.0	0.0	0.0	0.0	0.0	0.0	0.0	0.0	0.0	0.0	0.0	0.0	0.0	0.0	0.0	0.0	0.0	0.0	0.0	0.0	0.0	0.0	0.0	0.0	0.0	0.0	0.0	0.0	0.0	0.0	0.0
35	0.0	0.0	0.0	0.0	0.0	0.0	0.0	0.0	0.0	0.0	0.0	0.0	0.0	0.0	0.0	0.0	0.0	0.0	0.0	0.0	0.0	0.0	0.0	0.0	0.0	0.0	0.0	0.0	0.0	0.0	0.0	0.0	0.0	0.0	0.0	0.0	0.0	0.0	0.0

LISTED CALL OPTION PRICE WHEN EXERCISE PRICE IS 60

NUMBER OF WEEKS BEFORE THE OPTION EXPIRES

Common Stock Price

Price	1	2	3	4	5	6	7	8	9	10	11	12	13	14	15	16	17	18	19	20	21	22	23	24	25	26	27	28	29	30	31	32	33	34	35	36	37	38	39
78	18.1	18.2	18.2	18.3	18.3	18.4	18.5	18.6	18.6	18.7	18.8	18.8	18.9	19.0	19.1	19.1	19.2	19.3	19.3	19.4	19.5	19.5	19.6	19.7	19.8	19.8	19.9	19.9	20.0	20.1	20.2	20.2	20.3	20.4	20.4	20.5	20.6	20.7	20.7
77	17.1	17.2	17.2	17.3	17.3	17.4	17.5	17.5	17.7	17.8	17.8	17.9	18.0	18.1	18.1	18.2	18.3	18.4	18.4	18.5	18.6	18.7	18.7	18.8	18.9	19.0	19.0	19.1	19.2	19.3	19.3	19.4	19.5	19.6	19.6	19.7	19.8	19.9	19.9
76	16.1	16.2	16.2	16.3	16.3	16.5	16.5	16.6	16.7	16.8	16.9	17.0	17.0	17.1	17.2	17.3	17.4	17.4	17.5	17.6	17.6	17.7	17.8	17.9	18.0	18.1	18.2	18.2	18.3	18.4	18.5	18.6	18.6	18.7	18.8	18.9	19.0	19.0	19.1
75	15.1	15.2	15.3	15.3	15.4	15.5	15.6	15.7	15.8	15.9	15.9	16.0	16.1	16.2	16.3	16.4	16.4	16.5	16.6	16.7	16.8	16.9	17.0	17.0	17.1	17.2	17.3	17.4	17.5	17.6	17.6	17.7	17.8	17.9	18.0	18.1	18.2	18.2	18.3
74	14.1	14.2	14.3	14.4	14.4	14.5	14.6	14.7	14.8	14.9	14.9	15.0	15.1	15.3	15.4	15.4	15.5	15.6	15.7	15.7	15.8	16.0	16.1	16.2	16.3	16.4	16.4	16.5	16.6	16.7	16.8	16.9	17.0	17.1	17.2	17.3	17.3	17.4	17.5
73	13.1	13.2	13.3	13.4	13.4	13.5	13.6	13.7	13.8	13.9	14.0	14.0	14.1	14.2	14.3	14.4	14.5	14.6	14.7	14.8	14.9	15.0	15.1	15.2	15.3	15.4	15.5	15.6	15.7	15.8	15.9	16.0	16.1	16.2	16.3	16.4	16.5	16.6	16.7
72	12.1	12.2	12.3	12.4	12.4	12.5	12.6	12.7	12.8	12.9	13.0	13.1	13.2	13.3	13.4	13.5	13.6	13.7	13.8	13.9	14.0	14.1	14.3	14.4	14.4	14.5	14.6	14.8	14.9	15.0	15.1	15.2	15.3	15.4	15.5	15.6	15.7	15.8	15.9
71	11.1	11.2	11.3	11.4	11.5	11.6	11.6	11.7	11.8	12.0	12.1	12.2	12.2	12.3	12.5	12.6	12.7	12.8	13.0	13.1	13.1	13.2	13.3	13.4	13.5	13.6	13.8	13.9	14.0	14.1	14.2	14.3	14.4	14.5	14.6	14.7	14.8	15.0	15.1
70	10.1	10.2	10.3	10.3	10.4	10.6	10.6	10.7	10.8	11.0	11.1	11.1	11.3	11.4	11.6	11.7	11.8	11.9	12.0	12.1	12.2	12.3	12.4	12.6	12.7	12.8	12.9	13.0	13.1	13.2	13.3	13.4	13.6	13.7	13.8	13.9	14.0	14.1	14.3
69	9.1	9.2	9.3	9.5	9.6	9.7	9.8	9.9	10.0	10.2	10.3	10.4	10.5	10.6	10.7	10.9	11.0	11.1	11.2	11.3	11.4	11.6	11.7	11.8	11.9	12.0	12.1	12.3	12.4	12.5	12.6	12.7	12.8	12.9	13.0	13.1	13.3	13.4	13.5
68	8.1	8.2	8.4	8.5	8.6	8.7	8.8	8.9	9.1	9.2	9.3	9.5	9.6	9.7	9.8	9.9	10.1	10.2	10.4	10.5	10.6	10.7	10.8	11.0	11.1	11.2	11.3	11.4	11.5	11.6	11.7	11.8	11.9	12.1	12.2	12.4	12.5	12.6	12.7
67	7.1	7.3	7.4	7.5	7.6	7.8	7.9	8.0	8.1	8.3	8.4	8.5	8.6	8.8	8.9	9.0	9.1	9.3	9.4	9.5	9.7	9.8	9.9	10.0	10.2	10.3	10.4	10.5	10.7	10.8	10.9	11.0	11.2	11.3	11.4	11.6	11.7	11.8	11.9
66	6.2	6.3	6.4	6.6	6.7	6.9	7.0	7.1	7.2	7.4	7.5	7.6	7.7	7.9	8.0	8.1	8.2	8.4	8.5	8.6	8.8	8.9	9.0	9.1	9.3	9.4	9.5	9.6	9.8	9.9	10.0	10.1	10.3	10.4	10.5	10.7	10.8	10.9	11.0
65	5.2	5.4	5.5	5.8	5.8	6.1	6.2	6.3	6.5	6.6	6.6	6.8	7.1	7.3	7.4	7.5	7.7	7.8	8.0	8.2	8.3	8.3	8.4	8.5	8.7	8.8	8.9	9.1	9.1	9.2	9.3	9.4	9.6	9.7	9.8	9.9	9.9	10.0	10.1
64	4.2	4.4	4.5	4.9	5.0	5.1	5.2	5.4	5.6	5.7	5.8	6.0	6.2	6.3	6.5	6.6	6.9	7.0	7.0	7.1	7.2	7.4	7.5	7.6	7.7	7.9	8.1	8.1	8.2	8.3	8.4	8.5	8.7	8.8	8.9	9.0	9.1	9.2	9.3
63	3.3	3.4	3.7	3.8	4.1	4.3	4.4	4.6	4.8	5.0	5.1	5.2	5.3	5.5	5.6	5.7	5.8	5.9	6.1	6.2	6.3	6.4	6.7	6.8	6.9	7.0	7.1	7.2	7.3	7.5	7.6	7.7	7.9	8.0	8.1	8.2	8.3	8.4	8.5
62	2.3	2.5	2.8	3.1	3.4	3.6	3.8	4.0	4.2	4.4	4.5	4.6	4.9	5.1	5.2	5.3	5.4	5.6	5.7	5.9	6.0	6.1	6.2	6.3	6.4	6.5	6.6	6.8	6.9	7.0	7.1	7.2	7.4	7.5	7.5	7.6	7.7	7.7	7.8
61	1.5	1.9	2.2	2.5	2.8	3.0	3.2	3.4	3.6	3.8	3.9	4.1	4.2	4.4	4.5	4.7	4.8	4.9	5.1	5.2	5.3	5.4	5.5	5.6	5.7	5.9	6.0	6.1	6.2	6.3	6.4	6.5	6.6	6.7	6.8	6.9	7.0	7.0	7.1
60	1.1	1.5	1.8	2.1	2.4	2.6	2.8	3.0	3.2	3.4	3.5	3.7	3.8	4.0	4.1	4.3	4.4	4.5	4.7	4.8	4.9	5.0	5.1	5.2	5.3	5.4	5.5	5.6	5.7	5.8	5.9	6.0	6.1	6.2	6.3	6.4	6.5	6.6	6.7
59	0.7	1.1	1.4	1.7	2.0	2.2	2.4	2.6	2.8	3.0	3.1	3.3	3.4	3.6	3.7	3.9	4.0	4.1	4.3	4.4	4.5	4.6	4.7	4.8	4.9	5.0	5.1	5.2	5.3	5.4	5.5	5.6	5.7	5.8	5.9	6.0	6.1	6.2	6.3
58	0.3	0.7	1.0	1.3	1.6	1.8	2.0	2.2	2.4	2.6	2.7	2.9	3.0	3.2	3.3	3.5	3.6	3.7	3.8	4.0	4.1	4.2	4.3	4.4	4.5	4.6	4.7	4.8	4.9	5.0	5.1	5.2	5.3	5.4	5.5	5.6	5.7	5.8	5.9
57	0.0	0.3	0.6	0.9	1.2	1.4	1.6	1.8	2.0	2.2	2.3	2.5	2.6	2.8	2.9	3.1	3.2	3.3	3.5	3.6	3.7	3.8	3.9	4.0	4.1	4.2	4.3	4.4	4.5	4.6	4.7	4.8	4.9	5.0	5.1	5.2	5.3	5.4	5.5
56	0.0	0.0	0.2	0.5	0.8	1.0	1.2	1.4	1.6	1.8	1.9	2.1	2.2	2.4	2.5	2.7	2.8	2.9	3.1	3.2	3.3	3.4	3.5	3.6	3.7	3.8	3.9	4.0	4.1	4.2	4.3	4.4	4.5	4.6	4.7	4.8	4.9	5.0	5.1
55	0.0	0.0	0.1	0.4	0.6	0.9	1.0	1.2	1.4	1.5	1.7	1.8	2.0	2.1	2.3	2.4	2.5	2.7	2.8	2.9	3.0	3.1	3.2	3.3	3.4	3.5	3.6	3.7	3.8	3.9	4.0	4.1	4.2	4.3	4.4	4.5	4.6	4.7	4.7
54	0.0	0.0	0.0	0.1	0.4	0.6	0.8	1.0	1.2	1.4	1.5	1.7	1.8	1.9	2.1	2.2	2.4	2.5	2.6	2.7	2.9	3.0	3.1	3.2	3.3	3.4	3.5	3.6	3.7	3.8	3.9	3.9	4.0	4.1	4.2	4.2	4.3	4.3	4.3
53	0.0	0.0	0.0	0.0	0.1	0.3	0.5	0.6	0.8	1.0	1.1	1.3	1.4	1.6	1.7	1.9	2.0	2.1	2.3	2.4	2.5	2.6	2.7	2.8	3.0	3.1	3.2	3.3	3.4	3.5	3.6	3.6	3.7	3.8	3.8	3.9	3.9	3.9	3.9
52	0.0	0.0	0.0	0.0	0.0	0.1	0.3	0.4	0.6	0.7	0.9	1.1	1.2	1.3	1.5	1.6	1.7	1.9	2.0	2.1	2.2	2.3	2.4	2.5	2.6	2.7	2.8	2.8	2.9	3.0	3.1	3.2	3.2	3.3	3.3	3.4	3.4	3.5	3.5
51	0.0	0.0	0.0	0.0	0.0	0.0	0.1	0.2	0.4	0.5	0.6	0.8	0.9	1.1	1.2	1.3	1.4	1.5	1.7	1.8	1.9	2.0	2.1	2.1	2.3	2.3	2.5	2.6	2.6	2.7	2.8	2.9	2.9	3.0	3.0	3.1	3.1	3.1	3.1
50	0.0	0.0	0.0	0.0	0.0	0.0	0.0	0.1	0.2	0.3	0.5	0.6	0.7	0.9	1.0	1.1	1.2	1.3	1.5	1.6	1.7	1.8	1.8	1.9	2.0	2.1	2.2	2.3	2.4	2.4	2.5	2.5	2.6	2.6	2.7	2.7	2.7	2.7	2.7
49	0.0	0.0	0.0	0.0	0.0	0.0	0.0	0.0	0.1	0.2	0.3	0.5	0.6	0.7	0.8	0.9	1.1	1.2	1.3	1.5	1.6	1.7	1.8	1.9	2.0	2.1	2.2	2.2	2.3	2.3	2.3	2.3	2.3	2.3	2.3	2.3	2.3	2.3	2.3
48	0.0	0.0	0.0	0.0	0.0	0.0	0.0	0.0	0.1	0.1	0.2	0.3	0.4	0.5	0.6	0.7	0.8	0.9	1.0	1.1	1.2	1.3	1.3	1.4	1.5	1.5	1.6	1.6	1.7	1.7	1.8	1.8	1.8	1.9	1.9	1.9	1.9	1.9	1.9
47	0.0	0.0	0.0	0.0	0.0	0.0	0.0	0.0	0.0	0.0	0.1	0.1	0.2	0.2	0.3	0.3	0.4	0.5	0.5	0.6	0.7	0.8	0.8	0.9	0.9	1.0	1.0	1.1	1.1	1.2	1.2	1.3	1.3	1.4	1.4	1.5	1.5	1.5	1.5
46	0.0	0.0	0.0	0.0	0.0	0.0	0.0	0.0	0.0	0.0	0.0	0.1	0.1	0.2	0.2	0.3	0.3	0.4	0.4	0.5	0.5	0.6	0.6	0.7	0.7	0.8	0.8	0.8	0.9	0.9	1.0	1.0	1.0	1.1	1.1	1.1	1.1	1.1	1.1
45	0.0	0.0	0.0	0.0	0.0	0.0	0.0	0.0	0.0	0.0	0.0	0.0	0.1	0.1	0.1	0.2	0.2	0.3	0.3	0.4	0.4	0.4	0.5	0.5	0.5	0.6	0.6	0.6	0.6	0.6	0.7	0.7	0.7	0.7	0.7	0.7	0.7	0.7	0.7
44	0.0	0.0	0.0	0.0	0.0	0.0	0.0	0.0	0.0	0.0	0.0	0.0	0.0	0.0	0.1	0.1	0.1	0.1	0.1	0.2	0.2	0.2	0.2	0.2	0.2	0.2	0.3	0.3	0.3	0.3	0.3	0.3	0.3	0.3	0.3	0.3	0.3	0.3	0.3
43	0.0	0.0	0.0	0.0	0.0	0.0	0.0	0.0	0.0	0.0	0.0	0.0	0.0	0.0	0.0	0.0	0.0	0.0	0.0	0.0	0.0	0.0	0.0	0.0	0.0	0.0	0.0	0.0	0.0	0.0	0.0	0.0	0.0	0.0	0.0	0.0	0.0	0.0	0.0
42	0.0	0.0	0.0	0.0	0.0	0.0	0.0	0.0	0.0	0.0	0.0	0.0	0.0	0.0	0.0	0.0	0.0	0.0	0.0	0.0	0.0	0.0	0.0	0.0	0.0	0.0	0.0	0.0	0.0	0.0	0.0	0.0	0.0	0.0	0.0	0.0	0.0	0.0	0.0

LISTED CALL OPTION PRICE WHEN EXERCISE PRICE IS 70

NUMBER OF WEEKS BEFORE THE OPTION EXPIRES

Common Stock Price

Price	1	2	3	4	5	6	7	8	9	10	11	12	13	14	15	16	17	18	19	20	21	22	23	24	25	26	27	28	29	30	31	32	33	34	35	36	37	38	39
91	21.1	21.2	21.2	21.3	21.4	21.5	21.6	21.7	21.7	21.8	21.9	22.0	22.1	22.1	22.2	22.3	22.4	22.5	22.6	22.6	22.7	22.8	22.9	23.0	23.0	23.1	23.2	23.3	23.4	23.4	23.5	23.6	23.7	23.8	23.9	23.9	24.0	24.1	24.2
90	20.1	20.2	20.3	20.3	20.4	20.4	20.6	20.7	20.7	20.8	20.9	21.0	21.0	21.1	21.2	21.3	21.4	21.5	21.6	21.6	21.7	21.8	21.9	22.0	22.1	22.1	22.2	22.4	22.5	22.6	22.7	22.7	22.8	22.9	23.0	23.1	23.2	23.3	23.4
89	19.1	19.2	19.3	19.4	19.5	19.6	19.6	19.7	19.8	19.9	20.0	20.1	20.2	20.2	20.3	20.4	20.5	20.6	20.7	20.8	20.9	21.0	21.1	21.2	21.3	21.4	21.5	21.6	21.7	21.8	21.8	21.9	22.0	22.1	22.2	22.3	22.4	22.5	22.6
88	18.1	18.2	18.3	18.4	18.5	18.6	18.7	18.8	18.9	19.0	19.1	19.2	19.3	19.4	19.5	19.6	19.6	19.7	19.8	19.9	20.0	20.1	20.2	20.3	20.4	20.5	20.6	20.7	20.8	20.9	21.0	21.1	21.2	21.3	21.4	21.5	21.6	21.7	21.8
87	17.1	17.2	17.3	17.4	17.5	17.6	17.7	17.8	17.9	18.0	18.1	18.2	18.3	18.4	18.5	18.6	18.7	18.8	18.9	19.0	19.1	19.2	19.3	19.4	19.5	19.6	19.7	19.8	19.9	20.1	20.1	20.3	20.4	20.5	20.6	20.7	20.8	20.9	21.0
86	16.1	16.2	16.3	16.4	16.5	16.6	16.7	16.8	16.9	17.1	17.2	17.3	17.4	17.5	17.6	17.7	17.8	17.9	18.0	18.1	18.3	18.4	18.5	18.6	18.7	18.8	18.9	19.0	19.1	19.2	19.3	19.4	19.5	19.6	19.8	19.9	19.9	20.1	20.2
85	15.1	15.2	15.3	15.4	15.5	15.6	15.7	15.8	15.9	16.1	16.2	16.3	16.5	16.6	16.7	16.8	16.9	17.0	17.1	17.2	17.4	17.5	17.6	17.7	17.8	17.9	18.0	18.3	18.4	18.4	18.5	18.6	18.7	18.8	18.9	19.0	19.2	19.3	19.4
84	14.1	14.2	14.4	14.5	14.6	14.7	14.8	14.9	15.1	15.2	15.3	15.4	15.5	15.6	15.8	15.9	16.0	16.1	16.2	16.4	16.5	16.6	16.7	16.8	16.9	17.1	17.2	17.3	17.4	17.5	17.6	17.8	17.9	18.0	18.1	18.2	18.3	18.5	18.6
83	13.1	13.2	13.4	13.5	13.6	13.7	13.9	14.0	14.1	14.2	14.4	14.5	14.6	14.7	14.8	15.0	15.1	15.2	15.3	15.5	15.6	15.7	15.8	15.9	16.1	16.2	16.3	16.4	16.6	16.7	16.8	16.9	17.0	17.2	17.3	17.4	17.5	17.7	17.8
82	12.1	12.3	12.4	12.5	12.6	12.9	13.0	13.1	13.2	13.3	13.4	13.5	13.7	13.8	13.9	14.0	14.2	14.3	14.4	14.6	14.7	14.8	15.0	15.1	15.2	15.4	15.5	15.6	15.7	15.8	16.0	16.1	16.2	16.4	16.5	16.6	16.7	16.9	17.0
81	11.1	11.3	11.4	11.5	11.7	11.8	11.9	12.1	12.2	12.3	12.5	12.6	12.7	12.9	13.0	13.1	13.3	13.4	13.5	13.7	13.8	13.9	14.1	14.2	14.3	14.5	14.6	14.7	14.9	15.0	15.1	15.2	15.4	15.5	15.7	15.8	15.9	16.1	16.2
80	10.1	10.3	10.4	10.6	10.7	10.7	10.8	10.9	11.1	11.2	11.4	11.5	11.7	11.8	11.9	12.1	12.2	12.3	12.5	12.6	12.8	13.0	13.0	13.3	13.5	13.5	13.7	13.8	14.0	14.1	14.3	14.4	14.6	14.6	14.8	15.0	15.1	15.2	15.4
79	9.1	9.3	9.4	9.6	9.7	9.9	10.0	10.1	10.3	10.4	10.6	10.7	10.9	11.0	11.1	11.3	11.4	11.6	11.7	11.9	12.0	12.2	12.3	12.4	12.6	12.7	12.9	13.0	13.2	13.2	13.4	13.6	13.7	13.9	14.0	14.2	14.3	14.4	14.6
78	8.1	8.3	8.5	8.6	8.7	8.9	9.0	9.2	9.3	9.5	9.6	9.8	9.9	10.1	10.2	10.4	10.5	10.7	10.8	11.0	11.1	11.3	11.4	11.6	11.7	11.9	12.0	12.2	12.3	12.4	12.6	12.7	12.9	13.0	13.2	13.3	13.5	13.6	13.8
77	7.1	7.3	7.5	7.6	7.8	7.9	8.1	8.3	8.4	8.6	8.7	8.9	9.0	9.2	9.3	9.5	9.6	9.8	9.9	10.1	10.2	10.4	10.5	10.7	10.8	10.9	11.1	11.3	11.3	11.5	11.6	11.8	11.9	12.1	12.2	12.3	12.5	12.6	12.8
76	6.2	6.4	6.5	6.7	6.9	7.0	7.2	7.4	7.5	7.7	7.8	8.0	8.1	8.3	8.4	8.6	8.7	8.9	9.0	9.2	9.3	9.5	9.6	9.8	9.9	10.1	10.2	10.4	10.5	10.6	10.8	10.9	11.0	11.2	11.3	11.4	11.6	11.7	11.8
75	5.2	5.4	5.5	5.8	6.0	6.1	6.3	6.5	6.6	6.8	6.9	7.1	7.2	7.4	7.5	7.7	7.8	8.0	8.1	8.3	8.4	8.6	8.7	8.9	9.0	9.2	9.3	9.5	9.6	9.7	9.9	10.0	10.1	10.3	10.4	10.5	10.7	10.7	10.8
74	4.3	4.4	4.6	4.9	5.1	5.2	5.4	5.5	5.7	5.8	6.0	6.1	6.3	6.4	6.6	6.7	6.8	7.0	7.1	7.3	7.4	7.6	7.7	7.9	8.0	8.2	8.3	8.4	8.6	8.7	8.8	9.0	9.1	9.2	9.4	9.5	9.6	9.7	9.8
73	3.3	3.4	3.6	4.0	4.1	4.3	4.5	4.7	4.9	5.1	5.3	5.5	5.7	5.9	6.0	6.2	6.3	6.5	6.6	6.8	6.9	7.0	7.2	7.3	7.4	7.5	7.7	7.8	7.9	8.0	8.1	8.2	8.4	8.5	8.6	8.7	8.8	8.9	9.0
72	2.4	2.6	2.9	3.3	3.5	3.6	3.9	4.1	4.3	4.5	4.7	4.9	5.1	5.3	5.5	5.7	5.8	6.0	6.2	6.3	6.5	6.6	6.8	6.9	7.1	7.1	7.3	7.4	7.6	7.6	7.8	7.8	8.0	8.1	8.2	8.4	8.4	8.6	8.6
71	1.6	2.2	2.6	2.9	3.2	3.5	3.7	3.9	4.1	4.3	4.5	4.7	4.9	5.1	5.2	5.4	5.5	5.7	5.8	6.0	6.1	6.2	6.4	6.6	6.6	6.7	6.9	7.0	7.1	7.2	7.3	7.4	7.6	7.7	7.8	7.9	8.0	8.1	8.2
70	1.2	1.8	2.2	2.5	2.8	3.1	3.3	3.5	3.7	3.9	4.1	4.3	4.5	4.7	4.8	5.0	5.1	5.3	5.4	5.6	5.7	5.8	6.0	6.1	6.2	6.3	6.5	6.6	6.6	6.8	6.9	7.0	7.0	7.1	7.4	7.5	7.6	7.7	7.8
69	0.8	1.4	1.8	2.1	2.4	2.7	2.9	3.1	3.3	3.5	3.7	3.9	4.1	4.3	4.4	4.6	4.7	4.9	5.0	5.2	5.3	5.4	5.6	5.7	5.7	5.9	6.1	6.2	6.3	6.3	6.5	6.6	6.8	6.9	7.0	7.1	7.2	7.3	7.4
68	0.4	1.0	1.4	1.7	2.0	2.3	2.5	2.7	2.9	3.1	3.3	3.5	3.7	3.9	4.0	4.2	4.3	4.5	4.6	4.8	5.0	5.0	5.2	5.3	5.4	5.5	5.7	5.8	5.9	6.0	6.1	6.2	6.4	6.5	6.6	6.7	6.9	7.0	7.0
67	0.0	0.6	1.0	1.3	1.7	1.9	2.1	2.3	2.5	2.7	2.9	3.1	3.3	3.5	3.6	3.8	3.9	4.1	4.2	4.4	4.5	4.6	4.8	4.9	5.0	5.1	5.3	5.4	5.4	5.6	5.7	5.8	6.0	6.1	6.2	6.3	6.4	6.5	6.6
66	0.0	0.2	0.6	0.9	1.2	1.5	1.7	1.9	2.1	2.3	2.5	2.7	2.9	3.1	3.2	3.4	3.5	3.7	3.8	4.0	4.1	4.2	4.4	4.5	4.6	4.7	4.9	5.0	5.1	5.2	5.3	5.4	5.6	5.7	5.8	5.9	6.0	6.1	6.2
65	0.0	0.0	0.2	0.5	0.8	1.1	1.3	1.5	1.7	1.9	2.1	2.3	2.5	2.7	2.8	3.0	3.1	3.3	3.4	3.6	3.7	3.8	4.0	4.1	4.2	4.3	4.5	4.6	4.7	4.8	4.9	5.0	5.2	5.3	5.4	5.5	5.6	5.7	5.8
64	0.0	0.0	0.1	0.2	0.5	0.7	0.9	1.1	1.3	1.5	1.7	1.9	2.1	2.3	2.4	2.6	2.7	2.9	3.0	3.2	3.3	3.4	3.6	3.7	3.8	3.9	4.1	4.2	4.3	4.4	4.5	4.6	4.8	4.9	5.0	5.1	5.2	5.3	5.4
63	0.0	0.0	0.0	0.1	0.3	0.5	0.7	0.9	1.1	1.3	1.5	1.7	1.9	2.1	2.2	2.4	2.5	2.7	2.8	3.0	3.1	3.2	3.4	3.5	3.6	3.7	3.9	4.0	4.1	4.2	4.3	4.4	4.6	4.7	4.8	4.9	5.0	5.1	5.2
62	0.0	0.0	0.0	0.0	0.1	0.3	0.5	0.7	0.9	1.1	1.3	1.5	1.7	1.9	2.0	2.2	2.3	2.5	2.6	2.8	2.9	3.0	3.2	3.3	3.4	3.5	3.7	3.8	3.9	4.0	4.1	4.2	4.4	4.5	4.6	4.7	4.8	4.9	5.0
61	0.0	0.0	0.0	0.0	0.0	0.1	0.3	0.5	0.7	0.9	1.1	1.3	1.5	1.7	1.8	2.0	2.1	2.3	2.4	2.6	2.7	2.8	3.0	3.1	3.2	3.3	3.5	3.6	3.7	3.8	3.9	4.0	4.2	4.3	4.4	4.5	4.6	4.7	4.8
60	0.0	0.0	0.0	0.0	0.0	0.0	0.1	0.3	0.5	0.7	0.8	1.0	1.2	1.4	1.6	1.8	1.9	2.1	2.2	2.4	2.5	2.6	2.8	2.9	3.0	3.1	3.3	3.4	3.6	3.6	3.7	3.8	4.0	4.1	4.2	4.3	4.4	4.5	4.6
59	0.0	0.0	0.0	0.0	0.0	0.0	0.0	0.1	0.3	0.5	0.6	0.8	1.0	1.1	1.3	1.5	1.6	1.8	1.9	2.1	2.2	2.3	2.5	2.6	2.7	2.8	3.0	3.1	3.2	3.3	3.4	3.5	3.7	3.8	3.9	4.0	4.1	4.2	4.3
58	0.0	0.0	0.0	0.0	0.0	0.0	0.0	0.0	0.1	0.3	0.4	0.6	0.8	0.9	1.1	1.3	1.4	1.6	1.7	1.8	2.0	2.1	2.2	2.4	2.5	2.6	2.7	2.9	3.0	3.1	3.2	3.3	3.4	3.6	3.7	3.8	3.9	4.0	4.1
57	0.0	0.0	0.0	0.0	0.0	0.0	0.0	0.0	0.0	0.1	0.2	0.4	0.5	0.7	0.8	1.0	1.1	1.3	1.4	1.6	1.7	1.8	2.0	2.1	2.2	2.3	2.5	2.6	2.7	2.8	3.0	3.1	3.2	3.3	3.4	3.5	3.6	3.7	3.8
56	0.0	0.0	0.0	0.0	0.0	0.0	0.0	0.0	0.0	0.0	0.1	0.2	0.3	0.5	0.6	0.8	0.9	1.1	1.2	1.4	1.5	1.6	1.8	1.9	2.0	2.1	2.3	2.4	2.5	2.6	2.8	2.9	3.0	3.1	3.2	3.3	3.5	3.5	3.6
55	0.0	0.0	0.0	0.0	0.0	0.0	0.0	0.0	0.0	0.0	0.0	0.1	0.2	0.3	0.4	0.6	0.7	0.9	1.0	1.2	1.3	1.4	1.6	1.7	1.8	1.9	2.1	2.2	2.3	2.4	2.5	2.6	2.8	2.9	3.0	3.1	3.2	3.3	3.4
54	0.0	0.0	0.0	0.0	0.0	0.0	0.0	0.0	0.0	0.0	0.0	0.0	0.1	0.2	0.2	0.4	0.6	0.7	0.8	1.0	1.1	1.2	1.4	1.5	1.6	1.7	1.9	2.0	2.1	2.2	2.3	2.4	2.6	2.7	2.8	2.9	3.0	3.1	3.2
53	0.0	0.0	0.0	0.0	0.0	0.0	0.0	0.0	0.0	0.0	0.0	0.0	0.0	0.1	0.1	0.3	0.4	0.5	0.6	0.8	0.9	1.0	1.2	1.3	1.4	1.5	1.7	1.7	1.8	2.0	2.1	2.2	2.4	2.5	2.6	2.7	2.8	2.9	3.0
52	0.0	0.0	0.0	0.0	0.0	0.0	0.0	0.0	0.0	0.0	0.0	0.0	0.0	0.0	0.0	0.1	0.2	0.3	0.5	0.6	0.7	0.8	1.0	1.1	1.2	1.3	1.5	1.5	1.6	1.8	1.9	2.0	2.1	2.2	2.4	2.4	2.5	2.6	2.6
51	0.0	0.0	0.0	0.0	0.0	0.0	0.0	0.0	0.0	0.0	0.0	0.0	0.0	0.0	0.0	0.0	0.1	0.1	0.2	0.4	0.5	0.6	0.8	0.9	1.0	1.1	1.3	1.3	1.4	1.6	1.7	1.8	1.9	1.9	2.0	2.0	2.1	2.2	2.2
50	0.0	0.0	0.0	0.0	0.0	0.0	0.0	0.0	0.0	0.0	0.0	0.0	0.0	0.0	0.0	0.0	0.0	0.1	0.1	0.2	0.3	0.5	0.6	0.7	0.8	0.9	1.0	1.1	1.2	1.3	1.3	1.4	1.5	1.6	1.6	1.7	1.7	1.8	1.8
49	0.0	0.0	0.0	0.0	0.0	0.0	0.0	0.0	0.0	0.0	0.0	0.0	0.0	0.0	0.0	0.0	0.0	0.0	0.0	0.0	0.1	0.1	0.2	0.3	0.4	0.5	0.6	0.7	0.8	0.9	1.0	1.1	1.2	1.2	1.3	1.4	1.4	1.5	1.5

LISTED CALL OPTION PRICE WHEN EXERCISE PRICE IS 80

NUMBER OF WEEKS BEFORE THE OPTION EXPIRES

Common Stock Price	1	2	3	4	5	6	7	8	9	10	11	12	13	14	15	16	17	18	19	20	21	22	23	24	25	26	27	28	29	30	31	32	33	34	35	36	37	38	39
104	24.1	24.2	24.3	24.4	24.5	24.6	24.7	24.7	24.8	24.9	25.0	25.1	25.2	25.3	25.4	25.5	25.6	25.7	25.8	25.9	26.0	26.1	26.1	26.2	26.3	26.4	26.5	26.6	26.7	26.8	26.9	27.0	27.1	27.2	27.3	27.4	27.5	27.5	27.6
102	22.1	22.2	22.3	22.4	22.5	22.6	22.7	22.8	22.9	23.0	23.1	23.2	23.3	23.5	23.6	23.7	23.8	23.9	24.0	24.1	24.2	24.3	24.4	24.5	24.6	24.7	24.8	24.9	25.0	25.1	25.2	25.3	25.4	25.5	25.6	25.7	25.8	25.9	26.0
100	20.1	20.2	20.3	20.5	20.6	20.7	20.8	20.9	21.0	21.1	21.3	21.4	21.5	21.6	21.7	21.8	21.9	22.0	22.2	22.3	22.4	22.5	22.6	22.7	22.8	23.8	23.1	23.2	23.3	23.4	23.5	23.6	23.8	23.9	24.0	24.1	24.2	24.3	24.4
99	19.1	19.2	19.4	19.5	19.6	19.7	19.8	19.9	20.1	20.2	20.3	20.4	20.5	20.7	20.8	20.9	21.0	21.1	21.3	21.4	21.5	21.6	21.7	21.9	22.0	22.1	22.2	22.3	22.5	22.6	22.7	22.8	22.9	23.0	23.2	23.3	23.4	23.5	23.6
98	18.1	18.2	18.4	18.5	18.6	18.7	18.9	19.0	19.1	19.2	19.4	19.5	19.6	19.7	19.9	19.9	20.1	20.2	20.4	20.5	20.6	20.7	20.9	21.0	21.1	21.2	21.4	21.5	21.6	21.7	21.8	22.0	22.1	22.2	22.3	22.5	22.6	22.7	22.8
97	17.1	17.3	17.4	17.5	17.6	17.8	17.9	18.0	18.2	18.3	18.4	18.6	18.7	18.8	18.9	19.1	19.2	19.3	19.5	19.6	19.7	19.8	19.9	20.1	20.2	20.4	20.5	20.6	20.7	20.9	21.0	21.1	21.3	21.4	21.5	21.7	21.8	21.9	22.0
96	16.1	16.3	16.4	16.5	16.7	16.8	16.9	17.1	17.2	17.3	17.5	17.6	17.7	17.9	18.0	18.1	18.3	18.4	18.6	18.7	18.8	19.0	19.1	19.2	19.4	19.5	19.6	19.8	19.9	20.0	20.2	20.3	20.4	20.6	20.7	20.8	21.0	21.1	21.2
95	15.1	15.3	15.4	15.6	15.7	15.8	16.0	16.1	16.3	16.4	16.5	16.7	16.8	17.0	17.1	17.2	17.4	17.5	17.7	17.8	17.9	18.1	18.2	18.3	18.5	18.6	18.8	18.9	19.0	19.2	19.3	19.5	19.6	19.7	19.9	20.0	20.2	20.3	20.4
94	14.1	14.3	14.4	14.6	14.7	14.9	15.0	15.2	15.3	15.4	15.6	15.7	15.9	16.0	16.2	16.3	16.5	16.6	16.7	16.9	17.0	17.2	17.3	17.5	17.6	17.8	17.9	18.0	18.2	18.3	18.5	18.6	18.8	18.9	19.1	19.2	19.4	19.5	19.6
93	13.1	13.3	13.4	13.6	13.7	13.9	14.0	14.2	14.3	14.5	14.6	14.8	14.9	15.1	15.2	15.4	15.5	15.7	15.8	16.0	16.1	16.3	16.4	16.6	16.7	16.9	17.0	17.2	17.3	17.5	17.6	17.8	17.9	18.1	18.2	18.4	18.5	18.7	18.8
92	12.2	12.3	12.5	12.6	12.8	12.9	13.1	13.2	13.4	13.5	13.7	13.9	14.0	14.2	14.3	14.5	14.6	14.8	14.9	15.1	15.3	15.4	15.6	15.7	15.9	16.0	16.2	16.3	16.5	16.6	16.8	17.0	17.1	17.3	17.4	17.6	17.7	17.9	18.0
91	11.2	11.3	11.5	11.6	11.8	12.0	12.1	12.3	12.4	12.6	12.8	12.9	13.1	13.2	13.4	13.6	13.7	13.9	14.0	14.2	14.4	14.5	14.7	14.8	15.0	15.2	15.3	15.5	15.6	15.8	16.0	16.1	16.3	16.4	16.6	16.8	16.9	17.1	17.2
90	10.2	10.3	10.5	10.7	10.8	11.0	11.2	11.3	11.5	11.7	11.8	12.0	12.1	12.3	12.5	12.6	12.8	13.0	13.1	13.3	13.5	13.6	13.8	14.0	14.1	14.3	14.5	14.6	14.8	15.0	15.1	15.3	15.4	15.6	15.8	15.9	16.1	16.3	16.4
89	9.2	9.3	9.5	9.7	9.9	10.0	10.2	10.4	10.5	10.7	10.9	11.0	11.2	11.4	11.6	11.7	11.9	12.1	12.2	12.4	12.6	12.7	12.9	13.1	13.3	13.4	13.6	13.8	13.9	14.1	14.3	14.4	14.6	14.8	15.0	15.1	15.3	15.5	15.6
88	8.2	8.3	8.5	8.7	8.9	9.1	9.3	9.5	9.6	9.8	9.9	10.1	10.2	10.4	10.6	10.7	11.0	11.2	11.3	11.4	11.6	11.7	11.9	12.1	12.3	12.4	12.6	12.8	13.0	13.2	13.4	13.5	13.7	13.9	14.1	14.2	14.4	14.6	14.7
87	7.2	7.4	7.5	7.8	7.9	8.2	8.4	8.6	8.6	8.8	9.0	9.1	9.3	9.5	9.7	9.8	10.1	10.3	10.4	10.5	10.7	10.8	11.0	11.2	11.4	11.5	11.7	11.9	12.1	12.3	12.5	12.6	12.8	13.0	13.2	13.4	13.5	13.7	13.8
86	6.2	6.4	6.6	6.8	7.0	7.3	7.5	7.7	7.7	7.9	8.0	8.2	8.4	8.6	8.8	8.9	9.2	9.4	9.5	9.6	9.8	9.9	10.1	10.3	10.5	10.6	10.8	11.0	11.2	11.4	11.7	11.7	11.9	12.1	12.3	12.5	12.6	12.8	12.9
85	5.3	5.4	5.6	5.9	6.1	6.4	6.6	6.8	6.8	6.9	7.1	7.3	7.5	7.7	7.9	8.0	8.3	8.5	8.6	8.7	8.9	9.0	9.2	9.4	9.6	9.7	9.9	10.1	10.3	10.5	10.9	10.9	11.1	11.2	11.4	11.6	11.7	11.9	12.0
84	4.3	4.4	4.6	4.9	5.2	5.5	5.7	5.9	6.1	6.2	6.3	6.5	6.7	6.9	7.1	7.3	7.5	7.6	7.8	8.0	8.1	8.3	8.4	8.6	8.7	8.9	9.0	9.3	9.4	9.6	10.0	10.1	10.2	10.3	10.5	10.7	10.8	11.0	11.1
83	2.4	3.4	3.7	4.1	4.4	4.7	5.0	5.2	5.5	5.7	5.9	6.1	6.3	6.5	6.7	6.9	7.1	7.2	7.4	7.6	7.7	7.9	8.0	8.2	8.3	8.5	8.6	8.7	8.9	9.0	9.1	9.3	9.4	9.5	9.6	9.9	10.0	10.2	10.2
82	2.4	2.8	3.3	3.6	4.0	4.3	4.6	4.8	5.1	5.3	5.5	5.7	5.9	6.1	6.3	6.5	6.7	6.8	7.0	7.2	7.3	7.5	7.6	7.8	7.9	8.1	8.2	8.3	8.5	8.6	8.7	8.9	9.0	9.1	9.2	9.3	9.5	9.6	9.7
81	1.8	2.4	2.9	3.2	3.6	3.9	4.2	4.4	4.7	4.9	5.1	5.3	5.5	5.7	5.9	6.1	6.3	6.4	6.6	6.8	6.9	7.1	7.2	7.4	7.5	7.7	7.8	7.9	8.1	8.2	8.3	8.5	8.6	8.7	8.8	8.9	9.1	9.2	9.3
80	1.4	2.0	2.5	2.8	3.2	3.5	3.8	4.0	4.3	4.5	4.7	4.9	5.1	5.3	5.5	5.7	5.9	6.0	6.2	6.4	6.5	6.7	6.8	7.0	7.1	7.3	7.4	7.5	7.7	7.8	7.9	8.1	8.2	8.3	8.4	8.5	8.7	8.8	8.9
79	1.0	1.6	2.1	2.4	2.8	3.1	3.4	3.6	3.9	4.1	4.3	4.5	4.7	4.9	5.1	5.3	5.5	5.6	5.8	6.0	6.1	6.3	6.4	6.6	6.7	6.9	7.0	7.1	7.3	7.4	7.5	7.7	7.8	7.9	8.0	8.1	8.3	8.4	8.5
78	0.6	1.2	1.7	2.0	2.4	2.7	3.0	3.2	3.5	3.7	3.9	4.1	4.3	4.5	4.7	4.9	5.1	5.2	5.4	5.6	5.7	5.9	6.0	6.2	6.3	6.5	6.6	6.7	6.9	7.0	7.1	7.3	7.4	7.5	7.6	7.7	7.9	8.0	8.1
77	0.2	0.8	1.3	1.6	2.0	2.3	2.6	2.8	3.1	3.3	3.5	3.7	3.9	4.1	4.3	4.5	4.7	4.8	5.0	5.2	5.3	5.5	5.6	5.8	5.9	6.1	6.2	6.3	6.5	6.6	6.7	6.9	7.0	7.1	7.2	7.3	7.5	7.6	7.7
76	0.0	0.4	0.9	1.2	1.6	1.9	2.2	2.4	2.7	2.9	3.1	3.3	3.5	3.7	3.9	4.1	4.3	4.4	4.6	4.8	4.9	5.1	5.2	5.4	5.5	5.7	5.8	5.9	6.1	6.2	6.3	6.5	6.6	6.7	6.8	6.9	7.1	7.2	7.3
75	0.0	0.0	0.5	0.8	1.2	1.5	1.8	2.0	2.3	2.5	2.7	2.9	3.1	3.3	3.5	3.7	3.9	4.0	4.2	4.4	4.5	4.7	4.8	5.0	5.1	5.3	5.4	5.5	5.7	5.8	5.9	6.1	6.2	6.3	6.4	6.5	6.7	6.8	6.9
74	0.0	0.0	0.1	0.4	0.8	1.1	1.4	1.6	1.9	2.1	2.3	2.5	2.7	2.9	3.1	3.3	3.5	3.6	3.8	4.0	4.1	4.3	4.4	4.6	4.7	4.9	5.0	5.1	5.3	5.4	5.5	5.7	5.8	5.9	6.0	6.1	6.3	6.4	6.5
73	0.0	0.0	0.0	0.0	0.4	0.7	1.0	1.2	1.5	1.7	1.9	2.1	2.3	2.5	2.7	2.9	3.1	3.2	3.4	3.6	3.7	3.9	4.0	4.2	4.3	4.5	4.6	4.7	4.9	5.0	5.1	5.3	5.4	5.5	5.6	5.7	5.9	6.0	6.1
72	0.0	0.0	0.0	0.0	0.0	0.3	0.6	0.8	1.1	1.3	1.5	1.7	1.9	2.1	2.3	2.5	2.7	2.8	3.0	3.2	3.3	3.5	3.6	3.8	3.9	4.1	4.2	4.3	4.5	4.6	4.7	4.9	5.0	5.1	5.2	5.3	5.5	5.6	5.7
71	0.0	0.0	0.0	0.0	0.0	0.0	0.2	0.4	0.7	0.9	1.1	1.3	1.5	1.7	1.9	2.1	2.3	2.4	2.6	2.8	2.9	3.1	3.2	3.4	3.5	3.7	3.8	3.9	4.1	4.2	4.3	4.5	4.6	4.7	4.8	4.9	5.1	5.2	5.3
70	0.0	0.0	0.0	0.0	0.0	0.0	0.0	0.0	0.3	0.5	0.7	0.9	1.1	1.3	1.5	1.7	1.9	2.0	2.2	2.4	2.5	2.7	2.8	3.0	3.1	3.3	3.4	3.5	3.7	3.8	3.9	4.1	4.2	4.3	4.4	4.5	4.7	4.8	4.9
69	0.0	0.0	0.0	0.0	0.0	0.0	0.0	0.0	0.0	0.1	0.3	0.5	0.7	0.9	1.1	1.3	1.5	1.6	1.8	2.0	2.1	2.3	2.4	2.6	2.7	2.9	3.0	3.1	3.3	3.4	3.5	3.7	3.8	3.9	4.0	4.1	4.3	4.4	4.5
68	0.0	0.0	0.0	0.0	0.0	0.0	0.0	0.0	0.0	0.0	0.0	0.1	0.3	0.5	0.7	0.9	1.1	1.2	1.4	1.6	1.7	1.9	2.0	2.2	2.3	2.5	2.6	2.7	2.9	3.0	3.1	3.3	3.4	3.5	3.6	3.7	3.9	4.0	4.1
67	0.0	0.0	0.0	0.0	0.0	0.0	0.0	0.0	0.0	0.0	0.0	0.0	0.0	0.1	0.3	0.5	0.7	0.8	1.0	1.2	1.3	1.5	1.6	1.8	1.9	2.1	2.2	2.3	2.5	2.6	2.7	2.9	3.0	3.1	3.2	3.3	3.5	3.6	3.7
66	0.0	0.0	0.0	0.0	0.0	0.0	0.0	0.0	0.0	0.0	0.0	0.0	0.0	0.0	0.0	0.1	0.3	0.4	0.6	0.8	0.9	1.1	1.2	1.4	1.5	1.7	1.8	1.9	2.1	2.2	2.3	2.5	2.6	2.7	2.8	2.9	3.1	3.2	3.3
65	0.0	0.0	0.0	0.0	0.0	0.0	0.0	0.0	0.0	0.0	0.0	0.0	0.0	0.0	0.0	0.0	0.0	0.0	0.2	0.4	0.5	0.7	0.8	1.0	1.1	1.3	1.4	1.5	1.7	1.8	1.9	2.1	2.2	2.3	2.4	2.5	2.7	2.8	2.9
64	0.0	0.0	0.0	0.0	0.0	0.0	0.0	0.0	0.0	0.0	0.0	0.0	0.0	0.0	0.0	0.0	0.0	0.0	0.0	0.0	0.1	0.3	0.4	0.6	0.7	0.9	1.0	1.1	1.3	1.4	1.5	1.7	1.8	1.9	2.0	2.1	2.3	2.4	2.5
63	0.0	0.0	0.0	0.0	0.0	0.0	0.0	0.0	0.0	0.0	0.0	0.0	0.0	0.0	0.0	0.0	0.0	0.0	0.0	0.0	0.0	0.0	0.0	0.2	0.3	0.5	0.6	0.7	0.9	1.0	1.1	1.3	1.4	1.5	1.7	1.8	1.9	2.0	2.1
62	0.0	0.0	0.0	0.0	0.0	0.0	0.0	0.0	0.0	0.0	0.0	0.0	0.0	0.0	0.0	0.0	0.0	0.0	0.0	0.0	0.0	0.0	0.0	0.0	0.0	0.1	0.2	0.3	0.5	0.6	0.7	0.9	1.0	1.1	1.2	1.3	1.5	1.6	1.7
61	0.0	0.0	0.0	0.0	0.0	0.0	0.0	0.0	0.0	0.0	0.0	0.0	0.0	0.0	0.0	0.0	0.0	0.0	0.0	0.0	0.0	0.0	0.0	0.0	0.0	0.0	0.0	0.0	0.1	0.2	0.3	0.5	0.6	0.7	0.8	0.9	1.1	1.2	1.3
60	0.0	0.0	0.0	0.0	0.0	0.0	0.0	0.0	0.0	0.0	0.0	0.0	0.0	0.0	0.0	0.0	0.0	0.0	0.0	0.0	0.0	0.0	0.0	0.0	0.0	0.0	0.0	0.0	0.0	0.0	0.0	0.1	0.2	0.3	0.4	0.5	0.7	0.8	0.9
59	0.0	0.0	0.0	0.0	0.0	0.0	0.0	0.0	0.0	0.0	0.0	0.0	0.0	0.0	0.0	0.0	0.0	0.0	0.0	0.0	0.0	0.0	0.0	0.0	0.0	0.0	0.0	0.0	0.0	0.0	0.0	0.0	0.0	0.0	0.0	0.1	0.3	0.4	0.5
58	0.0	0.0	0.0	0.0	0.0	0.0	0.0	0.0	0.0	0.0	0.0	0.0	0.0	0.0	0.0	0.0	0.0	0.0	0.0	0.0	0.0	0.0	0.0	0.0	0.0	0.0	0.0	0.0	0.0	0.0	0.0	0.0	0.0	0.0	0.0	0.0	0.0	0.0	0.1
57	0.0	0.0	0.0	0.0	0.0	0.0	0.0	0.0	0.0	0.0	0.0	0.0	0.0	0.0	0.0	0.0	0.0	0.0	0.0	0.0	0.0	0.0	0.0	0.0	0.0	0.0	0.0	0.0	0.0	0.0	0.0	0.0	0.0	0.0	0.0	0.0	0.0	0.0	0.0

LISTED CALL OPTION PRICE WHEN EXERCISE PRICE IS 90

NUMBER OF WEEKS BEFORE THE OPTION EXPIRES

Common Stock Price	1	2	3	4	5	6	7	8	9	10	11	12	13	14	15	16	17	18	19	20	21	22	23	24	25	26	27	28	29	30	31	32	33	34	35	36	37	38	39
118	28.1	28.2	28.3	28.4	28.5	28.6	28.7	28.8	28.9	29.0	29.1	29.2	29.3	29.4	29.5	29.6	29.7	29.8	29.9	29.9	30.1	30.2	30.3	30.4	30.5	30.6	30.7	30.8	30.9	31.0	31.1	31.2	31.3	31.4	31.5	31.6	31.7	31.8	31.9
116	26.1	26.2	26.3	26.4	26.6	26.7	26.8	26.9	27.0	27.1	27.2	27.3	27.4	27.5	27.7	27.8	27.9	28.0	28.1	28.2	28.3	28.4	28.5	28.6	28.8	28.9	29.0	29.1	29.2	29.3	29.4	29.5	29.6	29.7	29.8	29.9	30.1	30.2	30.3
114	24.1	24.2	24.4	24.5	24.6	24.7	24.8	25.0	25.1	25.2	25.3	25.4	25.6	25.7	25.8	25.9	26.0	26.2	26.3	26.4	26.5	26.6	26.8	26.9	27.0	27.1	27.3	27.4	27.5	27.6	27.7	27.9	28.0	28.1	28.2	28.3	28.5	28.6	28.7
112	22.1	22.3	22.4	22.5	22.7	22.8	22.9	23.0	23.2	23.3	23.4	23.6	23.7	23.8	24.0	24.1	24.2	24.4	24.5	24.6	24.7	24.9	25.0	25.1	25.3	25.4	25.5	25.7	25.8	25.9	26.0	26.2	26.3	26.4	26.6	26.7	26.8	27.0	27.1
110	20.1	20.3	20.4	20.6	20.7	20.8	21.0	21.1	21.3	21.4	21.5	21.7	21.8	22.0	22.1	22.3	22.4	22.5	22.7	22.8	23.0	23.1	23.2	23.4	23.5	23.7	23.8	23.9	24.1	24.2	24.4	24.5	24.6	24.8	24.9	25.1	25.2	25.4	25.5
108	18.2	18.3	18.5	18.6	18.8	18.9	19.1	19.2	19.4	19.5	19.7	19.8	19.9	20.1	20.3	20.4	20.6	20.7	20.9	21.0	21.2	21.3	21.5	21.6	21.8	21.9	22.1	22.2	22.4	22.5	22.7	22.8	23.0	23.1	23.3	23.4	23.6	23.7	23.9
106	16.2	16.3	16.5	16.6	16.8	17.0	17.1	17.3	17.5	17.6	17.8	17.9	18.1	18.3	18.4	18.6	18.7	18.9	19.1	19.2	19.4	19.6	19.7	19.9	20.0	20.2	20.4	20.5	20.7	20.8	21.0	21.2	21.3	21.5	21.6	21.8	22.0	22.1	22.3
104	14.2	14.3	14.5	14.7	14.9	15.0	15.2	15.4	15.5	15.7	15.9	16.1	16.2	16.4	16.6	16.7	16.9	17.1	17.3	17.4	17.6	17.8	17.9	18.1	18.3	18.5	18.6	18.8	19.0	19.1	19.3	19.5	19.7	19.8	20.0	20.2	20.4	20.5	20.7
102	12.2	12.4	12.5	12.7	12.9	13.1	13.3	13.5	13.6	13.8	14.0	14.2	14.4	14.5	14.7	14.9	15.1	15.3	15.5	15.6	15.8	16.0	16.2	16.4	16.5	16.7	16.9	17.1	17.3	17.5	17.6	17.8	18.0	18.2	18.4	18.5	18.7	18.9	19.1
100	10.2	10.4	10.6	10.8	11.0	11.2	11.3	11.5	11.7	11.9	12.1	12.3	12.5	12.7	12.9	13.1	13.3	13.5	13.7	13.8	14.0	14.2	14.4	14.6	14.8	15.0	15.2	15.4	15.6	15.8	16.0	16.1	16.3	16.5	16.7	16.9	17.1	17.3	17.5
99	9.2	9.4	9.6	9.8	10.0	10.2	10.4	10.6	10.7	10.9	11.1	11.4	11.6	11.8	12.0	12.2	12.4	12.6	12.8	12.9	13.1	13.3	13.5	13.7	13.9	14.1	14.3	14.5	14.7	14.9	15.1	15.2	15.4	15.6	15.8	16.0	16.2	16.4	16.6
98	8.2	8.4	8.6	8.8	9.1	9.3	9.4	9.6	9.8	10.0	10.2	10.5	10.7	10.9	11.1	11.3	11.5	11.7	11.9	12.0	12.2	12.4	12.6	12.8	13.0	13.2	13.4	13.6	13.8	14.0	14.2	14.3	14.5	14.7	14.9	15.1	15.3	15.4	15.7
97	7.2	7.4	7.6	7.9	8.1	8.3	8.5	8.7	8.8	9.0	9.3	9.6	9.8	10.0	10.2	10.4	10.6	10.8	11.0	11.1	11.3	11.5	11.7	11.9	12.1	12.3	12.5	12.7	12.9	13.1	13.3	13.4	13.6	13.8	14.0	14.2	14.4	14.6	14.8
96	6.3	6.5	6.7	6.9	7.2	7.4	7.5	7.7	7.9	8.1	8.4	8.7	8.9	9.1	9.3	9.5	9.7	9.9	10.1	10.2	10.4	10.6	10.8	11.0	11.2	11.4	11.6	11.8	12.0	12.2	12.4	12.5	12.7	12.9	13.1	13.3	13.5	13.7	13.9
95	5.3	5.5	5.7	6.0	6.3	6.5	6.6	6.8	7.0	7.2	7.5	7.8	8.0	8.2	8.4	8.6	8.8	9.0	9.2	9.3	9.5	9.7	9.9	10.1	10.3	10.5	10.7	10.9	11.1	11.3	11.5	11.6	11.8	12.0	12.2	12.4	12.6	12.8	13.0
94	4.4	4.5	4.8	5.1	5.4	5.6	5.8	6.1	6.4	6.7	6.9	7.1	7.4	7.6	7.8	8.0	8.2	8.4	8.6	8.8	8.9	9.1	9.3	9.4	9.6	9.8	9.9	10.1	10.2	10.4	10.6	10.7	10.9	11.1	11.3	11.5	11.7	11.9	12.1
93	3.4	3.5	4.0	4.4	4.8	5.1	5.4	5.7	6.0	6.3	6.5	6.7	7.0	7.2	7.4	7.6	7.8	8.0	8.2	8.4	8.5	8.7	8.9	9.0	9.2	9.4	9.5	9.7	9.8	9.9	10.1	10.3	10.4	10.5	10.7	10.8	10.9	11.1	11.2
92	2.5	3.1	3.6	4.0	4.4	4.7	5.0	5.3	5.6	5.9	6.1	6.3	6.6	6.8	7.0	7.2	7.4	7.6	7.8	8.0	8.1	8.3	8.5	8.6	8.8	9.0	9.1	9.3	9.4	9.6	9.7	9.9	9.9	10.1	10.3	10.4	10.5	10.7	10.8
91	2.0	2.7	3.2	3.6	4.0	4.3	4.6	4.9	5.2	5.5	5.7	5.9	6.2	6.4	6.6	6.8	7.0	7.2	7.4	7.6	7.7	7.9	8.1	8.2	8.4	8.6	8.7	8.9	9.0	9.2	9.3	9.5	9.6	9.7	9.9	10.0	10.1	10.3	10.4
90	1.6	2.3	2.8	3.2	3.6	3.9	4.2	4.5	4.8	5.1	5.3	5.5	5.8	6.0	6.2	6.4	6.6	6.8	7.0	7.2	7.3	7.5	7.7	7.8	8.0	8.2	8.3	8.5	8.6	8.8	8.9	9.1	9.2	9.3	9.5	9.6	9.7	9.9	10.0
89	1.2	1.9	2.4	2.8	3.2	3.5	3.8	4.1	4.4	4.7	4.9	5.1	5.4	5.6	5.8	6.0	6.2	6.4	6.6	6.8	6.9	7.1	7.3	7.4	7.6	7.8	7.9	8.1	8.2	8.4	8.5	8.7	8.8	8.9	9.1	9.2	9.3	9.5	9.6
88	0.8	1.5	2.0	2.4	2.8	3.1	3.4	3.7	4.0	4.3	4.5	4.7	5.0	5.2	5.4	5.6	5.8	6.0	6.2	6.4	6.5	6.7	6.9	7.0	7.2	7.4	7.5	7.7	7.8	8.0	8.1	8.3	8.4	8.5	8.7	8.8	8.9	9.1	9.2
87	0.4	1.1	1.6	2.0	2.4	2.7	3.0	3.3	3.6	3.9	4.1	4.3	4.6	4.8	5.0	5.2	5.4	5.6	5.8	6.0	6.1	6.3	6.5	6.6	6.8	7.0	7.1	7.3	7.4	7.6	7.7	7.9	8.0	8.1	8.3	8.4	8.5	8.7	8.8
86	0.0	0.7	1.2	1.6	2.0	2.3	2.6	2.9	3.2	3.5	3.7	3.9	4.2	4.4	4.6	4.8	5.0	5.2	5.4	5.6	5.7	5.9	6.1	6.2	6.4	6.6	6.7	6.9	7.0	7.2	7.3	7.5	7.6	7.7	7.9	8.0	8.1	8.3	8.4
85	0.0	0.3	0.8	1.2	1.6	1.9	2.2	2.5	2.8	3.1	3.3	3.5	3.8	4.0	4.2	4.4	4.6	4.8	5.0	5.2	5.3	5.5	5.7	5.8	6.0	6.2	6.3	6.5	6.6	6.8	6.9	7.1	7.2	7.3	7.5	7.6	7.7	7.9	8.0
84	0.0	0.0	0.4	0.8	1.2	1.5	1.8	2.1	2.4	2.7	2.9	3.1	3.4	3.6	3.8	4.0	4.2	4.4	4.6	4.8	4.9	5.1	5.3	5.4	5.6	5.8	5.9	6.1	6.2	6.4	6.5	6.7	6.8	6.9	7.1	7.2	7.3	7.5	7.6
83	0.0	0.0	0.0	0.4	0.8	1.1	1.4	1.7	2.0	2.3	2.5	2.7	3.0	3.2	3.4	3.6	3.8	4.0	4.2	4.4	4.5	4.7	4.9	5.0	5.2	5.4	5.5	5.7	5.8	6.0	6.1	6.3	6.4	6.5	6.7	6.8	6.9	7.1	7.2
82	0.0	0.0	0.0	0.0	0.4	0.7	1.0	1.3	1.6	1.9	2.1	2.3	2.6	2.8	3.0	3.2	3.4	3.6	3.8	4.0	4.1	4.3	4.5	4.6	4.8	5.0	5.1	5.3	5.4	5.6	5.7	5.9	6.0	6.1	6.3	6.4	6.5	6.7	6.8
81	0.0	0.0	0.0	0.0	0.0	0.3	0.6	0.9	1.2	1.5	1.7	1.9	2.2	2.4	2.6	2.8	3.0	3.2	3.4	3.6	3.7	3.9	4.1	4.2	4.4	4.6	4.7	4.9	5.0	5.2	5.3	5.5	5.6	5.7	5.9	6.0	6.1	6.3	6.4
80	0.0	0.0	0.0	0.0	0.0	0.0	0.2	0.5	0.8	1.1	1.3	1.5	1.8	2.0	2.2	2.4	2.6	2.8	3.0	3.2	3.3	3.5	3.7	3.8	4.0	4.2	4.3	4.5	4.6	4.8	4.9	5.1	5.2	5.3	5.5	5.6	5.7	5.9	6.0
79	0.0	0.0	0.0	0.0	0.0	0.0	0.0	0.1	0.4	0.7	0.9	1.1	1.4	1.6	1.8	2.0	2.2	2.4	2.6	2.8	2.9	3.1	3.3	3.4	3.6	3.8	3.9	4.1	4.2	4.4	4.5	4.7	4.8	4.9	5.1	5.2	5.3	5.5	5.6
78	0.0	0.0	0.0	0.0	0.0	0.0	0.0	0.0	0.0	0.3	0.5	0.7	1.0	1.2	1.4	1.6	1.8	2.0	2.2	2.4	2.5	2.7	2.9	3.0	3.2	3.4	3.5	3.7	3.8	4.0	4.1	4.3	4.4	4.5	4.7	4.8	4.9	5.1	5.2
77	0.0	0.0	0.0	0.0	0.0	0.0	0.0	0.0	0.0	0.0	0.1	0.3	0.6	0.8	1.0	1.2	1.4	1.6	1.8	2.0	2.1	2.3	2.5	2.6	2.8	3.0	3.1	3.3	3.4	3.6	3.7	3.8	4.0	4.1	4.3	4.4	4.5	4.7	4.8
76	0.0	0.0	0.0	0.0	0.0	0.0	0.0	0.0	0.0	0.0	0.0	0.0	0.2	0.4	0.6	0.8	1.0	1.2	1.4	1.6	1.7	1.9	2.1	2.2	2.4	2.6	2.7	2.9	3.0	3.2	3.3	3.5	3.6	3.7	3.9	4.0	4.1	4.3	4.4
75	0.0	0.0	0.0	0.0	0.0	0.0	0.0	0.0	0.0	0.0	0.0	0.0	0.0	0.0	0.2	0.4	0.6	0.8	1.0	1.2	1.3	1.5	1.7	1.8	2.0	2.2	2.3	2.5	2.6	2.8	2.9	3.1	3.2	3.3	3.5	3.6	3.7	3.9	4.0
74	0.0	0.0	0.0	0.0	0.0	0.0	0.0	0.0	0.0	0.0	0.0	0.0	0.0	0.0	0.0	0.0	0.2	0.4	0.6	0.8	0.9	1.1	1.3	1.4	1.6	1.8	1.9	2.1	2.2	2.4	2.5	2.7	2.8	2.9	3.1	3.2	3.3	3.5	3.6
73	0.0	0.0	0.0	0.0	0.0	0.0	0.0	0.0	0.0	0.0	0.0	0.0	0.0	0.0	0.0	0.0	0.0	0.0	0.2	0.4	0.5	0.7	0.9	1.0	1.2	1.4	1.5	1.7	1.8	2.0	2.1	2.3	2.4	2.5	2.7	2.8	2.9	3.1	3.2
72	0.0	0.0	0.0	0.0	0.0	0.0	0.0	0.0	0.0	0.0	0.0	0.0	0.0	0.0	0.0	0.0	0.0	0.0	0.0	0.0	0.1	0.3	0.5	0.6	0.8	1.0	1.1	1.3	1.4	1.6	1.7	1.9	2.0	2.1	2.3	2.4	2.5	2.7	2.8
71	0.0	0.0	0.0	0.0	0.0	0.0	0.0	0.0	0.0	0.0	0.0	0.0	0.0	0.0	0.0	0.0	0.0	0.0	0.0	0.0	0.0	0.0	0.1	0.2	0.4	0.6	0.7	0.9	1.0	1.2	1.3	1.5	1.6	1.7	1.9	2.0	2.1	2.3	2.4
70	0.0	0.0	0.0	0.0	0.0	0.0	0.0	0.0	0.0	0.0	0.0	0.0	0.0	0.0	0.0	0.0	0.0	0.0	0.0	0.0	0.0	0.0	0.0	0.0	0.0	0.2	0.3	0.5	0.6	0.8	0.9	1.1	1.2	1.3	1.5	1.6	1.7	1.9	2.0
69	0.0	0.0	0.0	0.0	0.0	0.0	0.0	0.0	0.0	0.0	0.0	0.0	0.0	0.0	0.0	0.0	0.0	0.0	0.0	0.0	0.0	0.0	0.0	0.0	0.0	0.0	0.0	0.1	0.2	0.4	0.5	0.7	0.8	0.9	1.1	1.2	1.3	1.5	1.6
68	0.0	0.0	0.0	0.0	0.0	0.0	0.0	0.0	0.0	0.0	0.0	0.0	0.0	0.0	0.0	0.0	0.0	0.0	0.0	0.0	0.0	0.0	0.0	0.0	0.0	0.0	0.0	0.0	0.0	0.0	0.1	0.3	0.4	0.5	0.7	0.8	0.9	1.1	1.2
67	0.0	0.0	0.0	0.0	0.0	0.0	0.0	0.0	0.0	0.0	0.0	0.0	0.0	0.0	0.0	0.0	0.0	0.0	0.0	0.0	0.0	0.0	0.0	0.0	0.0	0.0	0.0	0.0	0.0	0.0	0.0	0.0	0.0	0.1	0.3	0.4	0.5	0.7	0.8
66	0.0	0.0	0.0	0.0	0.0	0.0	0.0	0.0	0.0	0.0	0.0	0.0	0.0	0.0	0.0	0.0	0.0	0.0	0.0	0.0	0.0	0.0	0.0	0.0	0.0	0.0	0.0	0.0	0.0	0.0	0.0	0.0	0.0	0.0	0.0	0.0	0.1	0.3	0.4
65	0.0	0.0	0.0	0.0	0.0	0.0	0.0	0.0	0.0	0.0	0.0	0.0	0.0	0.0	0.0	0.0	0.0	0.0	0.0	0.0	0.0	0.0	0.0	0.0	0.0	0.0	0.0	0.0	0.0	0.0	0.0	0.0	0.0	0.0	0.0	0.0	0.0	0.0	0.0
64	0.0	0.0	0.0	0.0	0.0	0.0	0.0	0.0	0.0	0.0	0.0	0.0	0.0	0.0	0.0	0.0	0.0	0.0	0.0	0.0	0.0	0.0	0.0	0.0	0.0	0.0	0.0	0.0	0.0	0.0	0.0	0.0	0.0	0.0	0.0	0.0	0.0	0.0	0.0

LISTED CALL OPTION PRICE WHEN EXERCISE PRICE IS 100

NUMBER OF WEEKS BEFORE THE OPTION EXPIRES

Common Stock Price	1	2	3	4	5	6	7	8	9	10	11	12	13	14	15	16	17	18	19	20	21	22	23	24	25	26	27	28	29	30	31	32	33	34	35	36	37	38	39
130	30.1	30.2	30.3	30.5	30.6	30.7	30.8	30.9	31.0	31.2	31.3	31.4	31.5	31.6	31.8	31.9	32.0	32.1	32.2	32.3	32.4	32.6	32.7	32.8	32.9	33.0	33.2	33.3	33.4	33.5	33.6	33.7	33.8	34.0	34.1	34.2	34.3	34.4	34.6
128	28.1	28.3	28.4	28.5	28.6	28.8	28.9	29.0	29.1	29.3	29.4	29.5	29.7	29.8	29.9	30.0	30.2	30.3	30.4	30.5	30.7	30.8	30.9	31.0	31.2	31.3	31.4	41.6	31.7	31.8	31.9	32.1	32.2	32.3	32.4	32.6	32.7	32.8	33.0
126	26.1	26.3	26.4	26.5	26.7	26.8	27.0	27.1	27.2	27.4	27.5	27.6	27.8	27.9	28.1	28.2	28.3	28.5	28.6	28.7	28.9	29.0	29.2	29.3	29.4	29.6	29.7	29.8	29.9	30.1	30.3	30.4	30.5	30.7	30.8	30.9	31.1	31.2	31.3
124	24.1	24.3	24.4	24.6	24.7	24.9	25.0	25.2	25.3	25.5	25.6	25.8	25.9	26.1	26.2	26.4	26.5	26.7	26.8	26.9	27.1	27.2	27.4	27.5	27.7	27.8	28.0	28.1	28.3	28.4	28.6	28.7	28.9	29.0	29.2	29.3	29.5	29.6	29.8
122	22.2	22.3	22.5	22.6	22.8	22.9	23.1	23.3	23.4	23.6	23.7	23.9	24.1	24.2	24.4	24.5	24.7	24.8	25.0	25.2	25.3	25.5	25.6	25.8	25.9	26.1	26.3	26.4	26.6	26.7	26.9	27.0	27.2	27.4	27.5	27.7	27.8	28.0	28.2
120	20.2	20.3	20.5	20.7	20.8	21.0	21.2	21.3	21.5	21.7	21.8	22.0	22.2	22.4	22.5	22.7	22.9	23.0	23.2	23.4	23.5	23.7	23.9	24.0	24.2	24.4	24.5	24.7	24.9	25.0	25.2	25.4	25.5	25.7	25.9	26.0	26.2	26.4	26.6
118	18.2	18.4	18.5	18.7	18.9	19.1	19.2	19.4	19.6	19.8	19.9	20.1	20.3	20.5	20.7	20.9	21.0	21.2	21.4	21.6	21.7	21.9	22.1	22.3	22.5	22.6	22.8	23.0	23.2	23.3	23.5	23.7	23.9	24.1	24.2	24.4	24.6	24.8	25.0
116	16.2	16.4	16.6	16.8	16.9	17.1	17.3	17.5	17.7	17.9	18.1	18.3	18.5	18.6	18.8	19.0	19.2	19.4	19.6	19.8	19.9	20.1	20.3	20.5	20.7	20.9	21.1	21.3	21.5	21.7	21.8	22.0	22.2	22.4	22.6	22.8	23.8	23.2	23.4
114	14.2	14.4	14.6	14.8	15.0	15.2	15.4	15.6	15.8	16.0	16.2	16.4	16.6	16.8	17.0	17.2	17.4	17.6	17.8	18.0	18.2	18.4	18.6	18.8	19.0	19.2	19.4	19.6	19.8	19.9	20.2	20.4	20.6	20.8	21.0	21.2	21.4	21.6	21.8
112	12.2	12.4	12.6	12.8	13.0	13.3	13.5	13.7	13.9	14.1	14.3	14.5	14.7	14.9	15.1	15.3	15.6	15.8	16.0	16.2	16.4	16.6	16.8	17.0	17.2	17.4	17.6	17.9	18.1	18.3	18.5	18.7	18.9	19.1	19.3	19.5	19.7	19.9	20.1
110	10.2	10.4	10.6	10.8	11.0	11.3	11.5	11.7	12.0	12.2	12.4	12.6	12.8	13.0	13.4	13.6	13.9	14.1	14.2	14.4	14.6	14.9	15.1	15.3	15.5	15.7	15.9	16.2	16.4	16.6	16.7	16.9	17.1	17.3	17.4	17.6	17.8	18.0	18.2
108	8.2	8.4	8.7	8.9	9.2	9.4	9.6	9.8	10.1	10.3	10.6	10.8	11.0	11.2	11.7	11.9	12.2	12.4	12.6	12.8	13.0	13.2	13.4	13.6	13.8	14.0	14.2	14.5	14.7	14.9	15.0	15.2	15.4	15.6	15.7	15.7	15.9	16.1	16.3
106	6.3	6.5	6.8	7.0	7.3	7.5	7.7	7.9	8.2	8.6	8.8	9.0	9.3	9.6	10.0	10.2	10.5	10.7	10.9	11.1	11.3	11.5	11.7	11.9	12.1	12.3	12.5	12.8	13.0	13.2	13.3	13.5	13.7	13.9	14.0	14.0	14.1	14.3	14.5
104	4.4	4.6	4.8	5.2	5.6	6.0	6.3	6.6	6.9	7.2	7.5	7.8	8.0	8.3	8.5	8.7	8.9	9.1	9.4	9.6	9.8	9.9	10.1	10.3	10.5	10.7	10.8	11.0	11.2	11.3	11.5	11.7	11.8	12.0	12.1	12.3	12.4	12.6	12.7
102	2.6	3.3	4.0	4.4	4.8	5.2	5.5	5.8	6.1	6.4	6.7	7.0	7.2	7.5	7.7	7.9	8.1	8.3	8.6	8.8	9.0	9.1	9.3	9.5	9.7	9.9	10.0	10.2	10.4	10.5	10.7	10.9	11.0	11.2	11.3	11.5	11.6	11.8	11.9
100	1.8	2.5	3.1	3.6	4.0	4.4	4.7	5.0	5.3	5.6	5.9	6.2	6.4	6.7	6.9	7.1	7.3	7.5	7.8	8.0	8.2	8.3	8.5	8.7	8.9	9.1	9.2	9.4	9.6	9.7	9.9	10.1	10.2	10.4	10.5	10.7	10.8	11.0	11.1
99	1.4	2.1	2.7	3.2	3.6	4.0	4.3	4.6	4.9	5.2	5.5	5.8	6.0	6.3	6.5	6.7	6.9	7.1	7.4	7.6	7.8	7.9	8.1	8.3	8.5	8.7	8.8	9.0	9.2	9.3	9.5	9.7	9.8	9.9	10.1	10.3	10.4	10.6	10.7
98	1.0	1.7	2.3	2.8	3.2	3.6	3.9	4.2	4.5	4.8	5.1	5.4	5.6	5.9	6.1	6.3	6.5	6.7	7.0	7.2	7.4	7.5	7.7	7.9	8.1	8.3	8.4	8.6	8.8	8.9	9.1	9.3	9.4	9.6	9.7	9.9	10.0	10.2	10.3
97	0.6	1.3	1.9	2.4	2.8	3.2	3.5	3.8	4.1	4.4	4.7	5.0	5.2	5.5	5.7	5.9	6.1	6.3	6.6	6.8	7.0	7.1	7.3	7.5	7.7	7.9	8.0	8.2	8.4	8.5	8.7	8.9	9.0	9.2	9.3	9.5	9.6	9.8	9.9
96	0.2	0.9	1.5	2.0	2.4	2.8	3.1	3.4	3.7	4.0	4.3	4.6	4.8	5.1	5.3	5.5	5.7	5.9	6.2	6.4	6.6	6.7	6.9	7.1	7.3	7.5	7.6	7.8	8.0	8.1	8.3	8.5	8.6	8.8	8.9	9.1	9.2	9.4	9.5
95	0.0	0.5	1.1	1.6	2.0	2.4	2.7	3.0	3.3	3.6	3.9	4.2	4.4	4.7	4.9	5.1	5.3	5.5	5.8	6.0	6.2	6.3	6.5	6.7	6.9	7.1	7.2	7.4	7.6	7.7	7.9	8.1	8.2	8.4	8.5	8.7	8.8	9.0	9.1
94	0.0	0.1	0.7	1.2	1.6	2.0	2.3	2.6	2.9	3.2	3.5	3.8	4.0	4.3	4.5	4.7	4.9	5.1	5.4	5.6	5.8	5.9	6.1	6.3	6.5	6.7	6.8	7.0	7.2	7.3	7.5	7.7	7.8	8.0	8.1	8.3	8.4	8.6	8.7
93	0.0	0.0	0.3	0.8	1.2	1.6	1.9	2.2	2.5	2.8	3.1	3.4	3.6	3.9	4.1	4.3	4.5	4.7	5.0	5.2	5.4	5.5	5.7	5.9	6.1	6.3	6.4	6.6	6.8	6.9	7.1	7.3	7.4	7.6	7.7	7.9	8.0	8.2	8.3
92	0.0	0.0	0.0	0.4	0.8	1.2	1.5	1.8	2.1	2.4	2.7	3.0	3.2	3.5	3.7	3.9	4.1	4.3	4.6	4.8	5.0	5.1	5.3	5.5	5.7	5.9	6.0	6.2	6.4	6.5	6.7	6.9	7.0	7.2	7.3	7.5	7.6	7.8	7.9
91	0.0	0.0	0.0	0.0	0.4	0.8	1.1	1.4	1.7	2.0	2.3	2.6	2.8	3.1	3.3	3.5	3.7	3.9	4.2	4.4	4.6	4.7	4.9	5.1	5.3	5.5	5.6	5.8	6.0	6.1	6.3	6.5	6.6	6.8	6.9	7.1	7.2	7.4	7.5
90	0.0	0.0	0.0	0.0	0.0	0.4	0.7	1.0	1.3	1.6	1.9	2.2	2.4	2.7	2.9	3.1	3.3	3.5	3.8	4.0	4.2	4.3	4.5	4.7	4.9	5.1	5.2	5.4	5.6	5.7	5.9	6.1	6.2	6.4	6.5	6.7	6.8	7.0	7.1
89	0.0	0.0	0.0	0.0	0.0	0.0	0.3	0.6	0.9	1.2	1.5	1.8	2.0	2.3	2.5	2.7	2.9	3.1	3.4	3.6	3.8	3.9	4.1	4.3	4.5	4.7	4.8	5.0	5.2	5.3	5.5	5.7	5.8	6.0	6.1	6.3	6.4	6.6	6.7
88	0.0	0.0	0.0	0.0	0.0	0.0	0.0	0.2	0.5	0.8	1.1	1.4	1.6	1.9	2.1	2.3	2.5	2.7	3.0	3.2	3.4	3.5	3.7	3.9	4.1	4.3	4.4	4.6	4.8	4.9	5.1	5.3	5.4	5.6	5.7	5.9	6.0	6.2	6.3
87	0.0	0.0	0.0	0.0	0.0	0.0	0.0	0.0	0.1	0.4	0.7	1.0	1.2	1.5	1.7	1.9	2.1	2.3	2.6	2.8	3.0	3.1	3.3	3.5	3.7	3.9	4.0	4.2	4.4	4.5	4.7	4.9	5.0	5.2	5.3	5.5	5.6	5.8	5.9
86	0.0	0.0	0.0	0.0	0.0	0.0	0.0	0.0	0.0	0.0	0.3	0.6	0.8	1.1	1.3	1.5	1.7	1.9	2.2	2.4	2.6	2.7	2.9	3.1	3.3	3.5	3.6	3.8	4.0	4.1	4.3	4.5	4.6	4.8	4.9	5.1	5.2	5.4	5.5
85	0.0	0.0	0.0	0.0	0.0	0.0	0.0	0.0	0.0	0.0	0.0	0.2	0.4	0.7	0.9	1.1	1.3	1.5	1.8	2.0	2.2	2.3	2.5	2.7	2.9	3.1	3.2	3.4	3.6	3.7	3.9	4.1	4.2	4.4	4.5	4.7	4.8	5.0	5.1
84	0.0	0.0	0.0	0.0	0.0	0.0	0.0	0.0	0.0	0.0	0.0	0.0	0.0	0.3	0.5	0.7	0.9	1.1	1.4	1.6	1.8	1.9	2.1	2.3	2.5	2.7	2.8	3.0	3.2	3.3	3.5	3.7	3.8	4.0	4.1	4.3	4.4	4.6	4.7
83	0.0	0.0	0.0	0.0	0.0	0.0	0.0	0.0	0.0	0.0	0.0	0.0	0.0	0.0	0.1	0.3	0.5	0.7	1.0	1.2	1.4	1.5	1.7	1.9	2.1	2.3	2.4	2.6	2.8	2.9	3.1	3.3	3.4	3.6	3.7	3.9	4.0	4.2	4.3
82	0.0	0.0	0.0	0.0	0.0	0.0	0.0	0.0	0.0	0.0	0.0	0.0	0.0	0.0	0.0	0.0	0.1	0.3	0.6	0.8	1.0	1.1	1.3	1.5	1.7	1.9	2.0	2.2	2.4	2.5	2.7	2.9	3.0	3.2	3.3	3.5	3.6	3.8	3.9
81	0.0	0.0	0.0	0.0	0.0	0.0	0.0	0.0	0.0	0.0	0.0	0.0	0.0	0.0	0.0	0.0	0.0	0.0	0.2	0.4	0.6	0.7	0.9	1.1	1.3	1.5	1.6	1.8	2.0	2.1	2.3	2.5	2.6	2.8	2.9	3.1	3.2	3.4	3.5
80	0.0	0.0	0.0	0.0	0.0	0.0	0.0	0.0	0.0	0.0	0.0	0.0	0.0	0.0	0.0	0.0	0.0	0.0	0.0	0.0	0.2	0.3	0.5	0.7	0.9	1.1	1.2	1.4	1.6	1.7	1.9	2.1	2.2	2.4	2.5	2.7	2.8	3.0	3.1
79	0.0	0.0	0.0	0.0	0.0	0.0	0.0	0.0	0.0	0.0	0.0	0.0	0.0	0.0	0.0	0.0	0.0	0.0	0.0	0.0	0.0	0.0	0.1	0.3	0.5	0.7	0.8	1.0	1.2	1.3	1.5	1.7	1.8	2.0	2.1	2.3	2.4	2.6	2.7
78	0.0	0.0	0.0	0.0	0.0	0.0	0.0	0.0	0.0	0.0	0.0	0.0	0.0	0.0	0.0	0.0	0.0	0.0	0.0	0.0	0.0	0.0	0.0	0.0	0.1	0.3	0.4	0.6	0.8	0.9	1.1	1.3	1.4	1.6	1.7	1.9	2.0	2.2	2.3
77	0.0	0.0	0.0	0.0	0.0	0.0	0.0	0.0	0.0	0.0	0.0	0.0	0.0	0.0	0.0	0.0	0.0	0.0	0.0	0.0	0.0	0.0	0.0	0.0	0.0	0.0	0.0	0.2	0.4	0.5	0.7	0.9	1.0	1.2	1.3	1.5	1.6	1.8	1.9
76	0.0	0.0	0.0	0.0	0.0	0.0	0.0	0.0	0.0	0.0	0.0	0.0	0.0	0.0	0.0	0.0	0.0	0.0	0.0	0.0	0.0	0.0	0.0	0.0	0.0	0.0	0.0	0.0	0.0	0.1	0.3	0.5	0.6	0.8	0.9	1.1	1.2	1.4	1.5
75	0.0	0.0	0.0	0.0	0.0	0.0	0.0	0.0	0.0	0.0	0.0	0.0	0.0	0.0	0.0	0.0	0.0	0.0	0.0	0.0	0.0	0.0	0.0	0.0	0.0	0.0	0.0	0.0	0.0	0.0	0.0	0.1	0.2	0.4	0.5	0.7	0.8	1.0	1.1
74	0.0	0.0	0.0	0.0	0.0	0.0	0.0	0.0	0.0	0.0	0.0	0.0	0.0	0.0	0.0	0.0	0.0	0.0	0.0	0.0	0.0	0.0	0.0	0.0	0.0	0.0	0.0	0.0	0.0	0.0	0.0	0.0	0.0	0.0	0.1	0.3	0.4	0.6	0.7
73	0.0	0.0	0.0	0.0	0.0	0.0	0.0	0.0	0.0	0.0	0.0	0.0	0.0	0.0	0.0	0.0	0.0	0.0	0.0	0.0	0.0	0.0	0.0	0.0	0.0	0.0	0.0	0.0	0.0	0.0	0.0	0.0	0.0	0.0	0.0	0.0	0.0	0.2	0.3
72	0.0	0.0	0.0	0.0	0.0	0.0	0.0	0.0	0.0	0.0	0.0	0.0	0.0	0.0	0.0	0.0	0.0	0.0	0.0	0.0	0.0	0.0	0.0	0.0	0.0	0.0	0.0	0.0	0.0	0.0	0.0	0.0	0.0	0.0	0.0	0.0	0.0	0.0	0.0
71	0.0	0.0	0.0	0.0	0.0	0.0	0.0	0.0	0.0	0.0	0.0	0.0	0.0	0.0	0.0	0.0	0.0	0.0	0.0	0.0	0.0	0.0	0.0	0.0	0.0	0.0	0.0	0.0	0.0	0.0	0.0	0.0	0.0	0.0	0.0	0.0	0.0	0.0	0.0
70	0.0	0.0	0.0	0.0	0.0	0.0	0.0	0.0	0.0	0.0	0.0	0.0	0.0	0.0	0.0	0.0	0.0	0.0	0.0	0.0	0.0	0.0	0.0	0.0	0.0	0.0	0.0	0.0	0.0	0.0	0.0	0.0	0.0	0.0	0.0	0.0	0.0	0.0	0.0

LISTED CALL OPTION PRICE WHEN EXERCISE PRICE IS 110

NUMBER OF WEEKS BEFORE THE OPTION EXPIRES

Common Stock Price	1	2	3	4	5	6	7	8	9	10	11	12	13	14	15	16	17	18	19	20	21	22	23	24	25	26	27	28	29	30	31	32	33	34	35	36	37	38	39
144	34.1	34.2	34.4	34.5	34.6	34.7	34.9	35.0	35.1	35.2	35.4	35.5	35.6	35.7	35.8	36.0	36.1	36.2	36.3	36.5	36.6	36.7	36.8	37.0	37.1	37.2	37.3	37.4	37.6	37.7	37.8	37.9	38.1	38.2	38.3	38.4	38.6	38.7	38.8
142	32.1	32.3	32.4	32.5	32.7	32.8	32.9	33.1	33.2	33.3	33.5	33.6	33.7	33.9	34.0	34.1	34.3	34.4	34.5	34.7	34.8	34.9	35.1	35.2	35.3	35.5	35.6	35.7	35.9	36.0	36.1	36.3	36.4	36.5	36.7	36.8	36.9	37.1	37.2
140	30.1	30.3	30.4	30.6	30.7	30.9	31.0	31.1	31.3	31.4	31.6	31.7	31.9	32.0	32.2	32.3	32.4	32.6	32.7	32.9	33.0	33.2	33.3	33.4	33.6	33.7	33.9	34.0	34.2	34.3	34.5	34.6	34.7	34.9	35.0	35.2	35.3	35.5	35.6
138	28.2	28.3	28.5	28.6	28.8	28.9	29.1	29.2	29.4	29.5	29.7	29.8	30.0	30.2	30.3	30.5	30.6	30.8	30.9	31.1	31.2	31.4	31.5	31.7	31.8	32.0	32.2	32.3	32.5	32.6	32.8	32.9	33.1	33.2	33.4	33.5	33.7	33.9	34.0
136	26.2	26.3	26.4	26.7	26.8	27.0	27.1	27.3	27.5	27.6	27.8	28.0	28.1	28.3	28.5	28.6	28.8	29.0	29.1	29.3	29.4	29.6	29.8	29.9	30.1	30.3	30.4	30.6	30.8	30.9	31.1	31.3	31.4	31.6	31.7	31.9	32.1	32.2	32.4
134	24.2	24.3	24.5	24.7	24.9	25.0	25.2	25.4	25.6	25.7	25.9	26.1	26.3	26.4	26.6	26.8	27.0	27.1	27.3	27.5	27.7	27.8	28.0	28.2	28.4	28.5	28.7	28.9	29.1	29.2	29.4	29.6	29.8	29.9	30.1	30.3	30.5	30.6	30.8
132	22.2	22.4	22.6	22.7	22.9	23.1	23.3	23.5	23.7	23.8	24.0	24.2	24.4	24.6	24.8	25.0	25.1	25.3	25.5	25.7	25.9	26.1	26.2	26.4	26.6	26.8	27.0	27.2	27.4	27.5	27.7	27.9	28.1	28.3	28.5	28.7	28.8	29.0	29.2
130	20.2	20.4	20.6	20.8	21.0	21.2	21.4	21.6	21.8	22.0	22.1	22.3	22.5	22.7	22.9	23.1	23.3	23.5	23.7	23.9	24.1	24.3	24.5	24.7	24.9	25.1	25.3	25.5	25.7	25.9	26.0	26.2	26.4	26.6	26.8	27.0	27.2	27.4	27.6
128	18.2	18.4	18.6	18.8	19.0	19.2	19.4	19.6	19.8	20.1	20.3	20.5	20.7	20.9	21.1	21.3	21.5	21.7	21.9	22.1	22.3	22.5	22.7	22.9	23.1	23.3	23.5	23.7	24.0	24.2	24.4	24.6	24.8	25.0	25.2	25.4	25.6	25.8	26.0
126	16.2	16.4	16.6	16.9	17.1	17.3	17.5	17.7	17.9	18.2	18.4	18.6	18.8	19.0	19.2	19.4	19.7	19.9	20.1	20.3	20.5	20.7	21.0	21.2	21.4	21.6	21.8	22.0	22.2	22.5	22.7	22.9	23.1	23.3	23.5	23.8	24.0	24.2	24.4
124	14.2	14.5	14.7	14.9	15.1	15.4	15.6	15.8	16.0	16.3	16.5	16.7	16.9	17.2	17.4	17.6	17.8	18.1	18.3	18.5	18.7	19.0	19.2	19.4	19.6	19.9	20.1	20.3	20.5	20.8	21.0	21.2	21.5	21.7	21.9	22.1	22.4	22.6	22.8
122	12.2	12.5	12.7	12.9	13.2	13.4	13.7	13.9	14.1	14.4	14.6	14.8	15.1	15.3	15.5	15.8	16.0	16.2	16.5	16.7	17.0	17.2	17.4	17.7	17.9	18.1	18.4	18.6	18.8	19.1	19.3	19.6	19.8	20.0	20.3	20.5	20.7	21.0	21.2
120	10.2	10.5	10.7	11.0	11.3	11.5	11.8	12.0	12.3	12.6	12.8	13.0	13.2	13.5	13.7	14.0	14.2	14.5	14.8	15.0	15.3	15.5	15.7	16.0	16.1	16.3	16.6	16.8	17.0	17.3	17.5	17.8	18.0	18.2	18.5	18.7	18.9	19.2	19.4
118	8.3	8.5	8.8	9.1	9.4	9.6	9.9	10.2	10.5	10.8	11.0	11.2	11.5	11.8	12.0	12.3	12.5	12.8	13.0	13.2	13.5	13.7	13.9	14.2	14.4	14.6	14.9	15.1	15.2	15.5	15.7	16.0	16.2	16.4	16.7	16.9	17.1	17.4	17.6
116	6.3	6.6	6.8	7.2	7.5	7.7	8.1	8.4	8.7	9.0	9.3	9.6	9.9	10.3	10.5	10.8	11.0	11.3	11.5	11.7	12.0	12.2	12.4	12.7	12.9	13.1	13.3	13.5	13.7	14.0	14.2	14.5	14.7	14.8	14.9	15.1	15.3	15.6	15.8
114	4.5	4.7	5.0	5.5	6.0	6.4	6.8	7.1	7.5	7.8	8.1	8.4	8.7	8.9	9.2	9.4	9.7	9.9	10.1	10.4	10.6	10.8	11.0	11.2	11.4	11.6	11.8	12.0	12.1	12.3	12.5	12.7	12.8	13.0	13.2	13.3	13.5	13.7	13.8
112	2.8	3.6	4.2	4.7	5.2	5.6	6.0	6.3	6.7	7.0	7.3	7.6	7.9	8.1	8.4	8.6	8.9	9.1	9.3	9.6	9.8	9.9	10.2	10.4	10.6	10.8	11.0	11.2	11.3	11.5	11.7	11.9	12.0	12.2	12.4	12.5	12.7	12.9	13.0
110	2.0	2.8	3.4	3.9	4.4	4.8	5.2	5.5	5.9	6.2	6.5	6.8	7.1	7.3	7.6	7.8	8.1	8.3	8.5	8.8	9.0	9.2	9.4	9.6	9.8	9.9	10.2	10.4	10.5	10.7	10.9	11.1	11.2	11.4	11.6	11.7	11.9	12.1	12.2
108	1.2	2.0	2.6	3.1	3.6	4.0	4.4	4.7	5.1	5.4	5.7	6.0	6.3	6.5	6.8	7.0	7.3	7.5	7.7	8.0	8.2	8.4	8.6	8.8	9.0	9.2	9.4	9.6	9.7	9.9	10.1	10.3	10.4	10.6	10.8	10.9	11.1	11.3	11.4
106	0.4	1.2	1.8	2.3	2.8	3.2	3.6	3.9	4.3	4.6	4.9	5.2	5.5	5.7	6.0	6.2	6.5	6.7	6.9	7.2	7.4	7.6	7.8	8.0	8.2	8.4	8.6	8.8	8.9	9.1	9.3	9.5	9.6	9.8	9.9	10.1	10.3	10.5	10.6
104	0.0	0.4	1.0	1.5	2.0	2.4	2.8	3.1	3.5	3.8	4.1	4.4	4.7	4.9	5.2	5.4	5.7	5.9	6.1	6.4	6.6	6.8	7.0	7.2	7.4	7.6	7.8	8.0	8.1	8.3	8.5	8.7	8.8	9.0	9.2	9.3	9.5	9.7	9.8
102	0.0	0.0	0.2	0.7	1.2	1.6	2.0	2.3	2.7	3.0	3.3	3.6	3.9	4.1	4.4	4.6	4.9	5.1	5.3	5.6	5.8	6.0	6.2	6.4	6.6	6.8	7.0	7.2	7.3	7.5	7.7	7.9	8.0	8.2	8.4	8.5	8.7	8.9	9.0
100	0.0	0.0	0.0	0.0	0.4	0.8	1.2	1.5	1.9	2.2	2.5	2.8	3.1	3.3	3.6	3.8	4.1	4.3	4.5	4.8	5.0	5.2	5.4	5.6	5.8	6.0	6.2	6.4	6.5	6.7	6.9	7.1	7.2	7.4	7.6	7.7	7.9	8.1	8.2
99	0.0	0.0	0.0	0.0	0.0	0.4	0.8	1.1	1.5	1.8	2.1	2.4	2.7	2.9	3.2	3.4	3.7	3.9	4.1	4.4	4.6	4.8	5.0	5.2	5.4	5.6	5.8	6.0	6.1	6.3	6.5	6.7	6.8	7.0	7.2	7.3	7.5	7.7	7.8
98	0.0	0.0	0.0	0.0	0.0	0.0	0.4	0.7	1.1	1.4	1.7	2.0	2.3	2.5	2.8	3.0	3.3	3.5	3.7	4.0	4.2	4.4	4.6	4.8	5.0	5.2	5.4	5.6	5.7	5.9	6.1	6.3	6.4	6.6	6.8	6.9	7.1	7.3	7.4
97	0.0	0.0	0.0	0.0	0.0	0.0	0.0	0.3	0.7	1.0	1.3	1.6	1.9	2.1	2.4	2.6	2.9	3.1	3.3	3.6	3.8	4.0	4.2	4.4	4.6	4.8	5.0	5.2	5.3	5.5	5.7	5.9	6.0	6.2	6.4	6.5	6.7	6.9	7.0
96	0.0	0.0	0.0	0.0	0.0	0.0	0.0	0.0	0.3	0.6	0.9	1.2	1.5	1.7	2.0	2.2	2.5	2.7	2.9	3.2	3.4	3.6	3.8	4.0	4.2	4.4	4.6	4.8	4.9	5.1	5.3	5.5	5.6	5.8	6.0	6.1	6.3	6.5	6.6
95	0.0	0.0	0.0	0.0	0.0	0.0	0.0	0.0	0.0	0.2	0.5	0.8	1.1	1.3	1.6	1.8	2.1	2.3	2.5	2.8	3.0	3.2	3.4	3.6	3.8	4.0	4.2	4.4	4.5	4.7	4.9	5.1	5.2	5.4	5.6	5.7	5.9	6.1	6.2
94	0.0	0.0	0.0	0.0	0.0	0.0	0.0	0.0	0.0	0.0	0.1	0.4	0.7	0.9	1.2	1.4	1.7	1.9	2.1	2.4	2.6	2.8	3.0	3.2	3.4	3.6	3.8	4.0	4.1	4.3	4.5	4.7	4.8	5.0	5.2	5.3	5.5	5.7	5.8
93	0.0	0.0	0.0	0.0	0.0	0.0	0.0	0.0	0.0	0.0	0.0	0.0	0.3	0.5	0.8	1.0	1.3	1.5	1.7	2.0	2.2	2.4	2.6	2.8	3.0	3.2	3.4	3.6	3.7	3.9	4.1	4.3	4.4	4.6	4.8	4.9	5.1	5.3	5.4
92	0.0	0.0	0.0	0.0	0.0	0.0	0.0	0.0	0.0	0.0	0.0	0.0	0.0	0.1	0.4	0.6	0.9	1.1	1.3	1.6	1.8	2.0	2.2	2.4	2.6	2.8	3.0	3.2	3.3	3.5	3.7	3.9	4.0	4.2	4.4	4.5	4.7	4.9	5.0
91	0.0	0.0	0.0	0.0	0.0	0.0	0.0	0.0	0.0	0.0	0.0	0.0	0.0	0.0	0.0	0.2	0.5	0.7	0.9	1.2	1.4	1.6	1.8	2.0	2.2	2.4	2.6	2.8	2.9	3.1	3.3	3.5	3.6	3.8	4.0	4.1	4.3	4.5	4.6
90	0.0	0.0	0.0	0.0	0.0	0.0	0.0	0.0	0.0	0.0	0.0	0.0	0.0	0.0	0.0	0.0	0.1	0.3	0.5	0.8	1.0	1.2	1.4	1.6	1.8	2.0	2.2	2.4	2.5	2.7	2.9	3.1	3.2	3.4	3.6	3.7	3.9	4.1	4.2
89	0.0	0.0	0.0	0.0	0.0	0.0	0.0	0.0	0.0	0.0	0.0	0.0	0.0	0.0	0.0	0.0	0.0	0.0	0.1	0.4	0.6	0.8	1.0	1.2	1.4	1.6	1.8	2.0	2.1	2.3	2.5	2.7	2.8	3.0	3.2	3.3	3.5	3.7	3.8
88	0.0	0.0	0.0	0.0	0.0	0.0	0.0	0.0	0.0	0.0	0.0	0.0	0.0	0.0	0.0	0.0	0.0	0.0	0.0	0.0	0.2	0.4	0.6	0.8	1.0	1.2	1.4	1.6	1.7	1.9	2.1	2.3	2.4	2.6	2.8	2.9	3.1	3.3	3.4
87	0.0	0.0	0.0	0.0	0.0	0.0	0.0	0.0	0.0	0.0	0.0	0.0	0.0	0.0	0.0	0.0	0.0	0.0	0.0	0.0	0.0	0.0	0.2	0.4	0.6	0.8	1.0	1.2	1.3	1.5	1.7	1.9	2.0	2.2	2.4	2.5	2.7	2.9	3.0
86	0.0	0.0	0.0	0.0	0.0	0.0	0.0	0.0	0.0	0.0	0.0	0.0	0.0	0.0	0.0	0.0	0.0	0.0	0.0	0.0	0.0	0.0	0.0	0.0	0.2	0.4	0.6	0.8	0.9	1.1	1.3	1.5	1.6	1.8	2.0	2.1	2.3	2.5	2.6
85	0.0	0.0	0.0	0.0	0.0	0.0	0.0	0.0	0.0	0.0	0.0	0.0	0.0	0.0	0.0	0.0	0.0	0.0	0.0	0.0	0.0	0.0	0.0	0.0	0.0	0.0	0.2	0.4	0.5	0.7	0.9	1.1	1.2	1.4	1.6	1.7	1.9	2.1	2.2
84	0.0	0.0	0.0	0.0	0.0	0.0	0.0	0.0	0.0	0.0	0.0	0.0	0.0	0.0	0.0	0.0	0.0	0.0	0.0	0.0	0.0	0.0	0.0	0.0	0.0	0.0	0.0	0.0	0.1	0.3	0.5	0.7	0.8	1.0	1.2	1.3	1.5	1.7	1.8
83	0.0	0.0	0.0	0.0	0.0	0.0	0.0	0.0	0.0	0.0	0.0	0.0	0.0	0.0	0.0	0.0	0.0	0.0	0.0	0.0	0.0	0.0	0.0	0.0	0.0	0.0	0.0	0.0	0.0	0.0	0.1	0.3	0.4	0.6	0.8	0.9	1.1	1.3	1.4
82	0.0	0.0	0.0	0.0	0.0	0.0	0.0	0.0	0.0	0.0	0.0	0.0	0.0	0.0	0.0	0.0	0.0	0.0	0.0	0.0	0.0	0.0	0.0	0.0	0.0	0.0	0.0	0.0	0.0	0.0	0.0	0.0	0.0	0.2	0.4	0.5	0.7	0.9	1.0
81	0.0	0.0	0.0	0.0	0.0	0.0	0.0	0.0	0.0	0.0	0.0	0.0	0.0	0.0	0.0	0.0	0.0	0.0	0.0	0.0	0.0	0.0	0.0	0.0	0.0	0.0	0.0	0.0	0.0	0.0	0.0	0.0	0.0	0.0	0.0	0.1	0.3	0.5	0.6
80	0.0	0.0	0.0	0.0	0.0	0.0	0.0	0.0	0.0	0.0	0.0	0.0	0.0	0.0	0.0	0.0	0.0	0.0	0.0	0.0	0.0	0.0	0.0	0.0	0.0	0.0	0.0	0.0	0.0	0.0	0.0	0.0	0.0	0.0	0.0	0.0	0.0	0.1	0.2
79	0.0	0.0	0.0	0.0	0.0	0.0	0.0	0.0	0.0	0.0	0.0	0.0	0.0	0.0	0.0	0.0	0.0	0.0	0.0	0.0	0.0	0.0	0.0	0.0	0.0	0.0	0.0	0.0	0.0	0.0	0.0	0.0	0.0	0.0	0.0	0.0	0.0	0.0	0.0
78	0.0	0.0	0.0	0.0	0.0	0.0	0.0	0.0	0.0	0.0	0.0	0.0	0.0	0.0	0.0	0.0	0.0	0.0	0.0	0.0	0.0	0.0	0.0	0.0	0.0	0.0	0.0	0.0	0.0	0.0	0.0	0.0	0.0	0.0	0.0	0.0	0.0	0.0	0.0
77	0.0	0.0	0.0	0.0	0.0	0.0	0.0	0.0	0.0	0.0	0.0	0.0	0.0	0.0	0.0	0.0	0.0	0.0	0.0	0.0	0.0	0.0	0.0	0.0	0.0	0.0	0.0	0.0	0.0	0.0	0.0	0.0	0.0	0.0	0.0	0.0	0.0	0.0	0.0

LISTED CALL OPTION PRICE WHEN EXERCISE PRICE IS 120

NUMBER OF WEEKS BEFORE THE OPTION EXPIRES

Common Stock Price	1	2	3	4	5	6	7	8	9	10	11	12	13	14	15	16	17	18	19	20	21	22	23	24	25	26	27	28	29	30	31	32	33	34	35	36	37	38	39
156	36.1	36.3	36.4	36.6	36.7	36.8	37.0	37.1	37.3	37.4	37.5	37.7	37.8	38.0	38.1	38.2	38.4	38.5	38.7	38.8	38.9	39.1	39.2	39.4	39.5	39.6	39.8	39.9	40.1	40.2	40.3	40.5	40.6	40.8	40.9	41.0	41.2	41.3	41.5
154	34.2	34.3	34.5	34.6	34.8	34.9	35.1	35.2	35.4	35.5	35.7	35.8	36.0	36.1	36.3	36.4	36.6	36.7	36.9	37.0	37.2	37.3	37.5	37.6	37.8	37.9	38.1	38.2	38.4	38.5	38.7	38.8	39.0	39.1	39.3	39.4	39.6	39.7	39.9
152	32.2	32.3	32.5	32.6	32.8	33.0	33.1	33.3	33.4	33.6	33.8	33.9	34.1	34.2	34.4	34.6	34.7	34.9	35.0	35.2	35.4	35.5	35.7	35.9	36.0	36.2	36.3	36.5	36.7	36.8	37.0	37.1	37.3	37.5	37.6	37.8	37.9	38.1	38.3
150	30.2	30.3	30.5	30.7	30.9	31.0	31.2	31.4	31.5	31.7	31.9	32.0	32.2	32.4	32.6	32.7	32.9	33.1	33.2	33.4	33.6	33.8	33.9	34.1	34.3	34.4	34.6	34.8	35.0	35.1	35.3	35.5	35.6	35.8	36.0	36.1	36.3	36.5	36.7
148	28.2	28.4	28.5	28.7	28.9	29.1	29.3	29.4	29.6	29.8	29.9	30.2	30.4	30.5	30.7	30.9	31.1	31.3	31.4	31.6	31.8	32.0	32.2	32.3	32.5	32.7	32.9	33.1	33.2	33.4	33.6	33.8	34.0	34.2	34.3	34.5	34.7	34.9	35.1
146	26.2	26.4	26.6	26.8	27.0	27.1	27.3	27.5	27.7	27.9	28.1	28.3	28.5	28.7	28.9	29.1	29.3	29.4	29.6	29.8	30.0	30.2	30.4	30.6	30.8	31.0	31.2	31.4	31.5	31.7	31.9	32.1	32.3	32.5	32.7	32.9	33.1	33.3	33.5
144	24.2	24.4	24.6	24.8	25.0	25.2	25.4	25.6	25.8	26.0	26.2	26.4	26.6	26.8	27.0	27.2	27.4	27.6	27.8	28.0	28.2	28.4	28.6	28.8	29.0	29.2	29.4	29.6	29.8	30.0	30.2	30.4	30.7	30.9	31.1	31.3	31.5	31.7	31.9
142	22.2	22.4	22.6	22.8	23.1	23.3	23.5	23.7	23.9	24.1	24.3	24.5	24.8	25.0	25.2	25.4	25.6	25.8	26.0	26.2	26.4	26.7	26.9	27.1	27.3	27.5	27.7	27.9	28.1	28.4	28.6	28.8	29.0	29.2	29.4	29.6	29.8	30.0	30.3
140	20.2	20.4	20.7	20.9	21.1	21.3	21.6	21.8	22.0	22.2	22.4	22.7	22.9	23.1	23.3	23.6	23.8	24.0	24.2	24.4	24.7	24.9	25.1	25.3	25.6	25.8	26.0	26.2	26.4	26.7	26.9	27.1	27.3	27.5	27.8	28.0	28.2	28.4	28.7
138	18.2	18.5	18.7	18.9	19.2	19.4	19.6	19.9	20.1	20.3	20.6	20.8	21.0	21.3	21.5	21.7	21.9	22.2	22.4	22.6	22.9	23.1	23.3	23.6	23.8	24.0	24.3	24.5	24.7	25.0	25.2	25.4	25.7	25.9	26.1	26.4	26.6	26.8	27.1
136	16.2	16.5	16.7	17.0	17.2	17.5	17.7	17.9	18.2	18.4	18.7	18.9	19.2	19.4	19.6	19.9	20.1	20.4	20.6	20.9	21.1	21.3	21.6	21.8	22.1	22.3	22.5	22.8	23.0	23.3	23.5	23.8	24.0	24.2	24.5	24.7	25.0	25.2	25.5
134	14.3	14.5	14.8	15.0	15.3	15.5	15.8	16.0	16.3	16.5	16.8	17.0	17.3	17.5	17.8	18.0	18.3	18.6	18.8	19.1	19.3	19.6	19.8	20.1	20.3	20.6	20.8	21.1	21.3	21.6	21.8	22.1	22.3	22.6	22.8	23.1	23.4	23.6	23.9
132	12.3	12.5	12.8	13.0	13.3	13.5	13.9	14.1	14.4	14.6	15.0	15.3	15.6	15.8	16.1	16.3	16.6	16.9	17.1	17.4	17.6	17.9	18.1	18.2	18.4	18.7	18.9	19.2	19.4	19.7	19.9	20.2	20.4	20.7	20.9	21.2	21.5	21.7	22.0
130	10.3	10.5	10.8	11.1	11.4	11.6	12.1	12.3	12.6	12.8	13.2	13.5	13.9	14.1	14.4	14.6	14.9	15.2	15.4	15.7	15.9	16.2	16.4	16.7	16.9	17.2	17.4	17.7	17.9	18.2	18.4	18.7	18.9	19.2	19.3	19.4	19.6	19.8	20.1
128	8.4	8.6	8.9	9.2	9.5	9.8	10.3	10.5	10.8	11.0	11.5	11.8	12.2	12.4	12.7	12.9	13.2	13.5	13.7	14.0	14.2	14.5	14.7	15.0	15.2	15.5	15.7	16.0	16.2	16.5	16.7	17.0	17.2	17.5	17.6	17.8	17.8	17.9	18.2
126	6.5	6.7	7.0	7.3	7.6	8.0	8.6	8.8	9.3	9.6	10.1	10.4	10.8	11.0	11.3	11.5	11.8	12.1	12.3	12.6	12.8	13.1	13.3	13.6	13.8	14.1	14.3	14.6	14.8	15.1	15.3	15.6	15.7	15.8	15.9	16.0	16.1	16.2	16.4
124	4.6	4.9	5.3	5.9	6.4	6.8	7.2	7.6	8.0	8.4	8.7	9.0	9.3	9.6	9.9	10.1	10.4	10.7	10.9	11.1	11.4	11.6	11.8	12.1	12.3	12.5	12.7	12.9	13.1	13.3	13.5	13.7	13.9	14.0	14.2	14.4	14.6	14.8	14.9
122	2.9	3.8	4.5	5.1	5.6	6.0	6.4	6.8	7.2	7.6	7.9	8.2	8.5	8.8	9.1	9.3	9.6	9.9	10.1	10.3	10.6	10.8	11.0	11.3	11.5	11.7	11.9	12.1	12.3	12.5	12.7	12.9	13.1	13.2	13.4	13.6	13.8	14.0	14.1
120	2.1	3.0	3.7	4.3	4.8	5.2	5.6	6.0	6.4	6.8	7.1	7.4	7.7	8.0	8.3	8.5	8.8	9.1	9.3	9.5	9.8	10.0	10.2	10.5	10.7	10.9	11.1	11.3	11.5	11.7	11.9	12.1	12.3	12.4	12.6	12.8	13.0	13.2	13.3
118	1.3	2.2	2.9	3.5	4.0	4.4	4.8	5.2	5.6	6.0	6.3	6.6	6.9	7.2	7.5	7.7	8.0	8.3	8.5	8.7	9.0	9.2	9.4	9.7	9.9	10.1	10.3	10.5	10.7	10.9	11.1	11.3	11.5	11.6	11.8	12.0	12.2	12.4	12.5
116	0.5	1.4	2.1	2.7	3.2	3.6	4.0	4.4	4.8	5.2	5.5	5.8	6.1	6.4	6.7	6.9	7.2	7.5	7.7	7.9	8.2	8.4	8.6	8.9	9.1	9.3	9.5	9.7	9.9	10.1	10.3	10.5	10.7	10.8	11.0	11.2	11.4	11.6	11.7
114	0.0	0.6	1.3	1.9	2.4	2.8	3.2	3.6	4.0	4.4	4.7	5.0	5.3	5.6	5.9	6.1	6.4	6.7	6.9	7.1	7.4	7.6	7.8	8.1	8.3	8.5	8.7	8.9	9.1	9.3	9.5	9.7	9.9	10.0	10.2	10.4	10.6	10.8	10.9
112	0.0	0.0	0.5	1.1	1.6	2.0	2.4	2.8	3.2	3.6	3.9	4.2	4.5	4.8	5.1	5.3	5.6	5.9	6.1	6.3	6.6	6.8	7.0	7.3	7.5	7.7	7.9	8.1	8.3	8.5	8.7	8.9	9.1	9.2	9.4	9.6	9.8	9.9	10.1
110	0.0	0.0	0.0	0.3	0.8	1.2	1.6	2.0	2.4	2.8	3.1	3.4	3.7	4.0	4.3	4.5	4.8	5.1	5.3	5.5	5.8	6.0	6.2	6.5	6.7	6.9	7.1	7.3	7.5	7.7	7.9	8.1	8.3	8.4	8.6	8.8	9.0	9.2	9.3
108	0.0	0.0	0.0	0.0	0.0	0.4	0.8	1.2	1.6	2.0	2.3	2.6	2.9	3.2	3.5	3.7	4.0	4.3	4.5	4.7	5.0	5.2	5.4	5.7	5.9	6.1	6.3	6.5	6.7	6.9	7.1	7.3	7.5	7.6	7.8	8.0	8.2	8.4	8.5
106	0.0	0.0	0.0	0.0	0.0	0.0	0.0	0.4	0.8	1.2	1.5	1.8	2.1	2.4	2.7	2.9	3.2	3.5	3.7	3.9	4.2	4.4	4.6	4.9	5.1	5.3	5.5	5.7	5.9	6.1	6.3	6.5	6.7	6.8	7.0	7.2	7.4	7.6	7.7
104	0.0	0.0	0.0	0.0	0.0	0.0	0.0	0.0	0.0	0.4	0.7	1.0	1.3	1.6	1.9	2.1	2.4	2.7	2.9	3.1	3.4	3.6	3.8	4.1	4.3	4.5	4.7	4.9	5.1	5.3	5.5	5.7	5.9	6.0	6.2	6.4	6.6	6.8	6.9
102	0.0	0.0	0.0	0.0	0.0	0.0	0.0	0.0	0.0	0.0	0.0	0.2	0.5	0.8	1.1	1.3	1.6	1.9	2.1	2.3	2.6	2.8	3.0	3.3	3.5	3.7	3.9	4.1	4.3	4.5	4.7	4.9	5.1	5.2	5.4	5.6	5.8	6.0	6.1
100	0.0	0.0	0.0	0.0	0.0	0.0	0.0	0.0	0.0	0.0	0.0	0.0	0.0	0.0	0.3	0.5	0.8	1.1	1.3	1.5	1.8	2.0	2.2	2.5	2.7	2.9	3.1	3.3	3.5	3.7	3.9	4.1	4.3	4.4	4.6	4.8	5.0	5.2	5.3
99	0.0	0.0	0.0	0.0	0.0	0.0	0.0	0.0	0.0	0.0	0.0	0.0	0.0	0.0	0.0	0.1	0.4	0.7	0.9	1.1	1.4	1.6	1.8	2.1	2.3	2.5	2.7	2.9	3.1	3.3	3.5	3.7	3.9	4.0	4.2	4.4	4.6	4.8	4.9
98	0.0	0.0	0.0	0.0	0.0	0.0	0.0	0.0	0.0	0.0	0.0	0.0	0.0	0.0	0.0	0.0	0.0	0.3	0.5	0.7	1.0	1.2	1.4	1.7	1.9	2.1	2.3	2.5	2.7	2.9	3.1	3.3	3.5	3.6	3.8	4.0	4.2	4.4	4.5
97	0.0	0.0	0.0	0.0	0.0	0.0	0.0	0.0	0.0	0.0	0.0	0.0	0.0	0.0	0.0	0.0	0.0	0.0	0.1	0.3	0.6	0.8	1.0	1.3	1.5	1.7	1.9	2.1	2.3	2.5	2.7	2.9	3.1	3.2	3.4	3.6	3.8	4.0	4.1
96	0.0	0.0	0.0	0.0	0.0	0.0	0.0	0.0	0.0	0.0	0.0	0.0	0.0	0.0	0.0	0.0	0.0	0.0	0.0	0.0	0.2	0.4	0.6	0.9	1.1	1.3	1.5	1.7	1.9	2.1	2.3	2.5	2.7	2.8	3.0	3.2	3.4	3.6	3.7
95	0.0	0.0	0.0	0.0	0.0	0.0	0.0	0.0	0.0	0.0	0.0	0.0	0.0	0.0	0.0	0.0	0.0	0.0	0.0	0.0	0.0	0.0	0.2	0.5	0.7	0.9	1.1	1.3	1.5	1.7	1.9	2.1	2.3	2.4	2.6	2.8	3.0	3.2	3.3
94	0.0	0.0	0.0	0.0	0.0	0.0	0.0	0.0	0.0	0.0	0.0	0.0	0.0	0.0	0.0	0.0	0.0	0.0	0.0	0.0	0.0	0.0	0.0	0.1	0.3	0.5	0.7	0.9	1.1	1.3	1.5	1.7	1.9	2.0	2.2	2.4	2.6	2.8	2.9
93	0.0	0.0	0.0	0.0	0.0	0.0	0.0	0.0	0.0	0.0	0.0	0.0	0.0	0.0	0.0	0.0	0.0	0.0	0.0	0.0	0.0	0.0	0.0	0.0	0.0	0.1	0.3	0.5	0.7	0.9	1.1	1.3	1.5	1.6	1.8	2.0	2.2	2.4	2.5
92	0.0	0.0	0.0	0.0	0.0	0.0	0.0	0.0	0.0	0.0	0.0	0.0	0.0	0.0	0.0	0.0	0.0	0.0	0.0	0.0	0.0	0.0	0.0	0.0	0.0	0.0	0.0	0.1	0.3	0.5	0.7	0.9	1.1	1.2	1.4	1.6	1.8	2.0	2.1
91	0.0	0.0	0.0	0.0	0.0	0.0	0.0	0.0	0.0	0.0	0.0	0.0	0.0	0.0	0.0	0.0	0.0	0.0	0.0	0.0	0.0	0.0	0.0	0.0	0.0	0.0	0.0	0.0	0.0	0.1	0.3	0.5	0.7	0.8	1.0	1.2	1.4	1.6	1.7
90	0.0	0.0	0.0	0.0	0.0	0.0	0.0	0.0	0.0	0.0	0.0	0.0	0.0	0.0	0.0	0.0	0.0	0.0	0.0	0.0	0.0	0.0	0.0	0.0	0.0	0.0	0.0	0.0	0.0	0.0	0.0	0.1	0.3	0.4	0.6	0.8	1.0	1.2	1.3
89	0.0	0.0	0.0	0.0	0.0	0.0	0.0	0.0	0.0	0.0	0.0	0.0	0.0	0.0	0.0	0.0	0.0	0.0	0.0	0.0	0.0	0.0	0.0	0.0	0.0	0.0	0.0	0.0	0.0	0.0	0.0	0.0	0.0	0.0	0.2	0.4	0.6	0.8	0.9
88	0.0	0.0	0.0	0.0	0.0	0.0	0.0	0.0	0.0	0.0	0.0	0.0	0.0	0.0	0.0	0.0	0.0	0.0	0.0	0.0	0.0	0.0	0.0	0.0	0.0	0.0	0.0	0.0	0.0	0.0	0.0	0.0	0.0	0.0	0.0	0.0	0.2	0.4	0.5
87	0.0	0.0	0.0	0.0	0.0	0.0	0.0	0.0	0.0	0.0	0.0	0.0	0.0	0.0	0.0	0.0	0.0	0.0	0.0	0.0	0.0	0.0	0.0	0.0	0.0	0.0	0.0	0.0	0.0	0.0	0.0	0.0	0.0	0.0	0.0	0.0	0.0	0.0	0.1
86	0.0	0.0	0.0	0.0	0.0	0.0	0.0	0.0	0.0	0.0	0.0	0.0	0.0	0.0	0.0	0.0	0.0	0.0	0.0	0.0	0.0	0.0	0.0	0.0	0.0	0.0	0.0	0.0	0.0	0.0	0.0	0.0	0.0	0.0	0.0	0.0	0.0	0.0	0.0
85	0.0	0.0	0.0	0.0	0.0	0.0	0.0	0.0	0.0	0.0	0.0	0.0	0.0	0.0	0.0	0.0	0.0	0.0	0.0	0.0	0.0	0.0	0.0	0.0	0.0	0.0	0.0	0.0	0.0	0.0	0.0	0.0	0.0	0.0	0.0	0.0	0.0	0.0	0.0
84	0.0	0.0	0.0	0.0	0.0	0.0	0.0	0.0	0.0	0.0	0.0	0.0	0.0	0.0	0.0	0.0	0.0	0.0	0.0	0.0	0.0	0.0	0.0	0.0	0.0	0.0	0.0	0.0	0.0	0.0	0.0	0.0	0.0	0.0	0.0	0.0	0.0	0.0	0.0

LISTED CALL OPTION PRICE WHEN EXERCISE PRICE IS 130

NUMBER OF WEEKS BEFORE THE OPTION EXPIRES

Common Stock Price	1	2	3	4	5	6	7	8	9	10	11	12	13	14	15	16	17	18	19	20	21	22	23	24	25	26	27	28	29	30	31	32	33	34	35	36	37	38	39
170	40.1	40.3	40.4	40.6	40.7	40.9	41.0	41.2	41.3	41.5	41.6	41.8	41.9	42.1	42.2	42.3	42.5	42.6	42.8	42.9	43.1	43.2	43.4	43.5	43.7	43.8	44.0	44.1	44.2	44.4	44.5	44.7	44.8	45.0	45.1	45.3	45.4	45.6	45.7
168	38.2	38.3	38.5	38.6	38.8	38.9	39.1	39.3	39.4	39.6	39.7	39.9	40.0	40.2	40.4	40.5	40.7	40.8	41.0	41.1	41.3	41.4	41.6	41.8	41.9	42.1	42.2	42.4	42.5	42.7	42.9	43.0	43.2	43.3	43.5	43.6	43.8	44.0	44.1
166	36.2	36.3	36.5	36.7	36.8	37.0	37.2	37.3	37.5	37.7	37.8	38.0	38.2	38.3	38.5	38.7	38.8	39.0	39.2	39.3	39.5	39.7	39.8	40.0	40.2	40.3	40.5	40.7	40.8	41.0	41.2	41.3	41.5	41.7	41.8	42.0	42.2	42.3	42.5
164	34.2	34.4	34.5	34.7	34.9	35.1	35.2	35.4	35.6	35.8	36.0	36.1	36.3	36.5	36.7	36.8	37.0	37.2	37.4	37.5	37.7	37.9	38.1	38.3	38.4	38.6	38.8	39.0	39.1	39.3	39.5	39.7	39.9	40.0	40.2	40.4	40.6	40.7	40.9
162	32.2	32.4	32.6	32.8	32.9	33.1	33.3	33.5	33.7	33.9	34.1	34.3	34.4	34.6	34.8	35.0	35.2	35.4	35.6	35.8	35.9	36.1	36.3	36.5	36.7	36.9	37.1	37.3	37.4	37.6	37.8	38.0	38.2	38.4	38.6	38.8	38.9	39.1	39.3
160	30.2	30.4	30.6	30.8	31.0	31.2	31.4	31.6	31.8	32.0	32.2	32.4	32.6	32.8	33.0	33.2	33.4	33.6	33.8	34.0	34.2	34.4	34.5	34.7	34.9	35.1	35.3	35.5	35.7	35.9	36.1	36.3	36.5	36.7	36.9	37.1	37.3	37.5	37.7
158	28.2	28.4	28.6	28.8	29.0	29.2	29.5	29.7	29.9	30.1	30.3	30.5	30.7	30.9	31.1	31.3	31.5	31.7	32.0	32.2	32.4	32.6	32.8	33.0	33.2	33.4	33.6	33.8	34.0	34.2	34.5	34.7	34.9	35.1	35.3	35.5	35.7	35.9	36.1
156	26.2	26.4	26.7	26.9	27.1	27.3	27.5	27.7	28.0	28.2	28.4	28.6	28.8	29.1	29.3	29.5	29.7	29.9	30.1	30.4	30.6	30.8	31.0	31.2	31.5	31.7	31.9	32.1	32.3	32.6	32.8	33.0	33.2	33.4	33.6	33.9	34.1	34.3	34.5
154	24.2	24.5	24.7	24.9	25.1	25.4	25.6	25.8	26.1	26.3	26.5	26.7	27.0	27.2	27.4	27.7	27.9	28.1	28.3	28.6	28.8	29.0	29.3	29.5	29.7	29.9	30.2	30.4	30.6	30.9	31.1	31.3	31.5	31.8	32.0	32.2	32.5	32.7	32.9
152	22.2	22.5	22.7	23.0	23.2	23.4	23.7	23.9	24.1	24.4	24.6	24.9	25.1	25.3	25.6	25.8	26.1	26.3	26.5	26.8	27.0	27.3	27.5	27.7	28.0	28.2	28.4	28.7	28.9	29.2	29.4	29.6	29.9	30.1	30.4	30.6	30.8	31.1	31.3
150	20.2	20.5	20.7	21.0	21.2	21.5	21.7	22.0	22.2	22.5	22.7	23.0	23.2	23.5	23.7	24.0	24.2	24.5	24.7	25.0	25.2	25.5	25.7	26.0	26.2	26.5	26.7	27.0	27.2	27.5	27.7	28.0	28.2	28.5	28.7	29.0	29.2	29.5	29.7
148	18.3	18.5	18.8	19.0	19.3	19.6	19.8	20.1	20.3	20.6	20.9	21.1	21.4	21.6	21.9	22.1	22.4	22.7	22.9	23.2	23.4	23.7	24.0	24.2	24.5	24.7	25.0	25.3	25.5	25.8	26.0	26.3	26.6	26.8	27.1	27.3	27.6	27.9	28.1
146	16.3	16.5	16.8	17.1	17.3	17.6	17.9	18.2	18.4	18.7	19.0	19.2	19.5	19.8	20.0	20.3	20.6	20.9	21.1	21.4	21.7	21.9	22.2	22.5	22.7	23.0	23.3	23.5	23.8	24.1	24.4	24.6	24.9	25.2	25.4	25.7	26.0	26.2	26.5
144	14.3	14.6	14.8	15.1	15.4	15.7	16.0	16.2	16.5	16.8	17.1	17.4	17.6	17.9	18.2	18.5	18.8	19.0	19.3	19.6	19.9	20.2	20.4	20.7	21.0	21.3	21.6	21.8	22.1	22.4	22.7	23.0	23.2	23.5	23.8	24.1	24.4	24.6	24.9
142	12.3	12.6	12.8	13.1	13.4	13.8	14.1	14.3	14.6	14.9	15.3	15.6	15.8	16.1	16.4	16.7	17.0	17.2	17.5	17.8	18.2	18.5	18.7	19.0	19.3	19.6	19.9	20.1	20.4	20.7	20.9	21.2	21.4	21.6	21.9	22.2	22.5	22.7	23.0
140	10.4	10.6	10.9	11.2	11.5	12.0	12.3	12.5	12.8	13.1	13.5	13.9	14.1	14.4	14.7	15.0	15.3	15.5	15.7	16.0	16.4	16.7	16.9	17.2	17.5	17.8	18.1	18.3	18.6	18.9	19.2	19.5	19.7	19.9	20.4	20.6	21.0	21.4	21.5
138	8.5	8.7	9.0	9.3	9.7	10.1	10.4	10.7	11.1	11.5	11.8	12.2	12.4	12.7	13.0	13.3	13.6	13.8	14.1	14.5	14.9	15.2	15.4	15.7	16.0	16.3	16.6	16.9	17.2	17.5	17.8	18.1	18.4	18.7	19.0	19.3	19.6	19.8	19.9
136	6.6	6.8	7.1	7.4	8.0	8.6	9.0	9.4	9.8	10.2	10.6	10.9	11.1	11.5	11.8	12.1	12.4	12.6	12.9	13.2	13.6	13.9	14.1	14.4	14.7	15.0	15.3	15.5	15.8	16.1	16.4	16.5	16.7	16.9	17.1	17.4	17.8	17.9	17.9
134	4.7	5.0	5.6	6.2	6.8	7.3	7.7	8.1	8.5	8.9	9.3	9.6	9.9	10.3	10.6	10.9	11.1	11.4	11.7	11.9	12.2	12.4	12.7	12.9	13.2	13.4	13.6	13.8	14.1	14.3	14.5	14.7	14.9	15.1	15.3	15.5	15.7	15.9	16.0
132	3.1	4.1	4.8	5.4	6.0	6.5	6.9	7.3	7.7	8.1	8.5	8.8	9.1	9.5	9.8	10.1	10.3	10.6	10.9	11.1	11.4	11.6	11.9	12.1	12.4	12.6	12.8	13.0	13.3	13.5	13.7	13.9	14.1	14.3	14.5	14.7	14.9	15.1	15.2
130	2.3	3.3	4.0	4.6	5.2	5.7	6.1	6.5	6.9	7.3	7.7	8.0	8.3	8.7	9.0	9.3	9.5	9.8	10.1	10.3	10.6	10.8	11.1	11.3	11.6	11.8	12.0	12.2	12.5	12.7	12.9	13.1	13.3	13.5	13.7	13.9	14.1	14.3	14.4
128	1.5	2.5	3.2	3.8	4.4	4.9	5.3	5.7	6.1	6.5	6.9	7.2	7.5	7.9	8.2	8.5	8.7	9.0	9.3	9.5	9.8	10.0	10.3	10.5	10.8	11.0	11.2	11.4	11.7	11.9	12.1	12.3	12.5	12.7	12.9	13.1	13.3	13.5	13.6
126	0.7	1.7	2.4	3.0	3.6	4.1	4.5	4.9	5.3	5.7	6.1	6.4	6.7	7.1	7.4	7.7	7.9	8.2	8.5	8.7	9.0	9.2	9.5	9.7	9.9	10.2	10.4	10.6	10.9	11.1	11.3	11.5	11.7	11.9	12.1	12.3	12.5	12.7	12.8
124	0.0	0.9	1.6	2.2	2.8	3.3	3.7	4.1	4.5	4.9	5.3	5.6	5.9	6.3	6.6	6.9	7.1	7.4	7.7	7.9	8.2	8.4	8.7	8.9	9.2	9.4	9.6	9.8	10.1	10.3	10.5	10.7	10.9	11.1	11.3	11.5	11.7	11.9	12.0
122	0.0	0.1	0.8	1.4	2.0	2.5	2.9	3.3	3.7	4.1	4.5	4.8	5.1	5.5	5.8	6.1	6.3	6.6	6.9	7.1	7.4	7.6	7.9	8.1	8.4	8.6	8.8	9.0	9.3	9.5	9.7	9.9	10.1	10.3	10.5	10.7	10.9	11.1	11.2
120	0.0	0.0	0.0	0.6	1.2	1.7	2.1	2.5	2.9	3.3	3.7	4.0	4.3	4.7	5.0	5.3	5.5	5.8	6.1	6.3	6.6	6.8	7.1	7.3	7.6	7.8	8.0	8.2	8.5	8.7	8.9	9.1	9.3	9.5	9.7	9.9	10.1	10.3	10.4
118	0.0	0.0	0.0	0.0	0.4	0.9	1.3	1.7	2.1	2.5	2.9	3.2	3.5	3.9	4.2	4.5	4.7	5.0	5.3	5.5	5.8	6.0	6.3	6.5	6.8	7.0	7.2	7.4	7.7	7.9	8.1	8.3	8.5	8.7	8.9	9.1	9.3	9.5	9.6
116	0.0	0.0	0.0	0.0	0.0	0.1	0.5	0.9	1.3	1.7	2.1	2.4	2.7	3.1	3.4	3.7	3.9	4.2	4.5	4.7	5.0	5.2	5.5	5.7	6.0	6.2	6.4	6.6	6.9	7.1	7.3	7.5	7.7	7.9	8.1	8.3	8.5	8.7	8.8
114	0.0	0.0	0.0	0.0	0.0	0.0	0.0	0.1	0.5	0.9	1.3	1.6	1.9	2.3	2.6	2.9	3.1	3.4	3.7	3.9	4.2	4.4	4.7	4.9	5.2	5.4	5.6	5.8	6.1	6.3	6.5	6.7	6.9	7.1	7.3	7.5	7.7	7.9	8.0
112	0.0	0.0	0.0	0.0	0.0	0.0	0.0	0.0	0.0	0.1	0.5	0.8	1.1	1.5	1.8	2.1	2.3	2.6	2.9	3.1	3.4	3.6	3.9	4.1	4.4	4.6	4.8	5.0	5.3	5.5	5.7	5.9	6.1	6.3	6.5	6.7	6.9	7.1	7.2
110	0.0	0.0	0.0	0.0	0.0	0.0	0.0	0.0	0.0	0.0	0.0	0.0	0.3	0.7	1.0	1.3	1.5	1.8	2.1	2.3	2.6	2.8	3.1	3.3	3.6	3.8	4.0	4.2	4.5	4.7	4.9	5.1	5.3	5.5	5.7	5.9	6.1	6.3	6.4
108	0.0	0.0	0.0	0.0	0.0	0.0	0.0	0.0	0.0	0.0	0.0	0.0	0.0	0.0	0.2	0.5	0.7	1.0	1.3	1.5	1.8	2.0	2.3	2.5	2.8	3.0	3.2	3.4	3.7	3.9	4.1	4.3	4.5	4.7	4.9	5.1	5.3	5.5	5.6
106	0.0	0.0	0.0	0.0	0.0	0.0	0.0	0.0	0.0	0.0	0.0	0.0	0.0	0.0	0.0	0.0	0.0	0.2	0.5	0.7	1.0	1.2	1.5	1.7	2.0	2.2	2.4	2.6	2.9	3.1	3.3	3.5	3.7	3.9	4.1	4.3	4.5	4.7	4.8
104	0.0	0.0	0.0	0.0	0.0	0.0	0.0	0.0	0.0	0.0	0.0	0.0	0.0	0.0	0.0	0.0	0.0	0.0	0.0	0.0	0.2	0.4	0.7	0.9	1.2	1.4	1.6	1.8	2.1	2.3	2.5	2.7	2.9	3.1	3.3	3.5	3.7	3.9	4.0
102	0.0	0.0	0.0	0.0	0.0	0.0	0.0	0.0	0.0	0.0	0.0	0.0	0.0	0.0	0.0	0.0	0.0	0.0	0.0	0.0	0.0	0.0	0.0	0.1	0.4	0.6	0.8	1.0	1.3	1.5	1.7	1.9	2.1	2.3	2.5	2.7	2.9	3.1	3.2
100	0.0	0.0	0.0	0.0	0.0	0.0	0.0	0.0	0.0	0.0	0.0	0.0	0.0	0.0	0.0	0.0	0.0	0.0	0.0	0.0	0.0	0.0	0.0	0.0	0.0	0.0	0.0	0.2	0.5	0.7	0.9	1.1	1.3	1.5	1.7	1.9	2.1	2.3	2.4
99	0.0	0.0	0.0	0.0	0.0	0.0	0.0	0.0	0.0	0.0	0.0	0.0	0.0	0.0	0.0	0.0	0.0	0.0	0.0	0.0	0.0	0.0	0.0	0.0	0.0	0.0	0.0	0.0	0.1	0.3	0.5	0.7	0.9	1.1	1.3	1.5	1.7	1.9	2.0
98	0.0	0.0	0.0	0.0	0.0	0.0	0.0	0.0	0.0	0.0	0.0	0.0	0.0	0.0	0.0	0.0	0.0	0.0	0.0	0.0	0.0	0.0	0.0	0.0	0.0	0.0	0.0	0.0	0.0	0.0	0.1	0.3	0.5	0.7	0.9	1.1	1.3	1.5	1.6
97	0.0	0.0	0.0	0.0	0.0	0.0	0.0	0.0	0.0	0.0	0.0	0.0	0.0	0.0	0.0	0.0	0.0	0.0	0.0	0.0	0.0	0.0	0.0	0.0	0.0	0.0	0.0	0.0	0.0	0.0	0.0	0.0	0.1	0.3	0.5	0.7	0.9	1.1	1.2
96	0.0	0.0	0.0	0.0	0.0	0.0	0.0	0.0	0.0	0.0	0.0	0.0	0.0	0.0	0.0	0.0	0.0	0.0	0.0	0.0	0.0	0.0	0.0	0.0	0.0	0.0	0.0	0.0	0.0	0.0	0.0	0.0	0.0	0.0	0.1	0.3	0.5	0.7	0.8
95	0.0	0.0	0.0	0.0	0.0	0.0	0.0	0.0	0.0	0.0	0.0	0.0	0.0	0.0	0.0	0.0	0.0	0.0	0.0	0.0	0.0	0.0	0.0	0.0	0.0	0.0	0.0	0.0	0.0	0.0	0.0	0.0	0.0	0.0	0.0	0.0	0.1	0.3	0.4
94	0.0	0.0	0.0	0.0	0.0	0.0	0.0	0.0	0.0	0.0	0.0	0.0	0.0	0.0	0.0	0.0	0.0	0.0	0.0	0.0	0.0	0.0	0.0	0.0	0.0	0.0	0.0	0.0	0.0	0.0	0.0	0.0	0.0	0.0	0.0	0.0	0.0	0.0	0.0
93	0.0	0.0	0.0	0.0	0.0	0.0	0.0	0.0	0.0	0.0	0.0	0.0	0.0	0.0	0.0	0.0	0.0	0.0	0.0	0.0	0.0	0.0	0.0	0.0	0.0	0.0	0.0	0.0	0.0	0.0	0.0	0.0	0.0	0.0	0.0	0.0	0.0	0.0	0.0
92	0.0	0.0	0.0	0.0	0.0	0.0	0.0	0.0	0.0	0.0	0.0	0.0	0.0	0.0	0.0	0.0	0.0	0.0	0.0	0.0	0.0	0.0	0.0	0.0	0.0	0.0	0.0	0.0	0.0	0.0	0.0	0.0	0.0	0.0	0.0	0.0	0.0	0.0	0.0
91	0.0	0.0	0.0	0.0	0.0	0.0	0.0	0.0	0.0	0.0	0.0	0.0	0.0	0.0	0.0	0.0	0.0	0.0	0.0	0.0	0.0	0.0	0.0	0.0	0.0	0.0	0.0	0.0	0.0	0.0	0.0	0.0	0.0	0.0	0.0	0.0	0.0	0.0	0.0

LISTED CALL OPTION PRICE WHEN EXERCISE PRICE IS 140

NUMBER OF WEEKS BEFORE THE OPTION EXPIRES

Common Stock Price	1	2	3	4	5	6	7	8	9	10	11	12	13	14	15	16	17	18	19	20	21	22	23	24	25	26	27	28	29	30	31	32	33	34	35	36	37	38	39
182	42.2	42.3	42.5	42.7	42.8	43.0	43.1	43.3	43.5	43.6	43.8	44.0	44.1	44.3	44.4	44.6	44.8	44.9	45.1	45.3	45.4	45.6	45.8	45.9	46.1	46.2	46.4	46.6	46.7	46.9	47.1	47.2	47.4	47.6	47.7	47.9	48.0	48.2	48.4
180	40.2	40.3	40.5	40.7	40.9	41.0	41.2	41.4	41.6	41.7	41.9	42.1	42.3	42.4	42.6	42.8	43.0	43.1	43.3	43.5	43.6	43.8	44.0	44.2	44.3	44.5	44.7	44.9	45.0	45.2	45.4	45.6	45.7	45.9	46.1	46.2	46.4	46.6	46.8
178	38.2	38.4	38.6	38.7	38.9	39.1	39.3	39.5	39.7	39.8	40.0	40.2	40.4	40.6	40.8	40.9	41.1	41.3	41.5	41.7	41.9	42.0	42.2	42.4	42.6	42.8	43.0	43.1	43.3	43.5	43.7	43.9	44.1	44.3	44.4	44.6	44.8	45.0	45.2
176	36.2	36.4	36.6	36.8	37.0	37.2	37.4	37.6	37.7	37.9	38.1	38.3	38.5	38.7	38.9	39.1	39.3	39.5	39.7	39.9	40.1	40.3	40.5	40.7	40.9	41.0	41.2	41.4	41.6	41.8	42.0	42.2	42.4	42.6	42.8	43.0	43.2	43.4	43.6
174	34.2	34.4	34.6	34.8	35.0	35.2	35.4	35.6	35.8	36.0	36.2	36.5	36.7	36.9	37.1	37.3	37.5	37.7	37.9	38.1	38.3	38.5	38.7	38.9	39.1	39.3	39.5	39.7	39.9	40.1	40.3	40.5	40.7	40.9	41.2	41.4	41.6	41.8	42.0
172	32.2	32.4	32.6	32.9	33.1	33.3	33.5	33.7	33.9	34.1	34.4	34.6	34.8	35.0	35.2	35.4	35.6	35.9	36.1	36.3	36.5	36.7	36.9	37.2	37.4	37.6	37.8	38.0	38.2	38.4	38.7	38.9	39.1	39.3	39.5	39.7	39.9	40.2	40.4
170	30.2	30.4	30.7	30.9	31.1	31.3	31.6	31.8	32.0	32.2	32.5	32.7	32.9	33.1	33.4	33.6	33.8	34.0	34.3	34.5	34.7	34.9	35.2	35.4	35.6	35.8	36.1	36.3	36.5	36.7	37.0	37.2	37.4	37.6	37.9	38.1	38.3	38.5	38.8
168	28.2	28.5	28.7	28.9	29.2	29.4	29.6	29.9	30.1	30.4	30.6	30.8	31.1	31.3	31.5	31.8	32.0	32.2	32.5	32.7	32.9	33.2	33.4	33.6	33.9	34.1	34.3	34.6	34.8	35.1	35.3	35.5	35.8	36.0	36.2	36.5	36.7	36.9	37.2
166	26.2	26.5	26.7	27.0	27.2	27.5	27.7	28.0	28.2	28.5	28.7	28.9	29.2	29.4	29.7	29.9	30.2	30.4	30.7	30.9	31.2	31.4	31.6	31.9	32.1	32.4	32.6	32.9	33.1	33.4	33.6	33.9	34.1	34.3	34.6	34.8	35.1	35.3	35.6
164	24.3	24.5	24.8	25.0	25.3	25.5	25.8	26.0	26.3	26.6	26.8	27.1	27.3	27.6	27.8	28.1	28.3	28.6	28.9	29.1	29.4	29.6	29.9	30.1	30.4	30.6	30.9	31.2	31.4	31.7	31.9	32.2	32.4	32.7	32.9	33.2	33.5	33.7	34.0
162	22.3	22.5	22.8	23.1	23.3	23.6	23.9	24.1	24.4	24.7	24.9	25.2	25.5	25.7	26.0	26.3	26.5	26.8	27.1	27.3	27.6	27.8	28.1	28.4	28.6	28.9	29.2	29.4	29.7	29.9	30.2	30.5	30.8	31.0	31.3	31.6	31.8	32.1	32.4
160	20.3	20.6	20.8	21.1	21.4	21.7	21.9	22.2	22.5	22.8	23.0	23.3	23.6	23.9	24.1	24.4	24.7	25.0	25.2	25.5	25.8	26.1	26.4	26.6	26.9	27.2	27.5	27.7	28.0	28.3	28.6	28.8	29.1	29.4	29.7	29.9	30.3	30.5	30.8
158	18.3	18.6	18.9	19.1	19.4	19.7	20.0	20.3	20.6	20.9	21.2	21.4	21.7	22.0	22.3	22.6	22.9	23.2	23.4	23.7	24.0	24.3	24.6	24.9	25.2	25.4	25.7	26.0	26.3	26.6	26.9	27.2	27.5	27.7	28.0	28.3	28.6	28.9	29.2
156	16.3	16.6	16.9	17.2	17.5	17.8	18.1	18.4	18.7	19.0	19.3	19.6	19.9	20.2	20.5	20.7	21.0	21.3	21.6	21.9	22.2	22.5	22.8	23.1	23.4	23.7	24.0	24.3	24.6	24.9	25.2	25.5	25.8	26.1	26.4	26.7	27.0	27.3	27.6
154	14.3	14.6	14.9	15.2	15.6	15.9	16.2	16.5	16.8	17.1	17.4	17.7	18.0	18.3	18.6	18.8	19.1	19.4	19.7	20.0	20.3	20.6	20.9	21.2	21.5	21.8	22.1	22.4	22.7	23.0	23.3	23.6	23.9	24.2	24.5	24.8	25.1	25.4	25.6
152	12.4	12.6	12.9	13.3	13.7	14.0	14.3	14.6	14.9	15.2	15.5	15.8	16.1	16.4	16.7	16.9	17.2	17.5	17.8	18.1	18.4	18.7	19.0	19.3	19.6	19.9	20.2	20.5	20.8	21.1	21.4	21.7	22.0	22.3	22.6	22.9	23.2	23.5	23.7
150	10.5	10.7	11.0	11.4	11.8	12.1	12.4	12.7	13.1	13.4	13.7	14.0	14.3	14.6	14.9	15.1	15.4	15.7	16.0	16.3	16.6	16.9	17.2	17.5	17.8	18.1	18.4	18.7	19.0	19.3	19.6	19.9	20.2	20.5	20.8	21.1	21.3	21.6	21.8
148	8.6	8.8	9.1	9.5	9.9	10.2	10.6	10.9	11.3	11.6	11.9	12.2	12.5	12.8	13.1	13.3	13.6	13.9	14.2	14.5	14.8	15.1	15.4	15.6	15.9	16.2	16.5	16.8	17.1	17.4	17.7	18.0	18.3	18.6	18.9	19.2	19.4	19.7	19.9
146	6.7	6.9	7.3	7.7	8.0	8.5	9.0	9.4	9.9	10.3	10.7	11.0	11.4	11.7	12.0	12.4	12.7	13.0	13.3	13.5	13.8	14.1	14.3	14.6	14.9	15.1	15.3	15.6	15.8	16.0	16.3	16.5	16.7	16.9	17.1	17.3	17.5	17.8	18.0
144	4.8	5.1	5.9	6.6	7.2	7.7	8.2	8.6	9.1	9.5	9.9	10.2	10.6	10.9	11.2	11.6	11.9	12.2	12.5	12.7	13.0	13.3	13.5	13.8	14.1	14.3	14.5	14.8	15.0	15.2	15.5	15.7	15.9	16.1	16.3	16.5	16.7	17.0	17.2
142	3.3	4.3	5.1	5.8	6.4	6.9	7.4	7.8	8.3	8.7	9.1	9.4	9.8	10.1	10.4	10.8	11.1	11.4	11.7	11.9	12.2	12.5	12.7	13.0	13.3	13.5	13.7	14.0	14.2	14.4	14.7	14.9	15.1	15.3	15.5	15.7	15.9	16.2	16.4
140	2.5	3.5	4.3	5.0	5.6	6.1	6.6	7.0	7.5	7.9	8.3	8.6	9.0	9.3	9.6	9.9	10.3	10.6	10.9	11.1	11.4	11.7	11.9	12.2	12.5	12.7	12.9	13.2	13.4	13.6	13.9	14.1	14.3	14.5	14.7	14.9	15.1	15.4	15.6
138	1.7	2.7	3.5	4.2	4.8	5.3	5.8	6.2	6.7	7.1	7.5	7.8	8.2	8.5	8.8	9.2	9.5	9.8	10.1	10.3	10.6	10.9	11.1	11.4	11.7	11.9	12.1	12.4	12.6	12.8	13.1	13.3	13.5	13.7	13.9	14.1	14.3	14.6	14.8
136	0.9	1.9	2.7	3.4	4.0	4.5	5.0	5.4	5.9	6.3	6.7	7.0	7.4	7.7	8.0	8.4	8.7	9.0	9.3	9.5	9.8	10.1	10.3	10.6	10.9	11.1	11.3	11.6	11.8	12.0	12.3	12.5	12.7	12.9	13.1	13.3	13.5	13.8	14.0
134	0.1	1.1	1.9	2.6	3.2	3.7	4.2	4.6	5.1	5.5	5.9	6.2	6.6	6.9	7.2	7.6	7.9	8.2	8.5	8.7	9.0	9.3	9.5	9.8	10.1	10.3	10.5	10.8	11.0	11.2	11.5	11.7	11.9	12.1	12.3	12.5	12.7	13.0	13.2
132	0.0	0.3	1.1	1.8	2.4	2.9	3.4	3.8	4.3	4.7	5.1	5.4	5.8	6.1	6.4	6.8	7.1	7.4	7.7	7.9	8.2	8.5	8.7	9.0	9.3	9.5	9.7	9.9	10.2	10.4	10.7	10.9	11.1	11.3	11.5	11.7	11.9	12.2	12.4
130	0.0	0.0	0.3	1.0	1.6	2.1	2.6	3.0	3.5	3.9	4.3	4.6	5.0	5.3	5.6	6.0	6.3	6.6	6.9	7.1	7.4	7.7	7.9	8.2	8.5	8.7	8.9	9.2	9.4	9.6	9.9	10.1	10.3	10.5	10.7	10.9	11.1	11.4	11.6
128	0.0	0.0	0.0	0.2	0.8	1.3	1.8	2.2	2.7	3.1	3.5	3.8	4.2	4.5	4.8	5.2	5.5	5.8	6.1	6.3	6.6	6.9	7.1	7.4	7.7	7.9	8.1	8.4	8.6	8.8	9.1	9.3	9.5	9.7	9.9	10.1	10.3	10.6	10.8
126	0.0	0.0	0.0	0.0	0.0	0.5	1.0	1.4	1.9	2.3	2.7	3.0	3.4	3.7	4.0	4.4	4.7	5.0	5.3	5.5	5.8	6.1	6.3	6.6	6.9	7.1	7.3	7.6	7.8	8.0	8.3	8.5	8.7	8.9	9.1	9.3	9.5	9.8	9.9
124	0.0	0.0	0.0	0.0	0.0	0.0	0.2	0.6	1.1	1.5	1.9	2.2	2.6	2.9	3.2	3.6	3.9	4.2	4.5	4.7	5.0	5.3	5.5	5.8	6.1	6.3	6.5	6.8	7.0	7.2	7.5	7.7	7.9	8.1	8.3	8.5	8.7	9.0	9.2
122	0.0	0.0	0.0	0.0	0.0	0.0	0.0	0.0	0.3	0.7	1.1	1.4	1.8	2.1	2.4	2.8	3.1	3.4	3.7	3.9	4.2	4.5	4.7	5.0	5.3	5.5	5.7	6.0	6.2	6.4	6.7	6.9	7.1	7.3	7.5	7.7	7.9	8.2	8.4
120	0.0	0.0	0.0	0.0	0.0	0.0	0.0	0.0	0.0	0.0	0.3	0.6	1.0	1.3	1.6	2.0	2.3	2.6	2.9	3.1	3.4	3.7	3.9	4.2	4.5	4.7	4.9	5.2	5.4	5.6	5.9	6.1	6.3	6.5	6.7	6.9	7.1	7.4	7.6
118	0.0	0.0	0.0	0.0	0.0	0.0	0.0	0.0	0.0	0.0	0.0	0.0	0.2	0.5	0.8	1.2	1.5	1.8	2.1	2.3	2.6	2.9	3.1	3.4	3.7	3.9	4.1	4.4	4.6	4.8	5.1	5.3	5.5	5.7	5.9	6.1	6.3	6.6	6.8
116	0.0	0.0	0.0	0.0	0.0	0.0	0.0	0.0	0.0	0.0	0.0	0.0	0.0	0.0	0.0	0.4	0.7	1.0	1.3	1.5	1.8	2.1	2.3	2.6	2.9	3.1	3.3	3.6	3.8	4.0	4.3	4.5	4.7	4.9	5.1	5.3	5.5	5.8	6.0
114	0.0	0.0	0.0	0.0	0.0	0.0	0.0	0.0	0.0	0.0	0.0	0.0	0.0	0.0	0.0	0.0	0.0	0.2	0.5	0.7	1.0	1.3	1.5	1.8	2.1	2.3	2.5	2.8	3.0	3.2	3.5	3.7	3.9	4.1	4.3	4.5	4.7	5.0	5.2
112	0.0	0.0	0.0	0.0	0.0	0.0	0.0	0.0	0.0	0.0	0.0	0.0	0.0	0.0	0.0	0.0	0.0	0.0	0.0	0.0	0.2	0.5	0.7	1.0	1.3	1.5	1.7	2.0	2.2	2.4	2.7	2.9	3.1	3.3	3.5	3.7	3.9	4.2	4.4
110	0.0	0.0	0.0	0.0	0.0	0.0	0.0	0.0	0.0	0.0	0.0	0.0	0.0	0.0	0.0	0.0	0.0	0.0	0.0	0.0	0.0	0.0	0.0	0.2	0.5	0.7	0.9	1.2	1.4	1.6	1.9	2.1	2.3	2.5	2.7	2.9	3.1	3.4	3.6
108	0.0	0.0	0.0	0.0	0.0	0.0	0.0	0.0	0.0	0.0	0.0	0.0	0.0	0.0	0.0	0.0	0.0	0.0	0.0	0.0	0.0	0.0	0.0	0.0	0.0	0.0	0.1	0.4	0.6	0.8	1.1	1.3	1.5	1.7	1.9	2.1	2.3	2.6	2.8
106	0.0	0.0	0.0	0.0	0.0	0.0	0.0	0.0	0.0	0.0	0.0	0.0	0.0	0.0	0.0	0.0	0.0	0.0	0.0	0.0	0.0	0.0	0.0	0.0	0.0	0.0	0.0	0.0	0.0	0.0	0.3	0.5	0.7	0.9	1.1	1.3	1.5	1.8	2.0
104	0.0	0.0	0.0	0.0	0.0	0.0	0.0	0.0	0.0	0.0	0.0	0.0	0.0	0.0	0.0	0.0	0.0	0.0	0.0	0.0	0.0	0.0	0.0	0.0	0.0	0.0	0.0	0.0	0.0	0.0	0.0	0.0	0.0	0.1	0.3	0.5	0.7	1.0	1.2
102	0.0	0.0	0.0	0.0	0.0	0.0	0.0	0.0	0.0	0.0	0.0	0.0	0.0	0.0	0.0	0.0	0.0	0.0	0.0	0.0	0.0	0.0	0.0	0.0	0.0	0.0	0.0	0.0	0.0	0.0	0.0	0.0	0.0	0.0	0.0	0.0	0.0	0.2	0.4
100	0.0	0.0	0.0	0.0	0.0	0.0	0.0	0.0	0.0	0.0	0.0	0.0	0.0	0.0	0.0	0.0	0.0	0.0	0.0	0.0	0.0	0.0	0.0	0.0	0.0	0.0	0.0	0.0	0.0	0.0	0.0	0.0	0.0	0.0	0.0	0.0	0.0	0.0	0.0
99	0.0	0.0	0.0	0.0	0.0	0.0	0.0	0.0	0.0	0.0	0.0	0.0	0.0	0.0	0.0	0.0	0.0	0.0	0.0	0.0	0.0	0.0	0.0	0.0	0.0	0.0	0.0	0.0	0.0	0.0	0.0	0.0	0.0	0.0	0.0	0.0	0.0	0.0	0.0
98	0.0	0.0	0.0	0.0	0.0	0.0	0.0	0.0	0.0	0.0	0.0	0.0	0.0	0.0	0.0	0.0	0.0	0.0	0.0	0.0	0.0	0.0	0.0	0.0	0.0	0.0	0.0	0.0	0.0	0.0	0.0	0.0	0.0	0.0	0.0	0.0	0.0	0.0	0.0

LISTED CALL OPTION PRICE WHEN EXERCISE PRICE IS 150

NUMBER OF WEEKS BEFORE THE OPTION EXPIRES

Common Stock Price	1	2	3	4	5	6	7	8	9	10	11	12	13	14	15	16	17	18	19	20	21	22	23	24	25	26	27	28	29	30	31	32	33	34	35	36	37	38	39
196	46.2	46.3	46.5	46.7	46.8	47.0	47.2	47.4	47.5	47.7	47.9	48.0	48.2	48.4	48.5	48.7	48.9	49.1	49.2	49.4	49.6	49.7	49.9	50.1	50.2	50.4	50.6	50.8	50.9	51.1	51.3	51.4	51.6	51.8	51.9	52.1	52.3	52.5	52.6
194	44.2	44.4	44.5	44.7	44.9	45.1	45.3	45.4	45.6	45.8	46.0	46.2	46.3	46.5	46.7	46.9	47.1	47.2	47.4	47.6	47.8	48.0	48.1	48.3	48.5	48.7	48.9	49.0	49.2	49.4	49.6	49.8	49.9	50.1	50.3	50.5	50.7	50.8	51.0
192	42.2	42.4	42.6	42.8	43.0	43.1	43.3	43.5	43.7	43.9	44.1	44.3	44.5	44.7	44.9	45.0	45.2	45.4	45.6	45.8	46.0	46.2	46.4	46.6	46.8	46.9	47.1	47.3	47.5	47.7	47.9	48.1	48.3	48.5	48.7	48.9	49.0	49.2	49.4
190	40.2	40.4	40.6	40.8	41.0	41.2	41.4	41.6	41.8	42.0	42.2	42.4	42.6	42.8	43.0	43.2	43.4	43.6	43.8	44.0	44.2	44.4	44.6	44.8	45.0	45.2	45.4	45.6	45.8	46.0	46.2	46.4	46.6	46.8	47.0	47.2	47.4	47.6	47.8
188	38.2	38.4	38.6	38.8	39.1	39.3	39.5	39.7	39.9	40.1	40.3	40.5	40.7	41.0	41.2	41.4	41.6	41.8	42.0	42.2	42.4	42.6	42.9	43.1	43.3	43.5	43.7	43.9	44.1	44.3	44.5	44.7	45.0	45.2	45.4	45.6	45.8	46.0	46.2
186	36.2	36.4	36.7	36.9	37.1	37.3	37.5	37.8	38.0	38.2	38.4	38.7	38.9	39.1	39.3	39.5	39.8	39.9	40.2	40.4	40.6	40.9	41.1	41.3	41.5	41.8	42.0	42.2	42.4	42.6	42.9	43.1	43.3	43.5	43.7	44.0	44.2	44.4	44.6
184	34.2	34.5	34.7	34.9	35.2	35.4	35.6	35.9	36.1	36.3	36.5	36.8	37.0	37.2	37.5	37.7	37.9	38.2	38.4	38.6	38.9	39.1	39.3	39.6	39.8	40.0	40.2	40.5	40.7	40.9	41.2	41.4	41.6	41.9	42.1	42.3	42.6	42.8	43.0
182	32.2	32.5	32.7	33.0	33.2	33.5	33.7	33.9	34.2	34.4	34.7	34.9	35.1	35.4	35.6	35.9	36.1	36.4	36.6	36.8	37.1	37.3	37.6	37.8	38.0	38.3	38.5	38.8	39.0	39.3	39.5	39.7	39.9	40.2	40.5	40.7	40.9	41.2	41.4
180	30.3	30.5	30.8	31.0	31.3	31.5	31.8	32.0	32.3	32.5	32.8	33.0	33.3	33.5	33.8	34.0	34.3	34.5	34.8	35.0	35.3	35.5	35.8	36.0	36.3	36.6	36.8	37.1	37.3	37.6	37.8	38.1	38.3	38.6	38.8	39.1	39.3	39.6	39.8
178	28.3	28.5	28.8	29.0	29.3	29.6	29.8	30.1	30.4	30.6	30.9	31.1	31.4	31.7	31.9	32.2	32.5	32.7	33.0	33.2	33.5	33.8	34.0	34.3	34.6	34.8	35.1	35.3	35.6	35.9	36.1	36.4	36.7	36.9	37.2	37.4	37.7	38.0	38.2
176	26.3	26.5	26.8	27.1	27.4	27.6	27.9	28.2	28.5	28.7	29.8	29.3	29.5	29.8	30.1	30.4	30.6	30.9	31.2	31.4	31.7	32.0	32.3	32.5	32.8	33.1	33.4	33.6	33.9	34.2	34.4	34.7	35.0	35.3	35.5	35.8	36.1	36.4	36.6
174	24.3	24.6	24.8	25.1	25.4	25.7	26.0	26.3	26.5	26.8	27.1	27.4	27.7	28.0	28.2	28.5	28.8	29.1	29.4	29.7	29.9	30.2	30.5	30.8	31.1	31.4	31.6	31.9	32.2	32.5	32.8	33.0	33.3	33.6	33.9	34.2	34.5	34.7	35.0
172	22.3	22.6	22.9	23.2	23.5	23.8	24.1	24.3	24.6	24.9	25.2	25.5	25.8	26.1	26.4	26.7	27.0	27.3	27.6	27.9	28.2	28.4	28.7	29.0	29.3	29.6	29.9	30.2	30.5	30.8	31.1	31.4	31.7	32.0	32.3	32.5	32.8	33.1	33.4
170	20.3	20.6	20.9	21.2	21.5	21.8	22.1	22.4	22.7	23.0	23.3	23.6	23.9	24.2	24.5	24.9	25.2	25.5	25.8	26.1	26.4	26.7	27.0	27.3	27.6	27.9	28.2	28.5	28.8	29.1	29.4	29.7	30.0	30.3	30.6	30.9	31.2	31.5	31.8
168	18.3	18.6	18.9	19.3	19.6	19.9	20.2	20.5	20.8	21.1	21.4	21.8	22.1	22.4	22.7	23.0	23.3	23.6	24.0	24.3	24.6	24.9	25.2	25.5	25.8	26.1	26.5	26.8	27.1	27.4	27.7	28.0	28.3	28.7	29.0	29.3	29.6	29.9	30.2
166	16.3	16.6	17.0	17.3	17.6	17.9	18.3	18.6	18.9	19.2	19.6	19.9	20.2	28.5	20.9	21.2	21.5	21.8	22.2	22.5	22.8	23.1	23.4	23.8	24.1	24.4	24.7	25.1	25.4	25.7	26.0	26.4	26.7	27.0	27.3	27.7	28.0	28.3	28.6
164	14.3	14.6	15.0	15.4	15.7	16.0	16.3	16.6	16.9	17.2	17.6	18.0	18.3	18.6	19.0	19.3	19.6	19.9	20.3	20.6	20.9	21.2	21.5	21.9	22.2	22.5	22.8	23.2	23.5	23.8	24.1	24.5	24.8	25.1	25.4	25.8	26.1	26.4	26.7
162	12.4	12.7	13.1	13.4	13.8	14.1	14.4	14.7	15.0	15.3	15.7	16.1	16.4	16.7	17.1	17.4	17.7	18.0	18.4	18.7	19.0	19.3	19.6	20.0	20.3	20.6	20.9	21.2	21.6	21.9	22.2	22.6	22.9	23.2	23.5	23.9	24.2	24.5	24.8
160	10.5	10.8	11.2	11.5	11.9	12.2	12.5	12.8	13.1	13.4	13.8	14.2	14.5	14.8	15.2	15.5	15.8	16.1	16.5	16.8	17.1	17.4	17.7	18.1	18.2	18.7	19.0	19.4	19.7	20.0	20.3	20.7	21.0	21.3	21.6	22.0	22.3	22.6	22.9
158	8.7	8.9	9.3	9.6	10.0	10.4	10.6	10.9	11.2	11.6	12.1	12.4	12.8	13.2	13.5	13.9	14.2	14.5	14.8	15.1	15.4	15.7	16.0	16.3	16.5	16.8	17.1	17.5	17.8	18.1	18.4	18.8	19.1	19.4	19.7	20.1	20.4	20.7	21.0
156	6.8	7.0	7.5	7.9	8.4	8.9	9.5	9.9	10.4	10.8	11.3	11.6	12.0	12.4	12.7	13.1	13.4	13.7	14.0	14.3	14.6	14.9	15.2	15.5	15.7	16.0	16.3	16.5	16.8	17.0	17.3	17.5	17.7	18.0	18.2	18.4	18.6	18.8	19.1
154	4.9	5.4	6.2	6.9	7.6	8.1	8.7	9.1	9.6	10.0	10.5	10.8	11.2	11.6	11.9	12.3	12.6	12.9	13.2	13.5	13.8	14.1	14.4	14.7	14.9	15.2	15.5	15.7	16.0	16.2	16.5	16.7	16.9	17.2	17.4	17.6	17.8	18.0	18.3
152	3.5	4.6	5.4	6.1	6.8	7.3	7.9	8.3	8.8	9.2	9.7	10.0	10.4	10.8	11.1	11.5	11.8	12.1	12.4	12.7	13.0	13.3	13.6	13.9	14.1	14.4	14.7	14.9	15.2	15.4	15.7	15.9	16.1	16.4	16.6	16.8	17.0	17.2	17.5
150	2.7	3.8	4.6	5.3	6.0	6.5	7.1	7.5	8.8	8.4	8.9	9.2	9.6	9.9	10.3	10.7	11.0	11.3	11.6	11.9	12.2	12.5	12.8	13.1	13.3	13.6	13.9	14.1	14.4	14.6	14.9	15.1	15.3	15.6	15.8	16.0	16.2	16.4	16.7
148	1.9	3.0	3.8	4.5	5.2	5.7	6.3	6.7	7.2	7.6	8.1	8.4	8.8	9.2	9.5	9.9	10.2	10.5	10.8	11.1	11.4	11.7	12.0	12.3	12.5	12.8	13.1	13.3	13.6	13.8	14.1	14.3	14.5	14.8	15.0	15.2	15.4	15.6	15.9
146	1.1	2.2	3.0	3.7	4.4	4.9	5.5	5.9	6.4	6.8	7.3	7.6	8.0	8.4	8.7	9.1	9.4	9.7	10.0	10.3	10.6	10.9	11.2	11.5	11.7	12.0	12.3	12.5	12.8	13.0	13.3	13.5	13.7	14.0	14.2	14.4	14.6	14.8	15.1
144	0.3	1.4	2.2	2.9	3.6	4.1	4.7	5.1	5.6	6.0	6.5	6.8	7.2	7.6	7.9	8.3	8.6	8.9	9.2	9.5	9.8	10.1	10.4	10.7	10.9	11.2	11.5	11.7	12.0	12.2	12.5	12.7	12.9	13.2	13.4	13.6	13.8	14.0	14.3
142	0.0	0.6	1.4	2.1	2.8	3.3	3.9	4.3	4.8	5.2	5.7	6.0	6.4	6.8	7.1	7.5	7.8	8.1	8.4	8.7	9.0	9.3	9.6	9.9	10.1	10.4	10.7	10.9	11.2	11.4	11.7	11.9	12.1	12.4	12.6	12.8	13.0	13.2	13.5
140	0.0	0.0	0.6	1.3	2.0	2.5	3.1	3.5	4.8	4.4	4.9	5.2	5.6	6.0	6.3	6.7	7.0	7.3	7.6	7.9	8.2	8.5	8.8	9.1	9.3	9.6	9.9	10.1	10.4	10.6	10.9	11.1	11.3	11.6	11.8	12.0	12.2	12.4	12.7
138	0.0	0.0	0.0	0.5	1.2	1.7	2.3	2.7	3.2	3.6	4.1	4.4	4.8	5.2	5.5	5.9	6.2	6.5	6.8	7.1	7.4	7.7	8.0	8.3	8.5	8.8	9.1	9.3	9.6	9.8	10.1	10.3	10.5	10.8	11.0	11.2	11.4	11.6	11.9
136	0.0	0.0	0.0	0.0	0.4	0.9	1.5	1.9	2.4	2.8	3.3	3.6	4.0	4.4	4.7	5.1	5.4	5.7	6.0	6.3	6.6	6.9	7.2	7.5	7.7	8.0	8.3	8.5	8.8	9.0	9.3	9.5	9.7	9.9	10.2	10.4	10.6	10.8	11.1
134	0.0	0.0	0.0	0.0	0.0	0.1	0.7	1.1	1.6	2.0	2.5	2.8	3.2	3.6	3.9	4.3	4.6	4.9	5.2	5.5	5.8	6.1	6.4	6.7	6.9	7.2	7.5	7.7	8.0	8.2	8.5	8.7	8.9	9.2	9.4	9.6	9.8	10.0	10.3
132	0.0	0.0	0.0	0.0	0.0	0.0	0.0	0.3	0.8	1.2	1.7	2.0	2.4	2.8	3.1	3.5	3.8	4.1	4.4	4.7	5.8	5.3	5.6	5.9	6.1	6.4	6.7	6.9	7.2	7.4	7.7	7.9	8.1	8.4	8.6	8.8	9.0	9.2	9.5
130	0.0	0.0	0.0	0.0	0.0	0.0	0.0	0.0	0.0	0.4	0.9	1.2	1.6	2.0	2.3	2.7	3.0	3.3	3.6	3.9	4.2	4.5	4.8	5.1	5.3	5.6	5.9	6.1	6.4	6.6	6.9	7.1	7.3	7.6	7.8	8.0	8.2	8.4	8.7
128	0.0	0.0	0.0	0.0	0.0	0.0	0.0	0.0	0.0	0.0	0.1	0.4	0.8	1.2	1.5	1.9	2.2	2.5	2.8	3.1	3.4	3.7	4.0	4.3	4.5	4.8	5.1	5.3	5.6	5.8	6.1	6.3	6.5	6.8	7.0	7.2	7.4	7.6	7.9
126	0.0	0.0	0.0	0.0	0.0	0.0	0.0	0.0	0.0	0.0	0.0	0.0	0.0	0.4	0.7	1.1	1.4	1.7	2.0	2.3	2.6	2.9	3.2	3.5	3.7	4.0	4.3	4.5	4.8	5.0	5.3	5.5	5.7	6.0	6.2	6.4	6.6	6.8	7.1
124	0.0	0.0	0.0	0.0	0.0	0.0	0.0	0.0	0.0	0.0	0.0	0.0	0.0	0.0	0.0	0.3	0.6	0.9	1.2	1.5	1.8	2.1	2.4	2.7	2.9	3.2	3.5	3.7	4.0	4.2	4.5	4.7	4.9	5.2	5.4	5.6	5.8	6.0	6.3
122	0.0	0.0	0.0	0.0	0.0	0.0	0.0	0.0	0.0	0.0	0.0	0.0	0.0	0.0	0.0	0.0	0.0	0.1	0.4	0.7	1.0	1.3	1.6	1.9	2.1	2.4	2.7	2.9	3.2	3.4	3.7	3.9	4.1	4.4	4.6	4.8	5.0	5.2	5.5
120	0.0	0.0	0.0	0.0	0.0	0.0	0.0	0.0	0.0	0.0	0.0	0.0	0.0	0.0	0.0	0.0	0.0	0.0	0.0	0.0	0.2	0.5	0.8	1.1	1.3	1.6	1.9	2.1	2.4	2.6	2.9	3.1	3.3	3.6	3.8	4.0	4.2	4.4	4.7
118	0.0	0.0	0.0	0.0	0.0	0.0	0.0	0.0	0.0	0.0	0.0	0.0	0.0	0.0	0.0	0.0	0.0	0.0	0.0	0.0	0.0	0.0	0.0	0.3	0.5	0.8	1.1	1.3	1.6	1.8	2.1	2.3	2.5	2.8	3.0	3.2	3.4	3.6	3.9
116	0.0	0.0	0.0	0.0	0.0	0.0	0.0	0.0	0.0	0.0	0.0	0.0	0.0	0.0	0.0	0.0	0.0	0.0	0.0	0.0	0.0	0.0	0.0	0.0	0.0	0.0	0.3	0.5	0.8	1.0	1.3	1.5	1.7	2.0	2.2	2.4	2.6	2.8	3.1
114	0.0	0.0	0.0	0.0	0.0	0.0	0.0	0.0	0.0	0.0	0.0	0.0	0.0	0.0	0.0	0.0	0.0	0.0	0.0	0.0	0.0	0.0	0.0	0.0	0.0	0.0	0.0	0.0	0.0	0.2	0.5	0.7	0.9	1.2	1.4	1.6	1.8	2.0	2.3
112	0.0	0.0	0.0	0.0	0.0	0.0	0.0	0.0	0.0	0.0	0.0	0.0	0.0	0.0	0.0	0.0	0.0	0.0	0.0	0.0	0.0	0.0	0.0	0.0	0.0	0.0	0.0	0.0	0.0	0.0	0.0	0.0	0.1	0.4	0.6	0.8	1.0	1.2	1.5
110	0.0	0.0	0.0	0.0	0.0	0.0	0.0	0.0	0.0	0.0	0.0	0.0	0.0	0.0	0.0	0.0	0.0	0.0	0.0	0.0	0.0	0.0	0.0	0.0	0.0	0.0	0.0	0.0	0.0	0.0	0.0	0.0	0.0	0.0	0.0	0.0	0.2	0.4	0.7
108	0.0	0.0	0.0	0.0	0.0	0.0	0.0	0.0	0.0	0.0	0.0	0.0	0.0	0.0	0.0	0.0	0.0	0.0	0.0	0.0	0.0	0.0	0.0	0.0	0.0	0.0	0.0	0.0	0.0	0.0	0.0	0.0	0.0	0.0	0.0	0.0	0.0	0.0	0.0
106	0.0	0.0	0.0	0.0	0.0	0.0	0.0	0.0	0.0	0.0	0.0	0.0	0.0	0.0	0.0	0.0	0.0	0.0	0.0	0.0	0.0	0.0	0.0	0.0	0.0	0.0	0.0	0.0	0.0	0.0	0.0	0.0	0.0	0.0	0.0	0.0	0.0	0.0	0.0

LISTED PUT OPTION PRICE WHEN EXERCISE PRICE IS 20

NUMBER OF WEEKS BEFORE THE OPTION EXPIRES

Common Stock Price	1	2	3	4	5	6	7	8	9	10	11	12	13	14	15	16	17	18	19	20	21	22	23	24	25	26	27	28	29	30	31	32	33	34	35	36	37	38	39
28	0.0	0.0	0.0	0.0	0.0	0.0	0.0	0.0	0.0	0.0	0.0	0.0	0.0	0.0	0.0	0.0	0.0	0.0	0.0	0.0	0.0	0.0	0.0	0.0	0.0	0.0	0.0	0.0	0.0	0.0	0.0	0.0	0.0	0.0	0.0	0.0	0.0	0.0	0.0
27	0.0	0.0	0.0	0.0	0.0	0.0	0.0	0.0	0.0	0.0	0.0	0.0	0.0	0.0	0.0	0.0	0.0	0.0	0.0	0.0	0.0	0.0	0.0	0.0	0.0	0.0	0.0	0.0	0.0	0.0	0.0	0.0	0.0	0.0	0.0	0.0	0.1	0.1	0.1
26	0.0	0.0	0.0	0.0	0.0	0.0	0.0	0.0	0.0	0.0	0.0	0.0	0.0	0.0	0.0	0.0	0.0	0.0	0.0	0.0	0.0	0.0	0.0	0.0	0.0	0.0	0.0	0.0	0.1	0.1	0.1	0.1	0.2	0.2	0.2	0.2	0.3	0.3	0.3
25	0.0	0.0	0.0	0.0	0.0	0.0	0.0	0.0	0.0	0.0	0.0	0.0	0.0	0.0	0.0	0.0	0.0	0.0	0.0	0.0	0.0	0.0	0.0	0.1	0.1	0.2	0.2	0.2	0.3	0.3	0.3	0.3	0.4	0.4	0.4	0.4	0.5	0.5	0.5
24	0.0	0.0	0.0	0.0	0.0	0.0	0.0	0.0	0.0	0.0	0.0	0.0	0.0	0.0	0.0	0.1	0.1	0.1	0.2	0.2	0.2	0.3	0.3	0.3	0.4	0.4	0.4	0.4	0.5	0.5	0.5	0.5	0.6	0.6	0.6	0.6	0.7	0.7	0.7
23	0.0	0.0	0.0	0.0	0.0	0.0	0.0	0.0	0.0	0.1	0.1	0.2	0.2	0.2	0.3	0.3	0.3	0.4	0.4	0.4	0.5	0.5	0.5	0.6	0.6	0.6	0.6	0.7	0.7	0.7	0.8	0.8	0.8	0.8	0.8	0.9	0.9	0.9	0.9
22	0.0	0.0	0.1	0.1	0.1	0.2	0.2	0.3	0.3	0.4	0.4	0.4	0.5	0.5	0.5	0.6	0.6	0.6	0.7	0.7	0.7	0.8	0.8	0.8	0.8	0.9	0.9	0.9	0.9	1.0	1.0	1.0	1.0	1.0	1.1	1.1	1.1	1.2	1.2
21	0.0	0.1	0.2	0.3	0.3	0.4	0.4	0.5	0.5	0.6	0.6	0.7	0.7	0.8	0.8	0.8	0.9	0.9	0.9	1.0	1.0	1.0	1.1	1.1	1.1	1.1	1.2	1.2	1.2	1.3	1.3	1.3	1.3	1.4	1.4	1.4	1.4	1.4	1.5
20	0.3	0.4	0.5	0.6	0.6	0.7	0.8	0.8	0.9	0.9	0.9	1.0	1.0	1.1	1.1	1.1	1.2	1.2	1.2	1.3	1.3	1.3	1.4	1.4	1.4	1.5	1.5	1.5	1.5	1.6	1.6	1.6	1.6	1.7	1.7	1.7	1.8	1.8	1.8
19	1.0	1.1	1.1	1.2	1.2	1.3	1.3	1.4	1.4	1.5	1.5	1.6	1.6	1.6	1.7	1.7	1.8	1.8	1.9	1.9	2.0	2.0	2.1	2.1	2.2	2.2	2.2	2.3	2.3	2.4	2.4	2.5	2.5	2.6	2.6	2.7	2.7	2.8	2.8
18	2.0	2.1	2.1	2.2	2.2	2.2	2.3	2.3	2.3	2.4	2.4	2.5	2.5	2.5	2.6	2.6	2.7	2.7	2.7	2.8	2.8	2.8	2.9	2.9	3.0	3.0	3.0	3.1	3.1	3.2	3.2	3.2	3.3	3.3	3.3	3.4	3.4	3.5	3.5
17	3.0	3.1	3.1	3.1	3.2	3.2	3.2	3.2	3.3	3.3	3.3	3.4	3.4	3.4	3.5	3.5	3.5	3.6	3.6	3.6	3.6	3.7	3.7	3.7	3.8	3.8	3.8	3.9	3.9	3.9	3.9	4.0	4.0	4.0	4.1	4.1	4.1	4.2	4.2
16	4.0	4.0	4.1	4.1	4.1	4.1	4.2	4.2	4.2	4.2	4.3	4.3	4.3	4.3	4.3	4.4	4.4	4.4	4.4	4.5	4.5	4.5	4.5	4.5	4.6	4.6	4.6	4.6	4.7	4.7	4.7	4.7	4.8	4.8	4.8	4.8	4.8	4.9	4.9
15	5.0	5.0	5.0	5.1	5.1	5.1	5.1	5.1	5.1	5.1	5.2	5.2	5.2	5.2	5.2	5.2	5.3	5.3	5.3	5.3	5.3	5.3	5.3	5.4	5.4	5.4	5.4	5.4	5.4	5.4	5.5	5.5	5.5	5.5	5.5	5.5	5.6	5.6	5.6
14.5	5.5	5.5	5.5	5.5	5.6	5.6	5.6	5.6	5.6	5.6	5.6	5.6	5.6	5.7	5.7	5.7	5.7	5.7	5.7	5.7	5.7	5.7	5.8	5.8	5.8	5.8	5.8	5.8	5.8	5.8	5.8	5.9	5.9	5.9	5.9	5.9	5.9	5.9	5.9
14	6.0	6.0	6.0	6.0	6.0	6.0	6.0	6.1	6.1	6.1	6.1	6.1	6.1	6.1	6.1	6.1	6.1	6.1	6.1	6.1	6.1	6.2	6.2	6.2	6.2	6.2	6.2	6.2	6.2	6.2	6.2	6.2	6.2	6.2	6.2	6.3	6.3	6.3	6.3
13.5	6.5	6.5	6.5	6.5	6.5	6.5	6.5	6.5	6.5	6.5	6.5	6.5	6.5	6.5	6.5	6.6	6.6	6.6	6.6	6.6	6.6	6.6	6.6	6.6	6.6	6.6	6.6	6.6	6.6	6.6	6.6	6.6	6.6	6.6	6.6	6.6	6.6	6.6	6.6
13	7.0	7.0	7.0	7.0	7.0	7.0	7.0	7.0	7.0	7.0	7.0	7.0	7.0	7.0	7.0	7.0	7.0	7.0	7.0	7.0	7.0	7.0	7.0	7.0	7.0	7.0	7.0	7.0	7.0	7.0	7.0	7.0	7.0	7.0	7.0	7.0	7.0	7.0	7.0
12.5	7.5	7.5	7.5	7.5	7.5	7.5	7.5	7.5	7.5	7.5	7.5	7.5	7.5	7.5	7.5	7.5	7.5	7.5	7.5	7.5	7.5	7.5	7.5	7.5	7.5	7.5	7.5	7.5	7.5	7.5	7.5	7.5	7.5	7.5	7.5	7.5	7.5	7.5	7.5
12	8.0	8.0	8.0	8.0	8.0	8.0	8.0	8.0	8.0	8.0	8.0	8.0	8.0	8.0	8.0	8.0	8.0	8.0	8.0	8.0	8.0	8.0	8.0	8.0	8.0	8.0	8.0	8.0	8.0	8.0	8.0	8.0	8.0	8.0	8.0	8.0	8.0	8.0	8.0

LISTED PUT OPTION PRICE WHEN EXERCISE PRICE IS 15

NUMBER OF WEEKS BEFORE THE OPTION EXPIRES

Common Stock Price	1	2	3	4	5	6	7	8	9	10	11	12	13	14	15	16	17	18	19	20	21	22	23	24	25	26	27	28	29	30	31	32	33	34	35	36	37	38	39
21	0.0	0.0	0.0	0.0	0.0	0.0	0.0	0.0	0.0	0.0	0.0	0.0	0.0	0.0	0.0	0.0	0.0	0.0	0.0	0.0	0.0	0.0	0.0	0.0	0.0	0.0	0.0	0.0	0.0	0.0	0.0	0.0	0.0	0.0	0.0	0.0	0.0	0.0	0.0
20	0.0	0.0	0.0	0.0	0.0	0.0	0.0	0.0	0.0	0.0	0.0	0.0	0.0	0.0	0.0	0.0	0.0	0.0	0.0	0.0	0.0	0.0	0.0	0.0	0.0	0.0	0.0	0.0	0.0	0.0	0.0	0.0	0.0	0.1	0.1	0.1	0.1	0.1	0.1
19	0.0	0.0	0.0	0.0	0.0	0.0	0.0	0.0	0.0	0.0	0.0	0.0	0.0	0.0	0.0	0.0	0.0	0.0	0.0	0.0	0.0	0.0	0.0	0.0	0.0	0.1	0.1	0.1	0.1	0.2	0.2	0.2	0.2	0.2	0.3	0.3	0.3	0.3	0.3
18	0.0	0.0	0.0	0.0	0.0	0.0	0.0	0.0	0.0	0.0	0.0	0.0	0.0	0.0	0.0	0.1	0.1	0.1	0.1	0.2	0.2	0.2	0.2	0.2	0.3	0.3	0.3	0.3	0.3	0.4	0.4	0.4	0.4	0.4	0.5	0.5	0.5	0.5	0.5
17	0.0	0.0	0.0	0.0	0.0	0.0	0.0	0.0	0.1	0.1	0.1	0.2	0.2	0.2	0.3	0.3	0.3	0.3	0.4	0.4	0.4	0.4	0.5	0.5	0.5	0.5	0.5	0.6	0.6	0.6	0.6	0.6	0.7	0.7	0.7	0.7	0.7	0.8	0.8
16	0.0	0.0	0.1	0.1	0.2	0.2	0.3	0.3	0.3	0.4	0.4	0.4	0.5	0.5	0.5	0.6	0.6	0.6	0.6	0.7	0.7	0.7	0.7	0.7	0.8	0.8	0.8	0.8	0.8	0.9	0.9	0.9	0.9	0.9	1.0	1.0	1.0	1.0	1.0
15	0.2	0.3	0.4	0.4	0.5	0.5	0.6	0.6	0.6	0.7	0.7	0.7	0.8	0.8	0.8	0.9	0.9	0.9	0.9	1.0	1.0	1.0	1.0	1.0	1.1	1.1	1.1	1.1	1.1	1.2	1.2	1.2	1.2	1.2	1.3	1.3	1.3	1.3	1.3
14.5	0.5	0.6	0.6	0.7	0.7	0.7	0.8	0.8	0.8	0.9	0.9	0.9	1.0	1.0	1.0	1.1	1.1	1.1	1.2	1.2	1.2	1.3	1.3	1.3	1.4	1.4	1.5	1.5	1.5	1.6	1.6	1.7	1.7	1.7	1.8	1.8	1.8	1.9	1.9
14	1.0	1.1	1.1	1.1	1.2	1.2	1.2	1.3	1.3	1.3	1.4	1.4	1.4	1.5	1.5	1.5	1.6	1.6	1.6	1.7	1.7	1.7	1.8	1.8	1.8	1.9	1.9	1.9	2.0	2.0	2.0	2.0	2.1	2.1	2.1	2.2	2.2	2.2	2.3
13.5	1.5	1.6	1.6	1.7	1.7	1.7	1.7	1.7	1.8	1.8	1.8	1.8	1.9	1.9	1.9	2.0	2.0	2.0	2.0	2.1	2.1	2.1	2.2	2.2	2.2	2.2	2.3	2.3	2.3	2.4	2.4	2.4	2.5	2.5	2.5	2.5	2.6	2.6	2.6
13	2.0	2.0	2.1	2.1	2.1	2.1	2.2	2.2	2.2	2.2	2.3	2.3	2.3	2.3	2.4	2.4	2.4	2.4	2.5	2.5	2.5	2.5	2.6	2.6	2.6	2.6	2.7	2.7	2.7	2.8	2.8	2.8	2.8	2.9	2.9	2.9	2.9	3.0	3.0
12.5	2.5	2.6	2.6	2.6	2.6	2.6	2.6	2.7	2.7	2.7	2.7	2.7	2.8	2.8	2.8	2.8	2.8	2.9	2.9	2.9	3.0	3.0	3.0	3.0	3.0	3.0	3.1	3.1	3.1	3.1	3.1	3.2	3.2	3.2	3.2	3.3	3.3	3.3	3.3
12	3.0	3.0	3.1	3.1	3.1	3.1	3.1	3.1	3.2	3.2	3.2	3.2	3.2	3.2	3.2	3.3	3.3	3.3	3.3	3.3	3.4	3.4	3.4	3.4	3.4	3.4	3.5	3.5	3.5	3.5	3.5	3.5	3.6	3.6	3.6	3.6	3.6	3.6	3.7
11.5	3.5	3.5	3.6	3.6	3.6	3.6	3.6	3.6	3.6	3.6	3.6	3.6	3.7	3.7	3.7	3.7	3.7	3.7	3.8	3.8	3.8	3.8	3.8	3.8	3.8	3.8	3.9	3.9	3.9	3.9	3.9	3.9	3.9	3.9	4.0	4.0	4.0	4.0	4.0
11	4.0	4.0	4.0	4.0	4.0	4.1	4.1	4.1	4.1	4.1	4.1	4.1	4.1	4.1	4.1	4.1	4.1	4.2	4.2	4.2	4.2	4.2	4.2	4.2	4.2	4.2	4.2	4.3	4.3	4.3	4.3	4.3	4.3	4.3	4.3	4.3	4.3	4.4	4.4
10.5	4.5	4.5	4.5	4.5	4.5	4.5	4.5	4.5	4.5	4.6	4.6	4.6	4.6	4.6	4.6	4.6	4.6	4.6	4.6	4.6	4.6	4.6	4.6	4.6	4.6	4.6	4.6	4.6	4.7	4.7	4.7	4.7	4.7	4.7	4.7	4.7	4.7	4.7	4.7
10	5.0	5.0	5.0	5.0	5.0	5.0	5.0	5.0	5.0	5.0	5.0	5.0	5.0	5.0	5.0	5.0	5.0	5.0	5.0	5.0	5.0	5.0	5.0	5.0	5.0	5.0	5.0	5.0	5.0	5.0	5.0	5.0	5.0	5.0	5.0	5.0	5.0	5.0	5.0
9.5	5.5	5.5	5.5	5.5	5.5	5.5	5.5	5.5	5.5	5.5	5.5	5.5	5.5	5.5	5.5	5.5	5.5	5.5	5.5	5.5	5.5	5.5	5.5	5.5	5.5	5.5	5.5	5.5	5.5	5.5	5.5	5.5	5.5	5.5	5.5	5.5	5.5	5.5	5.5
9	6.0	6.0	6.0	6.0	6.0	6.0	6.0	6.0	6.0	6.0	6.0	6.0	6.0	6.0	6.0	6.0	6.0	6.0	6.0	6.0	6.0	6.0	6.0	6.0	6.0	6.0	6.0	6.0	6.0	6.0	6.0	6.0	6.0	6.0	6.0	6.0	6.0	6.0	6.0

LISTED PUT OPTION PRICE WHEN EXERCISE PRICE IS 10

NUMBER OF WEEKS BEFORE THE OPTION EXPIRES

Common Stock Price	1	2	3	4	5	6	7	8	9	10	11	12	13	14	15	16	17	18	19	20	21	22	23	24	25	26	27	28	29	30	31	32	33	34	35	36	37	38	39
14	0.0	0.0	0.0	0.0	0.0	0.0	0.0	0.0	0.0	0.0	0.0	0.0	0.0	0.0	0.0	0.0	0.0	0.0	0.0	0.0	0.0	0.0	0.0	0.0	0.0	0.0	0.0	0.0	0.0	0.0	0.0	0.0	0.0	0.0	0.0	0.0	0.0	0.0	0.0
13.5	0.0	0.0	0.0	0.0	0.0	0.0	0.0	0.0	0.0	0.0	0.0	0.0	0.0	0.0	0.0	0.0	0.0	0.0	0.0	0.0	0.0	0.0	0.0	0.0	0.0	0.0	0.0	0.0	0.0	0.0	0.0	0.0	0.0	0.0	0.0	0.0	0.0	0.0	0.1
13	0.0	0.0	0.0	0.0	0.0	0.0	0.0	0.0	0.0	0.0	0.0	0.0	0.0	0.0	0.0	0.0	0.0	0.0	0.0	0.0	0.0	0.0	0.0	0.0	0.0	0.0	0.0	0.0	0.0	0.0	0.1	0.1	0.1	0.1	0.1	0.1	0.1	0.1	0.2
12.5	0.0	0.0	0.0	0.0	0.0	0.0	0.0	0.0	0.0	0.0	0.0	0.0	0.0	0.0	0.0	0.0	0.0	0.0	0.0	0.0	0.0	0.0	0.0	0.1	0.1	0.1	0.1	0.1	0.1	0.1	0.2	0.2	0.2	0.2	0.2	0.2	0.2	0.2	0.2
12	0.0	0.0	0.0	0.0	0.0	0.0	0.0	0.0	0.0	0.0	0.0	0.0	0.0	0.0	0.0	0.0	0.1	0.1	0.1	0.1	0.1	0.1	0.1	0.2	0.2	0.2	0.2	0.2	0.2	0.2	0.2	0.2	0.2	0.2	0.2	0.2	0.2	0.3	0.4
11.5	0.0	0.0	0.0	0.0	0.0	0.0	0.0	0.0	0.0	0.0	0.1	0.1	0.1	0.1	0.1	0.2	0.2	0.2	0.2	0.2	0.2	0.3	0.3	0.3	0.3	0.3	0.3	0.3	0.3	0.4	0.4	0.4	0.4	0.4	0.4	0.4	0.4	0.5	0.5
11	0.0	0.0	0.0	0.0	0.0	0.1	0.1	0.1	0.1	0.2	0.2	0.2	0.2	0.2	0.3	0.3	0.3	0.3	0.3	0.3	0.4	0.4	0.4	0.4	0.4	0.4	0.4	0.5	0.5	0.5	0.5	0.5	0.5	0.5	0.6	0.6	0.6	0.6	0.6
10.5	0.0	0.0	0.1	0.1	0.2	0.2	0.2	0.3	0.3	0.3	0.3	0.3	0.4	0.4	0.4	0.4	0.4	0.5	0.5	0.5	0.5	0.5	0.5	0.5	0.6	0.6	0.6	0.6	0.6	0.6	0.6	0.7	0.7	0.7	0.7	0.7	0.7	0.7	0.7
10	0.1	0.2	0.2	0.3	0.3	0.3	0.4	0.4	0.4	0.5	0.5	0.5	0.5	0.5	0.6	0.6	0.6	0.6	0.6	0.6	0.7	0.7	0.7	0.7	0.7	0.7	0.7	0.8	0.8	0.8	0.8	0.8	0.8	0.8	0.8	0.9	0.9	0.9	0.9
9.5	0.5	0.5	0.6	0.6	0.6	0.6	0.7	0.7	0.7	0.7	0.8	0.8	0.8	0.8	0.8	0.9	0.9	0.9	0.9	1.0	1.0	1.0	1.0	1.1	1.1	1.1	1.1	1.1	1.2	1.2	1.2	1.2	1.3	1.3	1.3	1.3	1.4	1.4	1.4
9	1.0	1.0	1.1	1.1	1.1	1.1	1.1	1.2	1.2	1.2	1.2	1.2	1.2	1.3	1.3	1.3	1.3	1.3	1.4	1.4	1.4	1.4	1.4	1.5	1.5	1.5	1.5	1.5	1.6	1.6	1.6	1.6	1.6	1.7	1.7	1.7	1.7	1.7	1.7
8.5	1.5	1.5	1.5	1.6	1.6	1.6	1.6	1.6	1.6	1.7	1.7	1.7	1.7	1.7	1.7	1.7	1.8	1.8	1.8	1.8	1.8	1.8	1.9	1.9	1.9	1.9	1.9	1.9	1.9	2.0	2.0	2.0	2.0	2.0	2.0	2.1	2.1	2.1	2.1
8	2.0	2.0	2.0	2.0	2.1	2.1	2.1	2.1	2.1	2.1	2.1	2.1	2.1	2.2	2.2	2.2	2.2	2.2	2.2	2.2	2.2	2.3	2.3	2.3	2.3	2.3	2.3	2.3	2.3	2.3	2.4	2.4	2.4	2.4	2.4	2.4	2.4	2.4	2.4
7.5	2.5	2.5	2.5	2.5	2.5	2.5	2.6	2.6	2.6	2.6	2.6	2.6	2.6	2.6	2.6	2.6	2.6	2.6	2.6	2.6	2.6	2.7	2.7	2.7	2.7	2.7	2.7	2.7	2.7	2.7	2.7	2.7	2.7	2.8	2.8	2.8	2.8	2.8	2.8
7	3.0	3.0	3.0	3.0	3.0	3.0	3.0	3.0	3.0	3.0	3.0	3.0	3.0	3.0	3.1	3.1	3.1	3.1	3.1	3.1	3.1	3.1	3.1	3.1	3.1	3.1	3.1	3.1	3.1	3.1	3.1	3.1	3.1	3.1	3.1	3.1	3.1	3.1	3.1
6.5	3.5	3.5	3.5	3.5	3.5	3.5	3.5	3.5	3.5	3.5	3.5	3.5	3.5	3.5	3.5	3.5	3.5	3.5	3.5	3.5	3.5	3.5	3.5	3.5	3.5	3.5	3.5	3.5	3.5	3.5	3.5	3.5	3.5	3.5	3.5	3.5	3.5	3.5	3.5
6	4.0	4.0	4.0	4.0	4.0	4.0	4.0	4.0	4.0	4.0	4.0	4.0	4.0	4.0	4.0	4.0	4.0	4.0	4.0	4.0	4.0	4.0	4.0	4.0	4.0	4.0	4.0	4.0	4.0	4.0	4.0	4.0	4.0	4.0	4.0	4.0	4.0	4.0	4.0

THE NORMAL
VALUE LISTED
PUT OPTION
TABLES

LISTED PUT OPTION PRICE WHEN EXERCISE PRICE IS 25

NUMBER OF WEEKS BEFORE THE OPTION EXPIRES

Common Stock Prices	1	2	3	4	5	6	7	8	9	10	11	12	13	14	15	16	17	18	19	20	21	22	23	24	25	26	27	28	29	30	31	32	33	34	35	36	37	38	39
35	0.0	0.0	0.0	0.0	0.0	0.0	0.0	0.0	0.0	0.0	0.0	0.0	0.0	0.0	0.0	0.0	0.0	0.0	0.0	0.0	0.0	0.0	0.0	0.0	0.0	0.0	0.0	0.0	0.0	0.0	0.0	0.0	0.0	0.0	0.0	0.0	0.0	0.0	0.0
34	0.0	0.0	0.0	0.0	0.0	0.0	0.0	0.0	0.0	0.0	0.0	0.0	0.0	0.0	0.0	0.0	0.0	0.0	0.0	0.0	0.0	0.0	0.0	0.0	0.0	0.0	0.0	0.0	0.0	0.0	0.0	0.0	0.0	0.0	0.0	0.0	0.0	0.1	0.1
33	0.0	0.0	0.0	0.0	0.0	0.0	0.0	0.0	0.0	0.0	0.0	0.0	0.0	0.0	0.0	0.0	0.0	0.0	0.0	0.0	0.0	0.0	0.0	0.0	0.0	0.0	0.0	0.0	0.0	0.1	0.1	0.1	0.1	0.1	0.2	0.2	0.2	0.3	0.3
32	0.0	0.0	0.0	0.0	0.0	0.0	0.0	0.0	0.0	0.0	0.0	0.0	0.0	0.0	0.0	0.0	0.0	0.0	0.0	0.0	0.0	0.0	0.0	0.0	0.0	0.0	0.1	0.1	0.2	0.2	0.2	0.3	0.3	0.3	0.4	0.4	0.4	0.4	0.5
31	0.0	0.0	0.0	0.0	0.0	0.0	0.0	0.0	0.0	0.0	0.0	0.0	0.0	0.0	0.0	0.0	0.0	0.0	0.0	0.0	0.1	0.1	0.1	0.2	0.2	0.3	0.3	0.3	0.4	0.4	0.4	0.5	0.5	0.5	0.6	0.6	0.6	0.6	0.7
30	0.0	0.0	0.0	0.0	0.0	0.0	0.0	0.0	0.0	0.0	0.0	0.0	0.0	0.0	0.0	0.1	0.1	0.2	0.2	0.3	0.3	0.3	0.4	0.4	0.4	0.5	0.5	0.5	0.6	0.6	0.6	0.7	0.7	0.7	0.8	0.8	0.8	0.9	0.9
29	0.0	0.0	0.0	0.0	0.0	0.0	0.0	0.0	0.0	0.0	0.1	0.1	0.2	0.2	0.3	0.3	0.4	0.4	0.4	0.5	0.5	0.6	0.6	0.6	0.7	0.7	0.7	0.8	0.8	0.8	0.9	0.9	0.9	1.0	1.0	1.0	1.1	1.1	1.1
28	0.0	0.0	0.0	0.0	0.0	0.0	0.1	0.1	0.2	0.3	0.3	0.4	0.4	0.5	0.5	0.6	0.6	0.7	0.7	0.7	0.8	0.8	0.8	0.9	0.9	1.0	1.0	1.0	1.1	1.1	1.1	1.2	1.2	1.2	1.2	1.3	1.3	1.3	1.4
27	0.0	0.0	0.0	0.1	0.2	0.3	0.3	0.4	0.5	0.5	0.6	0.6	0.7	0.7	0.8	0.8	0.9	0.9	1.0	1.0	1.0	1.1	1.1	1.2	1.2	1.2	1.3	1.3	1.3	1.4	1.4	1.4	1.5	1.5	1.5	1.5	1.6	1.6	1.6
26	0.0	0.2	0.3	0.4	0.5	0.6	0.6	0.7	0.8	0.8	0.9	0.9	1.0	1.0	1.1	1.1	1.2	1.2	1.2	1.3	1.3	1.4	1.4	1.4	1.5	1.5	1.5	1.6	1.6	1.6	1.7	1.7	1.7	1.8	1.8	1.8	1.9	1.9	1.9
25	0.4	0.5	0.6	0.7	0.8	0.9	0.9	1.0	1.1	1.1	1.2	1.2	1.3	1.3	1.4	1.4	1.5	1.5	1.6	1.6	1.6	1.7	1.7	1.7	1.8	1.8	1.8	1.9	1.9	1.9	2.0	2.0	2.0	2.1	2.1	2.1	2.2	2.2	2.2
24	1.1	1.1	1.2	1.2	1.3	1.4	1.4	1.5	1.5	1.6	1.7	1.7	1.8	1.8	1.9	2.0	2.0	2.1	2.1	2.2	2.3	2.3	2.4	2.4	2.5	2.6	2.6	2.7	2.7	2.8	2.9	2.9	3.0	3.0	3.2	3.2	3.3	3.4	3.4
23	2.1	2.1	2.2	2.2	2.3	2.3	2.4	2.4	2.5	2.5	2.6	2.6	2.7	2.7	2.8	2.8	2.9	2.9	3.0	3.0	3.1	3.1	3.2	3.2	3.3	3.4	3.4	3.5	3.5	3.6	3.6	3.7	3.7	3.8	3.8	3.9	3.9	4.0	4.0
22	3.0	3.1	3.1	3.2	3.2	3.3	3.3	3.4	3.4	3.4	3.5	3.5	3.6	3.6	3.7	3.7	3.8	3.8	3.8	3.9	3.9	4.0	4.0	4.1	4.1	4.1	4.2	4.2	4.3	4.3	4.4	4.4	4.5	4.5	4.5	4.6	4.6	4.7	4.7
21	4.0	4.1	4.1	4.1	4.2	4.2	4.3	4.3	4.3	4.4	4.4	4.4	4.5	4.5	4.5	4.6	4.6	4.7	4.7	4.7	4.8	4.8	4.8	4.9	4.9	4.9	5.0	5.0	5.1	5.1	5.1	5.2	5.2	5.2	5.3	5.3	5.3	5.4	5.4
20	5.0	5.1	5.1	5.1	5.2	5.2	5.2	5.2	5.3	5.3	5.3	5.3	5.4	5.4	5.4	5.5	5.5	5.5	5.5	5.6	5.6	5.6	5.7	5.7	5.7	5.7	5.8	5.8	5.9	5.9	5.9	5.9	5.9	6.0	6.0	6.0	6.1	6.1	6.1
19	6.0	6.0	6.1	6.1	6.1	6.1	6.1	6.2	6.2	6.2	6.2	6.2	6.3	6.3	6.3	6.3	6.4	6.4	6.4	6.4	6.4	6.5	6.5	6.5	6.5	6.5	6.6	6.6	6.6	6.6	6.6	6.7	6.7	6.7	6.7	6.7	6.8	6.8	6.8
18	7.0	7.0	7.0	7.1	7.1	7.1	7.1	7.1	7.1	7.1	7.1	7.2	7.2	7.2	7.2	7.2	7.2	7.2	7.2	7.3	7.3	7.3	7.3	7.3	7.3	7.3	7.3	7.4	7.4	7.4	7.4	7.4	7.4	7.4	7.4	7.5	7.5	7.5	7.5
17	8.0	8.0	8.0	8.0	8.0	8.0	8.0	8.0	8.0	8.0	8.1	8.1	8.1	8.1	8.1	8.1	8.1	8.1	8.1	8.1	8.1	8.1	8.1	8.1	8.1	8.1	8.1	8.1	8.1	8.1	8.2	8.2	8.2	8.2	8.2	8.2	8.2	8.2	8.2
16	9.0	9.0	9.0	9.0	9.0	9.0	9.0	9.0	9.0	9.0	9.0	9.0	9.0	9.0	9.0	9.0	9.0	9.0	9.0	9.0	9.0	9.0	9.0	9.0	9.0	9.0	9.0	9.0	9.0	9.0	9.0	9.0	9.0	9.0	9.0	9.0	9.0	9.0	9.0
15	10.0	10.0	10.0	10.0	10.0	10.0	10.0	10.0	10.0	10.0	10.0	10.0	10.0	10.0	10.0	10.0	10.0	10.0	10.0	10.0	10.0	10.0	10.0	10.0	10.0	10.0	10.0	10.0	10.0	10.0	10.0	10.0	10.0	10.0	10.0	10.0	10.0	10.0	10.0

LISTED PUT OPTION PRICE WHEN EXERCISE PRICE IS 30

NUMBER OF WEEKS BEFORE THE OPTION EXPIRES

Common Stock Price	1	2	3	4	5	6	7	8	9	10	11	12	13	14	15	16	17	18	19	20	21	22	23	24	25	26	27	28	29	30	31	32	33	34	35	36	37	38	39
42	0.0	0.0	0.0	0.0	0.0	0.0	0.0	0.0	0.0	0.0	0.0	0.0	0.0	0.0	0.0	0.0	0.0	0.0	0.0	0.0	0.0	0.0	0.0	0.0	0.0	0.0	0.0	0.0	0.0	0.0	0.0	0.0	0.0	0.0	0.0	0.0	0.0	0.0	0.0
41	0.0	0.0	0.0	0.0	0.0	0.0	0.0	0.0	0.0	0.0	0.0	0.0	0.0	0.0	0.0	0.0	0.0	0.0	0.0	0.0	0.0	0.0	0.0	0.0	0.0	0.0	0.0	0.0	0.0	0.0	0.0	0.0	0.0	0.0	0.0	0.0	0.0	0.1	0.1
40	0.0	0.0	0.0	0.0	0.0	0.0	0.0	0.0	0.0	0.0	0.0	0.0	0.0	0.0	0.0	0.0	0.0	0.0	0.0	0.0	0.0	0.0	0.0	0.0	0.0	0.0	0.0	0.1	0.1	0.1	0.2	0.2	0.2	0.2	0.2	0.2	0.2	0.2	0.3
39	0.0	0.0	0.0	0.0	0.0	0.0	0.0	0.0	0.0	0.0	0.0	0.0	0.0	0.0	0.0	0.0	0.0	0.0	0.0	0.0	0.0	0.0	0.1	0.1	0.1	0.2	0.2	0.2	0.3	0.3	0.3	0.4	0.4	0.4	0.4	0.4	0.4	0.4	0.5
38	0.0	0.0	0.0	0.0	0.0	0.0	0.0	0.0	0.0	0.0	0.0	0.0	0.0	0.0	0.0	0.0	0.0	0.0	0.0	0.0	0.1	0.1	0.2	0.2	0.2	0.3	0.3	0.4	0.4	0.4	0.5	0.5	0.5	0.5	0.5	0.6	0.6	0.6	0.6
37	0.0	0.0	0.0	0.0	0.0	0.0	0.0	0.0	0.0	0.0	0.0	0.0	0.0	0.0	0.0	0.0	0.0	0.0	0.1	0.1	0.2	0.2	0.3	0.3	0.4	0.4	0.5	0.5	0.5	0.6	0.6	0.7	0.7	0.7	0.8	0.8	0.8	0.8	0.9
36	0.0	0.0	0.0	0.0	0.0	0.0	0.0	0.0	0.0	0.0	0.1	0.1	0.2	0.2	0.3	0.3	0.4	0.4	0.5	0.5	0.6	0.6	0.6	0.7	0.7	0.8	0.8	0.8	0.9	0.9	0.9	1.0	1.0	1.0	1.0	1.0	1.0	1.0	1.1
35	0.0	0.0	0.0	0.0	0.0	0.0	0.0	0.1	0.1	0.2	0.2	0.3	0.3	0.4	0.4	0.5	0.5	0.6	0.6	0.7	0.7	0.8	0.8	0.9	0.9	0.9	1.0	1.0	1.0	1.1	1.1	1.1	1.2	1.2	1.2	1.2	1.2	1.3	1.3
34	0.0	0.0	0.0	0.0	0.0	0.0	0.1	0.1	0.2	0.2	0.3	0.3	0.4	0.4	0.5	0.5	0.6	0.6	0.7	0.7	0.8	0.8	0.9	0.9	1.0	1.0	1.0	1.1	1.1	1.2	1.2	1.3	1.3	1.3	1.4	1.4	1.5	1.5	1.5
33	0.0	0.0	0.0	0.1	0.1	0.2	0.2	0.3	0.4	0.4	0.5	0.6	0.6	0.7	0.7	0.8	0.9	0.9	1.0	1.0	1.1	1.1	1.2	1.2	1.3	1.3	1.3	1.4	1.4	1.5	1.5	1.5	1.6	1.6	1.7	1.7	1.7	1.8	1.8
32	0.0	0.0	0.1	0.3	0.4	0.4	0.5	0.6	0.7	0.8	0.8	0.9	1.0	1.0	1.1	1.1	1.2	1.2	1.3	1.3	1.4	1.4	1.5	1.5	1.6	1.6	1.7	1.7	1.8	1.8	1.9	1.9	1.9	2.0	2.0	2.0	2.0	2.0	2.1
31	0.1	0.3	0.4	0.5	0.6	0.7	0.8	0.9	1.0	1.0	1.1	1.2	1.2	1.3	1.3	1.4	1.5	1.5	1.6	1.6	1.6	1.7	1.7	1.8	1.8	1.9	1.9	1.9	2.0	2.0	2.1	2.1	2.1	2.2	2.2	2.3	2.3	2.3	2.4
30	0.4	0.6	0.7	0.9	1.0	1.0	1.1	1.2	1.3	1.4	1.4	1.5	1.5	1.6	1.7	1.7	1.8	1.8	1.9	1.9	2.0	2.0	2.0	2.1	2.1	2.2	2.2	2.3	2.3	2.3	2.4	2.4	2.5	2.5	2.5	2.6	2.6	2.6	2.7
29	1.1	1.2	1.2	1.3	1.4	1.4	1.5	1.6	1.7	1.7	1.8	1.9	2.0	2.0	2.1	2.2	2.2	2.3	2.4	2.5	2.5	2.6	2.7	2.8	2.8	2.9	3.0	3.0	3.1	3.2	3.2	3.3	3.4	3.4	3.4	3.5	3.5	3.5	3.6
28	2.1	2.1	2.2	2.3	2.3	2.4	2.5	2.5	2.6	2.7	2.7	2.8	2.9	2.9	3.0	3.0	3.1	3.2	3.2	3.3	3.4	3.4	3.5	3.6	3.6	3.7	3.8	3.8	3.9	4.0	4.0	4.1	4.2	4.2	4.3	4.3	4.4	4.4	4.5
27	3.1	3.1	3.2	3.2	3.3	3.3	3.4	3.5	3.5	3.6	3.6	3.7	3.7	3.8	3.9	3.9	4.0	4.0	4.1	4.2	4.2	4.3	4.3	4.4	4.4	4.5	4.6	4.6	4.7	4.7	4.8	4.8	4.9	5.0	5.0	5.1	5.1	5.2	5.2
26	4.0	4.1	4.1	4.2	4.2	4.3	4.3	4.4	4.4	4.5	4.5	4.6	4.6	4.7	4.7	4.8	4.8	4.9	4.9	5.0	5.0	5.1	5.1	5.2	5.2	5.3	5.3	5.4	5.4	5.5	5.5	5.6	5.6	5.7	5.7	5.8	5.8	5.9	5.9
25	5.0	5.1	5.1	5.2	5.2	5.2	5.3	5.3	5.4	5.4	5.5	5.5	5.5	5.6	5.6	5.7	5.7	5.7	5.8	5.8	5.8	5.9	5.9	6.0	6.0	6.1	6.1	6.2	6.2	6.3	6.3	6.3	6.4	6.4	6.5	6.5	6.6	6.6	6.6
24	6.0	6.1	6.1	6.1	6.2	6.2	6.2	6.3	6.3	6.3	6.4	6.4	6.4	6.5	6.5	6.5	6.6	6.6	6.6	6.7	6.7	6.8	6.8	6.8	6.9	6.9	6.9	7.0	7.0	7.0	7.1	7.1	7.1	7.2	7.2	7.2	7.3	7.3	7.3
23	7.0	7.1	7.1	7.1	7.1	7.2	7.2	7.2	7.2	7.3	7.3	7.3	7.3	7.4	7.4	7.4	7.4	7.5	7.5	7.5	7.6	7.6	7.6	7.6	7.7	7.7	7.7	7.7	7.8	7.8	7.8	7.8	7.9	7.9	7.9	7.9	8.0	8.0	8.0
22	8.0	8.0	8.1	8.1	8.1	8.2	8.2	8.2	8.2	8.2	8.2	8.2	8.2	8.3	8.3	8.3	8.3	8.3	8.4	8.4	8.4	8.4	8.4	8.4	8.5	8.5	8.5	8.5	8.5	8.6	8.6	8.6	8.6	8.6	8.6	8.7	8.7	8.7	8.7
21	9.0	9.0	9.0	9.0	9.1	9.1	9.1	9.1	9.1	9.1	9.1	9.1	9.1	9.1	9.2	9.2	9.2	9.2	9.2	9.2	9.2	9.2	9.2	9.3	9.3	9.3	9.3	9.3	9.3	9.3	9.3	9.3	9.4	9.4	9.4	9.4	9.4	9.4	9.4
20	10.0	10.0	10.0	10.0	10.0	10.0	10.0	10.0	10.0	10.0	10.0	10.0	10.0	10.0	10.0	10.0	10.0	10.0	10.0	10.0	10.1	10.1	10.1	10.1	10.1	10.1	10.1	10.1	10.1	10.1	10.1	10.1	10.1	10.1	10.1	10.1	10.1	10.1	10.1
19	11.0	11.0	11.0	11.0	11.0	11.0	11.0	11.0	11.0	11.0	11.0	11.0	11.0	11.0	11.0	11.0	11.0	11.0	11.0	11.0	11.0	11.0	11.0	11.0	11.0	11.0	11.0	11.0	11.0	11.0	11.0	11.0	11.0	11.0	11.0	11.0	11.0	11.0	11.0
18	12.0	12.0	12.0	12.0	12.0	12.0	12.0	12.0	12.0	12.0	12.0	12.0	12.0	12.0	12.0	12.0	12.0	12.0	12.0	12.0	12.0	12.0	12.0	12.0	12.0	12.0	12.0	12.0	12.0	12.0	12.0	12.0	12.0	12.0	12.0	12.0	12.0	12.0	12.0

LISTED PUT OPTION PRICE WHEN EXERCISE PRICE IS 35

NUMBER OF WEEKS BEFORE THE OPTION EXPIRES

Common Stock Price (leftmost column)

Stock	1	2	3	4	5	6	7	8	9	10	11	12	13	14	15	16	17	18	19	20	21	22	23	24	25	26	27	28	29	30	31	32	33	34	35	36	37	38	39
49	0.0	0.0	0.0	0.0	0.0	0.0	0.0	0.0	0.0	0.0	0.0	0.0	0.0	0.0	0.0	0.0	0.0	0.0	0.0	0.0	0.0	0.0	0.0	0.0	0.0	0.0	0.0	0.0	0.0	0.0	0.0	0.0	0.0	0.0	0.0	0.0	0.0	0.0	0.0
48	0.0	0.0	0.0	0.0	0.0	0.0	0.0	0.0	0.0	0.0	0.0	0.0	0.0	0.0	0.0	0.0	0.0	0.0	0.0	0.0	0.0	0.0	0.0	0.0	0.0	0.0	0.0	0.0	0.0	0.0	0.0	0.0	0.0	0.0	0.0	0.0	0.0	0.0	0.0
47	0.0	0.0	0.0	0.0	0.0	0.0	0.0	0.0	0.0	0.0	0.0	0.0	0.0	0.0	0.0	0.0	0.0	0.0	0.0	0.1	0.1	0.1	0.1	0.1	0.1	0.2	0.2	0.2	0.2	0.2	0.2	0.2	0.3	0.3	0.3	0.3	0.3	0.3	0.3
46	0.0	0.0	0.0	0.0	0.0	0.0	0.0	0.0	0.0	0.0	0.0	0.0	0.0	0.1	0.1	0.1	0.1	0.1	0.2	0.2	0.2	0.2	0.2	0.3	0.3	0.3	0.3	0.3	0.3	0.4	0.4	0.4	0.4	0.4	0.4	0.4	0.4	0.4	0.4
45	0.0	0.0	0.0	0.0	0.0	0.0	0.0	0.0	0.0	0.0	0.1	0.1	0.1	0.1	0.2	0.2	0.2	0.3	0.3	0.3	0.3	0.4	0.4	0.4	0.4	0.4	0.5	0.5	0.5	0.5	0.5	0.5	0.6	0.6	0.6	0.6	0.6	0.6	0.6
44	0.0	0.0	0.0	0.0	0.0	0.0	0.0	0.0	0.0	0.1	0.1	0.1	0.2	0.2	0.2	0.3	0.3	0.3	0.4	0.4	0.4	0.5	0.5	0.5	0.5	0.6	0.6	0.6	0.6	0.7	0.7	0.7	0.7	0.7	0.8	0.8	0.8	0.8	0.8
43	0.0	0.0	0.0	0.0	0.0	0.0	0.0	0.1	0.1	0.2	0.2	0.3	0.3	0.4	0.4	0.5	0.5	0.5	0.6	0.6	0.7	0.7	0.7	0.8	0.8	0.8	0.8	0.9	0.9	0.9	0.9	1.0	1.0	1.0	1.0	1.0	1.0	1.0	1.0
42	0.0	0.0	0.0	0.0	0.0	0.0	0.1	0.1	0.2	0.2	0.3	0.3	0.4	0.4	0.5	0.5	0.6	0.6	0.7	0.7	0.8	0.8	0.8	0.9	0.9	0.9	1.0	1.0	1.0	1.1	1.1	1.1	1.1	1.2	1.2	1.2	1.2	1.2	1.2
41	0.0	0.0	0.0	0.0	0.0	0.1	0.2	0.3	0.3	0.4	0.5	0.5	0.6	0.7	0.7	0.8	0.8	0.9	0.9	1.0	1.0	1.1	1.1	1.1	1.2	1.2	1.2	1.3	1.3	1.3	1.4	1.4	1.4	1.4	1.5	1.5	1.5	1.5	1.5
40	0.0	0.0	0.0	0.1	0.2	0.3	0.4	0.4	0.5	0.6	0.6	0.7	0.8	0.8	0.9	0.9	1.0	1.0	1.1	1.1	1.2	1.2	1.3	1.3	1.3	1.4	1.4	1.4	1.5	1.5	1.5	1.6	1.6	1.6	1.6	1.7	1.7	1.7	1.7
39	0.0	0.0	0.1	0.2	0.3	0.4	0.5	0.6	0.7	0.8	0.8	0.9	1.0	1.0	1.1	1.2	1.2	1.3	1.3	1.4	1.4	1.5	1.5	1.5	1.6	1.6	1.7	1.7	1.7	1.8	1.8	1.8	1.9	1.9	1.9	1.9	2.0	2.0	2.0
38	0.0	0.0	0.1	0.2	0.3	0.4	0.5	0.6	0.7	0.8	0.9	1.0	1.0	1.1	1.2	1.2	1.3	1.4	1.4	1.5	1.5	1.6	1.6	1.7	1.7	1.8	1.8	1.8	1.9	1.9	2.0	2.0	2.0	2.1	2.1	2.1	2.2	2.2	2.2
37	0.0	0.1	0.2	0.3	0.4	0.5	0.6	0.7	0.8	0.9	1.0	1.1	1.2	1.2	1.3	1.4	1.4	1.5	1.6	1.6	1.7	1.7	1.8	1.8	1.9	1.9	2.0	2.0	2.1	2.1	2.2	2.2	2.2	2.3	2.3	2.4	2.4	2.5	2.5
36	0.0	0.1	0.3	0.4	0.5	0.6	0.7	0.8	0.9	1.0	1.1	1.2	1.3	1.4	1.4	1.5	1.6	1.7	1.7	1.8	1.8	1.9	2.0	2.0	2.1	2.1	2.2	2.2	2.3	2.3	2.4	2.4	2.5	2.5	2.6	2.6	2.7	2.7	2.8
35	0.5	0.7	0.9	1.0	1.1	1.2	1.3	1.4	1.5	1.6	1.7	1.7	1.8	1.9	1.9	2.0	2.1	2.1	2.2	2.2	2.3	2.3	2.4	2.4	2.5	2.5	2.6	2.6	2.7	2.7	2.8	2.8	2.9	2.9	3.0	3.0	3.0	3.1	3.1
34	1.1	1.2	1.3	1.4	1.5	1.5	1.6	1.7	1.8	1.9	2.0	2.0	2.1	2.2	2.3	2.3	2.4	2.5	2.5	2.6	2.7	2.7	2.8	2.9	2.9	3.0	3.1	3.1	3.2	3.3	3.3	3.4	3.5	3.6	3.7	3.8	3.9	3.9	4.0
33	2.1	2.2	2.2	2.3	2.4	2.5	2.6	2.6	2.7	2.8	2.9	2.9	3.0	3.1	3.2	3.2	3.3	3.4	3.4	3.5	3.6	3.7	3.7	3.8	3.9	3.9	4.0	4.1	4.1	4.2	4.3	4.3	4.4	4.5	4.6	4.6	4.7	4.8	4.9
32	3.1	3.1	3.2	3.3	3.4	3.4	3.5	3.6	3.6	3.7	3.8	3.9	3.9	4.0	4.1	4.1	4.2	4.3	4.3	4.4	4.5	4.5	4.6	4.7	4.7	4.8	4.9	4.9	5.0	5.1	5.1	5.2	5.3	5.3	5.4	5.5	5.6	5.7	5.8
31	4.1	4.1	4.2	4.2	4.3	4.4	4.4	4.5	4.6	4.6	4.7	4.8	4.8	4.9	4.9	5.0	5.1	5.1	5.2	5.2	5.3	5.3	5.4	5.5	5.5	5.6	5.6	5.7	5.8	5.8	5.9	5.9	6.0	6.1	6.1	6.2	6.3	6.4	6.5
30	5.1	5.1	5.2	5.3	5.3	5.4	5.4	5.5	5.6	5.6	5.7	5.7	5.8	5.8	5.9	5.9	6.0	6.0	6.1	6.1	6.2	6.2	6.3	6.3	6.4	6.4	6.5	6.5	6.6	6.6	6.7	6.7	6.8	6.9	6.9	7.0	7.0	7.1	7.2
29	6.0	6.1	6.1	6.2	6.2	6.3	6.3	6.4	6.4	6.5	6.5	6.6	6.6	6.7	6.7	6.8	6.8	6.8	6.9	6.9	7.0	7.0	7.1	7.1	7.2	7.2	7.3	7.3	7.3	7.4	7.4	7.5	7.5	7.6	7.6	7.7	7.7	7.8	7.9
28	7.0	7.1	7.1	7.1	7.2	7.2	7.3	7.3	7.3	7.4	7.4	7.5	7.5	7.5	7.6	7.6	7.7	7.7	7.7	7.8	7.8	7.9	7.9	7.9	8.0	8.0	8.1	8.1	8.1	8.2	8.2	8.3	8.3	8.3	8.4	8.4	8.5	8.5	8.6
27	8.0	8.1	8.1	8.1	8.2	8.2	8.2	8.3	8.3	8.3	8.4	8.4	8.4	8.5	8.5	8.5	8.6	8.6	8.6	8.7	8.7	8.7	8.7	8.8	8.8	8.8	8.9	8.9	8.9	9.0	9.0	9.0	9.0	9.1	9.1	9.1	9.2	9.2	9.2
26	9.0	9.0	9.1	9.1	9.1	9.1	9.2	9.2	9.2	9.2	9.3	9.3	9.3	9.3	9.4	9.4	9.4	9.4	9.4	9.5	9.5	9.5	9.5	9.6	9.6	9.6	9.6	9.6	9.7	9.7	9.7	9.7	9.8	9.8	9.8	9.8	9.9	9.9	9.9
25	10.0	10.0	10.0	10.1	10.1	10.1	10.1	10.1	10.2	10.2	10.2	10.2	10.2	10.2	10.3	10.3	10.3	10.3	10.3	10.3	10.4	10.4	10.4	10.4	10.4	10.4	10.4	10.5	10.5	10.5	10.5	10.5	10.5	10.6	10.6	10.6	10.6	10.6	10.6
24	11.0	11.0	11.0	11.0	11.0	11.0	11.1	11.1	11.1	11.1	11.1	11.1	11.1	11.1	11.1	11.1	11.1	11.1	11.1	11.2	11.2	11.2	11.2	11.2	11.2	11.2	11.2	11.2	11.2	11.3	11.3	11.3	11.3	11.3	11.3	11.3	11.3	11.3	11.3

LISTED PUT OPTION PRICE WHEN EXERCISE PRICE IS 40

NUMBER OF WEEKS BEFORE THE OPTION EXPIRES

Common Stock Price	1	2	3	4	5	6	7	8	9	10	11	12	13	14	15	16	17	18	19	20	21	22	23	24	25	26	27	28	29	30	31	32	33	34	35	36	37	38	39
56	0.0	0.0	0.0	0.0	0.0	0.0	0.0	0.0	0.0	0.0	0.0	0.0	0.0	0.0	0.0	0.0	0.0	0.0	0.0	0.0	0.0	0.0	0.0	0.0	0.0	0.0	0.0	0.0	0.0	0.0	0.0	0.0	0.0	0.0	0.0	0.0	0.0	0.0	0.0
55	0.0	0.0	0.0	0.0	0.0	0.0	0.0	0.0	0.0	0.0	0.0	0.0	0.0	0.0	0.0	0.0	0.0	0.0	0.0	0.0	0.0	0.0	0.0	0.0	0.0	0.0	0.0	0.0	0.0	0.0	0.0	0.0	0.0	0.0	0.0	0.0	0.0	0.0	0.1
54	0.0	0.0	0.0	0.0	0.0	0.0	0.0	0.0	0.0	0.0	0.0	0.0	0.0	0.0	0.0	0.0	0.0	0.0	0.0	0.0	0.0	0.0	0.0	0.0	0.0	0.0	0.0	0.0	0.0	0.1	0.1	0.1	0.1	0.1	0.1	0.1	0.1	0.2	0.2
53	0.0	0.0	0.0	0.0	0.0	0.0	0.0	0.0	0.0	0.0	0.0	0.0	0.0	0.0	0.0	0.0	0.0	0.0	0.0	0.0	0.0	0.0	0.0	0.0	0.0	0.0	0.1	0.1	0.1	0.2	0.2	0.3	0.3	0.3	0.4	0.4	0.4	0.4	0.4
52	0.0	0.0	0.0	0.0	0.0	0.0	0.0	0.0	0.0	0.0	0.0	0.0	0.0	0.0	0.0	0.0	0.0	0.0	0.0	0.0	0.0	0.1	0.1	0.2	0.3	0.3	0.4	0.5	0.5	0.6	0.6	0.6	0.6	0.6	0.6	0.6	0.6	0.6	0.6
51	0.0	0.0	0.0	0.0	0.0	0.0	0.0	0.0	0.0	0.0	0.0	0.0	0.0	0.0	0.0	0.0	0.0	0.1	0.1	0.2	0.3	0.5	0.6	0.7	0.7	0.8	0.8	0.9	0.7	0.8	0.8	0.7	0.7	0.6	0.6	0.7	0.5	0.7	0.8
50	0.0	0.0	0.0	0.0	0.0	0.0	0.0	0.0	0.0	0.0	0.0	0.0	0.0	0.0	0.0	0.0	0.0	0.3	0.3	0.4	0.4	0.5	0.6	0.7	0.7	0.8	0.8	0.9	0.9	1.0	1.0	1.0	1.0	1.0	1.0	1.0	1.0	1.0	1.0
49	0.0	0.0	0.0	0.0	0.0	0.0	0.0	0.0	0.0	0.0	0.0	0.0	0.0	0.0	0.0	0.1	0.2	0.3	0.3	0.4	0.5	0.6	0.8	0.8	0.9	0.9	1.0	1.0	1.1	1.1	1.2	1.2	1.2	1.2	1.2	1.2	1.2	1.2	1.2
48	0.0	0.0	0.0	0.0	0.0	0.0	0.0	0.0	0.0	0.0	0.0	0.0	0.0	0.0	0.1	0.2	0.3	0.4	0.5	0.6	0.7	0.8	0.9	1.0	1.1	1.1	1.2	1.2	1.3	1.3	1.4	1.4	1.4	1.4	1.4	1.4	1.4	1.4	1.4
47	0.0	0.0	0.0	0.0	0.0	0.0	0.0	0.0	0.0	0.1	0.2	0.3	0.4	0.5	0.5	0.6	0.7	0.8	0.9	1.0	1.0	1.1	1.2	1.2	1.3	1.4	1.5	1.5	1.6	1.6	1.6	1.6	1.6	1.6	1.6	1.6	1.6	1.6	1.6
46	0.0	0.0	0.0	0.0	0.0	0.0	0.0	0.1	0.2	0.3	0.4	0.5	0.6	0.7	0.8	0.9	1.0	1.0	1.1	1.1	1.2	1.2	1.3	1.4	1.5	1.5	1.6	1.6	1.7	1.7	1.8	1.8	1.8	1.9	1.9	1.9	1.9	1.9	1.9
45	0.0	0.0	0.0	0.0	0.0	0.1	0.2	0.3	0.4	0.5	0.6	0.7	0.8	0.9	1.0	1.1	1.2	1.3	1.3	1.4	1.5	1.6	1.6	1.7	1.7	1.8	1.8	1.9	1.9	2.0	2.0	2.0	2.1	2.1	2.1	2.1	2.1	2.1	2.1
44	0.0	0.0	0.0	0.0	0.1	0.2	0.3	0.4	0.5	0.6	0.7	0.8	0.9	1.0	1.0	1.1	1.2	1.3	1.4	1.5	1.6	1.7	1.8	1.9	2.0	2.0	2.1	2.1	2.2	2.2	2.3	2.3	2.4	2.4	2.4	2.4	2.4	2.4	2.4
43	0.0	0.1	0.1	0.2	0.4	0.5	0.6	0.7	0.8	0.9	1.0	1.1	1.2	1.2	1.3	1.4	1.5	1.6	1.7	1.8	1.9	2.0	2.1	2.2	2.2	2.3	2.3	2.4	2.5	2.5	2.6	2.6	2.7	2.7	2.7	2.7	2.7	2.7	2.7
42	0.0	0.2	0.4	0.5	0.7	0.8	0.9	1.0	1.1	1.2	1.3	1.4	1.5	1.5	1.6	1.7	1.8	1.9	1.9	2.0	2.1	2.2	2.3	2.3	2.4	2.5	2.5	2.6	2.6	2.7	2.7	2.8	2.8	2.9	2.9	2.9	2.9	2.9	2.9
41	0.3	0.5	0.7	0.8	1.0	1.1	1.2	1.3	1.4	1.5	1.6	1.7	1.7	1.8	1.9	2.0	2.0	2.1	2.2	2.2	2.3	2.4	2.4	2.5	2.5	2.6	2.6	2.7	2.7	2.8	2.9	2.9	3.0	3.0	3.1	3.1	3.2	3.2	3.2
40	0.6	0.8	1.0	1.1	1.3	1.4	1.5	1.6	1.7	1.8	1.9	2.0	2.0	2.1	2.2	2.3	2.4	2.5	2.5	2.6	2.7	2.7	2.8	2.8	2.9	2.9	3.0	3.0	3.1	3.1	3.2	3.2	3.3	3.3	3.4	3.5	3.5	3.6	3.6
39	1.1	1.2	1.3	1.4	1.5	1.6	1.7	1.8	1.8	1.9	2.0	2.1	2.2	2.3	2.4	2.5	2.6	2.6	2.7	2.8	2.8	2.9	3.0	3.0	3.1	3.1	3.2	3.3	3.4	3.4	3.5	3.6	3.7	3.8	3.9	4.0	4.2	4.3	4.5
38	2.1	2.2	2.3	2.4	2.5	2.6	2.7	2.8	2.8	2.9	3.0	3.1	3.2	3.3	3.4	3.5	3.6	3.7	3.8	3.9	4.0	4.0	4.1	4.2	4.3	4.4	4.5	4.6	4.7	4.8	4.9	5.0	5.1	5.1	5.2	5.3	5.3	5.4	5.4
37	3.1	3.2	3.3	3.3	3.4	3.5	3.6	3.7	3.8	3.8	3.9	4.0	4.1	4.2	4.3	4.4	4.4	4.5	4.6	4.7	4.8	4.9	4.9	5.0	5.1	5.2	5.3	5.4	5.5	5.5	5.6	5.7	5.8	5.9	6.0	6.0	6.1	6.2	6.3
36	4.1	4.2	4.2	4.3	4.4	4.5	4.5	4.6	4.7	4.8	4.8	4.9	5.0	5.1	5.2	5.2	5.3	5.4	5.5	5.5	5.6	5.7	5.8	5.8	5.9	6.0	6.1	6.2	6.2	6.3	6.4	6.5	6.5	6.6	6.7	6.8	6.8	6.9	7.0
35	5.1	5.1	5.2	5.3	5.3	5.4	5.5	5.6	5.6	5.7	5.8	5.8	5.9	6.0	6.0	6.1	6.2	6.2	6.3	6.4	6.4	6.5	6.6	6.7	6.7	6.8	6.9	6.9	7.0	7.1	7.1	7.2	7.3	7.4	7.4	7.5	7.6	7.6	7.7
34	6.1	6.2	6.2	6.3	6.3	6.4	6.4	6.5	6.6	6.6	6.7	6.7	6.8	6.9	6.9	7.0	7.0	7.1	7.2	7.2	7.3	7.3	7.4	7.5	7.5	7.6	7.7	7.7	7.8	7.8	7.9	8.0	8.0	8.1	8.1	8.2	8.3	8.3	8.4
33	7.1	7.2	7.2	7.3	7.3	7.3	7.4	7.4	7.5	7.5	7.6	7.6	7.7	7.7	7.8	7.9	7.9	8.0	8.0	8.1	8.2	8.2	8.2	8.3	8.3	8.4	8.4	8.5	8.5	8.6	8.7	8.7	8.8	8.8	8.9	8.9	9.0	9.0	9.1
32	8.0	8.1	8.1	8.2	8.2	8.3	8.3	8.4	8.4	8.5	8.5	8.5	8.6	8.6	8.7	8.7	8.8	8.8	8.9	8.9	9.0	9.0	9.0	9.1	9.1	9.2	9.2	9.3	9.3	9.4	9.4	9.5	9.5	9.5	9.6	9.6	9.7	9.7	9.8
31	9.0	9.1	9.1	9.2	9.2	9.2	9.3	9.3	9.3	9.4	9.4	9.4	9.5	9.5	9.6	9.6	9.6	9.7	9.7	9.8	9.8	9.8	9.9	9.9	9.9	9.9	10.0	10.1	10.1	10.1	10.2	10.2	10.2	10.3	10.3	10.4	10.4	10.4	10.5
30	10.0	10.0	10.1	10.1	10.1	10.1	10.2	10.2	10.2	10.3	10.3	10.4	10.4	10.4	10.4	10.5	10.5	10.5	10.6	10.6	10.6	10.7	10.7	10.7	10.7	10.8	10.8	10.8	10.9	10.9	10.9	11.0	11.0	11.0	11.0	11.0	11.1	11.1	11.2
29	11.0	11.0	11.1	11.1	11.1	11.1	11.2	11.2	11.2	11.2	11.2	11.3	11.3	11.3	11.3	11.4	11.4	11.4	11.4	11.4	11.5	11.5	11.5	11.5	11.5	11.6	11.6	11.6	11.6	11.6	11.7	11.7	11.7	11.7	11.8	11.8	11.8	11.8	11.9
28	12.0	12.0	12.0	12.1	12.1	12.1	12.1	12.1	12.1	12.1	12.2	12.2	12.2	12.2	12.2	12.2	12.2	12.3	12.3	12.3	12.3	12.3	12.3	12.3	12.4	12.4	12.4	12.4	12.4	12.4	12.4	12.5	12.5	12.5	12.5	12.5	12.5	12.5	12.6
27	13.0	13.0	13.0	13.0	13.0	13.0	13.0	13.0	13.1	13.1	13.1	13.1	13.1	13.1	13.1	13.1	13.1	13.1	13.1	13.1	13.1	13.1	13.1	13.2	13.2	13.2	13.2	13.2	13.2	13.2	13.2	13.2	13.2	13.2	13.2	13.2	13.2	13.2	13.2

LISTED PUT OPTION PRICE WHEN EXERCISE PRICE IS 45

NUMBER OF WEEKS BEFORE THE OPTION EXPIRES

Common Stock Price

Price	1	2	3	4	5	6	7	8	9	10	11	12	13	14	15	16	17	18	19	20	21	22	23	24	25	26	27	28	29	30	31	32	33	34	35	36	37	38	39
63	0.0	0.0	0.0	0.0	0.0	0.0	0.0	0.0	0.0	0.0	0.0	0.0	0.0	0.0	0.0	0.0	0.0	0.0	0.0	0.0	0.0	0.0	0.0	0.0	0.0	0.0	0.0	0.0	0.0	0.0	0.0	0.0	0.0	0.0	0.0	0.0	0.0	0.0	0.0
62	0.0	0.0	0.0	0.0	0.0	0.0	0.0	0.0	0.0	0.0	0.0	0.0	0.0	0.0	0.0	0.0	0.0	0.0	0.0	0.0	0.0	0.0	0.0	0.0	0.0	0.0	0.0	0.0	0.0	0.0	0.0	0.0	0.0	0.0	0.0	0.0	0.0	0.0	0.1
61	0.0	0.0	0.0	0.0	0.0	0.0	0.0	0.0	0.0	0.0	0.0	0.0	0.0	0.0	0.0	0.0	0.0	0.0	0.0	0.0	0.0	0.0	0.0	0.0	0.0	0.0	0.0	0.0	0.0	0.0	0.0	0.0	0.0	0.0	0.0	0.1	0.1	0.2	0.2
60	0.0	0.0	0.0	0.0	0.0	0.0	0.0	0.0	0.0	0.0	0.0	0.0	0.0	0.0	0.0	0.0	0.0	0.0	0.0	0.0	0.0	0.0	0.0	0.0	0.0	0.0	0.0	0.0	0.0	0.0	0.0	0.1	0.1	0.2	0.2	0.3	0.3	0.3	0.4
59	0.0	0.0	0.0	0.0	0.0	0.0	0.0	0.0	0.0	0.0	0.0	0.0	0.0	0.0	0.0	0.0	0.0	0.0	0.0	0.0	0.0	0.0	0.0	0.0	0.0	0.0	0.0	0.0	0.1	0.1	0.2	0.2	0.3	0.3	0.4	0.4	0.5	0.5	0.6
58	0.0	0.0	0.0	0.0	0.0	0.0	0.0	0.0	0.0	0.0	0.0	0.0	0.0	0.0	0.0	0.0	0.0	0.0	0.0	0.0	0.0	0.0	0.0	0.0	0.1	0.1	0.2	0.2	0.3	0.3	0.4	0.4	0.5	0.5	0.6	0.6	0.7	0.7	0.8
57	0.0	0.0	0.0	0.0	0.0	0.0	0.0	0.0	0.0	0.0	0.0	0.0	0.0	0.0	0.0	0.0	0.0	0.0	0.0	0.0	0.1	0.1	0.2	0.2	0.3	0.3	0.4	0.4	0.5	0.5	0.6	0.6	0.7	0.7	0.8	0.8	0.9	0.9	1.0
56	0.0	0.0	0.0	0.0	0.0	0.0	0.0	0.0	0.0	0.0	0.0	0.0	0.0	0.0	0.0	0.0	0.1	0.1	0.2	0.2	0.3	0.3	0.4	0.4	0.5	0.5	0.6	0.6	0.7	0.7	0.8	0.8	0.9	0.9	1.0	1.0	1.1	1.1	1.2
55	0.0	0.0	0.0	0.0	0.0	0.0	0.0	0.0	0.0	0.0	0.0	0.0	0.0	0.1	0.1	0.2	0.2	0.3	0.4	0.4	0.5	0.5	0.6	0.6	0.7	0.8	0.8	0.9	0.9	1.0	1.0	1.1	1.1	1.2	1.2	1.3	1.3	1.3	1.4
54	0.0	0.0	0.0	0.0	0.0	0.0	0.0	0.0	0.0	0.0	0.0	0.1	0.1	0.2	0.3	0.4	0.4	0.5	0.5	0.6	0.7	0.7	0.8	0.8	0.9	0.9	1.0	1.1	1.1	1.2	1.2	1.3	1.3	1.4	1.4	1.5	1.5	1.5	1.6
53	0.0	0.0	0.0	0.0	0.0	0.0	0.0	0.0	0.0	0.1	0.1	0.2	0.3	0.4	0.4	0.5	0.6	0.6	0.7	0.8	0.8	0.9	0.9	1.0	1.1	1.1	1.2	1.3	1.3	1.4	1.4	1.5	1.5	1.6	1.6	1.7	1.7	1.8	1.8
52	0.0	0.0	0.0	0.0	0.0	0.0	0.0	0.0	0.1	0.1	0.2	0.3	0.4	0.5	0.6	0.6	0.7	0.8	0.9	0.9	1.0	1.1	1.1	1.2	1.3	1.3	1.4	1.5	1.5	1.6	1.6	1.7	1.8	1.8	1.9	1.9	2.0	2.0	2.1
51	0.0	0.0	0.0	0.0	0.0	0.0	0.0	0.1	0.2	0.3	0.4	0.5	0.6	0.7	0.8	0.9	0.9	1.0	1.1	1.2	1.2	1.3	1.4	1.4	1.5	1.6	1.6	1.7	1.7	1.8	1.9	1.9	2.0	2.0	2.1	2.1	2.2	2.2	2.3
50	0.0	0.0	0.0	0.0	0.0	0.0	0.1	0.1	0.3	0.4	0.5	0.6	0.7	0.8	0.9	1.0	1.1	1.2	1.2	1.3	1.4	1.5	1.5	1.6	1.7	1.8	1.8	1.9	2.0	2.0	2.1	2.2	2.2	2.3	2.3	2.4	2.5	2.5	2.6
49	0.0	0.0	0.0	0.1	0.2	0.3	0.4	0.5	0.6	0.7	0.8	0.9	1.0	1.1	1.2	1.3	1.4	1.5	1.6	1.7	1.8	1.8	1.9	2.0	2.0	2.1	2.2	2.2	2.3	2.3	2.4	2.4	2.5	2.6	2.6	2.7	2.7	2.8	2.8
48	0.0	0.0	0.2	0.4	0.5	0.7	0.8	0.9	1.0	1.1	1.2	1.3	1.4	1.5	1.5	1.6	1.7	1.8	1.9	2.0	2.0	2.1	2.2	2.2	2.3	2.4	2.4	2.5	2.5	2.6	2.7	2.7	2.8	2.8	2.9	2.9	3.0	3.0	3.1
47	0.0	0.3	0.5	0.7	0.8	1.0	1.1	1.2	1.4	1.5	1.6	1.6	1.7	1.8	1.9	2.0	2.0	2.1	2.2	2.3	2.3	2.4	2.5	2.5	2.6	2.7	2.7	2.8	2.9	2.9	3.0	3.0	3.1	3.1	3.2	3.2	3.3	3.3	3.4
46	0.3	0.6	0.8	1.0	1.1	1.3	1.4	1.5	1.6	1.7	1.8	1.9	2.0	2.1	2.2	2.2	2.3	2.4	2.5	2.6	2.6	2.7	2.8	2.8	2.9	3.0	3.0	3.1	3.1	3.2	3.3	3.3	3.4	3.4	3.5	3.5	3.6	3.6	3.7
45	0.6	0.9	1.1	1.3	1.4	1.6	1.7	1.8	1.9	2.0	2.1	2.2	2.3	2.4	2.5	2.6	2.6	2.7	2.8	2.9	2.9	3.0	3.1	3.1	3.2	3.3	3.3	3.4	3.4	3.5	3.6	3.6	3.7	3.7	3.8	3.8	3.9	3.9	4.0
44	1.1	1.2	1.3	1.5	1.7	1.8	1.9	2.0	2.2	2.3	2.4	2.5	2.6	2.7	2.8	2.9	3.0	3.1	3.2	3.3	3.4	3.5	3.6	3.7	3.8	4.0	4.1	4.2	4.3	4.4	4.5	4.5	4.6	4.6	4.7	4.7	4.8	4.8	4.9
43	2.1	2.2	2.3	2.5	2.6	2.7	2.8	2.9	3.0	3.1	3.2	3.3	3.4	3.5	3.6	3.7	3.8	3.9	4.0	4.1	4.2	4.3	4.4	4.5	4.6	4.7	4.8	4.9	5.0	5.1	5.2	5.3	5.4	5.4	5.5	5.6	5.6	5.7	5.8
42	3.1	3.2	3.3	3.4	3.5	3.6	3.7	3.8	3.9	4.0	4.1	4.2	4.3	4.4	4.5	4.6	4.7	4.8	4.9	5.0	5.1	5.2	5.3	5.4	5.5	5.6	5.7	5.8	5.9	6.0	6.0	6.1	6.2	6.3	6.4	6.5	6.5	6.6	6.7
41	4.1	4.2	4.3	4.4	4.5	4.5	4.6	4.7	4.8	4.9	5.0	5.1	5.2	5.3	5.4	5.4	5.5	5.6	5.7	5.8	5.9	6.0	6.1	6.2	6.3	6.4	6.4	6.5	6.6	6.7	6.8	6.9	7.0	7.1	7.2	7.3	7.3	7.4	7.5
40	5.1	5.2	5.3	5.4	5.4	5.5	5.6	5.7	5.8	5.8	5.9	6.0	6.1	6.2	6.2	6.3	6.4	6.5	6.6	6.7	6.7	6.8	6.9	7.0	7.1	7.1	7.2	7.3	7.4	7.5	7.6	7.6	7.7	7.8	7.9	8.0	8.1	8.1	8.2
39	6.1	6.1	6.2	6.3	6.4	6.4	6.5	6.6	6.7	6.7	6.8	6.9	7.0	7.0	7.1	7.2	7.3	7.3	7.4	7.5	7.6	7.6	7.7	7.8	7.9	7.9	8.0	8.1	8.2	8.2	8.3	8.4	8.5	8.5	8.6	8.7	8.8	8.8	8.9
38	7.1	7.1	7.2	7.3	7.3	7.4	7.5	7.5	7.6	7.7	7.7	7.8	7.9	7.9	8.0	8.1	8.1	8.2	8.3	8.3	8.4	8.5	8.5	8.6	8.7	8.7	8.8	8.9	8.9	9.0	9.1	9.1	9.2	9.3	9.3	9.4	9.5	9.5	9.6
37	8.1	8.1	8.2	8.2	8.3	8.3	8.4	8.5	8.5	8.6	8.6	8.7	8.8	8.8	8.9	8.9	9.0	9.0	9.1	9.2	9.2	9.3	9.3	9.4	9.5	9.5	9.6	9.6	9.7	9.7	9.8	9.9	9.9	10.0	10.0	10.1	10.1	10.2	10.3
36	9.1	9.2	9.2	9.3	9.3	9.4	9.4	9.5	9.5	9.6	9.6	9.7	9.7	9.8	9.8	9.9	9.9	10.0	10.0	10.1	10.1	10.2	10.2	10.2	10.3	10.3	10.4	10.4	10.5	10.5	10.6	10.6	10.7	10.7	10.8	10.8	10.9	10.9	11.0
35	10.0	10.1	10.1	10.2	10.2	10.3	10.3	10.3	10.4	10.4	10.5	10.5	10.6	10.6	10.7	10.7	10.7	10.8	10.8	10.9	10.9	11.0	11.0	11.1	11.1	11.1	11.2	11.2	11.3	11.3	11.3	11.4	11.4	11.5	11.5	11.6	11.6	11.6	11.7
34	11.0	11.1	11.1	11.1	11.2	11.2	11.2	11.3	11.3	11.4	11.4	11.4	11.5	11.5	11.5	11.6	11.6	11.6	11.7	11.7	11.7	11.8	11.8	11.9	11.9	11.9	12.0	12.0	12.0	12.1	12.1	12.1	12.2	12.2	12.2	12.3	12.3	12.4	12.4
33	12.0	12.1	12.1	12.1	12.1	12.2	12.2	12.2	12.2	12.3	12.3	12.3	12.4	12.4	12.4	12.4	12.5	12.5	12.5	12.6	12.6	12.6	12.6	12.7	12.7	12.7	12.7	12.8	12.8	12.8	12.9	12.9	12.9	12.9	13.0	13.0	13.0	13.1	13.1
32	13.0	13.0	13.1	13.1	13.1	13.1	13.1	13.2	13.2	13.2	13.2	13.2	13.2	13.3	13.3	13.3	13.3	13.3	13.4	13.4	13.4	13.4	13.5	13.5	13.5	13.5	13.5	13.6	13.6	13.6	13.6	13.6	13.7	13.7	13.7	13.7	13.7	13.8	13.8
31	14.0	14.0	14.0	14.0	14.1	14.1	14.1	14.1	14.1	14.1	14.1	14.1	14.2	14.2	14.2	14.2	14.2	14.2	14.2	14.3	14.3	14.3	14.3	14.3	14.3	14.3	14.3	14.3	14.3	14.4	14.4	14.4	14.4	14.4	14.4	14.4	14.4	14.5	14.5
30	15.0	15.0	15.0	15.0	15.0	15.0	15.0	15.0	15.0	15.0	15.0	15.1	15.1	15.1	15.1	15.1	15.1	15.1	15.1	15.1	15.1	15.1	15.1	15.1	15.1	15.1	15.1	15.1	15.1	15.1	15.1	15.1	15.1	15.1	15.1	15.2	15.2	15.2	15.2

LISTED PUT OPTION PRICE WHEN EXERCISE PRICE IS 50

NUMBER OF WEEKS BEFORE THE OPTION EXPIRES

Common Stock Price	1	2	3	4	5	6	7	8	9	10	11	12	13	14	15	16	17	18	19	20	21	22	23	24	25	26	27	28	29	30	31	32	33	34	35	36	37	38	39
65	0.0	0.0	0.0	0.0	0.0	0.0	0.0	0.0	0.0	0.0	0.0	0.0	0.0	0.0	0.0	0.0	0.0	0.0	0.0	0.0	0.0	0.0	0.0	0.0	0.0	0.0	0.0	0.1	0.1	0.2	0.3	0.3	0.4	0.5	0.5	0.6	0.6	0.7	0.8
64	0.0	0.0	0.0	0.0	0.0	0.0	0.0	0.0	0.0	0.0	0.0	0.0	0.0	0.0	0.0	0.0	0.0	0.0	0.0	0.0	0.0	0.0	0.0	0.0	0.0	0.1	0.1	0.2	0.3	0.3	0.4	0.5	0.5	0.6	0.7	0.8	0.8	0.9	0.9
63	0.0	0.0	0.0	0.0	0.0	0.0	0.0	0.0	0.0	0.0	0.0	0.0	0.0	0.0	0.0	0.0	0.0	0.0	0.0	0.0	0.0	0.0	0.1	0.2	0.3	0.3	0.4	0.5	0.5	0.6	0.7	0.7	0.8	0.9	1.0	1.0	1.1	1.1	1.1
62	0.0	0.0	0.0	0.0	0.0	0.0	0.0	0.0	0.0	0.0	0.0	0.0	0.0	0.0	0.0	0.0	0.0	0.0	0.0	0.1	0.2	0.2	0.3	0.4	0.5	0.5	0.6	0.7	0.7	0.8	0.9	0.9	1.0	1.1	1.1	1.2	1.2	1.3	1.3
61	0.0	0.0	0.0	0.0	0.0	0.0	0.0	0.0	0.0	0.0	0.0	0.0	0.0	0.0	0.0	0.0	0.0	0.1	0.2	0.3	0.4	0.5	0.5	0.6	0.7	0.7	0.8	0.9	0.9	1.0	1.1	1.1	1.2	1.3	1.3	1.4	1.4	1.5	1.6
60	0.0	0.0	0.0	0.0	0.0	0.0	0.0	0.0	0.0	0.0	0.0	0.0	0.0	0.0	0.0	0.2	0.3	0.4	0.4	0.5	0.6	0.7	0.7	0.8	0.9	1.0	1.0	1.1	1.2	1.2	1.3	1.4	1.4	1.5	1.6	1.6	1.7	1.7	1.8
59	0.0	0.0	0.0	0.0	0.0	0.0	0.0	0.0	0.0	0.0	0.0	0.0	0.1	0.2	0.3	0.4	0.5	0.6	0.6	0.7	0.8	0.9	0.9	1.0	1.1	1.2	1.2	1.3	1.3	1.4	1.5	1.6	1.6	1.7	1.8	1.8	1.9	1.9	2.0
58	0.0	0.0	0.0	0.0	0.0	0.0	0.0	0.0	0.0	0.0	0.2	0.3	0.4	0.5	0.6	0.7	0.7	0.8	0.9	1.0	1.1	1.1	1.2	1.3	1.4	1.4	1.5	1.6	1.6	1.7	1.7	1.8	1.9	1.9	2.0	2.1	2.1	2.2	2.2
57	0.0	0.0	0.0	0.0	0.0	0.0	0.0	0.0	0.2	0.3	0.4	0.5	0.6	0.7	0.8	0.9	1.0	1.1	1.1	1.2	1.3	1.4	1.4	1.5	1.6	1.7	1.7	1.8	1.9	1.9	2.0	2.1	2.1	2.2	2.2	2.3	2.4	2.4	2.5
56	0.0	0.0	0.0	0.0	0.0	0.0	0.2	0.3	0.5	0.6	0.6	0.8	0.9	1.0	1.1	1.1	1.2	1.3	1.4	1.5	1.5	1.6	1.7	1.8	1.8	1.9	2.0	2.1	2.1	2.2	2.2	2.3	2.4	2.4	2.5	2.6	2.6	2.7	2.7
55	0.0	0.0	0.0	0.0	0.1	0.3	0.4	0.6	0.7	0.8	0.9	1.0	1.1	1.2	1.3	1.4	1.5	1.6	1.7	1.7	1.8	1.9	2.0	2.0	2.1	2.2	2.3	2.3	2.4	2.4	2.5	2.6	2.6	2.7	2.8	2.8	2.9	2.9	3.0
54	0.0	0.0	0.1	0.2	0.4	0.6	0.7	0.8	1.0	1.1	1.2	1.3	1.4	1.5	1.6	1.7	1.7	1.8	1.9	2.0	2.1	2.2	2.2	2.3	2.4	2.4	2.5	2.6	2.6	2.7	2.7	2.8	2.9	2.9	3.0	3.1	3.1	3.2	3.3
53	0.0	0.1	0.3	0.5	0.7	0.8	1.0	1.1	1.2	1.3	1.5	1.6	1.7	1.7	1.9	1.9	2.0	2.1	2.2	2.3	2.4	2.4	2.5	2.6	2.7	2.8	2.8	2.9	2.9	3.0	3.1	3.1	3.2	3.2	3.3	3.4	3.4	3.5	3.5
52	0.1	0.4	0.6	0.8	1.0	1.1	1.3	1.4	1.5	1.6	1.7	1.8	1.9	2.0	2.1	2.2	2.3	2.4	2.5	2.6	2.6	2.7	2.8	2.9	2.9	3.0	3.1	3.2	3.2	3.3	3.3	3.4	3.5	3.5	3.6	3.7	3.7	3.8	3.8
51	0.4	0.7	1.0	1.1	1.3	1.4	1.6	1.7	1.8	2.0	2.0	2.2	2.3	2.3	2.4	2.5	2.6	2.7	2.8	2.9	2.9	3.0	3.1	3.2	3.2	3.3	3.4	3.5	3.5	3.6	3.6	3.7	3.8	3.8	3.9	4.0	4.0	4.1	4.1
50	0.7	1.0	1.2	1.4	1.6	1.7	1.9	2.0	2.1	2.3	2.4	2.5	2.6	2.7	2.8	2.8	2.9	3.0	3.1	3.2	3.3	3.4	3.4	3.5	3.6	3.6	3.7	3.8	3.8	3.9	4.0	4.0	4.1	4.1	4.2	4.3	4.3	4.4	4.4
49	1.1	1.3	1.4	1.6	1.8	1.9	2.1	2.2	2.3	2.4	2.5	2.7	2.7	2.9	3.0	3.0	3.2	3.3	3.3	3.5	3.5	3.6	3.8	3.8	3.9	4.0	4.1	4.2	4.3	4.4	4.5	4.6	4.7	4.8	4.8	5.0	5.1	5.2	5.3
48	2.2	2.4	2.6	2.7	2.9	3.1	3.1	3.3	3.4	3.5	3.6	3.7	3.8	3.9	4.0	4.2	4.3	4.4	4.5	4.6	4.8	4.8	5.0	5.1	5.2	5.3	5.4	5.5	5.6	5.6	5.7	5.7	5.8	5.8	6.0	6.1	6.1	6.2	6.2
47	3.1	3.2	3.4	3.4	3.6	3.7	3.8	3.9	4.0	4.1	4.2	4.3	4.5	4.6	4.7	4.8	4.9	5.0	5.1	5.2	5.3	5.5	5.6	5.7	5.8	5.9	6.0	6.1	6.2	6.4	6.5	6.5	6.6	6.6	6.8	7.0	7.0	7.1	7.1
46	4.1	4.2	4.3	4.4	4.5	4.6	4.7	4.8	4.9	5.0	5.1	5.2	5.4	5.5	5.6	5.7	5.8	5.9	6.0	6.1	6.2	6.3	6.4	6.5	6.6	6.7	6.8	6.9	7.0	7.1	7.2	7.3	7.4	7.5	7.6	7.7	7.8	7.9	8.0
45	5.1	5.2	5.3	5.4	5.5	5.5	5.6	5.8	5.8	6.0	6.1	6.2	6.2	6.3	6.4	6.5	6.6	6.7	6.8	6.9	6.9	7.0	7.1	7.2	7.4	7.4	7.5	7.6	7.7	7.9	8.0	8.1	8.2	8.3	8.4	8.5	8.6	8.7	8.7
44	6.2	6.3	6.4	6.4	6.4	6.5	6.6	6.7	6.7	6.9	7.0	7.1	7.1	7.2	7.3	7.4	7.5	7.6	7.7	7.8	7.9	7.9	8.0	8.1	8.2	8.3	8.4	8.5	8.6	8.6	8.7	8.8	8.9	9.0	9.0	9.1	9.2	9.3	9.4
43	7.1	7.2	7.3	7.4	7.4	7.5	7.6	7.6	7.7	7.7	7.9	8.0	8.0	8.1	8.2	8.3	8.4	8.4	8.5	8.6	8.6	8.7	8.8	8.9	9.0	9.1	9.1	9.2	9.3	9.4	9.5	9.6	9.6	9.7	9.8	9.9	9.9	10.1	10.1
42	8.1	8.2	8.3	8.4	8.4	8.4	8.5	8.6	8.7	8.7	8.8	8.9	8.9	9.0	9.1	9.2	9.2	9.3	9.4	9.5	9.5	9.6	9.7	9.7	9.8	9.9	9.9	10.0	10.1	10.2	10.3	10.3	10.4	10.5	10.5	10.6	10.7	10.8	10.8
41	9.1	9.2	9.2	9.3	9.3	9.4	9.5	9.5	9.6	9.6	9.7	9.8	9.8	9.9	9.9	10.0	10.1	10.2	10.2	10.3	10.4	10.4	10.5	10.6	10.6	10.7	10.7	10.8	10.9	10.9	11.0	11.1	11.1	11.2	11.3	11.3	11.4	11.5	11.5
40	10.1	10.2	10.2	10.3	10.3	10.3	10.4	10.5	10.5	10.6	10.6	10.7	10.7	10.8	10.9	10.9	11.0	11.0	11.1	11.1	11.2	11.2	11.3	11.4	11.4	11.5	11.5	11.6	11.7	11.7	11.8	11.8	11.9	11.9	12.0	12.0	12.1	12.2	12.2
39	11.0	11.1	11.1	11.2	11.2	11.3	11.3	11.4	11.4	11.5	11.5	11.6	11.6	11.7	11.7	11.7	11.8	11.9	11.9	12.0	12.0	12.1	12.1	12.2	12.2	12.3	12.4	12.4	12.5	12.5	12.6	12.6	12.7	12.7	12.8	12.8	12.9	12.9	12.9
38	12.0	12.1	12.1	12.2	12.2	12.3	12.3	12.4	12.4	12.5	12.5	12.5	12.6	12.6	12.7	12.7	12.7	12.8	12.8	12.8	12.9	12.9	12.9	13.0	13.0	13.1	13.1	13.2	13.2	13.2	13.3	13.3	13.4	13.4	13.4	13.5	13.5	13.6	13.6
37	13.0	13.1	13.1	13.1	13.2	13.2	13.2	13.3	13.3	13.3	13.4	13.4	13.4	13.5	13.5	13.5	13.6	13.6	13.6	13.7	13.7	13.7	13.8	13.8	13.8	13.9	13.9	13.9	14.0	14.0	14.0	14.1	14.1	14.1	14.2	14.2	14.2	14.3	14.3
36	14.0	14.1	14.1	14.1	14.1	14.2	14.2	14.2	14.2	14.2	14.3	14.3	14.3	14.4	14.4	14.4	14.4	14.5	14.5	14.5	14.5	14.6	14.6	14.6	14.6	14.7	14.7	14.7	14.7	14.8	14.8	14.8	14.8	14.9	14.9	14.9	14.9	15.0	15.0
35	15.0	15.0	15.1	15.1	15.1	15.1	15.1	15.1	15.2	15.2	15.2	15.2	15.2	15.2	15.3	15.3	15.3	15.3	15.3	15.3	15.4	15.4	15.4	15.4	15.4	15.5	15.5	15.5	15.5	15.5	15.5	15.6	15.6	15.6	15.6	15.7	15.7	15.7	15.7

LISTED PUT OPTION PRICE WHEN EXERCISE PRICE IS 60

NUMBER OF WEEKS BEFORE THE OPTION EXPIRES

Common Stock Price

Stock Price	1	2	3	4	5	6	7	8	9	10	11	12	13	14	15	16	17	18	19	20	21	22	23	24	25	26	27	28	29	30	31	32	33	34	35	36	37	38	39
78	0.0	0.0	0.0	0.0	0.0	0.0	0.0	0.0	0.0	0.0	0.0	0.0	0.0	0.0	0.0	0.0	0.0	0.0	0.0	0.0	0.0	0.0	0.0	0.0	0.0	0.0	0.0	0.1	0.2	0.2	0.3	0.4	0.5	0.5	0.6	0.7	0.8	0.8	0.9
77	0.0	0.0	0.0	0.0	0.0	0.0	0.0	0.0	0.0	0.0	0.0	0.0	0.0	0.0	0.0	0.0	0.0	0.0	0.0	0.0	0.0	0.0	0.0	0.1	0.1	0.2	0.2	0.3	0.4	0.4	0.5	0.6	0.6	0.7	0.8	0.9	1.0	1.0	1.1
76	0.0	0.0	0.0	0.0	0.0	0.0	0.0	0.0	0.0	0.0	0.0	0.0	0.0	0.0	0.0	0.0	0.0	0.0	0.0	0.0	0.0	0.1	0.1	0.2	0.2	0.3	0.4	0.5	0.5	0.6	0.7	0.8	0.8	0.9	1.0	1.1	1.1	1.2	1.3
75	0.0	0.0	0.0	0.0	0.0	0.0	0.0	0.0	0.0	0.0	0.0	0.0	0.0	0.0	0.0	0.0	0.0	0.0	0.0	0.0	0.1	0.2	0.2	0.3	0.4	0.5	0.6	0.6	0.7	0.8	0.9	1.0	1.0	1.1	1.2	1.3	1.3	1.4	1.5
74	0.0	0.0	0.0	0.0	0.0	0.0	0.0	0.0	0.0	0.0	0.0	0.0	0.0	0.0	0.0	0.0	0.0	0.0	0.1	0.1	0.2	0.3	0.4	0.5	0.6	0.7	0.8	0.9	1.0	1.0	1.1	1.2	1.3	1.3	1.4	1.5	1.6	1.6	1.7
73	0.0	0.0	0.0	0.0	0.0	0.0	0.0	0.0	0.0	0.0	0.0	0.0	0.0	0.0	0.0	0.0	0.0	0.1	0.2	0.3	0.4	0.5	0.6	0.7	0.8	0.9	1.0	1.1	1.2	1.2	1.3	1.4	1.5	1.6	1.6	1.7	1.8	1.8	1.9
72	0.0	0.0	0.0	0.0	0.0	0.0	0.0	0.0	0.0	0.0	0.0	0.0	0.0	0.0	0.0	0.0	0.1	0.2	0.3	0.4	0.5	0.6	0.7	0.8	0.9	1.0	1.1	1.2	1.3	1.4	1.5	1.6	1.6	1.7	1.8	1.9	2.0	2.0	2.1
71	0.0	0.0	0.0	0.0	0.0	0.0	0.0	0.0	0.0	0.0	0.0	0.0	0.0	0.0	0.0	0.1	0.2	0.3	0.4	0.5	0.6	0.7	0.8	0.9	1.0	1.1	1.2	1.3	1.4	1.5	1.6	1.7	1.8	1.9	2.0	2.1	2.2	2.3	2.4
70	0.0	0.0	0.0	0.0	0.0	0.0	0.0	0.0	0.0	0.0	0.0	0.0	0.0	0.1	0.2	0.3	0.4	0.5	0.6	0.7	0.8	0.9	1.0	1.1	1.2	1.3	1.4	1.5	1.6	1.7	1.8	1.9	2.0	2.1	2.2	2.3	2.4	2.5	2.6
69	0.0	0.0	0.0	0.0	0.0	0.0	0.0	0.0	0.0	0.0	0.0	0.0	0.1	0.2	0.3	0.4	0.5	0.6	0.7	0.8	0.9	1.1	1.2	1.3	1.4	1.5	1.6	1.7	1.8	1.9	2.1	2.2	2.3	2.4	2.5	2.6	2.7	2.7	2.8
68	0.0	0.0	0.0	0.0	0.0	0.0	0.0	0.0	0.0	0.0	0.0	0.1	0.2	0.3	0.4	0.6	0.7	0.8	0.9	1.1	1.2	1.3	1.4	1.6	1.7	1.8	1.9	2.0	2.2	2.3	2.4	2.5	2.6	2.7	2.8	2.9	3.0	3.0	3.1
67	0.0	0.0	0.0	0.0	0.0	0.0	0.0	0.0	0.0	0.0	0.1	0.2	0.3	0.5	0.6	0.7	0.9	1.0	1.1	1.3	1.4	1.5	1.7	1.8	1.9	2.0	2.1	2.3	2.4	2.5	2.6	2.7	2.8	2.9	3.0	3.1	3.2	3.2	3.3
66	0.0	0.0	0.0	0.0	0.0	0.0	0.0	0.0	0.0	0.1	0.2	0.4	0.5	0.7	0.8	1.0	1.1	1.3	1.4	1.5	1.7	1.8	1.9	2.1	2.2	2.3	2.5	2.6	2.7	2.8	2.9	3.0	3.1	3.2	3.3	3.4	3.5	3.5	3.6
65	0.0	0.0	0.0	0.0	0.0	0.0	0.0	0.0	0.1	0.2	0.3	0.5	0.6	0.8	0.9	1.1	1.3	1.4	1.6	1.7	1.9	2.0	2.2	2.3	2.4	2.6	2.7	2.8	2.9	3.1	3.2	3.3	3.4	3.5	3.6	3.7	3.8	3.8	3.9
64	0.0	0.0	0.0	0.0	0.0	0.0	0.0	0.1	0.2	0.3	0.5	0.6	0.8	0.9	1.1	1.3	1.4	1.6	1.8	1.9	2.1	2.2	2.4	2.5	2.6	2.8	2.9	3.0	3.1	3.3	3.4	3.5	3.6	3.7	3.8	3.9	4.0	4.0	4.1
63	0.0	0.0	0.0	0.0	0.0	0.0	0.1	0.2	0.4	0.5	0.7	0.8	1.0	1.2	1.3	1.5	1.7	1.8	2.0	2.1	2.3	2.4	2.6	2.7	2.8	3.0	3.1	3.2	3.4	3.5	3.6	3.7	3.8	3.9	4.0	4.1	4.2	4.3	4.4
62	0.2	0.3	0.4	0.6	0.7	0.8	0.9	1.0	1.1	1.3	1.4	1.5	1.6	1.7	1.9	2.0	2.1	2.2	2.3	2.5	2.6	2.7	2.8	2.9	3.0	3.2	3.3	3.4	3.5	3.6	3.8	3.9	4.0	4.1	4.2	4.3	4.5	4.6	4.7
61	0.5	0.6	0.7	0.9	1.0	1.1	1.2	1.3	1.4	1.6	1.7	1.8	1.9	2.0	2.2	2.3	2.4	2.5	2.6	2.8	2.9	3.0	3.1	3.2	3.3	3.5	3.6	3.7	3.8	3.9	4.1	4.2	4.3	4.4	4.5	4.6	4.8	4.9	5.0
60	0.9	1.0	1.1	1.2	1.4	1.5	1.6	1.7	1.8	1.9	2.1	2.2	2.3	2.4	2.5	2.6	2.7	2.9	3.0	3.1	3.2	3.3	3.4	3.6	3.7	3.8	3.9	4.0	4.1	4.3	4.4	4.5	4.6	4.7	4.8	4.9	5.1	5.2	5.3
59	1.2	1.3	1.5	1.6	1.7	1.9	2.0	2.1	2.3	2.4	2.5	2.6	2.8	2.9	3.0	3.2	3.3	3.4	3.6	3.7	3.8	4.0	4.1	4.2	4.4	4.5	4.6	4.8	4.9	5.0	5.1	5.3	5.4	5.5	5.7	5.8	5.9	6.1	6.2
58	2.1	2.2	2.4	2.5	2.6	2.8	2.9	3.0	3.2	3.3	3.4	3.5	3.7	3.8	3.9	4.1	4.2	4.3	4.5	4.6	4.7	4.9	5.0	5.1	5.3	5.4	5.5	5.7	5.8	5.9	6.1	6.2	6.3	6.5	6.6	6.7	6.8	7.0	7.1
57	3.1	3.2	3.4	3.5	3.6	3.8	3.9	4.0	4.1	4.3	4.4	4.5	4.6	4.8	4.9	5.0	5.2	5.3	5.4	5.6	5.7	5.8	5.9	6.1	6.2	6.3	6.5	6.6	6.7	6.8	7.0	7.1	7.2	7.4	7.5	7.6	7.7	7.9	8.0
56	4.1	4.2	4.4	4.5	4.6	4.7	4.9	5.0	5.1	5.2	5.4	5.5	5.6	5.7	5.9	6.0	6.1	6.2	6.4	6.5	6.6	6.8	6.9	7.0	7.2	7.3	7.4	7.5	7.7	7.8	7.9	8.0	8.2	8.3	8.4	8.5	8.7	8.8	8.9
55	5.1	5.2	5.3	5.5	5.6	5.7	5.8	6.0	6.1	6.2	6.3	6.5	6.6	6.7	6.8	7.0	7.1	7.2	7.3	7.5	7.6	7.7	7.8	8.0	8.1	8.2	8.3	8.5	8.6	8.7	8.8	9.0	9.1	9.2	9.3	9.4	9.6	9.7	9.8
54	6.1	6.2	6.3	6.4	6.6	6.7	6.8	6.9	7.0	7.1	7.3	7.4	7.5	7.6	7.7	7.8	7.9	8.1	8.2	8.3	8.4	8.5	8.6	8.8	8.9	9.0	9.1	9.2	9.3	9.5	9.6	9.7	9.8	9.9	10.0	10.1	10.3	10.4	10.5
53	7.1	7.2	7.3	7.4	7.5	7.6	7.7	7.9	8.0	8.1	8.2	8.3	8.4	8.5	8.6	8.7	8.8	9.0	9.1	9.2	9.3	9.4	9.5	9.6	9.7	9.8	9.9	10.0	10.1	10.2	10.3	10.4	10.6	10.7	10.8	10.9	11.0	11.1	11.2
52	8.1	8.2	8.3	8.4	8.5	8.6	8.7	8.8	8.9	9.0	9.1	9.2	9.3	9.4	9.5	9.6	9.7	9.8	9.9	10.0	10.1	10.2	10.3	10.4	10.5	10.6	10.7	10.8	10.9	11.0	11.1	11.2	11.3	11.4	11.5	11.6	11.7	11.8	11.9
51	9.1	9.2	9.3	9.4	9.5	9.6	9.7	9.7	9.8	9.9	10.0	10.1	10.2	10.3	10.4	10.5	10.6	10.7	10.8	10.9	10.9	11.0	11.1	11.2	11.3	11.4	11.5	11.6	11.7	11.8	11.9	11.9	12.0	12.1	12.2	12.3	12.4	12.5	12.6
50	10.1	10.2	10.3	10.4	10.4	10.5	10.6	10.7	10.8	10.9	11.0	11.0	11.1	11.2	11.3	11.4	11.4	11.5	11.6	11.7	11.8	11.9	11.9	12.0	12.1	12.2	12.3	12.4	12.5	12.5	12.6	12.7	12.8	12.9	13.0	13.0	13.1	13.2	13.3
49	11.1	11.2	11.2	11.3	11.4	11.5	11.6	11.6	11.7	11.8	11.9	11.9	12.0	12.1	12.2	12.2	12.3	12.4	12.5	12.5	12.6	12.7	12.8	12.9	12.9	13.0	13.1	13.2	13.2	13.3	13.4	13.5	13.5	13.6	13.7	13.8	13.8	13.9	14.0
48	12.1	12.2	12.2	12.3	12.4	12.4	12.5	12.6	12.6	12.7	12.8	12.8	12.9	13.0	13.0	13.1	13.2	13.3	13.3	13.4	13.5	13.5	13.6	13.7	13.7	13.8	13.9	13.9	14.0	14.1	14.1	14.2	14.3	14.4	14.4	14.5	14.6	14.6	14.7
47	13.1	13.2	13.2	13.3	13.3	13.4	13.5	13.5	13.6	13.7	13.7	13.8	13.8	13.9	14.0	14.0	14.1	14.1	14.2	14.3	14.3	14.4	14.4	14.5	14.6	14.6	14.7	14.7	14.8	14.9	14.9	15.0	15.0	15.1	15.2	15.2	15.3	15.3	15.4
46	14.1	14.2	14.2	14.3	14.3	14.4	14.4	14.5	14.5	14.6	14.6	14.7	14.7	14.8	14.8	14.9	14.9	15.0	15.0	15.1	15.1	15.2	15.3	15.3	15.4	15.4	15.5	15.5	15.6	15.6	15.7	15.7	15.8	15.8	15.9	15.9	16.0	16.0	16.1
45	15.0	15.1	15.1	15.1	15.2	15.2	15.3	15.3	15.4	15.4	15.4	15.5	15.5	15.6	15.6	15.7	15.7	15.8	15.8	15.9	15.9	15.9	16.0	16.0	16.1	16.1	16.2	16.2	16.3	16.3	16.3	16.4	16.4	16.5	16.5	16.6	16.6	16.6	16.7
44	16.0	16.0	16.1	16.1	16.1	16.2	16.2	16.3	16.3	16.3	16.4	16.4	16.4	16.5	16.5	16.6	16.6	16.6	16.7	16.7	16.7	16.8	16.8	16.8	16.9	16.9	17.0	17.0	17.0	17.1	17.1	17.1	17.2	17.2	17.3	17.3	17.3	17.4	17.4
43	17.0	17.0	17.1	17.1	17.1	17.1	17.2	17.2	17.2	17.3	17.3	17.3	17.4	17.4	17.4	17.4	17.5	17.5	17.5	17.6	17.6	17.6	17.6	17.7	17.7	17.7	17.8	17.8	17.8	17.8	17.9	17.9	17.9	18.0	18.0	18.0	18.0	18.1	18.1
42	18.0	18.0	18.1	18.1	18.1	18.1	18.1	18.2	18.2	18.2	18.2	18.3	18.3	18.3	18.3	18.3	18.4	18.4	18.4	18.4	18.4	18.5	18.5	18.5	18.5	18.6	18.6	18.6	18.6	18.6	18.7	18.7	18.7	18.7	18.7	18.8	18.8	18.8	18.8

LISTED PUT OPTION PRICE WHEN EXERCISE PRICE IS 70

NUMBER OF WEEKS BEFORE THE OPTION EXPIRES

Common Stock Price

Price	1	2	3	4	5	6	7	8	9	10	11	12	13	14	15	16	17	18	19	20	21	22	23	24	25	26	27	28	29	30	31	32	33	34	35	36	37	38	39
91	0.0	0.0	0.0	0.0	0.0	0.0	0.0	0.0	0.0	0.0	0.0	0.0	0.0	0.0	0.0	0.0	0.0	0.0	0.0	0.0	0.0	0.0	0.0	0.0	0.0	0.0	0.0	0.1	0.2	0.3	0.4	0.5	0.6	0.6	0.7	0.8	0.9	1.0	1.1
90	0.0	0.0	0.0	0.0	0.0	0.0	0.0	0.0	0.0	0.0	0.0	0.0	0.0	0.0	0.0	0.0	0.0	0.0	0.0	0.0	0.0	0.0	0.0	0.0	0.0	0.1	0.2	0.3	0.4	0.5	0.6	0.7	0.7	0.8	0.9	1.0	1.1	1.1	1.2
89	0.0	0.0	0.0	0.0	0.0	0.0	0.0	0.0	0.0	0.0	0.0	0.0	0.0	0.0	0.0	0.0	0.0	0.0	0.0	0.0	0.0	0.0	0.1	0.2	0.3	0.4	0.5	0.5	0.6	0.7	0.8	0.9	0.9	1.0	1.1	1.2	1.3	1.3	1.4
88	0.0	0.0	0.0	0.0	0.0	0.0	0.0	0.0	0.0	0.0	0.0	0.0	0.0	0.0	0.0	0.0	0.0	0.0	0.0	0.0	0.0	0.1	0.2	0.3	0.4	0.5	0.6	0.7	0.8	0.8	0.9	1.0	1.1	1.2	1.3	1.4	1.5	1.5	1.6
87	0.0	0.0	0.0	0.0	0.0	0.0	0.0	0.0	0.0	0.0	0.0	0.0	0.0	0.0	0.0	0.0	0.0	0.1	0.2	0.3	0.4	0.5	0.6	0.7	0.8	0.9	1.0	1.1	1.2	1.3	1.4	1.5	1.6	1.6	1.7	1.8	1.9	2.0	2.1
86	0.0	0.0	0.0	0.0	0.0	0.0	0.0	0.0	0.0	0.0	0.0	0.0	0.0	0.0	0.0	0.0	0.1	0.2	0.3	0.4	0.5	0.6	0.7	0.8	0.9	1.0	1.1	1.2	1.3	1.4	1.5	1.6	1.7	1.8	1.9	2.0	2.1	2.2	2.3
85	0.0	0.0	0.0	0.0	0.0	0.0	0.0	0.0	0.0	0.0	0.0	0.0	0.0	0.0	0.1	0.2	0.3	0.4	0.5	0.6	0.7	0.8	0.9	1.0	1.2	1.3	1.4	1.5	1.6	1.7	1.8	1.9	2.0	2.1	2.2	2.3	2.3	2.4	2.5
84	0.0	0.0	0.0	0.0	0.0	0.0	0.0	0.0	0.0	0.0	0.0	0.0	0.1	0.2	0.4	0.5	0.6	0.7	0.8	0.9	1.1	1.2	1.3	1.4	1.5	1.6	1.7	1.8	1.9	2.0	2.1	2.2	2.3	2.3	2.4	2.5	2.6	2.6	2.7
83	0.0	0.0	0.0	0.0	0.0	0.0	0.0	0.0	0.0	0.0	0.3	0.4	0.6	0.7	0.8	0.9	1.1	1.2	1.3	1.4	1.5	1.6	1.7	1.8	1.9	2.0	2.1	2.2	2.3	2.4	2.5	2.6	2.7	2.8	2.9	2.9	3.0	2.9	2.9
82	0.0	0.0	0.0	0.0	0.0	0.0	0.0	0.0	0.0	0.4	0.8	0.9	0.8	1.0	1.1	1.2	1.3	1.4	1.6	1.7	1.9	2.0	2.1	2.2	2.3	2.4	2.5	2.6	2.7	2.8	2.9	3.0	3.1	3.2	3.3	3.3	3.4	2.9	3.2
81	0.0	0.0	0.0	0.0	0.0	0.0	0.0	0.3	0.5	0.7	0.8	0.9	1.0	1.2	1.4	1.7	1.6	1.8	1.9	2.1	2.2	2.4	2.5	2.6	2.7	2.8	2.9	3.0	3.1	3.2	3.2	3.3	3.4	3.5	3.6	3.7	3.8	3.1	3.4
80	0.0	0.0	0.0	0.0	0.2	0.5	0.6	0.5	0.7	0.9	1.0	1.2	1.3	1.4	1.6	1.7	1.8	2.0	2.1	2.3	2.4	2.5	2.6	2.7	2.9	3.0	3.1	3.2	3.3	3.4	3.5	3.6	3.7	3.8	3.9	3.9	4.0	3.3	3.7
79	0.0	0.0	0.0	0.2	0.5	0.7	0.8	0.9	1.0	1.1	1.3	1.4	1.6	1.7	1.9	2.0	2.2	2.3	2.4	2.6	2.7	2.8	2.9	3.0	3.2	3.3	3.4	3.5	3.6	3.7	3.8	3.9	4.0	4.0	4.1	4.2	4.3	3.6	3.9
78	0.0	0.0	0.5	0.8	0.8	1.0	1.1	1.3	1.4	1.7	1.6	1.7	1.8	2.1	2.2	2.3	2.5	2.6	2.8	2.9	3.1	3.2	3.3	3.4	3.5	3.6	3.7	3.8	4.0	4.1	4.2	4.3	4.4	4.5	4.6	4.7	4.8	4.1	4.2
77	0.0	0.0	0.8	1.1	1.0	1.2	1.7	1.9	2.1	2.2	2.4	2.5	2.6	2.7	2.8	3.1	3.2	3.3	3.5	3.6	3.8	3.9	4.0	4.1	4.2	4.3	4.4	4.5	4.6	4.7	4.8	4.9	5.0	5.1	5.2	5.3	4.8	4.4	4.2
76	0.0	0.3	1.1	1.4	1.6	2.1	2.3	2.5	2.7	2.8	3.0	3.1	3.3	3.4	3.5	3.7	3.8	3.9	4.0	4.1	4.2	4.4	4.5	4.6	4.7	4.8	4.9	5.0	5.2	5.3	5.4	5.5	5.6	5.7	5.8	4.5	4.4	4.5	4.5
75	0.0	0.5	1.5	1.8	2.2	2.3	2.6	3.0	3.2	3.3	3.5	3.6	3.8	3.9	4.1	4.2	4.3	4.4	4.6	4.8	4.9	5.0	5.1	5.2	5.3	5.4	5.5	5.6	5.7	5.8	5.9	6.0	6.1	4.9	4.7	4.5	4.6	4.6	4.7
74	0.0	0.8	1.8	2.3	2.7	2.8	3.2	3.4	3.6	3.8	4.0	4.1	4.3	4.4	4.6	4.7	4.9	5.0	5.2	5.3	5.5	5.6	5.7	5.8	5.9	6.0	6.1	6.3	6.4	6.5	6.6	6.7	5.1	4.9	4.7	4.8	4.8	4.9	5.0
73	0.1	1.1	2.5	3.0	3.4	3.6	3.9	4.3	4.5	4.7	4.9	5.0	5.2	5.4	5.6	5.7	5.9	6.0	6.2	6.4	6.6	6.7	6.9	7.0	7.2	7.3	7.4	7.6	7.7	7.8	5.5	5.1	4.8	5.0	5.0	5.1	5.1	5.2	5.3
72	0.4	1.4	3.3	3.7	4.1	4.3	4.8	5.0	5.2	5.5	5.7	5.9	6.1	6.2	6.4	6.6	6.8	6.9	7.1	7.3	7.5	7.6	7.8	8.0	8.1	8.3	8.4	8.6	8.8	5.5	5.2	5.3	5.4	5.5	5.6	5.7	5.7	5.8	5.6
71	0.7	1.7	3.5	4.4	4.6	4.9	5.1	6.1	6.3	6.5	6.7	6.8	7.0	7.2	7.4	7.6	7.7	7.9	8.1	8.3	8.5	8.7	8.8	9.0	9.2	9.3	9.5	9.7	5.9	5.6	5.7	5.8	5.8	5.9	6.0	6.1	6.2	6.2	5.9
70	1.2	2.2	4.2	5.2	5.8	6.3	6.1	7.1	8.1	8.3	8.4	8.6	8.8	9.0	9.2	9.4	9.6	9.8	10.0	10.2	10.4	10.6	10.8	11.0	11.2	11.4	11.6	6.3	6.1	6.2	6.3	6.4	6.5	6.6	6.7	6.8	6.9	7.0	6.2
69	1.5	2.5	4.7	5.6	6.3	6.9	7.3	7.6	8.0	8.2	8.4	8.6	8.8	9.0	9.2	9.4	9.6	9.8	10.0	10.2	10.4	10.6	10.8	11.0	11.2	11.4	11.6	6.9	6.5	6.6	6.7	6.8	6.9	7.0	7.1	7.2	7.3	7.4	7.1
68	2.2	3.1	5.3	6.6	7.3	7.8	8.3	8.9	9.2	9.3	9.6	9.8	10.0	10.2	10.4	10.6	10.8	11.0	11.2	11.4	11.6	11.8	12.0	12.2	12.4	12.6	12.8	7.5	7.0	7.1	7.2	7.3	7.4	7.5	7.6	7.7	7.8	7.9	8.0
67	3.2	4.2	6.1	7.5	8.2	8.8	9.3	10.1	10.3	10.5	10.8	11.0	11.2	11.4	11.6	11.8	12.0	12.2	12.4	12.6	12.8	13.0	13.2	13.4	13.6	13.8	14.0	8.3	7.6	8.0	8.9	9.1	9.2	9.4	8.6	7.8	7.9	8.8	8.9
66	4.2	5.2	6.4	8.5	8.6	9.7	10.1	10.9	11.0	11.2	11.4	11.6	11.8	12.2	12.4	12.6	12.8	13.0	13.2	13.4	13.6	13.8	14.0	14.2	14.4	14.6	14.8	9.2	9.4	10.1	10.4	10.6	10.7	10.4	9.4	9.5	9.6	9.7	9.8
65	5.2	6.3	8.4	9.5	9.6	10.6	11.6	12.0	12.2	12.4	12.6	12.8	13.0	13.2	13.4	13.5	13.7	13.9	14.1	14.3	14.5	14.7	14.9	15.1	15.3	15.5	15.7	10.1	10.1	10.7	11.0	11.3	11.4	11.6	10.3	10.4	10.6	10.6	10.7
64	6.1	6.4	8.4	10.4	11.5	12.1	12.6	13.4	13.6	13.8	14.0	14.2	14.3	14.5	14.7	14.9	15.1	15.3	15.5	15.6	15.8	16.0	16.2	16.4	16.6	16.8	17.0	11.0	11.0	11.2	11.9	12.2	12.2	11.6	11.1	11.3	11.3	11.3	11.6
63	7.1	7.3	9.4	11.4	12.5	13.0	13.6	14.5	14.7	14.9	15.0	15.2	15.4	15.6	15.8	16.0	16.2	16.3	16.5	16.7	16.9	17.1	17.3	17.5	17.7	17.9	18.1	12.3	11.7	11.9	12.2	12.8	12.9	13.0	12.4	12.6	12.7	12.8	12.2
62	8.1	9.2	11.2	12.3	13.4	14.0	14.6	15.6	15.6	15.7	15.9	16.1	16.3	16.4	16.6	16.8	17.0	17.2	17.4	17.6	17.8	18.0	18.2	18.4	18.6	18.8	19.0	13.1	13.2	13.3	13.4	13.6	13.7	13.8	13.9	13.3	13.4	13.5	12.9
61	9.1	10.2	11.3	13.3	14.4	14.9	15.5	16.4	16.6	16.6	16.8	17.0	17.2	17.3	17.5	17.7	17.9	18.1	18.3	18.5	18.7	18.9	19.1	19.3	19.5	19.8	20.1	14.5	14.1	14.2	14.3	14.5	14.6	14.7	14.8	14.9	14.1	14.2	13.6
60	10.1	11.2	13.3	14.3	15.4	16.0	16.6	17.4	17.5	17.6	17.8	17.9	18.1	18.3	18.5	18.7	18.9	19.1	19.3	19.5	19.6	19.8	20.0	20.2	20.4	20.6	20.8	15.4	15.5	16.2	16.4	16.6	16.7	16.9	15.5	15.6	15.7	15.0	14.3
59	11.1	12.2	13.4	15.2	16.3	16.9	17.5	18.2	18.4	18.5	18.6	18.8	19.0	19.2	19.4	19.6	19.7	19.9	20.1	20.3	20.5	20.7	20.9	21.1	20.8	20.9	20.1	16.3	16.4	17.1	17.4	17.6	17.7	17.9	16.6	16.7	16.8	15.9	15.0
58	12.1	12.3	13.4	15.3	16.5	17.4	17.9	18.8	18.9	19.0	19.1	19.3	19.5	19.6	19.8	20.0	20.2	20.4	20.6	20.8	21.0	21.2	21.3	20.7	20.8	20.9	21.1	17.3	17.4	18.0	18.1	18.3	18.4	18.6	17.7	17.8	17.9	16.3	15.7
57	13.1	13.2	15.2	16.3	17.4	18.1	18.7	19.5	19.6	19.7	19.8	20.0	20.2	20.3	20.5	20.7	20.9	21.1	21.3	21.5	20.5	20.6	20.7	20.9	21.0	21.2	21.4	18.5	18.6	19.3	19.5	19.7	19.8	19.9	18.8	19.0	18.0	17.1	16.4
56	14.1	14.2	15.3	17.2	18.4	19.0	19.7	20.4	20.5	20.6	20.7	20.8	21.0	21.2	21.4	21.6	20.5	20.6	20.7	20.9	21.0	21.2	21.4	21.5	20.9	21.1	21.2	19.4	19.5	20.2	20.4	20.6	20.7	20.9	20.5	19.7	19.8	17.7	17.1
55	15.1	15.1	16.2	17.4	18.5	19.8	20.5	21.3	21.4	21.5	21.6	20.5	20.6	20.8	20.9	21.0	21.2	21.3	21.5	21.7	21.9	20.7	20.9	21.0	21.1	21.3	21.5	20.5	20.6	20.7	20.8	21.0	21.1	21.3	20.5	20.6	20.7	18.4	17.8
54	16.1	16.2	17.2	18.3	19.4	20.7	21.3	20.4	20.5	20.6	20.7	20.9	21.0	21.2	21.3	21.5	21.7	21.1	21.2	21.3	21.5	21.6	20.7	20.9	21.0	21.1	21.3	20.4	20.5	20.6	20.7	20.9	21.0	21.1	20.4	20.5	20.6	19.1	18.5
53	17.1	17.1	18.1	19.2	20.3	21.6	20.4	20.5	20.6	20.7	20.9	21.1	21.2	21.4	21.6	21.7	20.5	20.6	20.7	20.9	21.0	21.2	21.3	21.5	20.4	20.5	20.6	20.7	20.9	21.0	21.2	21.3	21.4	21.6	20.8	19.9	19.0	19.8	19.2
52	18.0	18.1	19.1	20.1	20.3	20.4	20.5	20.6	20.8	21.0	21.2	21.3	21.4	21.6	21.7	20.5	20.6	20.7	20.9	21.0	21.2	21.3	21.5	20.4	20.5	20.6	20.7	20.9	21.0	21.2	21.3	21.4	21.6	21.1	20.2	19.7	19.7	19.8	19.9
51	19.0	19.1	19.1	19.2	20.2	20.3	20.4	20.5	20.6	20.8	21.0	21.2	21.3	21.4	21.6	21.7	20.5	20.6	20.7	20.9	21.0	21.2	21.3	21.5	21.6	20.7	20.8	20.9	21.1	21.2	21.3	21.5	21.6	21.7	20.8	20.1	20.3	20.5	20.6
50	20.0	20.0	20.1	20.1	20.2	20.2	20.3	20.3	20.4	20.3	20.4	20.4	20.5	20.5	20.6	20.7	20.6	20.6	20.6	20.7	20.8	20.8	20.9	21.0	21.0	21.1	21.1	21.2	21.2	21.3	21.4	21.5	21.6	21.6	20.4	20.5	20.5	21.2	21.3
49	21.0	21.0	21.1	21.1	21.1	21.2	21.2	21.2	21.2	21.2	21.3	21.3	21.3	21.4	21.4	21.4	21.4	21.4	21.5	21.5	21.5	21.5	21.6	21.6	21.6	21.6	21.7	21.7	21.7	21.7	21.7	21.8	21.8	21.8	21.1	21.9	21.9	21.9	22.0

LISTED PUT OPTION PRICE WHEN EXERCISE PRICE IS 80

NUMBER OF WEEKS BEFORE THE OPTION EXPIRES

Common Stock Price	1	2	3	4	5	6	7	8	9	10	11	12	13	14	15	16	17	18	19	20	21	22	23	24	25	26	27	28	29	30	31	32	33	34	35	36	37	38	39
104	0.0	0.0	0.0	0.0	0.0	0.0	0.0	0.0	0.0	0.0	0.0	0.0	0.0	0.0	0.0	0.0	0.0	0.0	0.0	0.0	0.0	0.0	0.0	0.0	0.0	0.0	0.0	0.1	0.2	0.3	0.4	0.5	0.6	0.7	0.8	0.9	1.0	1.1	1.2
102	0.0	0.0	0.0	0.0	0.0	0.0	0.0	0.0	0.0	0.0	0.0	0.0	0.0	0.0	0.0	0.0	0.0	0.0	0.0	0.0	0.0	0.0	0.0	0.1	0.2	0.3	0.4	0.5	0.6	0.7	0.8	0.9	1.0	1.1	1.2	1.3	1.4	1.5	1.6
100	0.0	0.0	0.0	0.0	0.0	0.0	0.0	0.0	0.0	0.0	0.0	0.0	0.0	0.0	0.0	0.0	0.0	0.0	0.0	0.0	0.1	0.2	0.3	0.5	0.6	0.7	0.8	0.9	1.0	1.1	1.2	1.3	1.4	1.5	1.6	1.7	1.8	1.9	2.0
99	0.0	0.0	0.0	0.0	0.0	0.0	0.0	0.0	0.0	0.0	0.0	0.0	0.0	0.0	0.0	0.0	0.0	0.0	0.0	0.2	0.3	0.4	0.5	0.7	0.8	0.9	1.0	1.1	1.2	1.3	1.4	1.5	1.6	1.7	1.8	1.9	2.0	2.1	2.2
98	0.0	0.0	0.0	0.0	0.0	0.0	0.0	0.0	0.0	0.0	0.0	0.0	0.0	0.0	0.0	0.0	0.0	0.1	0.3	0.4	0.5	0.6	0.8	0.9	1.0	1.1	1.2	1.3	1.4	1.5	1.6	1.7	1.8	1.9	2.0	2.1	2.2	2.3	2.4
97	0.0	0.0	0.0	0.0	0.0	0.0	0.0	0.0	0.0	0.0	0.0	0.0	0.0	0.0	0.0	0.1	0.2	0.3	0.5	0.6	0.7	0.9	1.0	1.1	1.2	1.3	1.4	1.5	1.6	1.7	1.9	2.0	2.1	2.2	2.2	2.3	2.4	2.5	2.6
96	0.0	0.0	0.0	0.0	0.0	0.0	0.0	0.0	0.0	0.0	0.0	0.0	0.0	0.0	0.1	0.3	0.4	0.6	0.7	0.8	1.0	1.1	1.2	1.3	1.4	1.5	1.6	1.8	1.9	2.0	2.1	2.2	2.3	2.4	2.5	2.6	2.7	2.8	2.8
95	0.0	0.0	0.0	0.0	0.0	0.0	0.0	0.0	0.0	0.0	0.0	0.0	0.1	0.2	0.4	0.5	0.7	0.8	0.9	1.0	1.2	1.3	1.4	1.5	1.7	1.8	1.9	2.0	2.1	2.2	2.3	2.4	2.5	2.6	2.7	2.8	2.9	3.0	3.1
94	0.0	0.0	0.0	0.0	0.0	0.0	0.0	0.0	0.0	0.0	0.0	0.1	0.3	0.4	0.6	0.7	0.9	1.0	1.2	1.3	1.4	1.5	1.6	1.8	1.9	2.0	2.1	2.2	2.3	2.4	2.5	2.6	2.7	2.8	2.9	3.0	3.1	3.2	3.3
93	0.0	0.0	0.0	0.0	0.0	0.0	0.0	0.0	0.0	0.0	0.2	0.4	0.5	0.7	0.8	1.0	1.1	1.3	1.4	1.5	1.6	1.8	1.9	2.0	2.1	2.2	2.3	2.4	2.6	2.7	2.8	2.9	3.0	3.1	3.2	3.3	3.3	3.4	3.5
92	0.0	0.0	0.0	0.0	0.0	0.0	0.0	0.0	0.1	0.3	0.4	0.6	0.8	0.9	1.1	1.2	1.4	1.5	1.6	1.8	1.9	2.0	2.1	2.2	2.4	2.5	2.6	2.7	2.8	2.9	3.0	3.1	3.2	3.3	3.4	3.5	3.6	3.7	3.8
91	0.0	0.0	0.0	0.0	0.0	0.0	0.0	0.1	0.3	0.5	0.7	0.8	1.0	1.2	1.3	1.5	1.6	1.7	1.9	2.0	2.1	2.2	2.4	2.5	2.6	2.7	2.8	2.9	3.0	3.1	3.2	3.3	3.4	3.5	3.6	3.7	3.8	3.9	4.0
90	0.0	0.0	0.0	0.0	0.0	0.0	0.2	0.4	0.6	0.8	0.9	1.1	1.3	1.4	1.6	1.7	1.9	2.0	2.1	2.2	2.4	2.5	2.6	2.7	2.8	3.0	3.1	3.2	3.3	3.4	3.5	3.6	3.7	3.8	3.9	4.0	4.1	4.2	4.3
89	0.0	0.0	0.0	0.0	0.0	0.2	0.4	0.6	0.8	1.0	1.2	1.4	1.5	1.7	1.8	2.0	2.1	2.2	2.4	2.5	2.6	2.8	2.9	3.0	3.1	3.2	3.3	3.4	3.5	3.6	3.8	3.9	4.0	4.1	4.1	4.2	4.3	4.4	4.5
88	0.0	0.0	0.0	0.0	0.2	0.5	0.7	0.9	1.1	1.3	1.4	1.6	1.8	1.9	2.1	2.2	2.4	2.5	2.6	2.8	2.9	3.0	3.1	3.3	3.4	3.5	3.6	3.7	3.8	3.9	4.0	4.1	4.2	4.3	4.4	4.5	4.6	4.7	4.8
87	0.0	0.0	0.0	0.2	0.5	0.7	1.0	1.2	1.4	1.5	1.7	1.9	2.0	2.2	2.3	2.5	2.6	2.8	2.9	3.0	3.2	3.3	3.4	3.5	3.6	3.7	3.9	4.0	4.1	4.2	4.3	4.4	4.5	4.6	4.7	4.8	4.9	5.0	5.1
86	0.0	0.0	0.2	0.5	0.8	1.0	1.2	1.4	1.6	1.8	2.0	2.2	2.3	2.5	2.6	2.8	2.9	3.0	3.2	3.3	3.4	3.6	3.7	3.8	3.9	4.0	4.1	4.2	4.3	4.5	4.6	4.7	4.8	4.9	4.9	5.0	5.1	5.2	5.3
85	0.0	0.1	0.5	0.8	1.0	1.3	1.5	1.7	1.9	2.1	2.3	2.4	2.6	2.8	2.9	3.0	3.2	3.3	3.5	3.6	3.7	3.8	4.0	4.1	4.2	4.3	4.4	4.5	4.6	4.7	4.8	4.9	5.0	5.1	5.2	5.3	5.4	5.5	5.6
84	0.0	0.4	0.8	1.1	1.3	1.6	1.8	2.0	2.2	2.4	2.6	2.7	2.9	3.0	3.2	3.3	3.5	3.6	3.7	3.9	4.0	4.1	4.2	4.4	4.5	4.6	4.7	4.8	4.9	5.0	5.1	5.2	5.3	5.4	5.5	5.6	5.7	5.8	5.9
83	0.2	0.7	1.0	1.4	1.6	1.9	2.1	2.3	2.5	2.7	2.9	3.0	3.2	3.3	3.5	3.6	3.8	3.9	4.0	4.2	4.3	4.4	4.5	4.7	4.8	4.9	5.0	5.1	5.2	5.3	5.4	5.5	5.6	5.7	5.8	5.9	6.0	6.1	6.2
82	0.5	1.0	1.3	1.7	1.9	2.2	2.4	2.6	2.8	3.0	3.2	3.3	3.5	3.6	3.8	3.9	4.1	4.2	4.3	4.5	4.6	4.7	4.8	5.0	5.1	5.2	5.3	5.4	5.5	5.6	5.7	5.8	5.9	6.0	6.1	6.2	6.3	6.4	6.5
81	0.8	1.3	1.7	2.0	2.2	2.5	2.7	2.9	3.1	3.3	3.5	3.6	3.8	3.9	4.1	4.2	4.4	4.5	4.6	4.8	4.9	5.0	5.1	5.3	5.4	5.5	5.6	5.7	5.8	5.9	6.0	6.1	6.2	6.3	6.4	6.5	6.6	6.7	6.8
80	1.1	1.6	2.0	2.3	2.5	2.8	3.0	3.2	3.4	3.6	3.8	3.9	4.1	4.3	4.4	4.6	4.7	4.8	5.0	5.1	5.2	5.3	5.5	5.6	5.7	5.8	5.9	6.0	6.1	6.2	6.3	6.4	6.5	6.6	6.7	6.8	6.9	7.0	7.1
79	1.2	1.7	2.1	2.5	2.7	3.0	3.2	3.4	3.6	3.8	4.0	4.1	4.3	4.5	4.7	4.9	5.0	5.1	5.3	5.4	5.6	5.7	5.8	6.0	6.2	6.4	6.6	6.8	7.0	7.1	7.2	7.3	7.4	7.5	7.6	7.7	7.8	7.9	8.0
78	2.2	2.4	2.6	2.8	3.0	3.2	3.4	3.6	3.8	4.0	4.2	4.4	4.6	4.8	5.0	5.2	5.4	5.6	5.8	6.0	6.2	6.4	6.6	6.8	7.0	7.2	7.4	7.6	7.8	8.0	8.1	8.2	8.3	8.4	8.5	8.6	8.7	8.8	8.9
77	3.2	3.4	3.6	3.8	4.0	4.2	4.4	4.5	4.7	4.9	5.1	5.3	5.5	5.7	5.9	6.1	6.3	6.5	6.7	6.9	7.1	7.2	7.4	7.6	7.8	8.0	8.2	8.4	8.6	8.8	9.0	9.1	9.2	9.3	9.4	9.5	9.6	9.7	9.8
76	4.2	4.4	4.6	4.7	4.9	5.1	5.3	5.5	5.7	5.9	6.0	6.2	6.4	6.6	6.8	7.0	7.1	7.3	7.5	7.7	7.9	8.1	8.3	8.4	8.6	8.8	9.0	9.2	9.4	9.6	9.7	9.9	10.1	10.2	10.3	10.4	10.5	10.6	10.7
75	5.2	5.4	5.5	5.7	5.9	6.1	6.2	6.4	6.6	6.8	6.9	7.1	7.3	7.5	7.7	7.8	8.0	8.2	8.4	8.5	8.7	8.9	9.1	9.3	9.4	9.6	9.8	9.9	10.1	10.3	10.5	10.7	10.8	11.0	11.2	11.3	11.4	11.5	11.6
74	6.2	6.3	6.5	6.7	6.8	7.0	7.2	7.4	7.5	7.7	7.9	8.0	8.2	8.4	8.5	8.7	8.9	9.0	9.2	9.4	9.6	9.7	9.9	10.1	10.2	10.4	10.6	10.7	10.9	11.1	11.3	11.4	11.6	11.8	11.9	12.1	12.3	12.4	12.5
73	7.2	7.3	7.5	7.6	7.8	8.0	8.1	8.3	8.5	8.6	8.8	8.9	9.1	9.3	9.4	9.6	9.7	9.9	10.1	10.2	10.4	10.6	10.7	10.9	11.0	11.2	11.4	11.5	11.7	11.8	12.0	12.2	12.3	12.5	12.7	12.8	13.0	13.1	13.3
72	8.2	8.3	8.5	8.6	8.8	8.9	9.1	9.2	9.4	9.5	9.7	9.8	9.9	10.2	10.3	10.5	10.6	10.8	10.9	11.1	11.2	11.4	11.5	11.7	11.8	12.0	12.2	12.3	12.5	12.6	12.8	12.9	13.1	13.2	13.4	13.5	13.7	13.8	14.0
71	9.1	9.3	9.4	9.6	9.7	9.9	10.0	10.2	10.3	10.5	10.6	10.8	10.9	11.0	11.2	11.3	11.5	11.6	11.8	11.9	12.1	12.2	12.4	12.5	12.6	12.8	12.9	13.1	13.2	13.4	13.5	13.7	13.8	14.0	14.1	14.3	14.4	14.5	14.7
70	10.1	10.3	10.4	10.6	10.7	10.8	11.0	11.1	11.2	11.4	11.5	11.7	11.8	11.9	12.1	12.2	12.3	12.5	12.6	12.8	12.9	13.0	13.2	13.3	13.5	13.6	13.7	13.9	14.0	14.1	14.3	14.4	14.6	14.7	14.8	15.0	15.1	15.2	15.4
69	11.1	11.3	11.4	11.5	11.7	11.8	11.9	12.0	12.2	12.3	12.4	12.6	12.7	12.8	13.0	13.1	13.2	13.3	13.5	13.6	13.7	13.9	14.0	14.1	14.3	14.4	14.5	14.6	14.8	14.9	15.0	15.2	15.3	15.4	15.6	15.7	15.8	15.9	16.1
68	12.1	12.2	12.4	12.5	12.6	12.7	12.9	13.0	13.1	13.2	13.3	13.5	13.6	13.7	13.8	14.0	14.1	14.2	14.3	14.4	14.6	14.7	14.8	14.9	15.1	15.2	15.3	15.4	15.5	15.7	15.8	15.9	16.0	16.2	16.3	16.4	16.5	16.7	16.8
67	13.1	13.2	13.3	13.5	13.6	13.7	13.8	13.9	14.0	14.1	14.3	14.4	14.5	14.6	14.7	14.8	14.9	15.1	15.2	15.3	15.4	15.5	15.6	15.7	15.9	16.0	16.1	16.2	16.3	16.4	16.6	16.7	16.8	16.9	17.0	17.1	17.2	17.4	17.5
66	14.1	14.2	14.3	14.4	14.5	14.6	14.7	14.9	15.0	15.1	15.2	15.3	15.4	15.5	15.6	15.7	15.8	15.9	16.0	16.1	16.2	16.3	16.5	16.6	16.7	16.8	16.9	17.0	17.1	17.2	17.3	17.4	17.5	17.6	17.7	17.8	17.9	18.1	18.2
65	15.1	15.2	15.3	15.4	15.5	15.6	15.7	15.8	15.9	16.0	16.1	16.2	16.3	16.4	16.5	16.6	16.7	16.8	16.9	17.0	17.1	17.2	17.3	17.4	17.5	17.6	17.7	17.8	17.9	18.0	18.1	18.2	18.3	18.4	18.5	18.6	18.7	18.8	18.9
64	16.1	16.2	16.3	16.4	16.5	16.5	16.6	16.7	16.8	16.9	17.0	17.1	17.2	17.3	17.4	17.5	17.5	17.6	17.7	17.8	17.9	18.0	18.1	18.2	18.3	18.4	18.5	18.6	18.6	18.7	18.8	18.9	19.0	19.1	19.2	19.3	19.4	19.5	19.6
63	17.1	17.2	17.2	17.3	17.4	17.5	17.6	17.7	17.7	17.8	17.9	18.0	18.1	18.2	18.2	18.3	18.4	18.5	18.6	18.7	18.7	18.8	18.9	19.0	19.1	19.2	19.2	19.3	19.4	19.5	19.6	19.7	19.7	19.8	19.9	19.9	20.1	20.2	20.2
62	18.1	18.2	18.2	18.3	18.4	18.5	18.5	18.6	18.7	18.8	18.8	18.9	19.0	19.1	19.1	19.2	19.3	19.4	19.4	19.5	19.6	19.7	19.7	19.8	19.9	19.9	20.0	20.1	20.2	20.3	20.3	20.4	20.5	20.6	20.6	20.7	20.8	20.9	20.9
61	19.1	19.1	19.2	19.3	19.3	19.4	19.5	19.5	19.6	19.7	19.7	19.8	19.9	19.9	20.0	20.1	20.1	20.2	20.3	20.4	20.4	20.5	20.6	20.6	20.7	20.8	20.8	20.9	21.0	21.0	21.1	21.2	21.2	21.3	21.4	21.4	21.5	21.6	21.6
60	20.1	20.1	20.2	20.2	20.3	20.4	20.4	20.5	20.5	20.6	20.7	20.7	20.8	20.8	20.9	21.0	21.0	21.1	21.1	21.2	21.3	21.3	21.4	21.4	21.5	21.6	21.6	21.7	21.7	21.8	21.9	21.9	22.0	22.0	22.1	22.2	22.2	22.3	22.3
59	21.1	21.1	21.2	21.2	21.3	21.3	21.4	21.4	21.5	21.5	21.6	21.6	21.7	21.7	21.8	21.8	21.9	21.9	22.0	22.0	22.1	22.1	22.2	22.2	22.3	22.3	22.4	22.5	22.5	22.6	22.6	22.7	22.7	22.8	22.8	22.9	22.9	23.0	23.0
58	22.0	22.1	22.1	22.2	22.2	22.3	22.3	22.4	22.4	22.4	22.5	22.5	22.6	22.6	22.7	22.7	22.7	22.8	22.8	22.9	22.9	23.0	23.0	23.1	23.1	23.1	23.2	23.2	23.3	23.3	23.4	23.4	23.5	23.5	23.5	23.6	23.6	23.7	23.7
57	23.0	23.1	23.1	23.1	23.2	23.2	23.3	23.3	23.3	23.4	23.4	23.4	23.5	23.5	23.5	23.6	23.6	23.7	23.7	23.7	23.8	23.8	23.8	23.9	23.9	23.9	24.0	24.0	24.1	24.1	24.1	24.2	24.2	24.2	24.3	24.3	24.3	24.4	24.4

LISTED PUT OPTION PRICE WHEN EXERCISE PRICE IS 90

NUMBER OF WEEKS BEFORE THE OPTION EXPIRES

Common Stock Price	1	2	3	4	5	6	7	8	9	10	11	12	13	14	15	16	17	18	19	20	21	22	23	24	25	26	27	28	29	30	31	32	33	34	35	36	37	38	39
118	0.0	0.0	0.0	0.0	0.0	0.0	0.0	0.0	0.0	0.0	0.0	0.0	0.0	0.0	0.0	0.0	0.0	0.0	0.0	0.0	0.0	0.0	0.0	0.0	0.0	0.0	0.0	0.0	0.1	0.2	0.3	0.4	0.5	0.6	0.7	0.9	1.0	1.1	1.2
116	0.0	0.0	0.0	0.0	0.0	0.0	0.0	0.0	0.0	0.0	0.0	0.0	0.0	0.0	0.0	0.0	0.0	0.0	0.0	0.0	0.0	0.0	0.0	0.0	0.0	0.1	0.2	0.3	0.4	0.6	0.7	0.8	0.9	1.0	1.1	1.2	1.3	1.4	1.5
114	0.0	0.0	0.0	0.0	0.0	0.0	0.0	0.0	0.0	0.0	0.0	0.0	0.0	0.0	0.0	0.0	0.0	0.0	0.0	0.0	0.0	0.0	0.1	0.2	0.3	0.5	0.6	0.7	0.8	1.0	1.1	1.2	1.3	1.4	1.5	1.6	1.7	1.8	1.9
112	0.0	0.0	0.0	0.0	0.0	0.0	0.0	0.0	0.0	0.0	0.0	0.0	0.0	0.0	0.0	0.0	0.0	0.0	0.0	0.1	0.2	0.4	0.5	0.6	0.7	0.9	1.0	1.1	1.2	1.4	1.5	1.6	1.7	1.8	1.9	2.0	2.1	2.2	2.3
110	0.0	0.0	0.0	0.0	0.0	0.0	0.0	0.0	0.0	0.0	0.0	0.0	0.0	0.0	0.0	0.0	0.0	0.2	0.3	0.5	0.6	0.8	0.9	1.0	1.2	1.3	1.4	1.5	1.7	1.8	1.9	2.0	2.1	2.2	2.3	2.4	2.6	2.7	2.8
108	0.0	0.0	0.0	0.0	0.0	0.0	0.0	0.0	0.0	0.0	0.0	0.0	0.0	0.0	0.2	0.3	0.5	0.6	0.8	0.9	1.1	1.2	1.3	1.5	1.6	1.7	1.9	2.0	2.1	2.2	2.3	2.4	2.6	2.7	2.8	2.9	3.0	3.1	3.2
106	0.0	0.0	0.0	0.0	0.0	0.0	0.0	0.0	0.0	0.0	0.0	0.1	0.3	0.4	0.6	0.8	0.9	1.1	1.2	1.4	1.5	1.7	1.8	1.9	2.1	2.2	2.3	2.4	2.6	2.7	2.8	2.9	3.0	3.1	3.2	3.3	3.4	3.5	3.7
104	0.0	0.0	0.0	0.0	0.0	0.0	0.0	0.0	0.0	0.2	0.4	0.6	0.7	0.9	1.1	1.2	1.4	1.6	1.7	1.9	2.0	2.1	2.3	2.4	2.5	2.7	2.8	2.9	3.0	3.1	3.3	3.4	3.5	3.6	3.7	3.8	3.9	4.0	4.1
102	0.0	0.0	0.0	0.0	0.0	0.0	0.0	0.2	0.5	0.7	0.9	1.0	1.2	1.4	1.6	1.7	1.9	2.0	2.2	2.3	2.5	2.6	2.8	2.9	3.0	3.1	3.3	3.4	3.5	3.6	3.7	3.9	4.0	4.1	4.2	4.3	4.4	4.5	4.6
100	0.0	0.0	0.0	0.0	0.0	0.3	0.5	0.7	1.0	1.2	1.4	1.6	1.7	1.9	2.1	2.2	2.4	2.6	2.7	2.8	3.0	3.1	3.3	3.4	3.5	3.7	3.8	3.9	4.0	4.1	4.3	4.4	4.5	4.6	4.7	4.8	4.9	5.0	5.1
99	0.0	0.0	0.0	0.0	0.2	0.5	0.8	1.0	1.2	1.4	1.6	1.8	2.0	2.2	2.3	2.5	2.7	2.8	3.0	3.1	3.3	3.4	3.5	3.7	3.8	3.9	4.0	4.2	4.3	4.4	4.5	4.6	4.7	4.9	5.0	5.1	5.2	5.3	5.4
98	0.0	0.0	0.0	0.2	0.5	0.8	1.0	1.3	1.5	1.7	1.9	2.1	2.3	2.4	2.6	2.8	2.9	3.1	3.2	3.4	3.5	3.7	3.8	3.9	4.1	4.2	4.3	4.4	4.5	4.7	4.8	4.9	5.0	5.1	5.2	5.3	5.4	5.5	5.6
97	0.0	0.0	0.1	0.5	0.8	1.1	1.3	1.5	1.8	2.0	2.2	2.4	2.5	2.7	2.9	3.0	3.2	3.4	3.5	3.6	3.8	3.9	4.1	4.2	4.3	4.5	4.6	4.7	4.8	4.9	5.1	5.2	5.3	5.4	5.5	5.6	5.7	5.8	5.9
96	0.0	0.0	0.4	0.8	1.1	1.3	1.6	1.8	2.0	2.3	2.4	2.6	2.8	3.0	3.2	3.3	3.5	3.6	3.8	3.9	4.1	4.2	4.3	4.5	4.6	4.7	4.9	5.0	5.1	5.2	5.3	5.4	5.6	5.7	5.8	5.9	6.0	6.1	6.2
95	0.0	0.3	0.7	1.0	1.3	1.6	1.9	2.1	2.3	2.5	2.7	2.9	3.1	3.3	3.4	3.6	3.8	3.9	4.1	4.2	4.4	4.5	4.6	4.8	4.9	5.0	5.1	5.3	5.4	5.5	5.6	5.7	5.8	6.0	6.1	6.2	6.3	6.4	6.5
94	0.1	0.6	1.0	1.3	1.6	1.9	2.2	2.4	2.6	2.8	3.0	3.2	3.4	3.6	3.7	3.9	4.1	4.2	4.4	4.5	4.6	4.8	4.9	5.0	5.2	5.3	5.4	5.6	5.7	5.8	5.9	6.0	6.1	6.2	6.4	6.5	6.6	6.7	6.8
93	0.4	0.9	1.3	1.6	1.9	2.2	2.5	2.7	2.9	3.1	3.3	3.5	3.7	3.9	4.0	4.2	4.4	4.5	4.7	4.8	4.9	5.1	5.2	5.3	5.5	5.6	5.7	5.8	6.0	6.1	6.2	6.3	6.4	6.5	6.6	6.8	6.9	7.0	7.1
92	0.7	1.2	1.6	1.9	2.2	2.5	2.8	3.0	3.2	3.4	3.6	3.8	4.0	4.2	4.3	4.5	4.7	4.8	5.0	5.1	5.2	5.4	5.5	5.6	5.8	5.9	6.0	6.2	6.3	6.4	6.5	6.6	6.7	6.8	7.0	7.1	7.2	7.3	7.4
91	1.0	1.5	1.9	2.2	2.5	2.8	3.1	3.3	3.5	3.7	3.9	4.1	4.3	4.5	4.6	4.8	5.0	5.1	5.3	5.4	5.6	5.7	5.8	6.0	6.1	6.2	6.3	6.5	6.6	6.7	6.8	6.9	7.0	7.2	7.3	7.4	7.5	7.6	7.7
90	1.3	1.8	2.2	2.6	2.9	3.1	3.4	3.6	3.8	4.1	4.2	4.4	4.6	4.8	5.0	5.1	5.3	5.4	5.6	5.7	5.9	6.0	6.1	6.3	6.4	6.5	6.7	6.8	6.9	7.0	7.1	7.2	7.4	7.5	7.6	7.7	7.8	7.9	8.0
89	1.5	1.6	2.0	2.4	2.7	3.2	3.5	3.7	4.0	4.2	4.4	4.6	4.8	5.0	5.2	5.3	5.6	5.7	5.9	6.1	6.3	6.4	6.5	6.7	6.9	7.1	7.4	7.6	7.8	7.9	8.0	8.1	8.3	8.4	8.5	8.6	8.7	8.8	8.9
88	2.2	2.5	2.7	2.9	3.1	3.4	3.6	3.8	4.1	4.3	4.5	4.7	5.0	5.2	5.4	5.6	5.9	6.1	6.3	6.6	6.8	7.0	7.2	7.5	7.7	7.9	8.2	8.4	8.6	8.8	8.9	9.0	9.2	9.3	9.4	9.5	9.6	9.7	9.8
87	3.2	3.4	3.7	3.9	4.1	4.3	4.5	4.8	5.0	5.2	5.4	5.6	5.9	6.1	6.3	6.5	6.7	7.0	7.2	7.4	7.6	7.8	8.1	8.3	8.5	8.7	8.9	9.2	9.4	9.6	9.8	9.9	10.1	10.2	10.3	10.4	10.5	10.6	10.7
86	4.2	4.4	4.6	4.8	5.1	5.3	5.5	5.7	5.9	6.1	6.3	6.5	6.8	7.0	7.2	7.4	7.6	7.8	8.0	8.2	8.5	8.7	8.9	9.1	9.3	9.5	9.7	9.9	10.2	10.4	10.6	10.8	11.0	11.1	11.2	11.3	11.4	11.5	11.6
85	5.2	5.4	5.6	5.8	6.0	6.2	6.4	6.6	6.8	7.0	7.2	7.5	7.7	7.9	8.1	8.3	8.5	8.7	8.9	9.1	9.3	9.5	9.7	9.9	10.1	10.3	10.5	10.7	10.9	11.1	11.3	11.5	11.7	11.9	12.1	10.2	12.3	12.4	12.5
84	6.2	6.4	6.6	6.8	7.0	7.2	7.4	7.6	7.8	8.0	8.2	8.4	8.6	8.8	8.9	9.1	9.3	9.5	9.7	9.9	10.1	10.3	10.5	10.7	10.9	11.1	11.3	11.5	11.7	11.9	12.1	12.3	12.5	12.7	12.9	13.1	13.2	13.3	13.4
83	7.2	7.4	7.6	7.8	7.9	8.1	8.3	8.5	8.7	8.9	9.1	9.3	9.5	9.6	9.8	10.0	10.2	10.4	10.6	10.8	11.0	11.1	11.3	11.5	11.7	11.9	12.1	12.3	12.5	12.7	12.8	13.0	13.2	13.4	13.6	13.8	14.0	14.2	14.3
82	8.2	8.4	8.5	8.7	8.9	9.1	9.3	9.4	9.6	9.8	9.9	10.2	10.4	10.5	10.7	10.9	11.1	11.3	11.4	11.6	11.8	12.0	12.2	12.3	12.5	12.7	12.9	13.1	13.2	13.4	13.6	13.8	14.0	14.1	14.3	14.5	14.7	14.9	15.1
81	9.2	9.3	9.5	9.7	9.9	10.0	10.2	10.4	10.6	10.7	10.9	11.1	11.2	11.4	11.6	11.8	11.9	12.1	12.3	12.5	12.6	12.8	13.0	13.2	13.3	13.5	13.7	13.8	14.0	14.2	14.4	14.5	14.7	14.9	15.1	15.2	15.4	15.6	15.7
80	10.2	10.3	10.5	10.7	10.8	11.0	11.2	11.3	11.5	11.7	11.8	12.0	12.1	12.3	12.5	12.6	12.8	13.0	13.1	13.3	13.5	13.6	13.8	14.0	14.1	14.3	14.5	14.6	14.8	15.0	15.1	15.3	15.4	15.6	15.8	15.9	16.1	16.3	16.4
79	11.2	11.3	11.5	11.6	11.8	11.9	12.1	12.3	12.4	12.6	12.7	12.9	13.0	13.2	13.4	13.5	13.7	13.8	14.0	14.1	14.3	14.5	14.6	14.8	14.9	15.1	15.2	15.4	15.6	15.7	15.9	16.0	16.2	16.3	16.5	16.7	16.8	17.0	17.1
78	12.1	12.3	12.4	12.6	12.7	12.9	13.0	13.2	13.3	13.5	13.6	13.8	13.9	14.1	14.2	14.4	14.5	14.7	14.8	15.0	15.1	15.3	15.4	15.6	15.7	15.9	16.0	16.2	16.3	16.5	16.6	16.8	16.9	17.1	17.2	17.4	17.5	17.7	17.8
77	13.1	13.3	13.4	13.6	13.7	13.8	14.0	14.1	14.3	14.4	14.6	14.7	14.8	15.0	15.1	15.3	15.4	15.5	15.7	15.8	16.0	16.1	16.3	16.4	16.5	16.7	16.8	17.0	17.1	17.2	17.4	17.5	17.7	17.8	18.0	18.1	18.2	18.4	18.5
76	14.1	14.3	14.4	14.5	14.7	14.8	14.9	15.1	15.2	15.3	15.5	15.6	15.7	15.9	16.0	16.1	16.3	16.4	16.5	16.7	16.8	16.9	17.1	17.2	17.3	17.5	17.6	17.7	17.9	18.0	18.1	18.3	18.4	18.5	18.7	18.8	19.0	19.1	19.2
75	15.1	15.3	15.4	15.5	15.6	15.8	15.9	16.0	16.1	16.3	16.4	16.5	16.6	16.8	16.9	17.0	17.1	17.3	17.4	17.5	17.6	17.8	17.9	18.0	18.1	18.3	18.4	18.5	18.7	18.8	18.9	19.0	19.2	19.3	19.4	19.5	19.7	19.8	19.9
74	16.1	16.2	16.4	16.5	16.6	16.7	16.8	16.9	17.1	17.2	17.3	17.4	17.5	17.7	17.8	17.9	18.0	18.1	18.2	18.4	18.5	18.6	18.7	18.8	19.0	19.1	19.2	19.3	19.4	19.5	19.7	19.8	19.9	20.0	20.1	20.3	20.4	20.5	20.6
73	17.1	17.2	17.3	17.4	17.6	17.7	17.8	17.9	18.0	18.1	18.2	18.3	18.4	18.5	18.7	18.8	18.9	19.0	19.1	19.2	19.3	19.4	19.5	19.6	19.8	19.9	19.9	20.1	20.2	20.3	20.4	20.5	20.6	20.8	20.9	21.0	21.1	21.2	21.3
72	18.1	18.2	18.3	18.4	18.5	18.6	18.7	18.8	18.9	19.0	19.1	19.2	19.3	19.4	19.5	19.6	19.7	19.8	19.9	20.0	20.2	20.3	20.4	20.5	20.6	20.7	20.8	20.9	21.0	21.1	21.2	21.3	21.4	21.5	21.6	21.7	21.8	21.9	22.0
71	19.1	19.2	19.3	19.4	19.5	19.6	19.7	19.8	19.9	19.9	20.0	20.1	20.2	20.3	20.4	20.5	20.6	20.7	20.8	20.9	21.0	21.1	21.2	21.3	21.4	21.5	21.6	21.6	21.7	21.8	21.9	22.0	22.1	22.2	22.3	22.4	22.5	22.6	22.7
70	20.1	20.2	20.3	20.3	20.4	20.5	20.6	20.7	20.8	20.9	21.0	21.0	21.1	21.2	21.3	21.4	21.5	21.6	21.6	21.7	21.8	21.9	22.8	22.1	22.2	22.3	22.3	22.4	22.5	22.6	22.7	22.8	22.9	23.0	23.0	23.1	23.2	23.3	23.4
69	21.1	21.2	21.2	21.3	21.4	21.5	21.6	21.6	21.7	21.8	21.9	21.9	22.0	22.1	22.2	22.3	22.3	22.4	22.5	22.6	22.7	22.7	22.8	22.9	23.0	23.1	23.1	23.2	23.3	23.4	23.4	23.5	23.6	23.7	23.8	23.8	23.9	24.0	24.1
68	22.1	22.1	22.2	22.0	22.4	22.4	22.5	22.6	22.6	22.7	22.8	22.9	22.9	23.0	23.1	23.1	23.2	23.3	23.4	23.4	23.5	23.6	23.6	23.7	23.8	23.8	23.9	24.0	24.1	24.1	24.2	24.3	24.3	24.4	24.5	24.6	24.6	24.7	24.8
67	23.1	23.1	23.2	23.3	23.3	23.4	23.4	23.5	23.6	23.6	23.7	23.8	23.8	23.9	23.9	24.0	24.1	24.1	24.2	24.3	24.3	24.4	24.5	24.5	24.6	24.6	24.7	24.8	24.8	24.9	25.0	25.0	25.1	25.2	25.2	25.3	25.3	25.4	25.5
66	24.1	24.1	24.2	24.2	24.3	24.3	24.4	24.4	24.5	24.6	24.6	24.7	24.7	24.8	24.8	24.9	24.9	25.0	25.1	25.1	25.2	25.2	25.3	25.3	25.4	25.4	25.5	25.6	25.6	25.7	25.7	25.8	25.8	25.9	25.9	26.0	26.1	26.1	26.2
65	25.0	25.1	25.1	25.2	25.2	25.3	25.3	25.4	25.4	25.5	25.5	25.6	25.6	25.7	25.7	25.8	25.8	25.9	25.9	26.0	26.8	26.0	26.1	26.1	26.2	26.2	26.3	26.3	26.4	26.4	26.5	26.5	26.6	26.6	26.7	26.7	26.8	26.8	26.9
64	26.0	26.1	26.1	26.2	26.2	26.2	26.3	26.3	26.4	26.4	26.4	26.5	26.5	26.6	26.6	26.6	26.7	26.7	26.8	26.8	26.8	26.9	26.9	27.0	27.0	27.0	27.1	27.1	27.2	27.2	27.2	27.3	27.3	27.4	27.4	27.4	27.5	27.5	27.6

LISTED PUT OPTION PRICE WHEN EXERCISE PRICE IS 100

NUMBER OF WEEKS BEFORE THE OPTION EXPIRES

Common Stock Price

Stock Price	1	2	3	4	5	6	7	8	9	10	11	12	13	14	15	16	17	18	19	20	21	22	23	24	25	26	27	28	29	30	31	32	33	34	35	36	37	38	39
130	0.0	0.0	0.0	0.0	0.0	0.0	0.0	0.0	0.0	0.0	0.0	0.0	0.0	0.0	0.0	0.0	0.0	0.0	0.0	0.0	0.0	0.0	0.0	0.0	0.0	0.0	0.0	0.1	0.2	0.4	0.5	0.6	0.8	0.9	1.0	1.2	1.3	1.4	1.5
128	0.0	0.0	0.0	0.0	0.0	0.0	0.0	0.0	0.0	0.0	0.0	0.0	0.0	0.0	0.0	0.0	0.0	0.0	0.0	0.0	0.0	0.0	0.0	0.0	0.0	0.1	0.2	0.4	0.5	0.7	0.8	1.0	1.1	1.2	1.4	1.5	1.7	1.8	1.9
126	0.0	0.0	0.0	0.0	0.0	0.0	0.0	0.0	0.0	0.0	0.0	0.0	0.0	0.0	0.0	0.0	0.0	0.0	0.0	0.0	0.0	0.0	0.1	0.2	0.4	0.5	0.7	0.8	1.0	1.2	1.3	1.5	1.6	1.8	1.9	2.1	2.2	2.3	2.3
124	0.0	0.0	0.0	0.0	0.0	0.0	0.0	0.0	0.0	0.0	0.0	0.0	0.0	0.0	0.0	0.0	0.0	0.0	0.0	0.0	0.1	0.3	0.4	0.6	0.7	0.9	1.0	1.2	1.4	1.5	1.7	1.8	2.0	2.1	2.3	2.4	2.6	2.6	2.7
122	0.0	0.0	0.0	0.0	0.0	0.0	0.0	0.0	0.0	0.0	0.0	0.0	0.0	0.0	0.0	0.0	0.0	0.0	0.0	0.1	0.3	0.4	0.6	0.7	0.9	1.1	1.2	1.4	1.6	1.7	1.9	2.0	2.2	2.4	2.5	2.7	2.8	3.0	3.1
120	0.0	0.0	0.0	0.0	0.0	0.0	0.0	0.0	0.0	0.0	0.0	0.0	0.0	0.0	0.0	0.0	0.0	0.1	0.3	0.4	0.6	0.7	0.9	1.1	1.3	1.4	1.6	1.8	1.9	2.1	2.3	2.4	2.6	2.8	2.9	3.1	3.3	3.4	3.6
118	0.0	0.0	0.0	0.0	0.0	0.0	0.0	0.0	0.0	0.0	0.0	0.0	0.0	0.0	0.0	0.0	0.1	0.3	0.5	0.6	0.8	1.0	1.2	1.3	1.5	1.7	1.9	2.0	2.2	2.4	2.6	2.7	2.9	3.1	3.3	3.4	3.6	3.8	4.0
116	0.0	0.0	0.0	0.0	0.0	0.0	0.0	0.0	0.0	0.0	0.0	0.0	0.0	0.0	0.1	0.3	0.5	0.6	0.8	1.0	1.2	1.4	1.6	1.7	1.9	2.1	2.3	2.5	2.7	2.8	3.0	3.2	3.4	3.6	3.8	3.9	4.1	4.3	4.5
114	0.0	0.0	0.0	0.0	0.0	0.0	0.0	0.0	0.0	0.0	0.0	0.0	0.0	0.1	0.3	0.5	0.7	0.9	1.1	1.3	1.5	1.6	1.8	2.0	2.2	2.4	2.6	2.8	3.0	3.2	3.4	3.6	3.8	4.0	4.2	4.4	4.6	4.8	5.0
112	0.0	0.0	0.0	0.0	0.0	0.0	0.0	0.0	0.0	0.0	0.0	0.0	0.1	0.3	0.5	0.7	0.9	1.1	1.4	1.6	1.8	2.0	2.2	2.4	2.6	2.9	3.1	3.3	3.5	3.7	3.9	4.1	4.3	4.6	4.8	5.0	5.2	5.4	5.5
110	0.0	0.0	0.0	0.0	0.0	0.0	0.0	0.0	0.0	0.0	0.1	0.3	0.5	0.7	0.9	1.1	1.4	1.6	1.8	2.0	2.3	2.5	2.7	2.9	3.2	3.4	3.6	3.8	4.1	4.3	4.5	4.7	5.0	5.2	5.4	5.6	5.8	5.9	6.0
108	0.0	0.0	0.0	0.0	0.0	0.0	0.0	0.0	0.1	0.3	0.5	0.7	1.0	1.2	1.4	1.6	1.9	2.1	2.3	2.5	2.8	3.0	3.2	3.4	3.7	3.9	4.1	4.3	4.6	4.8	5.0	5.2	5.5	5.7	5.9	6.1	6.3	6.4	6.5
106	0.0	0.0	0.0	0.0	0.0	0.1	0.3	0.5	0.7	1.0	1.2	1.4	1.6	1.8	2.0	2.2	2.5	2.7	2.9	3.1	3.3	3.5	3.7	3.9	4.2	4.4	4.6	4.8	5.0	5.2	5.4	5.6	5.9	6.1	6.3	6.5	6.7	6.9	7.1
104	0.2	0.4	0.6	0.8	1.0	1.2	1.4	1.6	1.8	2.0	2.2	2.4	2.6	2.8	3.0	3.1	3.3	3.5	3.7	3.9	4.1	4.3	4.5	4.7	4.9	5.1	5.3	5.5	5.7	5.9	6.1	6.3	6.5	6.7	6.9	7.1	7.3	7.5	7.7
102	0.8	1.0	1.2	1.4	1.6	1.8	2.0	2.2	2.4	2.6	2.8	3.0	3.2	3.4	3.6	3.8	3.9	4.1	4.3	4.5	4.7	4.9	5.1	5.3	5.5	5.7	5.9	6.1	6.3	6.5	6.7	6.9	7.1	7.3	7.5	7.7	7.9	8.1	8.3
100	1.4	1.6	1.8	2.0	2.2	2.4	2.6	2.8	3.0	3.2	3.4	3.6	3.8	4.0	4.2	4.4	4.5	4.7	4.9	5.1	5.3	5.5	5.7	5.9	6.1	6.3	6.5	6.7	6.9	7.1	7.3	7.5	7.7	7.9	8.1	8.3	8.5	8.7	8.9
99	1.6	1.8	2.0	2.3	2.5	2.7	2.9	3.1	3.3	3.5	3.8	4.0	4.2	4.4	4.6	4.8	5.0	5.3	5.5	5.7	5.9	6.1	6.3	6.5	6.8	7.0	7.2	7.4	7.6	7.8	8.0	8.3	8.5	8.7	8.9	9.1	9.3	9.6	9.8
98	2.3	2.5	2.8	3.0	3.2	3.4	3.6	3.9	4.1	4.3	4.5	4.7	5.0	5.2	5.4	5.6	5.8	6.1	6.3	6.5	6.7	6.9	7.2	7.4	7.6	7.8	8.0	8.3	8.5	8.7	8.9	9.1	9.4	9.6	9.8	10.0	10.2	10.5	10.7
97	3.2	3.4	3.7	3.9	4.1	4.3	4.5	4.8	5.0	5.2	5.4	5.6	5.9	6.1	6.3	6.5	6.7	7.0	7.2	7.4	7.6	7.8	8.1	8.3	8.5	8.7	8.9	9.2	9.4	9.6	9.8	10.0	10.3	10.5	10.7	10.9	11.1	11.4	11.6
96	4.2	4.4	4.7	4.9	5.1	5.3	5.5	5.7	6.0	6.2	6.4	6.6	6.8	7.0	7.2	7.5	7.7	7.9	8.1	8.3	8.5	8.7	9.0	9.2	9.4	9.6	9.8	10.0	10.2	10.5	10.7	10.9	11.1	11.3	11.5	11.8	12.0	12.3	12.5
95	5.2	5.4	5.7	5.9	6.1	6.3	6.5	6.7	6.9	7.1	7.4	7.6	7.8	8.0	8.2	8.4	8.6	8.9	9.1	9.3	9.5	9.7	9.9	10.1	10.4	10.6	10.8	11.0	11.2	11.4	11.6	11.9	12.1	12.3	12.5	12.7	12.9	13.2	13.4
94	6.2	6.4	6.6	6.8	7.1	7.3	7.5	7.7	7.9	8.1	8.3	8.5	8.8	9.0	9.2	9.4	9.6	9.8	10.0	10.2	10.4	10.6	10.9	11.1	11.3	11.5	11.7	11.9	12.1	12.3	12.5	12.7	13.0	13.2	13.4	13.6	13.8	14.0	14.3
93	7.2	7.4	7.6	7.8	8.0	8.3	8.5	8.7	8.9	9.1	9.3	9.5	9.7	9.9	10.1	10.4	10.6	10.8	11.0	11.2	11.4	11.6	11.8	12.0	12.3	12.5	12.7	12.9	13.1	13.3	13.5	13.7	13.9	14.1	14.4	14.6	14.8	15.0	15.2
92	8.2	8.4	8.6	8.8	9.0	9.3	9.5	9.7	9.9	10.1	10.3	10.5	10.7	10.9	11.1	11.3	11.5	11.7	11.9	12.1	12.3	12.5	12.7	12.9	13.1	13.3	13.5	13.7	13.9	14.2	14.4	14.6	14.8	15.0	15.2	15.4	15.6	15.8	16.1
91	9.2	9.4	9.6	9.8	10.0	10.2	10.4	10.6	10.8	11.0	11.2	11.4	11.6	11.8	12.0	12.2	12.4	12.6	12.8	13.0	13.2	13.4	13.6	13.8	14.0	14.2	14.4	14.6	14.8	15.0	15.2	15.4	15.6	15.8	16.0	16.2	16.4	16.6	16.8
90	10.2	10.4	10.6	10.8	11.0	11.2	11.3	11.5	11.7	11.9	12.1	12.3	12.5	12.7	12.8	13.0	13.2	13.4	13.6	13.8	14.0	14.2	14.4	14.5	14.7	14.9	15.1	15.3	15.5	15.7	15.9	16.0	16.3	16.5	16.7	16.9	17.1	17.3	17.5
89	11.2	11.4	11.6	11.7	11.9	12.1	12.3	12.5	12.6	12.8	13.0	13.2	13.4	13.5	13.7	13.9	14.1	14.3	14.4	14.6	14.8	15.0	15.2	15.3	15.5	15.7	15.9	16.1	16.3	16.4	16.6	16.8	17.0	17.2	17.3	17.6	17.8	18.0	18.2
88	12.2	12.4	12.5	12.7	12.9	13.0	13.2	13.4	13.5	13.7	13.9	14.0	14.2	14.4	14.6	14.7	14.9	15.1	15.2	15.4	15.6	15.7	15.9	16.1	16.3	16.4	16.6	16.8	16.9	17.1	17.3	17.4	17.6	17.8	18.0	18.3	18.5	18.7	18.9
87	13.2	13.4	13.5	13.7	13.9	14.0	14.2	14.3	14.5	14.7	14.8	15.0	15.2	15.3	15.5	15.7	15.8	16.0	16.2	16.3	16.5	16.7	16.8	17.0	17.2	17.3	17.5	17.6	17.8	18.0	18.2	18.3	18.5	18.6	18.9	19.1	19.2	19.4	19.6
86	14.2	14.4	14.5	14.7	14.8	15.0	15.1	15.3	15.5	15.6	15.8	15.9	16.1	16.3	16.4	16.6	16.7	16.9	17.1	17.2	17.4	17.5	17.7	17.9	18.0	18.2	18.3	18.5	18.7	18.8	19.0	19.1	19.3	19.5	19.6	19.8	20.0	20.1	20.3
85	15.2	15.4	15.5	15.6	15.8	15.9	16.1	16.2	16.4	16.6	16.7	16.9	17.0	17.2	17.3	17.5	17.6	17.8	18.0	18.1	18.3	18.4	18.6	18.7	18.9	19.0	19.2	19.4	19.5	19.7	19.8	20.0	20.1	20.3	20.4	20.6	20.7	20.9	21.0
84	16.1	16.3	16.4	16.5	16.7	16.8	17.0	17.1	17.3	17.4	17.6	17.7	17.9	18.0	18.2	18.3	18.4	18.6	18.7	18.9	19.0	19.2	19.3	19.5	19.6	19.8	19.9	20.1	20.2	20.4	20.5	20.7	20.8	21.0	21.1	21.3	21.4	21.6	21.7
83	17.1	17.2	17.4	17.5	17.6	17.8	17.9	18.1	18.2	18.4	18.5	18.6	18.8	18.9	19.1	19.2	19.4	19.5	19.6	19.8	19.9	20.1	20.2	20.4	20.5	20.6	20.8	20.9	21.1	21.2	21.4	21.5	21.6	21.8	21.9	22.1	22.2	22.3	22.4
82	18.1	18.2	18.4	18.5	18.6	18.8	18.9	19.0	19.2	19.3	19.4	19.6	19.7	19.9	20.0	20.1	20.3	20.4	20.6	20.7	20.8	21.0	21.1	21.2	21.4	21.5	21.7	21.8	21.9	22.1	22.2	22.3	22.5	22.6	22.7	22.9	23.0	23.1	23.1
81	19.1	19.2	19.3	19.5	19.6	19.7	19.8	20.0	20.1	20.2	20.3	20.5	20.6	20.7	20.8	21.0	21.1	21.2	21.4	21.5	21.6	21.7	21.9	22.0	22.1	22.2	22.4	22.5	22.6	22.7	22.9	23.0	23.1	23.2	23.4	23.5	23.6	23.7	23.7
80	20.1	20.2	20.3	20.4	20.6	20.7	20.8	20.9	21.0	21.2	21.3	21.4	21.5	21.6	21.8	21.9	22.0	22.1	22.2	22.4	22.5	22.6	22.7	22.8	23.0	23.1	23.2	23.3	23.4	23.6	23.7	23.8	23.9	24.0	24.1	24.2	24.3	23.7	24.4
79	21.1	21.2	21.3	21.4	21.5	21.6	21.8	21.9	22.0	22.1	22.2	22.3	22.4	22.6	22.7	22.8	22.9	23.0	23.1	23.2	23.4	23.5	23.6	23.7	23.8	23.9	24.0	24.2	24.3	24.4	24.5	24.6	24.7	24.8	24.9	25.0	25.1	25.0	25.1
78	22.1	22.2	22.3	22.4	22.5	22.6	22.7	22.8	22.9	23.0	23.2	23.3	23.4	23.5	23.6	23.7	23.8	23.9	24.0	24.1	24.2	24.3	24.4	24.5	24.6	24.7	24.9	25.0	25.1	25.2	25.3	25.4	25.5	25.6	25.7	25.8	25.8	25.7	25.8
77	23.1	23.2	23.3	23.4	23.5	23.5	23.6	23.7	23.8	23.9	24.0	24.1	24.2	24.3	24.4	24.5	24.6	24.7	24.8	24.9	25.0	25.1	25.2	25.3	25.4	25.5	25.6	25.7	25.8	25.9	26.0	26.1	26.2	26.3	26.3	26.4	26.4	26.5	26.5
76	24.1	24.2	24.3	24.3	24.4	24.5	24.6	24.7	24.8	24.8	24.9	25.0	25.1	25.2	25.3	25.3	25.4	25.5	25.6	25.7	25.8	25.8	25.9	26.0	26.1	26.2	26.3	26.3	26.4	26.5	26.6	26.7	26.8	26.8	26.9	27.0	27.1	27.2	27.2
75	25.1	25.2	25.2	25.3	25.4	25.5	25.5	25.6	25.7	25.7	25.8	25.9	26.0	26.1	26.1	26.2	26.3	26.4	26.4	26.5	26.6	26.7	26.7	26.8	26.9	27.0	27.0	27.1	27.2	27.3	27.3	27.4	27.5	27.6	27.6	27.7	27.8	27.9	27.9
74	26.1	26.2	26.2	26.3	26.3	26.4	26.5	26.6	26.6	26.7	26.8	26.8	26.9	27.0	27.0	27.1	27.2	27.2	27.3	27.4	27.4	27.5	27.6	27.6	27.7	27.8	27.8	27.9	28.0	28.1	28.1	28.2	28.3	28.3	28.4	28.5	28.5	28.6	28.6
73	27.1	27.1	27.2	27.2	27.3	27.4	27.4	27.5	27.5	27.6	27.6	27.7	27.8	27.8	27.9	27.9	28.0	28.1	28.1	28.2	28.2	28.4	28.4	28.4	28.5	28.6	28.6	28.7	28.7	28.8	28.8	28.9	29.0	29.0	29.1	29.1	29.2	29.3	29.3
72	28.1	28.1	28.2	28.2	28.3	28.3	28.4	28.4	28.5	28.5	28.6	28.6	28.7	28.7	28.8	28.8	28.9	28.9	29.0	29.0	29.1	29.1	29.2	29.2	29.3	29.3	29.4	29.4	29.5	29.5	29.6	29.6	29.7	29.7	29.8	29.8	29.9	29.9	30.0
71	29.0	29.1	29.1	29.2	29.2	29.3	29.3	29.4	29.4	29.4	29.5	29.5	29.6	29.6	29.6	29.7	29.7	29.8	29.8	29.8	29.9	29.9	29.9	30.0	30.0	30.1	30.1	30.2	30.2	30.3	30.3	30.3	30.4	30.4	30.5	30.5	30.6	30.6	30.7
70	30.0	30.0	30.1	30.1	30.1	30.2	30.2	30.2	30.3	30.3	30.3	30.4	30.4	30.4	30.5	30.5	30.6	30.6	30.6	30.7	30.7	30.7	30.8	30.8	30.9	30.9	30.9	31.0	31.0	31.1	31.1	31.1	31.2	31.2	31.2	31.3	31.3	31.3	31.4

LISTED PUT OPTION PRICE WHEN EXERCISE PRICE IS 110

NUMBER OF WEEKS BEFORE THE OPTION EXPIRES

Common Stock Price	1	2	3	4	5	6	7	8	9	10	11	12	13	14	15	16	17	18	19	20	21	22	23	24	25	26	27	28	29	30	31	32	33	34	35	36	37	38	39
144	0.0	0.0	0.0	0.0	0.0	0.0	0.0	0.0	0.0	0.0	0.0	0.0	0.0	0.0	0.0	0.0	0.0	0.0	0.0	0.0	0.0	0.0	0.0	0.0	0.0	0.0	0.0	0.0	0.1	0.3	0.4	0.5	0.7	0.8	1.0	1.1	1.2	1.3	1.5
142	0.0	0.0	0.0	0.0	0.0	0.0	0.0	0.0	0.0	0.0	0.0	0.0	0.0	0.0	0.0	0.0	0.0	0.0	0.0	0.0	0.0	0.0	0.0	0.0	0.0	0.1	0.2	0.4	0.5	0.6	0.8	0.9	1.1	1.2	1.3	1.5	1.6	1.7	1.8
140	0.0	0.0	0.0	0.0	0.0	0.0	0.0	0.0	0.0	0.0	0.0	0.0	0.0	0.0	0.0	0.0	0.0	0.0	0.0	0.0	0.0	0.0	0.0	0.1	0.3	0.4	0.6	0.7	0.9	1.0	1.2	1.3	1.5	1.6	1.7	1.9	2.0	2.1	2.2
138	0.0	0.0	0.0	0.0	0.0	0.0	0.0	0.0	0.0	0.0	0.0	0.0	0.0	0.0	0.0	0.0	0.0	0.0	0.0	0.0	0.0	0.2	0.4	0.5	0.7	0.8	1.0	1.1	1.3	1.4	1.6	1.7	1.9	2.0	2.1	2.3	2.4	2.5	2.6
136	0.0	0.0	0.0	0.0	0.0	0.0	0.0	0.0	0.0	0.0	0.0	0.0	0.0	0.0	0.0	0.0	0.0	0.0	0.1	0.3	0.4	0.6	0.8	0.9	1.1	1.3	1.4	1.6	1.7	1.8	2.0	2.1	2.3	2.4	2.5	2.7	2.8	2.9	3.0
134	0.0	0.0	0.0	0.0	0.0	0.0	0.0	0.0	0.0	0.0	0.0	0.0	0.0	0.0	0.0	0.0	0.2	0.3	0.5	0.7	0.9	1.0	1.2	1.4	1.5	1.7	1.8	2.0	2.1	2.3	2.4	2.6	2.7	2.8	3.0	3.1	3.2	3.3	3.5
132	0.0	0.0	0.0	0.0	0.0	0.0	0.0	0.0	0.0	0.0	0.0	0.0	0.0	0.0	0.2	0.4	0.6	0.8	1.0	1.1	1.3	1.5	1.6	1.8	2.0	2.1	2.3	2.4	2.6	2.7	2.8	3.0	3.1	3.3	3.4	3.5	3.7	3.8	3.9
130	0.0	0.0	0.0	0.0	0.0	0.0	0.0	0.0	0.0	0.0	0.0	0.0	0.2	0.4	0.6	0.8	1.0	1.2	1.4	1.6	1.8	1.9	2.1	2.3	2.4	2.6	2.7	2.9	3.0	3.2	3.3	3.4	3.6	3.7	3.8	4.0	4.1	4.2	4.4
128	0.0	0.0	0.0	0.0	0.0	0.0	0.0	0.0	0.0	0.0	0.2	0.5	0.7	0.9	1.1	1.3	1.5	1.7	1.9	2.1	2.2	2.4	2.6	2.7	2.9	3.0	3.2	3.3	3.5	3.6	3.8	3.9	4.0	4.2	4.3	4.4	4.6	4.7	4.8
126	0.0	0.0	0.0	0.0	0.0	0.0	0.0	0.0	0.2	0.5	0.7	1.0	1.2	1.4	1.6	1.8	2.0	2.2	2.4	2.5	2.7	2.9	3.0	3.2	3.4	3.5	3.7	3.8	4.0	4.1	4.2	4.4	4.5	4.7	4.8	4.9	5.1	5.2	5.3
124	0.0	0.0	0.0	0.0	0.0	0.0	0.2	0.5	0.7	1.0	1.2	1.4	1.7	1.9	2.1	2.3	2.5	2.7	2.8	3.0	3.2	3.4	3.5	3.7	3.9	4.0	4.2	4.3	4.5	4.6	4.7	4.9	5.0	5.2	5.3	5.4	5.5	5.7	5.8
122	0.0	0.0	0.0	0.0	0.0	0.4	0.7	1.0	1.2	1.5	1.7	2.0	2.2	2.4	2.6	2.8	3.0	3.2	3.4	3.5	3.7	3.9	4.0	4.2	4.4	4.5	4.7	4.8	5.0	5.1	5.3	5.4	5.5	5.7	5.8	5.9	6.1	6.2	6.3
120	0.0	0.0	0.0	0.2	0.6	0.9	1.2	1.5	1.8	2.0	2.3	2.5	2.7	2.9	3.1	3.3	3.5	3.7	3.9	4.1	4.2	4.4	4.6	4.7	4.9	5.0	5.2	5.4	5.5	5.6	5.8	5.9	6.1	6.2	6.3	6.5	6.6	6.7	6.8
118	0.0	0.0	0.3	0.7	1.1	1.4	1.8	2.0	2.3	2.6	2.8	3.0	3.3	3.5	3.7	3.9	4.1	4.3	4.4	4.6	4.8	5.0	5.1	5.3	5.4	5.6	5.7	5.9	6.0	6.2	6.3	6.5	6.6	6.7	6.9	7.0	7.1	7.3	7.4
116	0.0	0.4	0.9	1.3	1.7	2.0	2.3	2.6	2.9	3.1	3.4	3.6	3.8	4.0	4.2	4.4	4.6	4.8	5.0	5.2	5.4	5.5	5.7	5.8	6.0	6.2	6.3	6.5	6.6	6.8	6.9	7.0	7.2	7.3	7.4	7.6	7.7	7.8	8.0
114	0.3	1.0	1.5	1.9	2.3	2.6	2.9	3.2	3.5	3.7	4.0	4.2	4.4	4.6	4.8	5.0	5.2	5.4	5.6	5.8	5.9	6.1	6.3	6.4	6.6	6.7	6.9	7.0	7.2	7.3	7.5	7.6	7.8	7.9	8.0	8.2	8.3	8.4	8.5
112	0.9	1.6	2.1	2.5	2.9	3.2	3.5	3.8	4.1	4.3	4.6	4.8	5.0	5.2	5.4	5.6	5.8	6.0	6.2	6.4	6.5	6.7	6.9	7.0	7.2	7.4	7.5	7.7	7.8	7.9	8.1	8.2	8.4	8.5	8.6	8.8	8.9	9.0	9.1
110	1.6	2.2	2.7	3.1	3.5	3.8	4.1	4.4	4.7	5.0	5.2	5.4	5.6	5.9	6.1	6.3	6.5	6.6	6.8	7.0	7.2	7.3	7.5	7.7	7.8	8.0	8.1	8.3	8.4	8.6	8.7	8.9	9.0	9.1	9.3	9.4	9.5	9.7	9.8
108	2.3	2.6	3.0	3.3	3.7	4.0	4.3	4.6	4.9	5.2	5.5	5.7	6.0	6.4	6.6	6.8	7.0	7.2	7.4	7.6	7.9	8.2	8.5	8.8	9.0	9.3	9.6	9.9	10.2	10.4	10.5	10.7	10.8	10.9	11.1	11.2	11.3	11.5	11.6
106	4.3	4.5	4.8	5.1	5.3	5.6	5.9	6.1	6.4	6.7	6.9	7.2	7.5	7.7	8.0	8.3	8.5	8.8	9.1	9.3	9.6	9.9	10.1	10.4	10.7	10.9	11.2	11.5	11.7	12.0	12.3	12.5	12.6	12.7	12.8	12.9	13.1	13.3	13.4
104	6.3	6.5	6.8	7.0	7.3	7.5	7.8	8.0	8.3	8.5	8.8	9.0	9.3	9.5	9.8	10.0	10.3	10.5	10.8	11.0	11.3	11.5	11.8	12.0	12.3	12.5	12.8	13.0	13.3	13.5	13.8	14.0	14.3	14.5	14.6	14.7	14.9	15.1	15.2
102	8.2	8.5	8.7	8.9	9.2	9.4	9.6	9.9	10.1	10.3	10.6	10.8	11.1	11.3	11.5	11.8	12.0	12.2	12.5	12.7	12.9	13.2	13.4	13.6	13.9	14.1	14.3	14.6	14.8	15.0	15.3	15.5	15.8	16.0	16.2	16.5	16.7	16.9	17.0
100	10.2	10.4	10.7	10.9	11.1	11.3	11.5	11.8	12.0	12.2	12.4	12.6	12.8	13.1	13.3	13.5	13.7	13.9	14.2	14.4	14.6	14.8	15.0	15.3	15.5	15.7	15.9	16.1	16.4	16.6	16.8	17.0	17.2	17.5	17.7	17.9	18.1	18.3	18.5
99	11.2	11.4	11.6	11.8	12.1	12.3	12.5	12.7	12.9	13.1	13.3	13.5	13.7	14.0	14.2	14.4	14.6	14.8	15.0	15.2	15.4	15.7	15.9	16.1	16.3	16.5	16.7	16.9	17.1	17.3	17.6	17.8	18.0	18.2	18.4	18.6	18.8	19.0	19.2
98	12.2	12.4	12.6	12.8	13.0	13.2	13.4	13.6	13.8	14.0	14.2	14.4	14.6	14.8	15.1	15.3	15.5	15.7	15.9	16.1	16.3	16.5	16.7	16.9	17.1	17.3	17.5	17.7	17.9	18.1	18.3	18.5	18.7	18.9	19.1	19.3	19.5	19.7	19.9
97	13.2	13.4	13.6	13.8	14.0	14.2	14.4	14.6	14.8	15.0	15.2	15.3	15.5	15.7	15.9	16.1	16.3	16.5	16.7	16.9	17.1	17.3	17.5	17.7	17.9	18.1	18.3	18.5	18.7	18.9	19.1	19.3	19.5	19.7	19.9	20.0	20.2	20.4	20.6
96	14.2	14.4	14.6	14.8	14.9	15.1	15.3	15.5	15.7	15.9	16.1	16.3	16.4	16.6	16.8	17.0	17.2	17.4	17.6	17.8	17.9	18.1	18.3	18.5	18.7	18.9	19.1	19.3	19.4	19.6	19.8	20.0	20.2	20.4	20.6	20.8	21.0	21.1	21.3
95	15.2	15.4	15.5	15.7	15.9	16.1	16.3	16.4	16.6	16.8	17.0	17.2	17.3	17.5	17.7	17.9	18.1	18.2	18.4	18.6	18.8	19.0	19.1	19.3	19.5	19.7	19.9	20.0	20.2	20.4	20.6	20.8	20.9	21.1	21.3	21.5	21.7	21.8	22.0
94	16.2	16.3	16.5	16.7	16.9	17.0	17.2	17.4	17.6	17.7	17.9	18.1	18.2	18.4	18.6	18.8	18.9	19.1	19.3	19.4	19.6	19.8	19.9	20.1	20.3	20.5	20.7	20.8	21.0	21.2	21.3	21.5	21.7	21.9	22.0	22.2	22.4	22.5	22.7
93	17.2	17.3	17.5	17.7	17.8	18.0	18.2	18.3	18.5	18.6	18.8	19.0	19.1	19.3	19.5	19.6	19.8	19.9	20.1	20.3	20.5	20.6	20.8	20.9	21.1	21.3	21.4	21.6	21.8	21.9	22.1	22.3	22.6	22.6	22.8	22.9	23.1	23.2	23.4
92	18.2	18.3	18.5	18.6	18.8	18.9	19.1	19.3	19.4	19.6	19.7	19.9	20.0	20.2	20.3	20.5	20.7	20.8	21.0	21.1	21.3	21.4	21.6	21.8	21.9	22.1	22.2	22.4	22.5	22.7	22.9	23.0	23.2	23.3	23.5	23.6	23.8	23.9	24.1
91	19.1	19.3	19.4	19.6	19.7	19.9	20.0	20.2	20.3	20.5	20.6	20.8	20.9	21.1	21.2	21.4	21.5	21.7	21.8	22.0	22.1	22.3	22.4	22.6	22.7	22.9	23.0	23.2	23.3	23.5	23.6	23.8	23.9	24.1	24.0	24.4	24.5	24.7	24.8
90	20.1	20.3	20.4	20.6	20.7	20.8	21.0	21.1	21.3	21.4	21.5	21.7	21.8	22.0	22.1	22.3	22.4	22.5	22.7	22.8	23.0	23.1	23.2	23.4	23.5	23.7	23.8	23.9	24.1	24.2	24.4	24.5	24.6	24.8	24.9	25.1	25.2	25.4	25.5
89	21.1	21.3	21.4	21.5	21.7	21.8	21.9	22.1	22.2	22.3	22.5	22.6	22.7	22.9	23.0	23.1	23.3	23.4	23.5	23.7	23.8	23.9	24.1	24.2	24.3	24.5	24.6	24.7	24.9	25.0	25.1	25.3	25.4	25.5	25.7	25.8	25.9	26.1	26.2
88	22.1	22.3	22.4	22.5	22.6	22.8	22.9	23.0	23.1	23.3	23.4	23.5	23.6	23.8	23.9	24.0	24.1	24.3	24.4	24.5	24.6	24.8	24.9	25.0	25.1	25.3	25.4	25.5	25.6	25.8	25.9	26.0	26.1	26.3	26.4	26.5	26.6	26.8	26.9
87	23.1	23.2	23.4	23.5	23.6	23.7	23.8	23.9	24.1	24.2	24.3	24.4	24.5	24.6	24.8	24.9	25.0	25.1	25.2	25.3	25.5	25.6	25.7	25.8	25.9	26.1	26.2	26.3	26.4	26.5	26.6	26.8	26.9	27.0	27.1	27.2	27.3	27.5	27.6
86	24.1	24.2	24.3	24.4	24.5	24.7	24.8	24.9	25.0	25.1	25.2	25.3	25.4	25.5	25.6	25.8	25.9	26.0	26.1	26.2	26.3	26.4	26.5	26.6	26.7	26.8	27.0	27.1	27.2	27.3	27.4	27.5	27.6	27.7	27.8	27.9	28.1	28.2	28.3
85	25.1	25.2	25.3	25.4	25.5	25.6	25.7	25.8	25.9	26.0	26.1	26.2	26.3	26.4	26.5	26.6	26.7	26.8	26.9	27.0	27.1	27.2	27.3	27.4	27.5	27.6	27.7	27.8	28.0	28.1	28.2	28.3	28.4	28.5	28.6	28.7	28.8	28.9	29.0
84	26.1	26.2	26.3	26.4	26.5	26.6	26.7	26.8	26.8	26.9	27.0	27.1	27.2	27.3	27.4	27.5	27.6	27.7	27.8	27.9	28.0	28.1	28.2	28.3	28.3	28.4	28.5	28.6	28.7	28.8	28.9	29.0	29.1	29.2	29.3	29.4	29.5	29.6	29.7
83	27.1	27.2	27.3	27.3	27.4	27.5	27.6	27.7	27.8	27.9	27.9	28.0	28.1	28.2	28.3	28.4	28.5	28.5	28.6	28.7	28.8	28.9	29.0	29.1	29.2	29.2	29.3	29.4	29.5	29.6	29.7	29.8	29.8	29.9	30.0	30.1	30.2	30.3	30.4
82	28.1	28.2	28.2	28.3	28.4	28.5	28.5	28.6	28.7	28.8	28.9	28.9	29.0	29.1	29.2	29.3	29.3	29.4	29.5	29.6	29.6	29.7	29.8	29.9	29.9	30.0	30.1	30.2	30.3	30.3	30.4	30.5	30.6	30.7	30.8	30.9	30.9	31.0	31.1
81	29.1	29.1	29.2	29.3	29.4	29.4	29.5	29.6	29.6	29.7	29.8	29.8	29.9	29.9	30.1	30.1	30.2	30.3	30.3	30.4	30.5	30.5	30.6	30.7	30.8	30.8	30.9	31.0	31.0	31.1	31.2	31.3	31.3	31.4	31.5	31.5	31.6	31.7	31.7
80	30.1	30.1	30.2	30.3	30.3	30.4	30.4	30.5	30.6	30.6	30.7	30.8	30.8	30.9	30.9	31.0	31.1	31.1	31.0	31.3	31.3	31.4	31.4	31.5	31.6	31.6	31.7	31.8	31.8	31.9	31.9	32.0	32.1	32.1	32.2	32.3	32.3	32.4	32.4
79	31.1	31.1	31.2	31.2	31.3	31.3	31.4	31.4	31.5	31.5	31.6	31.7	31.7	31.8	31.8	31.9	31.9	32.0	32.0	32.1	32.1	32.2	32.3	32.3	32.4	32.4	32.5	32.5	32.6	32.6	32.7	32.8	32.8	32.9	32.9	33.0	33.0	33.1	33.1
78	32.0	32.1	32.1	32.2	32.2	32.3	32.3	32.4	32.4	32.5	32.5	32.6	32.6	32.7	32.7	32.8	32.8	32.8	32.9	32.9	33.0	33.0	33.1	33.1	33.2	33.2	33.3	33.3	33.4	33.4	33.5	33.5	33.5	33.6	33.6	33.7	33.7	33.8	33.8
77	33.0	33.1	33.1	33.2	33.2	33.2	33.3	33.3	33.4	33.4	33.4	33.5	33.5	33.5	33.6	33.6	33.7	33.7	33.7	33.8	33.8	33.9	33.9	33.9	34.0	34.0	34.1	34.1	34.1	34.2	34.2	34.3	34.3	34.3	34.4	34.4	34.4	34.5	34.5

LISTED PUT OPTION PRICE WHEN EXERCISE PRICE IS 120

NUMBER OF WEEKS BEFORE THE OPTION EXPIRES

Common Stock Price	1	2	3	4	5	6	7	8	9	10	11	12	13	14	15	16	17	18	19	20
156	0.0	0.0	0.0	0.0	0.0	0.0	0.0	0.0	0.0	0.0	0.0	0.0	0.0	0.0	0.0	0.0	0.0	0.0	0.0	0.0
154	0.0	0.0	0.0	0.0	0.0	0.0	0.0	0.0	0.0	0.0	0.0	0.0	0.0	0.0	0.0	0.0	0.0	0.0	0.0	0.0
152	0.0	0.0	0.0	0.0	0.0	0.0	0.0	0.0	0.0	0.0	0.0	0.0	0.0	0.0	0.0	0.0	0.0	0.0	0.0	0.0
150	0.0	0.0	0.0	0.0	0.0	0.0	0.0	0.0	0.0	0.0	0.0	0.0	0.0	0.0	0.0	0.0	0.0	0.0	0.0	0.0
148	0.0	0.0	0.0	0.0	0.0	0.0	0.0	0.0	0.0	0.0	0.0	0.0	0.0	0.0	0.0	0.0	0.0	0.0	0.2	0.4
146	0.0	0.0	0.0	0.0	0.0	0.0	0.0	0.0	0.0	0.0	0.0	0.0	0.0	0.0	0.0	0.0	0.2	0.4	0.6	0.8
144	0.0	0.0	0.0	0.0	0.0	0.0	0.0	0.0	0.0	0.0	0.0	0.0	0.0	0.0	0.2	0.4	0.6	0.8	1.0	1.2
142	0.0	0.0	0.0	0.0	0.0	0.0	0.0	0.0	0.0	0.0	0.0	0.0	0.2	0.4	0.7	0.9	1.1	1.3	1.5	1.7
140	0.0	0.0	0.0	0.0	0.0	0.0	0.0	0.0	0.0	0.0	0.2	0.4	0.7	0.9	1.1	1.3	1.6	1.8	2.0	2.2
138	0.0	0.0	0.0	0.0	0.0	0.0	0.0	0.0	0.1	0.4	0.7	0.9	1.1	1.4	1.6	1.8	2.0	2.2	2.4	2.6
136	0.0	0.0	0.0	0.0	0.0	0.0	0.0	0.3	0.6	0.9	1.1	1.4	1.6	1.9	2.1	2.3	2.5	2.7	2.9	3.1
134	0.0	0.0	0.0	0.0	0.0	0.2	0.5	0.8	1.1	1.4	1.7	1.9	2.1	2.4	2.6	2.8	3.0	3.2	3.4	3.6
132	0.0	0.0	0.0	0.0	0.3	0.7	1.0	1.3	1.6	1.9	2.2	2.4	2.7	2.9	3.1	3.3	3.6	3.8	4.0	4.1
130	0.0	0.0	0.0	0.5	0.9	1.2	1.6	1.9	2.2	2.4	2.7	3.0	3.2	3.4	3.7	3.9	4.1	4.3	4.5	4.7
128	0.0	0.0	0.6	1.0	1.4	1.8	2.1	2.4	2.7	3.0	3.3	3.5	3.8	4.0	4.2	4.4	4.6	4.8	5.0	5.2
126	0.0	0.6	1.1	1.6	2.0	2.4	2.7	3.0	3.3	3.6	3.8	4.1	4.3	4.6	4.8	5.0	5.2	5.4	5.6	5.8
124	0.5	1.2	1.7	2.2	2.6	2.9	3.3	3.6	3.9	4.2	4.4	4.7	4.9	5.2	5.4	5.6	5.8	6.0	6.2	6.4
122	1.1	1.8	2.3	2.8	3.2	3.6	3.9	4.2	4.5	4.8	5.0	5.3	5.5	5.8	6.0	6.2	6.4	6.6	6.8	7.0
120	1.7	2.4	3.0	3.4	3.8	4.2	4.5	4.8	5.1	5.4	5.7	5.9	6.2	6.4	6.6	6.8	7.0	7.2	7.4	7.6
118	2.3	2.7	3.2	3.7	4.2	4.4	4.7	5.0	5.4	5.7	6.1	6.3	6.7	6.9	7.1	7.3	7.5	7.7	7.9	8.2
116	4.3	4.6	4.9	5.2	5.5	5.8	6.1	6.3	6.6	6.9	7.2	7.5	7.8	8.1	8.4	8.7	9.0	9.3	9.6	9.9
114	6.3	6.6	6.8	7.1	7.4	7.7	7.9	8.2	8.5	8.8	9.1	9.3	9.6	9.9	10.2	10.4	10.7	11.0	11.3	11.6
112	8.3	8.5	8.8	9.0	9.3	9.6	9.8	10.1	10.4	10.6	10.9	11.1	11.4	11.7	11.9	12.2	12.5	12.7	13.0	13.2
110	10.2	10.5	10.7	11.0	11.2	11.5	11.7	12.0	12.2	12.5	12.7	13.0	13.2	13.4	13.7	13.9	14.2	14.4	14.7	14.9
108	12.2	12.5	12.7	12.9	13.2	13.4	13.6	13.8	14.1	14.3	14.5	14.8	15.0	15.2	15.5	15.7	15.9	16.2	16.4	16.6
106	14.2	14.4	14.6	14.9	15.1	15.3	15.5	15.7	15.9	16.1	16.4	16.6	16.8	17.0	17.2	17.4	17.7	17.9	18.1	18.3
104	16.2	16.4	16.6	16.8	17.0	17.2	17.4	17.6	17.8	18.0	18.2	18.4	18.6	18.8	19.0	19.2	19.4	19.6	19.8	19.9
102	18.2	18.4	18.6	18.7	18.9	19.1	19.3	19.5	19.7	19.8	20.0	20.2	20.4	20.6	20.8	20.9	21.1	21.3	21.5	21.7
100	20.2	20.3	20.5	20.7	20.8	21.0	21.2	21.3	21.5	21.7	21.8	22.0	22.2	22.4	22.5	22.7	22.9	23.0	23.2	23.4
99	21.2	21.3	21.5	21.6	21.8	22.0	22.1	22.3	22.4	22.6	22.8	22.9	23.1	23.2	23.4	23.6	23.7	23.9	24.0	24.2
98	22.2	22.3	22.5	22.6	22.8	22.9	23.1	23.2	23.4	23.5	23.7	23.8	24.0	24.1	24.3	24.4	24.6	24.7	24.9	25.0
97	23.1	23.3	23.4	23.6	23.7	23.9	24.0	24.2	24.3	24.4	24.6	24.7	24.9	25.0	25.2	25.3	25.5	25.6	25.7	25.9
96	24.1	24.3	24.4	24.5	24.7	24.8	25.0	25.1	25.2	25.4	25.5	25.6	25.8	25.9	26.0	26.2	26.3	26.5	26.6	26.7
95	25.1	25.3	25.4	25.5	25.6	25.8	25.9	26.0	26.2	26.3	26.4	26.5	26.7	26.8	26.9	27.1	27.2	27.3	27.4	27.6
94	26.1	26.2	26.4	26.5	26.6	26.7	26.8	27.0	27.1	27.2	27.3	27.5	27.6	27.7	27.8	27.9	28.1	28.2	28.3	28.4
93	27.1	27.2	27.3	27.5	27.6	27.7	27.8	27.9	28.0	28.1	28.2	28.4	28.5	28.6	28.7	28.8	28.9	29.0	29.1	29.3
92	28.1	28.2	28.3	28.4	28.5	28.6	28.7	28.8	28.9	29.1	29.2	29.3	29.4	29.5	29.6	29.7	29.8	29.9	30.0	30.1
91	29.1	29.2	29.3	29.4	29.5	29.6	29.7	29.8	29.9	29.9	30.1	30.2	30.3	30.4	30.5	30.6	30.7	30.8	30.9	30.9
90	30.1	30.2	30.3	30.4	30.4	30.5	30.6	30.7	30.8	30.9	31.0	31.1	31.2	31.3	31.3	31.4	31.5	31.6	31.7	31.8
89	31.1	31.2	31.2	31.3	31.4	31.5	31.6	31.7	31.7	31.8	31.9	32.0	32.1	32.1	32.2	32.3	32.4	32.5	32.6	32.6
88	32.1	32.1	32.2	32.3	32.4	32.4	32.5	32.6	32.7	32.7	32.8	32.9	33.0	33.0	33.1	33.2	33.3	33.3	33.4	33.5
87	33.1	33.1	33.2	33.3	33.3	33.4	33.5	33.5	33.6	33.7	33.7	33.8	33.9	33.9	34.0	34.1	34.1	34.2	34.3	34.3
86	34.1	34.1	34.2	34.2	34.3	34.3	34.4	34.5	34.5	34.6	34.6	34.7	34.8	34.8	34.9	34.9	35.0	35.0	35.1	35.2
85	35.1	35.1	35.2	35.2	35.3	35.3	35.4	35.4	35.5	35.5	35.6	35.6	35.7	35.7	35.8	35.8	35.9	35.9	36.0	36.0
84	36.0	36.1	36.1	36.2	36.2	36.3	36.3	36.3	36.4	36.4	36.5	36.5	36.6	36.6	36.6	36.7	36.7	36.8	36.8	36.9

Common Stock Price	21	22	23	24	25	26	27	28	29	30	31	32	33	34	35	36	37	38	39
156	0.0	0.0	0.0	0.0	0.0	0.0	0.0	0.2	0.3	0.5	0.6	0.8	0.9	1.1	1.2	1.4	1.5	1.7	1.8
154	0.0	0.0	0.0	0.0	0.1	0.2	0.4	0.6	0.7	0.9	1.0	1.2	1.3	1.5	1.6	1.8	1.9	2.1	2.2
152	0.0	0.0	0.1	0.3	0.5	0.6	0.8	1.0	1.1	1.3	1.4	1.6	1.7	1.9	2.0	2.2	2.3	2.4	2.6
150	0.1	0.3	0.5	0.7	0.9	1.0	1.2	1.4	1.5	1.7	1.8	2.0	2.1	2.3	2.4	2.6	2.7	2.8	3.0
148	0.6	0.7	0.9	1.1	1.3	1.4	1.6	1.8	1.9	2.1	2.2	2.4	2.5	2.7	2.8	3.0	3.1	3.3	3.4
146	1.0	1.2	1.4	1.5	1.7	1.9	2.0	2.2	2.4	2.5	2.7	2.8	3.0	3.1	3.3	3.4	3.6	3.7	3.8
144	1.4	1.6	1.8	2.0	2.1	2.3	2.5	2.6	2.8	3.0	3.1	3.3	3.4	3.6	3.7	3.8	4.0	4.1	4.3
142	1.9	2.1	2.2	2.4	2.6	2.8	2.9	3.1	3.2	3.4	3.6	3.7	3.9	4.0	4.2	4.3	4.4	4.6	4.7
140	2.3	2.5	2.7	2.9	3.1	3.2	3.4	3.6	3.7	3.9	4.0	4.2	4.3	4.5	4.6	4.8	4.9	5.0	5.2
138	2.8	3.0	3.2	3.4	3.5	3.7	3.9	4.0	4.2	4.3	4.5	4.7	4.8	4.9	5.1	5.2	5.4	5.5	5.7
136	3.3	3.5	3.7	3.8	4.0	4.2	4.4	4.5	4.7	4.8	5.0	5.1	5.3	5.4	5.6	5.7	5.9	6.0	6.1
134	3.8	4.0	4.2	4.4	4.5	4.7	4.9	5.0	5.2	5.3	5.5	5.6	5.8	5.9	6.1	6.2	6.4	6.5	6.7
132	4.3	4.5	4.7	4.9	5.0	5.2	5.4	5.5	5.7	5.9	6.0	6.2	6.3	6.5	6.6	6.8	6.9	7.0	7.2
130	4.9	5.1	5.2	5.4	5.6	5.8	5.9	6.1	6.2	6.4	6.6	6.7	6.9	7.0	7.2	7.3	7.4	7.6	7.7
128	5.4	5.6	5.8	6.0	6.1	6.3	6.5	6.6	6.8	7.0	7.1	7.3	7.4	7.6	7.7	7.8	8.0	8.1	8.3
126	6.0	6.2	6.4	6.5	6.7	6.9	7.0	7.2	7.4	7.5	7.7	7.8	8.0	8.1	8.3	8.4	8.6	8.7	8.8
124	6.6	6.8	7.0	7.1	7.3	7.5	7.6	7.8	8.0	8.1	8.3	8.4	8.6	8.7	8.9	9.0	9.1	9.3	9.4
122	7.2	7.4	7.6	7.7	7.9	8.1	8.2	8.4	8.6	8.7	8.9	9.0	9.2	9.3	9.5	9.6	9.8	9.9	10.0
120	7.8	8.0	8.2	8.4	8.5	8.7	8.9	9.0	9.2	9.4	9.5	9.7	9.8	9.9	10.1	10.2	10.4	10.5	10.7
118	8.5	8.8	9.1	9.4	9.7	10.0	10.3	10.7	11.0	11.2	11.3	11.5	11.6	11.7	11.9	12.0	12.2	12.3	12.4
116	10.2	10.5	10.7	11.0	11.3	11.6	11.9	12.2	12.5	12.8	13.1	13.3	13.4	13.5	13.7	13.8	14.0	14.1	14.2
114	11.8	12.1	12.4	12.7	12.9	13.2	13.5	13.8	14.1	14.3	14.6	14.9	15.2	15.3	15.5	15.6	15.8	15.9	16.0
112	13.5	13.8	14.0	14.3	14.5	14.8	15.1	15.3	15.6	15.9	16.1	16.4	16.6	16.9	17.2	17.4	17.6	17.7	17.8
110	15.2	15.4	15.7	15.9	16.2	16.4	16.6	16.9	17.1	17.4	17.6	17.9	18.1	18.4	18.6	18.9	18.8	18.9	19.0
108	16.8	17.1	17.3	17.5	17.8	18.0	18.2	18.5	18.7	18.9	19.1	19.4	19.6	19.8	20.1	20.3	20.5	20.7	20.8
106	18.5	18.7	18.9	19.2	19.4	19.6	19.8	20.0	20.2	20.4	20.7	20.9	21.1	21.3	21.5	21.7	22.0	22.2	22.4
104	20.2	20.4	20.6	20.8	21.0	21.2	21.4	21.6	21.8	22.0	22.2	22.4	22.6	22.8	23.0	23.2	23.4	23.6	23.8
102	21.9	22.0	22.2	22.4	22.6	22.8	23.0	23.1	23.3	23.5	23.7	23.9	24.1	24.2	24.4	24.6	24.8	25.0	25.2
100	23.5	23.7	23.9	24.0	24.2	24.4	24.5	24.7	24.9	25.0	25.2	25.4	25.5	25.7	25.9	26.0	26.2	26.4	26.6
99	24.4	24.5	24.7	24.8	25.0	25.2	25.3	25.5	25.6	25.8	26.0	26.1	26.3	26.4	26.6	26.8	26.9	27.1	27.2
98	25.2	25.4	25.5	25.7	25.3	26.0	26.1	26.3	26.4	26.6	26.7	26.9	27.0	27.2	27.3	27.5	27.6	27.8	27.9
97	26.0	26.2	26.3	26.5	26.6	26.8	26.9	27.0	27.2	27.3	27.5	27.6	27.8	27.9	28.1	28.2	28.3	28.5	28.6
96	26.9	27.0	27.1	27.3	27.4	27.6	27.7	27.8	28.0	28.1	28.2	28.4	28.5	28.6	28.8	28.9	29.1	29.2	29.3
95	27.7	27.8	28.0	28.1	28.2	28.3	28.5	28.6	28.7	28.9	29.0	29.1	29.2	29.4	29.5	29.6	29.8	29.9	30.0
94	28.5	28.7	28.8	28.9	29.0	29.1	29.3	29.4	29.5	29.6	29.7	29.9	29.9	30.1	30.2	30.4	30.5	30.6	30.7
93	29.4	29.5	29.6	29.7	29.8	29.9	30.1	30.2	30.3	30.4	30.5	30.6	30.7	30.8	31.0	31.1	31.2	31.3	31.4
92	30.2	30.3	30.4	30.5	30.6	30.7	30.8	30.9	31.1	31.2	31.3	31.4	31.5	31.6	31.7	31.8	31.9	32.0	32.1
91	31.0	31.1	31.2	31.3	31.4	31.5	31.6	31.7	31.8	31.9	32.0	32.1	32.2	32.3	32.4	32.5	32.6	32.7	32.8
90	31.9	32.0	32.1	32.2	32.2	32.3	32.4	32.5	32.6	32.7	32.8	32.9	33.0	33.0	33.1	33.2	33.3	33.4	33.5
89	32.7	32.8	32.9	33.0	33.0	33.1	33.2	33.3	33.4	33.5	33.5	33.6	33.7	33.8	33.9	33.9	34.0	34.1	34.2
88	33.6	33.6	33.7	33.8	33.8	33.9	34.0	34.1	34.1	34.2	34.3	34.4	34.4	34.5	34.6	34.7	34.7	34.8	34.9
87	34.4	34.5	34.5	34.6	34.7	34.7	34.8	34.9	34.9	35.0	35.0	35.1	35.2	35.2	35.3	35.4	35.4	35.5	35.6
86	35.2	35.3	35.3	35.4	35.5	35.5	35.6	35.6	35.7	35.7	35.8	35.9	35.9	36.0	36.0	36.1	36.2	36.2	36.3
85	36.1	36.1	36.2	36.2	36.3	36.3	36.4	36.4	36.5	36.5	36.6	36.6	36.7	36.7	36.8	36.8	36.9	36.9	37.0
84	36.9	36.9	37.0	37.0	37.1	37.1	37.2	37.2	37.2	37.3	37.3	37.4	37.4	37.4	37.5	37.5	37.6	37.6	37.7

LISTED PUT OPTION PRICE WHEN EXERCISE PRICE IS 130

NUMBER OF WEEKS BEFORE THE OPTION EXPIRES

Common Stock Price	1	2	3	4	5	6	7	8	9	10	11	12	13	14	15	16	17	18	19	20	21	22	23	24	25	26	27	28	29	30	31	32	33	34	35	36	37	38	39
170	0.0	0.0	0.0	0.0	0.0	0.0	0.0	0.0	0.0	0.0	0.0	0.0	0.0	0.0	0.0	0.0	0.0	0.0	0.0	0.0	0.0	0.0	0.0	0.0	0.0	0.0	0.0	0.0	0.2	0.3	0.5	0.7	0.8	1.0	1.2	1.3	1.5	1.6	1.8
168	0.0	0.0	0.0	0.0	0.0	0.0	0.0	0.0	0.0	0.0	0.0	0.0	0.0	0.0	0.0	0.0	0.0	0.0	0.0	0.0	0.0	0.0	0.0	0.0	0.0	0.0	0.2	0.4	0.6	0.7	0.9	1.1	1.2	1.4	1.5	1.7	1.8	2.0	2.1
166	0.0	0.0	0.0	0.0	0.0	0.0	0.0	0.0	0.0	0.0	0.0	0.0	0.0	0.0	0.0	0.0	0.0	0.0	0.0	0.0	0.0	0.0	0.0	0.0	0.2	0.4	0.6	0.8	0.9	1.1	1.3	1.4	1.6	1.8	1.9	2.1	2.2	2.4	2.5
164	0.0	0.0	0.0	0.0	0.0	0.0	0.0	0.0	0.0	0.0	0.0	0.0	0.0	0.0	0.0	0.0	0.0	0.0	0.0	0.0	0.0	0.1	0.2	0.4	0.6	0.8	1.0	1.2	1.3	1.5	1.7	1.8	2.0	2.2	2.3	2.5	2.6	2.8	2.9
162	0.0	0.0	0.0	0.0	0.0	0.0	0.0	0.0	0.0	0.0	0.0	0.0	0.0	0.0	0.0	0.0	0.0	0.0	0.0	0.1	0.3	0.5	0.7	0.8	1.0	1.2	1.4	1.6	1.7	1.9	2.1	2.2	2.4	2.6	2.7	2.9	3.0	3.2	3.3
160	0.0	0.0	0.0	0.0	0.0	0.0	0.0	0.0	0.0	0.0	0.0	0.0	0.0	0.0	0.0	0.0	0.0	0.0	0.3	0.5	0.7	0.9	1.1	1.3	1.5	1.6	1.8	2.0	2.2	2.3	2.5	2.7	2.8	3.0	3.1	3.3	3.5	3.6	3.8
158	0.0	0.0	0.0	0.0	0.0	0.0	0.0	0.0	0.0	0.0	0.0	0.0	0.0	0.0	0.0	0.0	0.3	0.5	0.7	0.9	1.1	1.3	1.5	1.7	1.9	2.1	2.2	2.4	2.6	2.8	2.9	3.1	3.3	3.4	3.6	3.7	3.9	4.0	4.2
156	0.0	0.0	0.0	0.0	0.0	0.0	0.0	0.0	0.0	0.0	0.0	0.0	0.0	0.0	0.2	0.5	0.7	0.9	1.1	1.3	1.5	1.7	1.9	2.1	2.3	2.5	2.7	2.9	3.0	3.2	3.4	3.5	3.7	3.9	4.0	4.2	4.3	4.5	4.6
154	0.0	0.0	0.0	0.0	0.0	0.0	0.0	0.0	0.0	0.0	0.0	0.0	0.2	0.4	0.7	0.9	1.1	1.4	1.6	1.8	2.0	2.2	2.4	2.6	2.8	3.0	3.1	3.3	3.5	3.7	3.8	4.0	4.1	4.3	4.5	4.6	4.8	4.9	5.1
152	0.0	0.0	0.0	0.0	0.0	0.0	0.0	0.0	0.0	0.0	0.1	0.4	0.6	0.9	1.1	1.4	1.6	1.8	2.0	2.3	2.5	2.7	2.9	3.0	3.2	3.4	3.6	3.8	3.9	4.1	4.3	4.4	4.6	4.8	4.9	5.1	5.2	5.4	5.5
150	0.0	0.0	0.0	0.0	0.0	0.0	0.0	0.0	0.0	0.3	0.6	0.9	1.1	1.4	1.6	1.9	2.1	2.3	2.5	2.7	2.9	3.1	3.3	3.5	3.7	3.9	4.1	4.2	4.4	4.6	4.8	4.9	5.1	5.2	5.4	5.6	5.7	5.9	6.0
148	0.0	0.0	0.0	0.0	0.0	0.0	0.0	0.2	0.5	0.8	1.1	1.3	1.6	1.9	2.1	2.3	2.6	2.8	3.0	3.2	3.4	3.6	3.8	4.0	4.2	4.4	4.6	4.7	4.9	5.1	5.2	5.4	5.6	5.7	5.9	6.0	6.2	6.3	6.5
146	0.0	0.0	0.0	0.0	0.0	0.0	0.3	0.7	1.0	1.3	1.6	1.9	2.1	2.4	2.6	2.8	3.1	3.3	3.5	3.7	3.9	4.1	4.3	4.5	4.7	4.9	5.1	5.2	5.4	5.6	5.7	5.9	6.1	6.2	6.4	6.5	6.7	6.8	7.0
144	0.0	0.0	0.0	0.0	0.1	0.5	0.9	1.2	1.5	1.8	2.1	2.4	2.6	2.9	3.1	3.4	3.6	3.8	4.0	4.2	4.4	4.6	4.8	5.0	5.2	5.4	5.6	5.7	5.9	6.1	6.3	6.4	6.6	6.7	6.9	7.1	7.2	7.4	7.5
142	0.0	0.0	0.0	0.2	0.6	1.0	1.4	1.7	2.0	2.3	2.6	2.9	3.2	3.4	3.7	3.9	4.1	4.3	4.5	4.8	5.0	5.2	5.4	5.5	5.7	5.9	6.1	6.3	6.4	6.6	6.8	7.0	7.1	7.3	7.4	7.6	7.7	7.9	8.0
140	0.0	0.0	0.2	0.7	1.2	1.6	1.9	2.3	2.6	2.9	3.2	3.4	3.7	4.0	4.2	4.4	4.7	4.9	5.1	5.3	5.5	5.7	5.9	6.1	6.3	6.5	6.6	6.8	7.0	7.2	7.3	7.5	7.7	7.8	8.0	8.1	8.3	8.4	8.6
138	0.0	0.2	0.8	1.3	1.7	2.1	2.5	2.8	3.1	3.4	3.7	4.0	4.3	4.5	4.8	5.0	5.2	5.4	5.7	5.9	6.1	6.3	6.5	6.7	6.8	7.0	7.2	7.4	7.6	7.7	7.9	8.1	8.2	8.4	8.5	8.7	8.8	9.0	9.1
136	0.0	0.8	1.4	1.9	2.3	2.7	3.1	3.4	3.7	4.0	4.3	4.6	4.8	5.1	5.3	5.6	5.8	6.0	6.2	6.4	6.6	6.8	7.0	7.2	7.4	7.6	7.8	8.0	8.1	8.3	8.5	8.6	8.8	9.0	9.1	9.3	9.4	9.6	9.7
134	0.6	1.4	2.0	2.5	2.9	3.3	3.7	4.0	4.3	4.6	4.9	5.2	5.4	5.7	5.9	6.2	6.4	6.6	6.8	7.0	7.2	7.4	7.6	7.8	8.0	8.2	8.4	8.5	8.7	8.9	9.1	9.2	9.4	9.5	9.7	9.9	10.0	10.2	10.3
132	1.2	2.0	2.6	3.1	3.5	3.9	4.3	4.6	4.9	5.2	5.5	5.8	6.0	6.3	6.5	6.8	7.0	7.2	7.4	7.6	7.8	8.0	8.2	8.4	8.6	8.8	9.0	9.2	9.3	9.5	9.7	9.8	9.9	10.2	10.3	10.5	10.6	10.8	10.9
130	1.9	2.6	3.2	3.7	4.1	4.5	4.9	5.2	5.6	5.9	6.1	6.4	6.7	6.9	7.2	7.4	7.6	7.8	8.1	8.3	8.5	8.7	8.9	9.1	9.3	9.4	9.6	9.8	9.9	10.1	10.3	10.5	10.6	10.8	10.9	11.1	11.3	11.4	11.6
128	2.5	2.8	3.4	3.9	4.4	4.8	5.2	5.5	5.9	6.2	6.4	6.7	7.1	7.3	7.6	7.8	8.0	8.2	8.5	8.7	9.1	9.4	9.7	10.1	10.4	10.7	11.1	11.4	11.7	11.9	12.1	12.3	12.4	12.6	12.7	12.9	13.1	13.2	13.4
126	4.3	4.6	5.0	5.3	5.6	5.9	6.2	6.6	6.9	7.2	7.5	7.8	8.2	8.5	8.8	9.1	9.4	9.8	10.1	10.4	10.7	11.0	11.4	11.7	12.0	12.3	12.6	13.0	13.3	13.6	13.9	14.1	14.2	14.4	14.5	14.7	14.9	15.0	15.2
124	6.3	6.6	6.9	7.2	7.5	7.8	8.1	8.4	8.7	9.0	9.4	9.7	9.9	10.3	10.6	10.9	11.2	11.5	11.8	12.1	12.4	12.7	13.0	13.3	13.6	13.9	14.2	14.5	14.8	15.1	15.4	15.7	16.0	16.2	16.3	16.5	16.7	16.8	17.0
122	8.3	8.6	8.9	9.2	9.4	9.7	10.0	10.3	10.6	10.9	11.2	11.5	11.8	12.0	12.3	12.6	12.9	13.2	13.5	13.8	14.1	14.4	14.6	14.9	15.2	15.5	15.8	16.1	16.4	16.7	17.0	17.2	17.5	17.8	18.1	18.3	18.5	18.6	18.8
120	10.3	10.5	10.8	11.1	11.4	11.6	11.9	12.2	12.5	12.7	13.0	13.3	13.6	13.8	14.1	14.4	14.6	14.9	15.2	15.5	15.7	16.0	16.3	16.6	16.8	17.1	17.4	17.7	17.9	18.2	18.5	18.7	19.0	19.3	19.6	19.8	20.1	20.4	20.6
118	12.3	12.5	12.8	13.0	13.3	13.5	13.8	14.1	14.3	14.6	14.8	15.1	15.3	15.6	15.9	16.1	16.4	16.6	16.9	17.2	17.4	17.7	17.9	18.2	18.4	18.7	19.0	19.2	19.5	19.7	19.9	20.2	20.5	20.8	21.0	21.3	21.5	21.8	22.0
116	14.2	14.5	14.7	15.0	15.2	15.5	15.7	15.9	16.2	16.4	16.7	16.9	17.1	17.4	17.6	17.9	18.1	18.4	18.6	18.8	19.1	19.3	19.6	19.8	20.0	20.3	20.5	20.8	21.0	21.3	21.5	21.7	22.0	22.2	22.5	22.7	23.0	23.2	23.4
114	16.2	16.5	16.7	16.9	17.1	17.4	17.6	17.8	18.0	18.3	18.5	18.7	18.9	19.2	19.4	19.6	19.8	20.1	20.3	20.5	20.8	21.0	21.2	21.4	21.7	21.9	22.1	22.3	22.6	22.8	23.0	23.2	23.5	23.7	23.9	24.1	24.4	24.6	24.8
112	18.2	18.4	18.6	18.8	19.1	19.3	19.5	19.7	19.9	20.1	20.3	20.5	20.7	20.9	21.2	21.4	21.6	21.8	22.0	22.2	22.4	22.6	22.8	23.1	23.3	23.5	23.7	23.9	24.1	24.3	24.5	24.7	25.0	25.2	25.4	25.6	25.8	26.0	26.2
110	20.2	20.4	20.6	20.8	21.0	21.2	21.4	21.6	21.8	22.0	22.1	22.3	22.5	22.7	22.9	23.1	23.3	23.5	23.7	23.9	24.1	24.3	24.5	24.7	24.9	25.1	25.3	25.5	25.7	25.9	26.0	26.2	26.4	26.6	26.8	27.0	27.2	27.4	27.6
108	22.2	22.4	22.5	22.7	22.9	23.1	23.3	23.4	23.6	23.8	24.0	24.2	24.3	24.5	24.7	24.9	25.0	25.2	25.4	25.6	25.8	25.9	26.1	26.3	26.5	26.7	26.8	27.0	27.2	27.4	27.6	27.7	27.9	28.1	28.3	28.5	28.6	28.8	29.0
106	24.2	24.3	24.5	24.7	24.8	25.0	25.1	25.3	25.5	25.6	25.8	26.0	26.1	26.3	26.5	26.6	26.8	26.9	27.1	27.3	27.4	27.6	27.8	27.9	28.1	28.3	28.4	28.6	28.7	28.9	29.1	29.2	29.4	29.6	29.7	29.9	30.1	30.2	30.4
104	26.1	26.3	26.4	26.6	26.7	26.9	27.8	27.2	27.3	27.5	27.6	27.8	27.9	28.1	28.2	28.4	28.5	28.7	28.8	29.0	29.1	29.3	29.4	29.6	29.7	29.8	29.9	30.1	30.3	30.4	30.6	30.7	30.9	31.0	31.2	31.3	31.5	31.6	31.8
102	28.1	28.3	28.4	28.5	28.7	28.8	28.9	29.1	29.2	29.3	29.5	29.6	29.7	29.9	29.9	30.1	30.2	30.4	30.5	30.6	30.8	30.9	31.0	31.2	31.3	31.4	31.6	31.7	31.8	32.0	32.1	32.2	32.4	32.5	32.6	32.8	32.9	33.0	33.2
100	30.1	30.2	30.3	30.5	30.6	30.7	30.8	30.9	31.0	31.2	31.3	31.4	31.5	31.6	31.8	31.9	32.0	32.1	32.2	32.3	32.4	32.6	32.7	32.8	32.9	33.0	33.2	33.3	33.4	33.5	33.6	33.7	33.8	34.0	34.1	34.2	34.3	34.4	34.6
99	31.1	31.2	31.3	31.4	31.5	31.7	31.8	31.9	32.0	32.1	32.2	32.3	32.4	32.5	32.6	32.7	32.9	33.0	33.1	33.2	33.3	33.4	33.5	33.6	33.7	33.8	33.9	34.0	34.2	34.3	34.4	34.5	34.6	34.7	34.8	34.9	35.0	35.1	35.2
98	32.1	32.2	32.3	32.4	32.5	32.6	32.7	32.8	32.9	33.0	33.1	33.2	33.3	33.4	33.5	33.6	33.7	33.8	33.9	34.0	34.1	34.2	34.3	34.4	34.5	34.6	34.7	34.8	34.9	35.0	35.1	35.2	35.3	35.4	35.5	35.6	35.7	35.8	35.9
97	33.1	33.2	33.3	33.4	33.5	33.6	33.7	33.7	33.8	33.9	34.0	34.1	34.2	34.3	34.4	34.5	34.6	34.7	34.8	34.9	35.0	35.0	35.1	35.2	35.3	35.4	35.5	35.6	35.7	35.8	35.9	36.0	36.1	36.2	36.3	36.4	36.4	36.5	36.6
96	34.1	34.2	34.3	34.3	34.4	34.5	34.6	34.7	34.8	34.9	34.9	35.0	35.1	35.2	35.3	35.4	35.5	35.5	35.6	35.7	35.8	35.9	36.0	36.0	36.1	36.2	36.3	36.4	36.5	36.6	36.6	36.7	36.8	36.9	37.0	37.1	37.2	37.2	37.3
95	35.1	35.2	35.2	35.3	35.4	35.5	35.5	35.6	35.7	35.8	35.9	35.9	36.0	36.1	36.2	36.2	36.3	36.4	36.5	36.6	36.6	36.7	36.8	36.9	36.9	37.0	37.1	37.2	37.2	37.3	37.4	37.5	37.6	37.6	37.7	37.8	37.9	37.9	38.0
94	36.1	36.1	36.2	36.3	36.3	36.4	36.5	36.6	36.6	36.7	36.8	36.8	36.9	37.0	37.0	37.1	37.2	37.3	37.3	37.4	37.5	37.5	37.6	37.7	37.7	37.8	37.9	38.0	38.0	38.1	38.2	38.2	38.3	38.4	38.4	38.5	38.6	38.6	38.7
93	37.1	37.1	37.2	37.2	37.3	37.4	37.4	37.5	37.6	37.6	37.7	37.7	37.8	37.9	37.9	38.0	38.1	38.1	38.2	38.2	38.3	38.4	38.4	38.5	38.5	38.6	38.7	38.7	38.8	38.9	38.9	39.0	39.0	39.1	39.2	39.2	39.3	39.3	39.4
92	38.1	38.1	38.2	38.2	38.3	38.3	38.4	38.4	38.5	38.5	38.6	38.6	38.7	38.8	38.8	38.9	38.9	39.0	39.0	39.1	39.1	39.2	39.2	39.3	39.4	39.4	39.5	39.5	39.6	39.6	39.7	39.7	39.8	39.8	39.9	39.9	39.9	40.1	40.1
91	39.0	39.1	39.1	39.2	39.2	39.3	39.3	39.4	39.4	39.5	39.5	39.6	39.6	39.6	39.7	39.7	39.8	39.8	39.9	39.9	39.9	40.0	40.1	40.1	40.2	40.2	40.2	40.3	40.3	40.4	40.4	40.5	40.5	40.6	40.6	40.7	40.7	40.8	40.8

Common
Stock
Price

LISTED PUT OPTION PRICE WHEN EXERCISE PRICE IS 140

NUMBER OF WEEKS BEFORE THE OPTION EXPIRES

Price	1	2	3	4	5	6	7	8	9	10	11	12	13	14	15	16	17	18	19	20	21	22	23	24	25	26	27	28	29	30	31	32	33	34	35	36	37	38	39
182	0.0	0.0	0.0	0.0	0.0	0.0	0.0	0.0	0.0	0.0	0.0	0.0	0.0	0.0	0.0	0.0	0.0	0.0	0.0	0.0	0.0	0.0	0.0	0.0	0.0	0.0	0.0	0.2	0.4	0.6	0.8	0.9	1.1	1.3	1.4	1.6	1.8	1.9	2.1
180	0.0	0.0	0.0	0.0	0.0	0.0	0.0	0.0	0.0	0.0	0.0	0.0	0.0	0.0	0.0	0.0	0.0	0.0	0.0	0.0	0.0	0.0	0.0	0.0	0.0	0.2	0.4	0.6	0.8	1.0	1.1	1.3	1.5	1.7	1.8	2.0	2.2	2.3	2.5
178	0.0	0.0	0.0	0.0	0.0	0.0	0.0	0.0	0.0	0.0	0.0	0.0	0.0	0.0	0.0	0.0	0.0	0.0	0.0	0.0	0.0	0.0	0.0	0.2	0.4	0.6	0.8	1.0	1.2	1.3	1.5	1.7	1.9	2.1	2.2	2.4	2.6	2.7	2.9
176	0.0	0.0	0.0	0.0	0.0	0.0	0.0	0.0	0.0	0.0	0.0	0.0	0.0	0.0	0.0	0.0	0.0	0.0	0.0	0.0	0.0	0.0	0.3	0.5	0.7	0.9	1.1	1.3	1.5	1.7	1.9	2.1	2.3	2.5	2.6	2.8	3.0	3.1	3.3
174	0.0	0.0	0.0	0.0	0.0	0.0	0.0	0.0	0.0	0.0	0.0	0.0	0.0	0.0	0.0	0.0	0.0	0.0	0.0	0.0	0.0	0.4	0.6	0.8	1.0	1.2	1.4	1.6	1.8	2.1	2.3	2.5	2.7	2.9	3.0	3.2	3.4	3.5	3.7
172	0.0	0.0	0.0	0.0	0.0	0.0	0.0	0.0	0.0	0.0	0.0	0.0	0.0	0.0	0.0	0.0	0.0	0.0	0.0	0.0	0.4	0.6	0.8	1.0	1.2	1.4	1.6	1.8	2.0	2.2	2.8	3.0	3.1	3.3	3.5	3.6	3.8	3.9	4.1
170	0.0	0.0	0.0	0.0	0.0	0.0	0.0	0.0	0.0	0.0	0.0	0.0	0.0	0.0	0.0	0.0	0.0	0.0	0.0	0.4	0.6	0.8	1.2	1.6	2.1	2.4	2.9	3.1	3.3	3.4	3.6	3.8	4.0	4.2	4.3	4.5	4.7	4.8	5.0
168	0.0	0.0	0.0	0.0	0.0	0.0	0.0	0.0	0.0	0.0	0.0	0.0	0.0	0.0	0.0	0.1	0.3	0.5	0.8	1.0	1.7	1.9	2.1	2.3	2.5	2.7	2.9	3.1	3.3	3.9	4.1	4.3	4.4	4.6	4.8	4.9	5.1	5.3	5.4
166	0.0	0.0	0.0	0.0	0.0	0.0	0.0	0.0	0.0	0.0	0.0	0.0	0.2	0.4	1.2	1.4	1.7	1.9	2.1	2.4	2.6	2.8	3.0	3.2	3.4	3.6	3.8	4.0	4.2	4.4	4.5	4.7	4.9	5.1	5.2	5.4	5.6	5.7	5.9
164	0.0	0.0	0.0	0.0	0.0	0.0	0.0	0.0	0.0	0.0	0.1	0.3	0.6	0.9	1.6	1.9	2.1	2.4	2.6	2.8	3.0	3.3	3.5	3.7	3.9	4.1	4.3	4.5	4.6	4.8	5.0	5.2	5.4	5.5	5.7	5.9	6.0	6.2	6.4
162	0.0	0.0	0.0	0.0	0.0	0.0	0.0	0.0	0.0	0.1	0.5	0.8	1.1	1.4	2.1	2.4	2.6	2.9	3.1	3.4	3.6	3.8	4.0	4.2	4.4	4.6	4.8	5.0	5.2	5.3	5.5	5.7	5.9	6.1	6.2	6.4	6.5	6.7	6.8
160	0.0	0.0	0.0	0.0	0.0	0.0	0.0	0.0	0.4	0.7	1.0	1.3	1.7	2.4	2.6	2.9	3.1	3.3	3.6	3.8	4.0	4.2	4.5	4.7	4.9	5.1	5.2	5.4	5.6	5.8	6.0	6.2	6.4	6.5	6.7	6.9	7.0	7.2	7.3
158	0.0	0.0	0.0	0.0	0.0	0.3	0.7	0.5	0.9	1.2	1.5	1.8	2.1	2.9	3.1	3.3	3.6	3.9	4.1	4.3	4.5	4.8	5.0	5.2	5.4	5.6	5.8	5.9	6.1	6.3	6.5	6.7	6.9	7.0	7.2	7.4	7.5	7.7	7.8
156	0.0	0.0	0.0	0.0	0.4	0.8	1.2	1.6	1.4	1.7	2.0	2.3	2.6	3.4	3.6	3.9	4.1	4.4	4.6	4.8	5.1	5.3	5.5	5.7	5.9	6.1	6.3	6.5	6.7	6.8	7.0	7.2	7.4	7.5	7.7	7.9	8.0	8.2	8.4
154	0.0	0.0	0.0	0.4	0.9	1.4	1.7	2.1	1.9	2.2	2.5	2.8	3.1	3.9	4.2	4.4	4.7	4.9	5.2	5.4	5.6	5.8	6.0	6.2	6.4	6.6	6.8	7.0	7.2	7.4	7.6	7.7	7.9	8.1	8.2	8.4	8.6	8.7	8.9
152	0.0	0.0	0.5	1.0	1.5	2.0	2.3	2.6	2.4	2.8	3.1	3.4	3.7	4.4	4.7	5.0	5.2	5.5	5.7	5.9	6.1	6.4	6.6	6.8	7.0	7.2	7.4	7.6	7.8	7.9	8.1	8.3	8.5	8.6	8.8	9.0	9.1	9.3	9.5
150	0.0	0.4	1.0	1.6	2.0	2.5	2.9	3.2	3.0	3.4	3.6	3.9	4.2	5.0	5.2	5.5	5.8	6.0	6.3	6.5	6.7	6.9	7.1	7.3	7.5	7.7	7.9	8.1	8.3	8.5	8.7	8.8	9.0	9.2	9.4	9.5	9.7	9.9	10.0
148	0.0	1.0	1.6	2.2	2.7	3.1	3.5	3.8	3.6	4.0	4.2	4.5	4.8	5.5	5.8	6.0	6.3	6.6	6.8	7.0	7.3	7.5	7.7	7.9	8.1	8.3	8.5	8.7	8.9	9.1	9.3	9.4	9.6	9.8	10.0	10.1	10.3	10.4	10.6
146	0.2	1.5	2.1	2.7	3.2	3.6	4.0	4.3	4.1	4.5	4.8	5.1	5.4	6.1	6.4	6.7	6.9	7.2	7.4	7.6	7.9	8.1	8.3	8.5	8.7	8.9	9.1	9.3	9.5	9.7	9.8	10.0	10.2	10.4	10.6	10.7	10.9	11.0	11.2
144	0.7	2.0	2.7	3.2	3.8	4.2	4.6	4.9	4.7	5.1	5.4	5.7	5.9	6.7	7.0	7.3	7.5	7.8	8.0	8.3	8.5	8.7	8.9	9.1	9.3	9.5	9.7	9.9	10.1	10.3	10.5	10.6	10.8	11.0	11.2	11.3	11.5	11.7	11.8
142	1.4	2.2	3.4	3.9	4.5	4.9	5.3	5.6	5.3	5.7	6.0	6.3	6.6	7.3	7.6	7.9	8.2	8.5	8.7	8.9	9.2	9.3	9.6	9.8	10.0	10.2	10.4	10.5	10.7	10.9	11.1	11.3	11.4	11.6	11.8	12.0	12.1	12.3	12.4
140	2.0	2.8	3.5	4.0	4.5	5.0	5.4	5.7	6.0	6.3	6.6	6.9	7.2	7.5	7.7	8.0	8.2	8.5	8.7	8.9	9.1	9.3	9.6	9.8	9.9	10.2	10.4	10.5	10.7	10.9	11.1	11.3	11.4	11.6	11.7	11.9	12.1	12.3	12.4
138	2.6	3.5	3.7	4.6	5.0	5.9	6.4	6.7	7.1	6.6	6.9	7.2	7.5	7.8	8.1	8.4	8.6	8.9	9.1	9.3	9.9	9.9	10.4	10.7	11.1	11.4	11.8	12.2	12.5	12.7	12.9	13.1	13.2	13.4	13.6	13.8	13.9	14.1	14.2
136	4.3	4.7	5.0	5.4	5.7	6.1	6.4	6.8	7.1	6.6?	6.9	7.2	7.5	7.9	8.2	8.4	8.6	8.9	9.1	9.3	9.9	9.9	10.4	10.7	11.1	11.4	11.8	12.2	12.5	12.7	12.9	13.1	13.2	13.4	13.6	13.8	13.9	14.1	14.2
134	6.3	6.7	7.0	7.3	7.7	8.0	8.3	8.7	9.0	9.3	9.6	9.9	10.3	10.6	11.0	11.3	11.6	12.0	12.3	12.6	13.0	13.3	13.6	13.9	14.3	14.6	15.0	15.3	15.6	16.0	16.3	16.6	16.8	15.2	15.4	15.6	15.7	15.9	16.0
132	8.6	9.0	9.3	9.6	9.6	9.9	10.2	10.5	10.8	11.2	11.5	11.8	12.1	12.4	12.7	13.1	13.4	13.7	14.0	14.3	14.6	14.9	15.3	15.6	15.9	16.2	16.5	16.9	17.2	17.5	17.8	18.1	18.4	18.7	19.0	19.0	19.3	19.5	16.0
130	10.3	10.6	10.9	11.2	11.5	11.9	12.1	12.5	12.7	13.0	13.3	13.6	13.9	14.2	14.5	15.1	15.4	15.7	16.0	16.3	16.6	16.6	16.9	17.3	17.6	17.9	18.2	18.4	18.7	19.0	19.4	19.6	19.9	20.2	20.5	20.8	21.1	21.4	17.8
128	12.3	12.6	12.9	13.1	13.4	13.7	14.0	14.3	14.6	14.8	15.1	15.4	15.7	16.0	16.3	16.6	16.8	17.1	17.4	17.7	18.0	18.3	18.5	18.8	19.1	19.4	19.7	19.9	20.3	20.5	20.8	21.1	21.4	21.7	22.0	22.2	22.5	22.8	23.1
126	14.3	14.5	14.8	15.1	15.3	15.6	15.9	16.2	16.4	16.7	17.0	17.2	17.5	17.8	18.0	18.3	18.6	18.8	19.1	19.4	19.7	19.9	20.2	20.5	20.7	21.0	21.3	21.5	21.8	22.1	22.3	22.6	22.9	23.1	23.4	23.7	24.0	24.2	24.5
124	16.3	16.5	16.8	17.0	17.3	17.5	17.8	18.1	18.3	18.5	18.8	19.0	19.3	19.5	19.8	20.1	20.3	20.6	20.8	21.1	21.3	21.6	21.8	22.1	22.3	22.6	22.8	23.1	23.3	23.6	23.9	24.1	24.4	24.6	24.9	25.1	25.4	25.6	25.9
122	18.2	18.5	18.7	20.9	19.2	19.4	19.7	19.9	20.1	20.4	20.6	20.9	21.1	21.3	21.6	21.8	22.0	22.3	22.5	22.8	23.0	23.2	23.5	23.7	23.9	24.2	24.4	24.7	24.9	25.1	25.4	25.6	25.8	26.1	26.3	26.6	26.8	27.0	27.3
120	20.2	20.4	20.7	20.9	21.1	21.3	21.6	21.8	22.0	22.2	22.4	22.7	22.9	23.1	23.3	23.6	23.8	24.0	24.2	24.4	24.7	24.9	25.1	25.3	25.6	25.8	26.0	26.2	26.4	26.7	26.9	27.1	27.3	27.5	27.8	28.0	28.2	28.4	28.7
118	22.2	22.4	22.6	22.8	23.0	23.2	23.4	23.7	23.9	24.1	24.3	24.5	24.7	24.9	25.1	25.3	25.5	25.7	25.9	26.1	26.3	26.5	26.7	27.0	27.2	27.4	27.6	27.8	28.0	28.2	28.4	28.6	28.8	29.0	29.2	29.4	29.6	29.8	30.0
116	24.2	24.4	24.6	24.8	25.0	25.1	25.3	25.5	25.7	25.9	26.1	26.3	26.5	26.7	26.9	27.1	27.3	27.4	27.6	27.8	28.0	28.2	28.4	28.6	28.8	29.0	29.1	29.3	29.5	29.7	29.9	30.1	30.3	30.5	30.7	30.9	31.1	31.2	31.4
114	26.2	26.4	26.5	26.7	26.9	27.1	27.2	27.4	27.6	27.8	27.9	28.1	28.3	28.5	28.6	28.8	29.0	29.2	29.3	29.5	29.7	29.9	30.0	30.2	30.4	30.6	30.7	30.9	31.1	31.3	31.4	31.6	31.8	32.0	32.1	32.3	32.5	32.7	32.8
112	28.2	28.3	28.5	28.6	28.8	29.0	29.1	29.3	29.4	29.6	29.8	29.9	30.1	30.2	30.4	30.6	30.7	30.9	31.0	31.2	31.3	31.5	31.7	31.8	32.0	32.1	32.3	32.5	32.6	32.8	32.9	33.1	33.3	33.4	33.6	33.7	33.9	34.1	34.2
110	30.3	30.3	30.4	30.6	30.7	30.9	31.0	31.2	31.3	31.4	31.6	31.7	31.9	32.0	32.2	32.3	32.5	32.6	32.8	32.9	33.1	33.2	33.3	33.5	33.6	33.7	33.9	34.0	34.2	34.3	34.5	34.6	34.7	34.9	35.0	35.2	35.3	35.5	35.6
108	32.1	32.3	32.4	32.5	32.6	32.8	32.9	33.0	33.2	33.3	33.4	33.5	33.7	33.8	33.9	34.0	34.2	34.3	34.4	34.6	34.7	34.8	34.9	35.1	35.2	35.3	35.4	35.6	35.7	35.8	36.0	36.1	36.2	36.4	36.5	36.6	36.7	36.9	37.0
106	34.1	34.2	34.3	34.4	34.6	34.7	34.8	34.9	35.0	35.1	35.2	35.4	35.5	35.6	35.7	35.8	35.9	36.0	36.1	36.2	36.4	36.5	36.6	36.7	36.8	36.9	37.0	37.1	37.3	37.4	37.5	37.6	37.7	37.8	37.9	38.0	38.2	38.3	38.4
104	36.1	36.2	36.3	36.4	36.5	36.6	36.7	36.8	36.9	37.0	37.1	37.2	37.3	37.4	37.5	37.6	37.6	37.9	38.0	38.1	38.2	38.3	38.4	38.5	38.6	38.7	38.8	38.9	39.0	39.1	39.1	39.2	39.3	39.4	39.5	39.6	39.6	39.8	39.8
102	38.1	38.2	38.2	38.3	38.4	38.5	38.6	38.6	38.7	38.8	38.9	39.0	39.1	39.1	39.2	39.3	39.4	39.5	39.6	39.6	39.7	39.8	39.9	39.9	40.0	40.1	40.2	40.3	40.4	40.4	40.5	40.6	40.7	40.8	40.8	40.9	41.0	41.1	41.2
100	40.1	40.1	40.2	40.3	40.3	40.4	40.5	40.5	40.6	40.7	40.7	40.8	40.9	40.9	41.0	41.1	41.1	41.2	41.3	41.3	41.4	41.5	41.5	41.6	41.6	41.7	41.8	41.8	41.9	42.0	42.0	42.1	42.2	42.2	42.3	42.4	42.4	42.5	42.6
99	41.1	41.1	41.1	41.2	41.3	41.3	41.4	41.4	41.5	41.6	41.6	41.7	41.7	41.8	41.9	41.9	42.0	42.0	42.1	42.1	42.2	42.3	42.3	42.4	42.4	42.5	42.5	42.6	42.7	42.7	42.8	42.8	42.9	43.0	43.0	43.1	43.1	43.2	43.2
98	42.0	42.1	42.1	42.2	42.2	42.3	42.3	42.4	42.4	42.5	42.5	42.6	42.6	42.7	42.7	42.8	42.8	42.9	42.9	43.0	43.0	43.1	43.1	43.2	43.2	43.3	43.3	43.4	43.4	43.5	43.5	43.6	43.6	43.7	43.7	43.8	43.8	43.9	43.9

LISTED PUT OPTION PRICE WHEN EXERCISE PRICE IS 150

NUMBER OF WEEKS BEFORE THE OPTION EXPIRES

Common Stock Price	1	2	3	4	5	6	7	8	9	10	11	12	13	14	15	16	17	18	19	20	21	22	23	24	25	26	27	28	29	30	31	32	33	34	35	36	37	38	39
196	0.0	0.0	0.0	0.0	0.0	0.0	0.0	0.0	0.0	0.0	0.0	0.0	0.0	0.0	0.0	0.0	0.0	0.0	0.0	0.0	0.0	0.0	0.0	0.0	0.0	0.0	0.0	0.0	0.2	0.4	0.6	0.8	1.0	1.2	1.4	1.5	1.7	1.9	2.1
194	0.0	0.0	0.0	0.0	0.0	0.0	0.0	0.0	0.0	0.0	0.0	0.0	0.0	0.0	0.0	0.0	0.0	0.0	0.0	0.0	0.0	0.0	0.0	0.0	0.0	0.0	0.2	0.4	0.6	0.8	1.0	1.2	1.4	1.6	1.7	1.9	2.1	2.3	2.4
192	0.0	0.0	0.0	0.0	0.0	0.0	0.0	0.0	0.0	0.0	0.0	0.0	0.0	0.0	0.0	0.0	0.0	0.0	0.0	0.0	0.0	0.0	0.0	0.0	0.2	0.4	0.6	0.8	1.0	1.2	1.4	1.6	1.8	1.9	2.1	2.3	2.5	2.7	2.8
190	0.0	0.0	0.0	0.0	0.0	0.0	0.0	0.0	0.0	0.0	0.0	0.0	0.0	0.0	0.0	0.0	0.0	0.0	0.0	0.0	0.0	0.0	0.1	0.4	0.6	0.8	1.0	1.2	1.4	1.6	1.8	2.0	2.2	2.3	2.5	2.7	2.9	3.1	3.2
188	0.0	0.0	0.0	0.0	0.0	0.0	0.0	0.0	0.0	0.0	0.0	0.0	0.0	0.0	0.0	0.0	0.0	0.0	0.0	0.0	0.1	0.3	0.5	0.8	1.0	1.2	1.4	1.6	1.8	2.0	2.2	2.4	2.6	2.7	2.9	3.1	3.3	3.5	3.6
186	0.0	0.0	0.0	0.0	0.0	0.0	0.0	0.0	0.0	0.0	0.0	0.0	0.0	0.0	0.0	0.0	0.0	0.0	0.0	0.3	0.5	0.7	0.9	1.2	1.4	1.6	1.8	2.0	2.2	2.4	2.6	2.8	3.0	3.2	3.3	3.5	3.7	3.9	4.0
184	0.0	0.0	0.0	0.0	0.0	0.0	0.0	0.0	0.0	0.0	0.0	0.0	0.0	0.0	0.0	0.0	0.0	0.2	0.4	0.7	0.9	1.1	1.4	1.6	1.8	2.0	2.2	2.4	2.6	2.8	3.0	3.2	3.4	3.6	3.8	3.9	4.1	4.3	4.5
182	0.0	0.0	0.0	0.0	0.0	0.0	0.0	0.0	0.0	0.0	0.0	0.0	0.0	0.0	0.0	0.1	0.4	0.6	0.9	1.1	1.3	1.6	1.8	2.0	2.2	2.4	2.7	2.9	3.1	3.3	3.4	3.6	3.8	4.0	4.2	4.4	4.5	4.7	4.9
180	0.0	0.0	0.0	0.0	0.0	0.0	0.0	0.0	0.0	0.0	0.0	0.0	0.0	0.0	0.3	0.5	0.8	1.1	1.3	1.5	1.8	2.0	2.2	2.5	2.7	2.9	3.1	3.3	3.5	3.7	3.9	4.1	4.3	4.4	4.6	4.8	5.0	5.2	5.3
178	0.0	0.0	0.0	0.0	0.0	0.0	0.0	0.0	0.0	0.0	0.0	0.0	0.1	0.4	0.7	1.0	1.3	1.5	1.8	2.0	2.2	2.5	2.7	2.9	3.1	3.3	3.5	3.7	3.9	4.1	4.3	4.5	4.7	4.9	5.1	5.3	5.4	5.6	5.8
176	0.0	0.0	0.0	0.0	0.0	0.0	0.0	0.0	0.0	0.0	0.0	0.3	0.6	0.9	1.2	1.4	1.7	2.0	2.2	2.5	2.7	2.9	3.1	3.4	3.6	3.8	4.0	4.2	4.4	4.6	4.8	5.0	5.2	5.4	5.5	5.7	5.9	6.1	6.2
174	0.0	0.0	0.0	0.0	0.0	0.0	0.0	0.0	0.0	0.1	0.5	0.8	1.1	1.4	1.6	1.9	2.2	2.4	2.7	2.9	3.2	3.4	3.6	3.8	4.1	4.3	4.5	4.7	4.9	5.1	5.3	5.5	5.6	5.8	6.0	6.2	6.4	6.5	6.7
172	0.0	0.0	0.0	0.0	0.0	0.0	0.0	0.0	0.3	0.6	0.9	1.3	1.6	1.8	2.1	2.4	2.7	2.9	3.2	3.4	3.6	3.9	4.1	4.3	4.5	4.7	5.0	5.2	5.4	5.6	5.7	5.9	6.1	6.3	6.5	6.7	6.8	7.0	7.2
170	0.0	0.0	0.0	0.0	0.0	0.0	0.0	0.4	0.8	1.1	1.4	1.7	2.1	2.3	2.6	2.9	3.2	3.4	3.7	3.9	4.1	4.4	4.6	4.8	5.0	5.2	5.4	5.6	5.8	6.0	6.2	6.4	6.6	6.8	7.0	7.2	7.3	7.5	7.7
168	0.0	0.0	0.0	0.0	0.0	0.1	0.5	0.9	1.3	1.6	1.9	2.3	2.6	2.8	3.1	3.4	3.7	3.9	4.2	4.4	4.6	4.9	5.1	5.3	5.5	5.7	6.0	6.2	6.4	6.6	6.7	6.9	7.1	7.3	7.5	7.7	7.8	8.0	8.2
166	0.0	0.0	0.0	0.0	0.1	0.6	1.0	1.4	1.8	2.1	2.5	2.8	3.1	3.4	3.6	3.9	4.2	4.4	4.7	4.9	5.2	5.4	5.6	5.8	6.0	6.3	6.5	6.7	6.9	7.1	7.3	7.4	7.6	7.8	8.0	8.2	8.4	8.5	8.7
164	0.0	0.0	0.0	0.2	0.7	1.1	1.6	1.9	2.3	2.7	3.0	3.3	3.6	3.9	4.2	4.4	4.7	5.0	5.2	5.4	5.7	5.9	6.1	6.4	6.6	6.8	7.0	7.2	7.4	7.6	7.8	8.0	8.2	8.4	8.5	8.7	8.9	9.1	9.2
162	0.0	0.0	0.1	0.7	1.2	1.7	2.1	2.5	2.8	3.2	3.5	3.8	4.1	4.4	4.7	5.0	5.2	5.5	5.7	6.0	6.2	6.5	6.7	6.9	7.1	7.3	7.5	7.7	7.9	8.1	8.3	8.5	8.7	8.9	9.1	9.3	9.4	9.6	9.8
160	0.0	0.0	0.7	1.3	1.8	2.2	2.6	3.0	3.4	3.8	4.1	4.4	4.7	5.0	5.3	5.5	5.8	6.1	6.3	6.5	6.8	7.0	7.2	7.5	7.7	7.9	8.1	8.3	8.5	8.7	8.9	9.1	9.3	9.4	9.6	9.8	9.9	10.2	10.3
158	0.0	0.6	1.3	1.8	2.3	2.8	3.2	3.6	4.0	4.3	4.7	5.0	5.3	5.6	5.8	6.1	6.4	6.6	6.9	7.1	7.4	7.6	7.8	8.0	8.2	8.5	8.7	8.9	9.1	9.3	9.5	9.6	9.8	10.0	10.2	10.4	10.6	10.7	10.9
156	0.3	1.2	1.9	2.4	2.9	3.4	3.8	4.2	4.6	4.9	5.2	5.5	5.9	6.1	6.4	6.7	7.0	7.2	7.5	7.7	7.9	8.2	8.4	8.6	8.8	9.0	9.2	9.5	9.7	9.8	10.0	10.2	10.4	10.6	10.8	11.0	11.1	11.3	11.5
154	0.9	1.8	2.5	3.0	3.5	4.0	4.4	4.8	5.2	5.5	5.8	6.1	6.5	6.7	7.0	7.3	7.6	7.8	8.1	8.3	8.5	8.8	9.0	9.2	9.4	9.6	9.8	10.0	10.2	10.4	10.6	10.8	11.0	11.2	11.4	11.6	11.7	11.9	12.1
152	1.5	2.4	3.1	3.6	4.1	4.6	5.0	5.4	5.8	6.1	6.4	6.8	7.1	7.4	7.6	7.9	8.2	8.4	8.7	8.9	9.2	9.4	9.6	9.8	10.0	10.3	10.5	10.7	10.9	11.1	11.3	11.4	11.6	11.8	12.0	12.2	12.4	12.5	12.7
150	2.1	3.0	3.7	4.3	4.8	5.2	5.6	6.0	6.4	6.8	7.1	7.4	7.7	8.0	8.3	8.5	8.8	9.1	9.3	9.5	9.8	10.0	10.2	10.5	10.7	10.9	11.1	11.3	11.5	11.7	11.9	12.1	12.3	12.4	12.6	12.8	13.0	13.2	13.3
148	2.7	3.2	3.9	4.5	5.0	5.4	5.8	6.3	6.7	7.1	7.4	7.7	8.0	8.3	8.7	8.9	9.2	9.5	9.7	9.9	10.2	10.6	11.0	11.4	11.8	12.1	12.5	12.9	13.3	13.5	13.7	13.9	14.1	14.2	14.4	14.6	14.8	15.0	15.1
146	4.4	4.7	5.1	5.5	5.9	6.2	6.6	7.0	7.4	7.7	8.1	8.5	8.9	9.2	9.6	9.9	10.4	10.7	11.1	11.5	11.9	12.2	12.6	13.0	13.4	13.7	14.1	14.5	14.9	15.2	15.5	15.7	15.9	16.0	16.2	16.4	16.6	16.8	16.9
144	6.4	6.7	7.1	7.4	7.8	8.2	8.5	8.9	9.2	9.6	9.9	10.3	10.7	11.0	11.4	11.7	12.1	12.5	12.8	13.2	13.5	13.9	14.3	14.6	15.0	15.3	15.7	16.0	16.4	16.8	17.1	17.5	17.7	17.8	18.0	18.2	18.4	18.6	18.7
142	8.3	8.7	9.0	9.4	9.7	10.1	10.4	10.7	11.1	11.4	11.8	12.1	12.5	12.8	13.1	13.5	13.8	14.2	14.5	14.9	15.2	15.5	15.9	16.2	16.6	16.9	17.3	17.6	17.9	18.3	18.6	19.0	19.3	19.6	19.8	20.0	20.2	20.4	20.5
140	10.3	10.7	11.0	11.3	11.6	12.0	12.3	12.6	12.9	13.3	13.6	13.9	14.3	14.6	14.9	15.2	15.6	15.9	16.2	16.5	16.9	17.2	17.5	17.9	18.2	18.5	18.8	19.2	19.5	19.8	20.2	20.5	20.8	21.1	21.5	21.8	22.0	22.1	22.3
138	12.3	12.6	12.9	13.2	13.6	13.9	14.2	14.5	14.8	15.1	15.4	15.7	16.1	16.4	16.7	17.0	17.3	17.6	17.9	18.2	18.5	18.9	19.2	19.5	19.8	20.1	20.4	20.7	21.0	21.4	21.7	22.0	22.3	22.6	22.9	23.2	23.5	23.8	24.1
136	14.3	14.6	14.9	15.2	15.5	15.8	16.1	16.4	16.7	17.0	17.3	17.6	17.8	18.1	18.4	18.7	19.0	19.3	19.6	19.9	20.2	20.5	20.8	21.1	21.4	21.7	22.0	22.3	22.6	22.9	23.2	23.5	23.8	24.1	24.4	24.7	25.0	25.3	25.5
134	16.3	16.6	16.8	17.1	17.4	17.7	18.0	18.2	18.5	18.8	19.1	19.4	19.6	19.9	20.2	20.5	20.8	21.0	21.3	21.6	21.9	22.2	22.5	22.7	23.0	23.3	23.6	23.9	24.1	24.4	24.7	25.0	25.3	25.5	25.8	26.1	26.4	26.7	26.9
132	18.3	18.5	18.8	19.1	19.3	19.6	19.9	20.1	20.4	20.6	20.9	21.2	21.4	21.7	22.0	22.2	22.5	22.8	23.0	23.3	23.6	23.8	24.1	24.4	24.6	24.9	25.1	25.4	25.7	25.9	26.2	26.5	26.7	27.0	27.3	27.5	27.8	28.1	28.3
130	20.2	20.5	20.7	21.0	21.2	21.5	21.7	22.0	22.2	22.5	22.7	23.0	23.2	23.5	23.7	24.0	24.2	24.5	24.7	25.0	25.2	25.5	25.7	26.0	26.2	26.5	26.7	27.0	27.2	27.5	27.7	28.0	28.2	28.5	28.7	29.0	29.2	29.5	29.7
128	22.2	22.5	22.7	22.9	23.2	23.4	23.6	23.9	24.1	24.3	24.6	24.8	25.0	25.3	25.5	25.7	26.0	26.2	26.4	26.7	26.9	27.1	27.4	27.6	27.8	28.1	28.3	28.5	28.8	29.0	29.2	29.5	29.7	29.9	30.2	30.4	30.6	30.9	31.1
126	24.2	24.4	24.7	24.9	25.1	25.3	25.5	25.7	26.0	26.2	26.4	26.6	26.8	27.0	27.3	27.5	27.7	27.9	28.1	28.4	28.6	28.8	29.0	29.2	29.4	29.7	29.9	30.1	30.3	30.5	30.8	31.0	31.2	31.4	31.6	31.8	32.1	32.3	32.5
124	26.2	26.4	26.6	26.8	27.0	27.2	27.4	27.6	27.8	28.0	28.2	28.4	28.6	28.8	29.0	29.2	29.4	29.6	29.8	30.0	30.2	30.4	30.6	30.9	31.1	31.3	31.5	31.7	31.9	32.1	32.3	32.5	32.7	32.9	33.1	33.3	33.5	33.7	33.9
122	28.2	28.4	28.6	28.7	28.9	29.1	29.3	29.5	29.7	29.9	30.1	30.2	30.4	30.6	30.8	31.0	31.2	31.4	31.5	31.7	31.9	32.1	32.3	32.5	32.7	32.8	33.0	33.2	33.4	33.6	33.8	34.0	34.2	34.3	34.5	34.7	34.9	35.1	35.3
120	30.2	30.3	30.5	30.7	30.9	31.0	31.2	31.4	31.5	31.7	31.9	32.0	32.2	32.4	32.6	32.7	32.9	33.1	33.2	33.4	33.6	33.8	33.9	34.1	34.3	34.4	34.6	34.8	35.0	35.1	35.3	35.5	35.6	35.8	36.0	36.1	36.3	36.5	36.7
118	32.2	32.3	32.5	32.6	32.8	32.9	33.1	33.2	33.4	33.6	33.7	33.9	34.0	34.2	34.3	34.5	34.6	34.8	34.9	35.1	35.3	35.4	35.6	35.7	35.9	36.0	36.2	36.3	36.5	36.7	36.8	37.0	37.1	37.3	37.4	37.6	37.7	37.9	38.0
116	34.1	34.3	34.4	34.6	34.7	34.8	35.0	35.1	35.3	35.4	35.5	35.7	35.8	36.0	36.1	36.2	36.4	36.5	36.6	36.8	36.9	37.1	37.2	37.3	37.5	37.6	37.8	37.9	38.0	38.2	38.3	38.5	38.6	38.7	38.9	39.0	39.2	39.3	39.4
114	36.1	36.2	36.4	36.5	36.6	36.7	36.9	37.0	37.1	37.2	37.4	37.5	37.6	37.7	37.9	38.8	38.1	38.2	38.4	38.5	38.6	38.7	38.8	39.0	39.1	39.2	39.3	39.5	39.6	39.7	39.8	39.9	40.1	40.2	40.3	40.5	40.6	40.7	40.8
112	38.1	38.2	38.3	38.4	38.5	38.6	38.8	38.9	39.0	39.1	39.2	39.3	39.4	39.5	39.6	39.7	39.8	39.9	40.1	40.2	40.3	40.4	40.5	40.6	40.7	40.8	40.9	41.0	41.1	41.2	41.4	41.5	41.6	41.7	41.8	41.9	42.0	42.1	42.2
110	40.1	40.2	40.3	40.4	40.5	40.6	40.6	40.7	40.8	40.9	41.0	41.1	41.2	41.3	41.4	41.5	41.6	41.7	41.8	41.8	41.9	42.0	42.1	42.2	42.3	42.4	42.5	42.6	42.7	42.8	42.9	43.0	43.1	43.1	43.2	43.3	43.4	43.5	43.6
108	42.1	42.2	42.2	42.3	42.4	42.5	42.5	42.6	42.7	42.8	42.8	42.9	43.0	43.1	43.2	43.2	43.3	43.4	43.5	43.5	43.6	43.7	43.8	43.8	43.9	44.0	44.1	44.1	44.2	44.3	44.4	44.5	44.5	44.6	44.7	44.8	44.8	44.9	45.0
106	44.1	44.1	44.2	44.2	44.3	44.4	44.4	44.5	44.5	44.6	44.7	44.7	44.8	44.9	44.9	45.0	45.0	45.1	45.2	45.2	45.3	45.3	45.4	45.5	45.5	45.6	45.6	45.7	45.8	45.8	45.9	46.0	46.0	46.1	46.1	46.2	46.3	46.3	46.4

Index

About the Author

Kenneth R. Trester is recognized as a leading international options advisor. A popular speaker at financial conventions and options trading seminars, he is credited with originating many of the options strategies that are industry standards today. He is the author of The Complete Option Player, 101 Option Trading Secrets, Sure Bet Investing, and The Option Player's Advanced Guidebook.